Fashioning the Dandy

Fashioning the Dandy

Style and Manners

Olga Vainshtein

Translated by Sofia Horujaya-Cook

ANTHEM PRESS

Anthem Press
An imprint of Wimbledon Publishing Company
www.anthempress.com

This edition first published in UK and USA 2023
by ANTHEM PRESS
75–76 Blackfriars Road, London SE1 8HA, UK
or PO Box 9779, London SW19 7ZG, UK
and
244 Madison Ave #116, New York, NY 10016, USA

Copyright © Olga Vainshtein 2023

The author asserts the moral right to be identified as the author of this work.

All rights reserved. Without limiting the rights under copyright reserved above,
no part of this publication may be reproduced, stored or introduced into
a retrieval system, or transmitted, in any form or by any means
(electronic, mechanical, photocopying, recording or otherwise),
without the prior written permission of both the copyright
owner and the above publisher of this book.

British Library Cataloguing-in-Publication Data
A catalogue record for this book is available from the British Library.

Library of Congress Cataloging-in-Publication Data
A catalog record for this book has been requested.
2023931241

ISBN-13: 978-1-83998-444-0 (Hbk)
ISBN-10: 1-83998-444-9 (Hbk)

Cover Credit: J.C. Leyendecker. The Arrow Collar Advertisement. 1912.
WikiArt. Public domain.

This title is also available as an e-book.

In memory of my father
Boris Vainshtein, crystallographer.

CONTENTS

List of Illustrations — ix

Acknowledgements — xi

Introduction — 1

Chapter One   **Fashioning the Dandy**
- Apollos in Double-Breasted Coats — 7
- Brummell the Innovator — 13
- On Cravats — 17
- Styling Interiors — 20

Chapter Two   **Literature and Legends**
- Brummell: Constructing the Legend — 27
- The Biographer's Gaze: Brummell in the Mirror — 30
- The Poetics of Dandyism: Fashion and Fiction — 32
- Aphorism as Dandy's Genre of Speech — 43

Chapter Three   **Charisma and Chameleonism**
- Chameleonism — 47
- The Charisma of Count d'Orsay — 49

Chapter Four   **Manners**
- Rules of Behaviour — 65
- Visual Games and the Optical Strategies — 69
- Dandyism and the Disdain for Vulgarity: A History of Meanings — 81
- The Fine Art of Scandal — 87
- Be Insolent! — 92
- Sugared Wigs and Luminous Rabbits: Practical Jokes in Dandyism — 97

Chapter Five   **The Body**
- The Dandy's Body — 113
- The Sporting Dandy — 118
- Corporeality: Poses and Gestures — 123
- Corporeality: Inscrutable Face — 125

	The Quest for Cleanliness: Dandy's Hygiene	127
	Festina Lente: Slowness in Dandy Culture	137
Chapter Six	**Oscar Wilde**	
	Oscar Wilde: The Dandy-Aesthete	145
	Dandyism after Oscar Wilde	158
Chapter Seven	**Russian Dandyism**	
	Russian 'Petit Maître': Occupational Hazards	163
	'Fashion's Loyal Devotee': Russian Dandies of the Nineteenth Century	167
	The Silver Age Masters of Elegance	184
	Dandyism after the Revolution (Pre-war Years)	192
	Orange Jackets and Pea Green Pants: The Fashion of Stilyagi in the Soviet Post-war Culture	196
Chapter Eight	**Dandyism Revisited**	
	Three Periods of Nineteenth-Century European Dandyism	213
	Modern Dandies and Two Trends in the History of Dandyism	215
	The New Bespoke Movement	219
	The Sapeurs	222

Conclusion 233

Bibliography 239

Subject Index 251

Name Index 253

LIST OF ILLUSTRATIONS

1	Measures. Illustration from J. Wyatt. The Taylor's Friendly Instructor. 1822.	2
2	Philip Dawe. The Macaroni. A Real Character at the Late Masquerade. 1773.	7
3	G.Cruikshank, I.R.Cruikshank. Jerry in training for a 'swell'. Illustration from 'Life in London' by Pierce Egan. 1821.	9
4	George 'Beau' Brummell, watercolor by Richard Dighton. 1805.	14
5	Prince Esterhazy, Lord Fife, Hughes Ball, Lord Winter. Illustration from R.H. Gronow. Reminiscences of Captain Gronow, being anecdotes of the camp, the court and the clubs at the close of the last war with France. L.: Smith, Elder and Co, 1862.	15
6	Daniel Maclise. Disraeli as a young man. 1833–1834.	37
7	Edmund J. Sullivan. The Dandies' Holy of Holies. Illustration from Sartor Resartus by Thomas Carlyle. 1898.	39
8	Sem (Georges Goursat). Green album. 1905.	44
9	Daniel Maclise. Portrait of Count Alfred D'Orsay. Middle of 19th century.	50
10	Quizzing glass. c.1820.	71
11	Brass jealousy glass for surreptitious sideways viewing. Paris, early 19th century.	72
12	Ebony walking stick with an ivory and brass spyglass. Early 19th century.	72
13	Pair of French opera glasses in brass and ivory. Early 19th century.	74
14	Pair of early folding opera glasses, made of delicate tortoiseshell with four folding lenses. c.1830.	75
15	Spring lorgnette with in-built watch and with gold watch key and Regulator. Early-mid 19th century.	76
16	Lover's eye portrait miniature. Circa 1810–1820.	80
17	Daniel Maclise. Portrait of Theodore Hook. 1831.	102
18	The first quadrille at Almacks. Illustration from R.H Gronow. Reminiscences of Captain Gronow, being anecdotes of the camp, the court and the clubs at the close of the last war with France. L.: Smith, Elder and Co, 1862.	115

19	Sir Henry Smyth. John Jackson at his boxing academy. Illustration from Pierce Egan. Boxiana; Or, Sketches of Ancient and Modern Pugilism. (1830).	117
20	Dandies of 1831. Journal des Dames et des Modes. 1831.	124
21	Paul Gavarni. Dolce Far Niente. 1831.	139
22	Paul Gavarni. Pelisse Russe. 1830.	171
23	Illustration from Russian magazine "The Dandy". 1910.	186
24	Lev Bakst. Portrait of Diaghilev. 1906.	189
25	Konstantin Vainshtein. 1916.	191
26	Stilyagi from Baku. Jazz-rock band of the faculty of physics of Baku University. Emil Gasanov, Hikmet Haji-zada, Vagif Aliev. 1976.	203
27	Georgy Dobrovolsky, Soviet cosmonaut. 1952.	216
28	Julio Mompó, Savile Row tailor. 2023.	218
29	Daniele Tamagni. Three 'Grand sapeurs' of Brazzaville: Willy Covary, Severin Mayembo, Germain le Doyen. 2008.	228
30	Ayres Gonçalo, bespoke tailor. 2018.	237

ACKNOWLEDGEMENTS

I am pleased to thank the copyright holders for kindly permitting me to use the photographs: British Optical Association Museum and the College of Optometrists, London; The Three Graces Antique Jewelry; Bahar Haji-zada; Marina Dobrovolskaya; Lee Osborne @sartorialee; Giordano Tamagni at Daniele Tamagni Foundation; bespoke tailors Julio Mompó and Ayres Gonçalo.

Parts of chapters appeared as articles in different books and journals. My grateful acknowledgements are made to the publishers for permission to reprint my previous English articles.

The sections on interiors and chameleonism were published originally in *The New Man*, edited by José Teunissen, Hanka van der Voet et al., Arnhem: ArtEZ Press, d'jonge Hond, 2010, pp. 119–132.

Parts of Chapter 4 on visual games were printed in *The Men's Fashion Reader*, edited by Peter McNeil and Vicki Karaminas. Oxford, New York: Berg Publishers, an imprint of Bloomsbury Publishing Plc., 2009, pp. 84–108.

Parts of Chapter 7 appeared in the book *Russian Masculinities in History and Culture*, edited by Barbara Clements, Rebecca Friedman and Dan Healey. New York, London: Palgrave Press, 2002, pp. 51–75. Reproduced with permission of Springer Nature Customer Service Center.

Parts of Chapter 5 on slow life and Conclusion were published in the journal *Fashion, Style & Popular Culture*, Volume 4, Issue 1, January 2017, pp. 81–104 (Intellect Journals).

The section on Stilyagi was published in *Fashion Theory*, Volume 22, Issue 2, 2018, pp. 167–185 (Taylor & Francis Journals).

Parts of Chapter 8 on Dandyism Revisited were published in *Fashionable Masculinities: Queers, Pimp Daddies, and Lumbersexuals*, edited by Vicki Karaminas, Adam Geczy and Pamela Church Gibson. New Brunswick, New Jersey: Rutgers University Press, 2022, pp.177–191.

I would like to express heartfelt thanks to all those who found time to read my drafts and offer valuable comments: my late mother Ariadna Nurok (1922–2019), friends and colleagues Raisa Kirsanova, Bruce Grant, Sergei Nekliudov, Liudmila Aliabieva and Dmitry Arkhipov. My special thanks go to the editors of the book series Vicki Karaminas and Adam Geczy for their continuous support. The translator Sofia Horujaya-Cook strove always to provide an engaging and accurate translation, and I am profoundly grateful for her hard work, and for our friendship. I must also give thanks to Anthem Press editors and to the publisher's anonymous reviewers.

And finally, this book would have been impossible without my husband, Aydin Dzhebrailov. A lawyer and collector of antique rugs and carpets, who has written on Shakespeare, Aydin always provided feedback when I needed it. Many a pleasurable hour was spent debating its future fabric. As a result of our discussions, the conceptual chameleon of dandyism took on the clear outlines of a book.

INTRODUCTION

When we speak of dandies, what images go through our minds? In our imagination, the dandy is an elegant man, impeccably dressed, perhaps wearing a dinner jacket and bow tie. He smokes a smart pipe, his unhurried gestures are languorous, lazy. His smile is condescending. What is it about dandies that instantly captures our attention? To this day, the dandies possess in our eyes a mysterious charisma; they are often seen as eccentric aesthetes, sharp dressers, capable of the most brazen, unexpected actions.

Who are the dandies? Larousse dictionary offers the following definition: A dandy is 'a man who affects supreme elegance in his toilet, his manners, and his tastes'.[1] Yet is dandyism really but an elegant pose? Nothing but a fashionable gesture, a chic lifestyle? The nineteenth-century dictionary compiled by Felix Toll provides a less glamorous, yet more specific definition. A dandy, it suggests, is a man 'always dressed according to the latest fashion, of high birth, possessing sufficient income, and good taste'.[2] Dandies, unsurprisingly, have long been associated with good taste and good breeding. A great many of them, indeed, were of noble birth: recall Count d'Orsay, Count Robert de Montesquiou, the Duke of Windsor. Yet others, originally, were of bourgeois background, including the founder of the tradition Beau Brummell.

Besides always being smartly dressed, dandies are famous for their manners conforming to a special code of conduct, and their costume is merely part of a bigger, well-structured system. So, let us formulate a working definition of the dandy as a fashionable male who achieves social influence by distinctive elegance in dress and sophisticated self-presentation.

In my research, I focused on fashion, literature and lifestyle – areas which, upon closer study, appear more interconnected than one might suspect, and detailed analysis reveals a multitude of unexpected links. On this entrancing journey, we will be concerned not only with fashion but also with many other aspects of everyday life, such as corporeality and hygiene, codes of conduct, practical jokes, high society scandals, notions of charisma and vulgarity. We will probe the origins of the principle of slowness and examine the roots of the dandy minimalist aesthetic. Our particular attention will go to contemporary dandyism, the tailors of Savile Row, and to the Sapeurs of Africa.

Where will we source our knowledge, to find reliable accounts of this appealing, yet also ephemeral world? The most prized and rare material in the study of fashion history is invariably from documentary sources such as tailors' treatises, fashion magazines, dandies' diaries, albums of men and ladies of fashion and, of course, dress collections. Of particular interest are albums containing samples of textiles and examples of outfits. Once a common genre, these combined features of a diary and household accounts. The Victoria and Albert Museum in London holds an album compiled by Barbara Johnson between 1746 and 1823. Pasting textile samples into a book, this lady wrote brief descriptions of dress styles, amount of fabric used and cost of dressmaking, as well as keeping a diary of life events.[3] Thus, text shifts seamlessly into textile – an example of connection, a symbolic link between the threads of language and fabric.[4]

Accounts exist of an album by Prince Kurakin, a beau from the times of Catherine the Great. Each page contained samples of fabrics used for his fabulous outfits, as well as descriptions of the most eye-catching outfits, which included swords, buckles, rings and snuff boxes.[5] Intended to aid the fop in creating the most effective combinations of dress and accessories, the album was a working instrument for his refined taste, a textbook for the 'grammar of glamour'.

Another valuable source of information can be found in treatises on fashion. At times, these came in the form of purely technical tailors' manuals, with patterns and instructions on taking measurements (Figure 1).[6] Others, however, contained detailed advice on matters such as tying one's cravat, presented in an entertaining, playful manner.[7] Some treatises were created with the lofty aim of providing a universal encyclopaedia for those wishing to look their best. One of these was the 1830 English treatise on 'The Whole Art

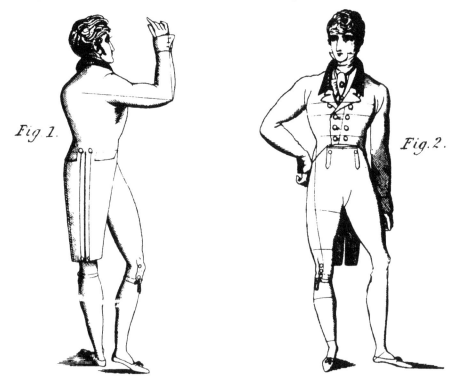

Figure 1 Measures. Illustration from Wyatt J. The Taylor's Friendly Instructor. 1822.

of Dress! Or, the Road to Elegance and Fashion', written by a cavalry officer. The full title of this intriguing work was a most imposing one:

> The Whole Art of Dress! Or, the Road to Elegance and Fashion, at the Enormous Saving of Thirty Per Cent! Being a treatise upon that essential and much-cultivated requisite of the present day, gentlemen's costume. Explains and clearly defines, by a series of beautifully engraved illustrations, the most becoming assortments of colours, and style of dress and undress in all varieties; suited to different ages and complexions, so as to render the human figure most symmetrical and imposing to their eyes. Also, directions in the purchase of all kinds of wearing apparel: accompanied by hints for the toilette, containing a few valuable and original recipes; likewise, some advice to the improvement of defects in the person and carriage. Together with a dissertation on uniform in general and the selection of fine dress. By a cavalry officer.[8]

Naturally, works such as these serve to give a flavour of an era, its manners and morals. Inevitably, such treatises are subjective, coloured by the tastes and opinions of the writer. Still more personal, textual sources such as biographies, letters, memoirs, diaries and travel journals are nonetheless valuable companions in guiding us through times gone by. Much of their substance is gossip, popular rumour recorded by an enthusiastic contemporary. At times, persistent repetition may lend hearsay an air of authenticity. When studying England's eighteenth-century macaronis, fashion historian Peter McNeil spent quite some time dutifully researching the whereabouts of a mysterious macaroni club mentioned by contemporary sources. Eventually, his studies concluded that this was either an ironic reference to Almack's, or, most likely, simply a fashionable society.[9]

Upon closer inspection, a number of dandy legends likewise appear of an apocryphal nature. The story of Beau Brummell using three tailors to make his gloves is, most likely, pure invention, yet this does not diminish its value. In the subtle matter of cultural self-fashioning, urban legends constitute a particularly substantial layer, with philologists treating them as folkloric texts.[10] In this area, philological approaches are especially relevant, considering the literary aspect of dandyism. Many notable dandies were writers: Lord Byron, Edward Bulwer-Lytton and Oscar Wilde in England; Alexander Pushkin and Mikhail Lermontov in Russia; Stendhal, Balzac, Barbey d'Aurevilly, Charles Baudelaire, Joris-Karl Huysmans and Marcel Proust in France. Besides portraying men of fashion in their works – recall the classical novels *Against Nature* (*À Rebours*) by Huysmans and Wilde's *The Picture of Dorian Gray* – these writers also left spirited treatises on dandyism, the best known being by Balzac, Barbey d'Aurevilly and Baudelaire. Finally, of course, they themselves liked to shine in their extravagant outfits. Almost any serious study of dandyism involves delving into its literary aspects.

Thus, our broad array of sources widens to include fiction. Mikhail Bakhtin once termed the efforts of certain critics to combine literature and life, 'naïve realism'. At the same time, he acknowledged that some human lives possess a completeness reminiscent of a literary character. Trusting the text, surely, is a more fruitful approach. Otherwise, one risks never discovering the dandies from the novels, never appreciating the fine details of their dress, lovingly described to conjure up a vivid, lifelike picture. Such descriptions, after all, introduce us to a world of costume and objects that is both rich and sumptuous. Thus, by reconsidering the well-known sources for dandyism – the biographies of dandies, fashion magazines and etiquette books – and including 'fashionable' novels, I argue that the dandyism of the English Regency period established the models of self-fashioning that became stereotypes of men's behaviour in society during the nineteenth century.

Another important and entertaining source for our research can be found in satirical depictions of dandies. Much satirised, men of fashion were the subject of cutting poems,[11] humorous passages in novels and merciless cartoons. To this day, the prints of George Cruikshank remain a key source of information on butterfly dandies, just as the caricatures in Krokodil magazine provide a key to the Soviet Stilyagi. More often than not, several types of sources can be used simultaneously, providing a balanced approach. Thus, our knowledge of Stilyagi adventures is also drawn from their own accounts, as many are still living. The tradition of self-description is continued today through luxurious albums with pictures of contemporary dandies and their brief autobiographies.[12]

The dandy cultural tradition has been the subject of many critical works, both popular[13] and academic. Recent critical books and essays on dandyism have tended to concentrate on dandies as precursors of modernity, heroes of urban consumerism, camp style and self-fashioning.[14] In the last decade, a number of new works on the theory and history of dandyism appeared, affirming the importance of this theme.[15] Some notable men of fashion, however, have not received due attention. Count Robert de Montesquiou, for instance, remains evidently under-researched, as do contemporary African dandies, although a number of academic books on Sapeurs have recently been published.[16]

Although much has been written on European dandyism, very few authors have attempted to offer a structural description of dandyism. The aim of this book is to provide a consistent interpretation of dandyism in the context of fashion, literature and the history of everyday life. The first Russian edition of this book was published by the *New Literary Observer* in 2005, and since then, it has been reprinted five times.[17] For the English edition, the original Russian text was abridged and reworked, and a new chapter added. This book is dedicated to my father Boris Vainshtein, crystallographer, whose influence was decisive in my life and who taught me that serious academic research could be combined with humour and practical jokes.

Notes

1. Pierre Larousse, *Grand Dictionnaire Universel Du XIXe Siècle*, 6: 63. https://www.larousse.fr/dictionnaires/francais/dandy/21602. Accessed 22 May 2022.
2. Felix Toll, *Nastolniy slovar' dlia spravok po vsem otrasliam znania* [Table Dictionary for all Fields of Knowledge] (Sankt Peterburg: Izdanie F. Tollya, 1864), 2: 21.
3. *A Lady of Fashion: Barbara Johnson's Album of Styles and Fabrics*, ed. Natalie Rothstein (New York: Thames & Hudson, 1987).
4. Etymologically, both words are connected with the Latin verb 'texere', to weave, and imply interweaving.
5. Mikhail Pyliayev, *Zamechatelniye Chudaki i Originaly* [*Memorable Eccentrics and Originals*] (Moscow: Interbuk, 1990), 90–91. For more on Prince Kurakin, see the chapter on Russian dandyism in our book.

6 See, for instance, James Wyatt, *The Taylor's Friendly Instructor, being an easy guide for finding the principal and leading points essential to the art of fitting the human shape, forming a complete system delineating the different parts according to the proportions of the human figures, illustrated with twenty four engraved models of different garments, designed on the principles of practical geometry, displaying in the most familiar manner the variety of forms produced by the variation of fashion; with notes containing the reason of every rule; also remarks on numerous systems in practice by different authors* (London: J. Harris, 1822).

7 *Neckclothitania; or Tietania: Being an Essay on Starchers. By One of the Cloth* (London: Stockdale, 1818).

8 *The Whole Art of Dress! Or, the Road to Elegance and Fashion, at the Enormous Saving of Thirty Per Cent! Being a treatise upon that essential and much-cultivated requisite of the present day, gentlemen's costume. Explains and clearly defines, by a series of beautifully engraved illustrations, the most becoming assortments of colours, and style of dress and undress in all varieties; suited to different ages and complexions, so as to render the human figure most symmetrical and imposing to their eyes. Also, directions in the purchase of all kinds of wearing apparel: accompanied by hints for the toilette, containing a few valuable and original recipes; likewise, some advice to the improvement of defects in the person and carriage. Together with a dissertation on uniform in general and the selection of fine dress. By a cavalry officer* (London: E. Wilson, 1830).

9 Peter McNeil, 'Macaroni Masculinities', *Fashion Theory* 4, no. 4 (2000): 377–378.

10 See https://www.ruthenia.ru/folklore/postfolk.htm. Accessed 1 July 2022.

11 *The Dandies' Ball, or High Life in the City* (London: John Marshall, 1819).

12 Nathaniel Adams, Rose Callahan and Glenn O'Brien, *I am Dandy: The Return of the Elegant Gentleman* (Berlin: Die Gestalten Verlag, 2013). Nathaniel Adams, *We Are Dandy: The Elegant Gentleman Around the World* (Berlin: Die Gestalten Verlag, 2016).

13 See George Walden, *Who Is a Dandy?* (London: Gibson Square Books, 2002); Ian Kelly, *Beau Brummell: The Ultimate Man of Style* (New York: Free Press, 2006).

14 See Rhonda Garelick, *Rising Star: Dandyism, Gender and Performance in the Fin de Siècle* (Princeton, NJ; Chichester: Princeton University Press, 1998); Susan Fillin-Yeh, ed., *Dandies: Fashion and Finesse in Art and Culture* (New York: New York University Press, 2001); Anne Kristin Tietenberg, *Der Dandy als Grenzgänger der Moderne: Selbststilisierungen in Literatur und Popkultur* (Berlin: Lit, 2013).

15 Dominic Janes, *British Dandies: Engendering Scandal and Fashioning a Nation* (Oxford: Bodleian Library Publishing, 2022); *Dandy Style: 250 Years of British Men's Fashion*, eds. Shaun Cole and Miles Lambert (New Haven, CT: Yale University Press, 2021); Len Gutkin, *Dandyism: Forming Fiction from Modernism to the Present* (Charlottesville: University of Virginia Press, 2020); Phillip Mann, *The Dandy at Dusk: Taste and Melancholy in the Twentieth Century* (London: Head of Zeus, 2018); Geertjan de Vugt, *Political Dandyism in Literature and Art: Genealogy of a Paradigm* (London, New York: Palgrave Macmillan, Springer International Publishing, 2018).

16 Monica L. Miller, *Slaves to Fashion: Black Dandyism and the Styling of Black Diasporic Identity* (Durham, NC: Duke University Press, 2009); Shantrelle P. Lewis, *Dandy Lion: The Black Dandy and Street Style* (New York: Aperture, 2017).

17 Olga Vainshtein, *Dendi: moda, literatura, stil' zhizni* [Dandy: Fashion, Literature, Lifestyle] (Moscow: New Literary Review, 2005, 2006, 2012, 2017, 2021).

Chapter One

FASHIONING THE DANDY

Apollos in Double-Breasted Coats

Tracing the roots of the classic men's suit, we inevitably find ourselves returning to early nineteenth-century England. The strict canon of male elegance developed by English dandies still retains much of its influence today; yet in those times, their style was seen as a radical break with tradition. What were the striking differences that distinguished the new canon of dandyism from the tastes of the previous era?

Delving into this intriguing matter, we may find ourselves revisiting the history of European costume. The dandy appeared as a fashion type from the mid-1790s in England. The nearest ancestors of the Dandy were the British Beaux and Macaroni of the eighteenth-century, preferring vibrant colours and sparkling fabrics (Figure 2).

Figure 2 Philip Dawe. The Macaroni. A Real Character at the Late Masquerade (1773). Wikimedia Commons.

The precursor to dandy style is late seventeenth-century male dress: around that time, the buttoned justacorps overcoat emerged as a universal element of male clothing (in French, its name 'surtout' literally means 'over everything'). This was usually worn with short full trousers, stockings, and a long vest.[1] Habitually half-buttoned, the vest concealed the wearer's waist. The shirts with their soft collars allowed for the use of neckerchiefs, which would later be followed by ties. All this together, justacorps, vest, shirt, tie, and trousers, formed the basic model of male dress.

The most striking and artificial-looking elements in late seventeenth – early eighteenth-century male costume remained, of course, the wigs and heels, remnants of the Rococo era. Overall, the most conservative aspect of contemporary men's fashion was perhaps the pear-shaped silhouette itself: decidedly at odds with later trends, it remained in vogue until 1780. Narrow across the shoulders, justacorps were frequently made without collars, as these would inevitably be covered in powder and pomade[2] from wigs. At the same time, the lower half of the body was exaggerated by the full, spreading tails of the justacorps, which sometimes included whalebone rods sewn into them to preserve their shape.

The focal point of the male silhouette was thus inevitably the stomach, protruding above the low-cut trouser waist. The boundary between short, full trouser leg and stocking, decorated as it often was with a bow or buckle, split the leg visually in two, making even tall gentlemen appear shorter. The resulting effect was a pear-shaped outline, appearing almost to encourage plumpness in the stomach area, much to the satisfaction of the portlier gentlemen.

By the end of the eighteenth century, the pear-shaped silhouette began to give way to the new dandy look. The new fashion brought together multiple trends, one of these, the simple, austere Protestant style of the English Puritans. Following the Reformation and revolutionary years, the clerical look in England became associated with loyalty to the new powers. Even in aristocratic circles, beaux favoured sombre, dark outfits, showing off their snow-white shirt collars to great effect.

The beginning of the nineteenth century brought with it the 'Great Male Renunciation'[3] described by British psychologist John Carl Flügel. Seen as a unification and simplification of male attire, this process also involved the disappearance of bright colours, luxurious fabrics and other 'excessive' detail. Renouncing brash looks in favour of qualities such as good taste, usefulness, and efficiency,[4] men espoused the new style as both practical and dignified. The reasons behind this shift were, according to Flügel, primarily political. The aristocratic aesthetic that saw dress as a means of denoting status and nobility was gradually disappearing; instead, under the influence of Europe's revolutions, a process of democratization was underway, calling for all external signs of social status to be eradicated. With the growth of industrial capitalism, a new bourgeois urban modernity was formed, with a burgeoning service industry and ever-growing number of jobs for clerks and officials. The need for a simple universal dark suit was becoming increasingly clear.

Another style contributing to the dandy canon was the English country squire look. Lovers of hunting and other outdoor pursuits, in the countryside these gentlemen would

Figure 3 G.Cruikshank, I.R.Cruikshank. Jerry in training for a 'swell' (1821). Illustration from 'Life in London' by Pierce Egan. Wikimedia Commons.

often be seen on horseback, rather than in a carriage – hence, the need for appropriate dress. Overcoats constituted a simplified version of the justacorps with no front tails, thus, more convenient for riding. For outdoor activities, natural colours, greens, browns, greys, and beiges were preferred. The most popular fabrics were wool, linen, and leather, with classic English wool the overall favourite.

With its ability to stretch and take on the desired shape, wool wore well, preserving its appearance for long periods. The world-famous English tailors working with the material invented dozens of ingenious techniques to achieve their chosen effect (Figure 3). The wool would be steamed to prevent wrinkling, or to give bulk where needed; virtually invisible tucks and pads could be inserted, turning the fabric into a smooth body-hugging suit. 'A coat should always sit easy and close to the shoulders, and close in at the back, the skirts hanging smoothly, without the slightest crumple,' one contemporary fashion treatise stated.[5] The fashions of the previous Rococo period had not only allowed for wrinkles in one's attire, but had encouraged them for special aesthetic effect. A myriad of shimmering creases in silk or velvet was seen as evoking the play of sunlight on water, a stippled surface all the better suited to show the fabric's beauty.

In the new dandy style, however, smooth, understated fabrics and close, easy fits were used to create a backdrop for the *fundamental structure* of the silhouette. This was highlighted by visible seams, well-balanced proportions, and the absence of bright colors or accessories.

The basic, bare construction is more important than the ornamental surface. This logic could be seen later as underpinning a number of areas of modern art, like Constructivist architecture, for example. In the history of dress, it is through late eighteenth – early nineteenth century dandy fashion in particular that contemporary minimalist aesthetic manifested itself.

How did this radically modernist change come about? Paradoxically, the main source of dandyism is to be found in ancient Greek and Roman cultures. In the second half of the eighteenth century, following archaeological excavations in Pompeii and Herculaneum, Europe was gripped by a classical antiquity craze. If previously, the main celebrated works were the Apollo Belvedere and statue of Laocoön and His Sons from the Vatican collection, at the turn of the century, the world became aware of new masterpieces. In 1806, a set of colossal sculptures that had adorned the Parthenon was brought to England by Lord Elgin, and a whole generation of young English people was raised with these ideals of classical beauty.[6]

In France, antique heritage found new expression in the work of architect Claude-Nicolas Ledoux, painter of the Revolution Jacques-Louis David, and actor François-Joseph Talma. Thus, from the second half of the eighteenth century, a neoclassical[7] canon was formed. As often happens in times of change, this was seen as the latest expression of humanist values.

Contemporary views on antiquity were best defined in the writings of German art historian Johann Joachim Winckelmann. In his analysis, Winckelmann stressed the importance of contour, explaining how its exquisite grace was perhaps the main feature of classical sculpture:

> The finest contour combines or defines all aspects of what is most beautiful in nature and of the qualities of ideal beauty in the figures of the Greeks. Or rather it is the highest concept in both cases.[8]

For this reason, Winckelmann was not overly fond of Baroque art, in which effect is often achieved through the use of plentiful extravagant detail. The art historian's views were extremely well-respected. What he proposed was not merely a reappraisal of the heritage of classical antiquity, but a new frame of cultural vision.

Thus, the new criterion for perfection was the body's outline. This trend was quick to manifest itself in fashion: we might conclude that *the importance of clear contour in ancient sculpture bore directly on the huge importance accorded to silhouette and construction in the dandy dress code*. Swiss art historian Heinrich Wölfflin's description of Greek sculpture, indeed, could well be applied to male fashion of the early nineteenth century:

> Classic art aims at boundaries: there is no form that does not express itself within a definite line-motive, no figure of which we could not say with an eye to what view it is conceived... The silhouette is here more than the fortuitous cessation of the visibility of the form: it asserts, beside the figure, a kind of independence, just because it represents something self-sufficing.[9]

By extension, we may conclude that *the distinct neoclassical silhouette was the main feature to determine the development of male dress over the following two centuries*. Let us recall the words of Jim, columnist for the Russian magazine Dandy in 1910:

> There was a time, in the days of our great-grandfathers, when male dress was enhanced with gaudy colors, precious gems, lace and plumes. Nowadays, the only feature that matters in men's fashion is the outline – it is this line, in its exquisite form that makes up the appearance of the contemporary dandy.[10]

The aesthetics of antique sculpture had a direct bearing on contemporary notions of ideal beauty: comparing a man's body to that of a Greek statue was extremely common. 'He is in plain view: the crowd gazes at him, as if he were an ancient statue,'[11] wrote the novelist Ivan Goncharov of his fashionable hero. In ancient Greek sculpture, men were most commonly depicted nude, athletic bodies rippling with well-developed muscles, broad in the shoulders and chest. Fashion-conscious males would often adopt a characteristic pose typical of Greek statues

> ...in a state of rest, in which one leg bears the weight and the other rests playfully, then the latter was placed only so far back as was necessary to remove the figure from a vertical position.[12]

Known as 'chiastic', this pose was often to be seen in portraits and engravings in fashionable magazines. To be told that one resembles a Greek god or ancient hero was, at that time, the greatest compliment. Two of the best-known dandies were considered to recall Apollo: Lord Byron's facial features were often compared to those of the god, while George Brummell was said to resemble Apollo in physique.

The cult of antiquity brought about a unique moment in fashion, with contemporary views on the ideal Greek body promoting a new silhouette in dress. In his praise of pure line, Winckelmann paid special attention to the beauty of the body's contours:

> ...beneath the garments of the Greek figures the masterly contour is still prominent and is clearly the main concern of the artist, who reveals the beautiful build of the body through the marble as though through a Kos garment.[13]

The antique model of corporeality can be seen as something of a Platonic ideal, a Form of Forms. The ideal body was a visible abstraction waiting to be incorporated in a practical, modern way. The neoclassical empire style brought with it a set of completely new aims. Dress was not to conceal or alter the body, but to outline its Greek-influenced contours. In other words, clothing was to produce an effect similar to that of nudity, with the nude body likened to that of Apollo.

How, then, could the dandies of the time pursue the ideal of the Hellenic body? Old-fashioned outfits did not match the idealized muscular torsos of neo-antiquity. The new 'body beautiful' demanded a different cut, straining at the familiar silhouette. The narrow shoulders of the old pear-shaped figure opened out, revealing strong biceps beneath close-cut sleeves. The top part of the male costume grew in size, as the rippling torso burst through its double row of flimsy fastenings: the old silhouette, with its pathetic paunch, was rendered obsolete.

The new style was more compact, coat tails narrowing in, bulky pockets and cuffs disappearing altogether. Trousers became tighter, hugging the legs and creating a lengthened silhouette to replace the familiar pear shape.

The top part of the ensemble grew to accommodate the antique-style torso. Padded shoulders and sleeves, widened in the shoulder area to suggest muscular arms, conveyed an impression of well-built, athletic body structure.

The new corporeal canon demanded new standards of dress: the old look, with its pear-shaped outline and protruding paunch, was no longer relevant. The main ingredient of the new look was the country gentleman's coat, the only one to sport a collar. Even so, it required extensive remodelling, the collar growing higher in order to present the wearer's 'heroic' neck and position the head in the most striking way. The head itself was no longer adorned with a powdered wig, but instead boasted an elegant coiffure à la Titus,[14] a short cut named after a Roman character in a Voltaire play. With the new double-breasted coat and waistcoat, the wearer's chest was flatteringly exaggerated. If the previous pear-shaped silhouette had been reminiscent of an isosceles triangle, the new outfit's lapels formed an inverted triangle, pointing down towards a new centre of focus, the wearer's manhood. Where previously, the folds of men's full trousers and long waistcoat tails had served as 'fig leaves', dandy costume introduced a candid style harking back to the Renaissance with its skin-tight breeches. The Russian writer Nikolai Grech described the new look thus:

> The fabric is smooth, with no wrinkles. It hugs the figure. There is no decoration; the shirt is exceptionally snowy-white.[15]

The tight one-piece trousers, shorter waistcoats, and coats with no front tails served to accentuate men's sexual charm. Handsome legs were highly prized in society, eliciting comments and comparisons, and offering ladies a pleasant and safe opportunity to pay gentlemen compliments.

The neoclassical look in women's fashion of that time was also highly eroticized due to the play of layers of see-through fabric. The cut of the tunic was low, with bare shoulders and arms, the chest was but half-covered – thus, the new empire style was in marked contrast to women's dress of the previous decades, as ladies were now permitted to show off far more of their curves.

Flesh-colored underclothes were worn, or occasionally, the semi-transparent gauze dress would be worn without any undergarments. In order better to flatter their curves, women would often wet their costumes before a ball, creating a look reminiscent of the Nike of Samothrace. Wetting fabric was, it seems, a technique used by the sculptors of antiquity themselves also, as Winckelmann suggests:

> Greek drapery was mostly made in imitation of thin and wet garments, and the result of this, as artists know, is that they cling close to the skin and the body, and allow the nudity of the latter to be perceived.[16]

In the nineteenth century, naturally, such risqué methods evoked much debate on morals: 'The Lacedæmonian ladies, who were veiled only by public opinion, were better covered from profane eyes than some English ladies are in wet drapery,'[17] dryly notes the perspicacious Mr. Percival in Maria Edgeworth's *Belinda* (1801). In countries with a cold climate such as Russia, such experiments with thin, wetted clothing could naturally lead to the wearer's catching cold. One of the fashion victims was the famous beauty Aleksandra Tiufiakina – she caught a cold at a ball and died of fever.

The Hellenic body craze played a formative role in the development of both men's and women's costume. Thus, with the revival of classical antiquity, the new corporeal canon was molded. In men's fashion the flowing, smooth outlines of the light-coloured trousers made the wearer's legs appear longer and shapelier – especially with thinner gentlemen. 'Excessive corpulence is a real physical shortcoming,' mused Horace Raisson, the author of numerous texts on fashion.[18] At once visible and invisible, the new dandy outfit did everything to create a skillful illusion of 'Greek' proportions, rhetorically denuding and heroizing the wearer.

Today's beaux, indubitably, still reap the benefits of the neoclassical period in men's fashion. And, whilst our evocation of Apollo may cause some to smile incredulously, variations on the dandy style continue to crop up in leading designers' collections worldwide, time and time again, confirming the stimulating potential of the classical tradition.

Brummell the Innovator

The most legendary of the dandies in the Regency period was George Bryan 'Beau' Brummell (1778–1840), originating from middle-class family. He had the reputation of being 'England's prime minister of taste' and was a celebrity. He may be remembered for an endless variety of exploits, yet his main legacy was as an innovator in men's style.

George Brummel's exemplary perfection of style was based on or the principle of 'conspicuous inconspicuousness'. It meant the imperative of dressing elegantly, yet unobtrusively, avoiding undesirable attention and marked ostentation.

This was a very important and essentially modern principle of the vestimentary behaviour, implying the blurring of class distinctions, since the new tactics erased the aristocratic pretensions to demonstrate wealth and noble origin through clothes. In many ways, Brummell's effortless career anticipated the modern world of social mobility in which taste is privileged above birth and wealth.

How, then, did this fascinating dandy dress? (Figure 4). Brummell's biographer Captain William Jesse offers a detailed description of the Beau's costume:

> His morning dress was similar to that of every other gentleman – Hessians and pantaloons, or top-boots and buckskins, with a blue coat, and a light or buff-coloured waistcoat; of course, fitting to admiration, on the best figure in England. His dress of an evening was a blue coat and white waistcoat, black pantaloons which buttoned tight to the ankle, striped silk stockings, and opera-hat; in fact, he was always carefully dressed, but never the slave of fashion.[19]

The only adornments to Brummell's costume were the brass buttons on his coat, a simple ring, and his gold watch chain.

For all their seeming simplicity, Brummell's outfits nevertheless demanded frequent changing of clothes.

> An élégant then requires per week twenty shirts, twenty-four pocket-handkerchiefs, nine or ten pair of summer trousers, thirty neck-handkerchiefs, (unless he wears black ones), a dozen waistcoats, and stockings à discretion.[20]

Figure 4 George 'Beau' Brummell, watercolor by Richard Dighton (1805). Wikimedia Commons.

Such, then, was the new code of gentlemanly consumerism: refined, yet never demonstrative.

The key principles of dandy style, according to Brummell, were simplicity and understatement. 'No perfumes', he insisted, 'but very fine linen, plenty of it, and country washing'.[21] 'If John Bull turns around to look at you, you are not well dressed but either too stiff, too tight, or too fashionable,' the Beau liked to repeat. Or, in other words, 'let it not be said of a man, what a well-dressed person he is, but how gentlemanly he dresses!'[22] A maxim which holds true to this day for followers of classical men's fashion around the world.

Hailing Brummell as the father of modern dress, the essayist and critic Max Beerbohm stressed the importance of the Beau's innovations:

> The costume of the nineteenth century, as shadowed for us first by Mr. Brummell, so quiet, so reasonable, and, I say emphatically, so beautiful; free from folly or affectation, yet susceptible to exquisite ordering; plastic, austere, economical, may not be ignored. I spoke of the doom of swift rebellions, but I doubt even if any soever gradual evolution will lead us astray from the general precepts of Mr. Brummell's code. At every step in the progress of democracy those precepts will be strengthened.[23]

A happy compromise between the decorative outfits of the macaronis and the traditional austere English country gentleman look,[24] Brummell's style could be seen as universal bourgeois dress. His materials were wool, leather, and linen. With the help of nearly imperceptible padding, curved streams, discreet darts, and steam pressing the coat was refined into an exquisitely balanced garment that fitted smoothly without wrinkles and buttoned without strain. The fit, the perfection of line, and texture transformed the body into a streamlined silhouette, following the neoclassic empire fashion.

Rejecting affectation and effeminacy in dress characteristic for Macaroni, George Brummell achieved the universal look, suitable for all classes and occupations. It was relieved from drabness by personal touches, such as Brummell's waistcoats and ties.

Perfect neckties were not Beau Brummell's only contribution to male fashion. Another of his innovations, stirrup trousers, is, though no less radical, far less known. In the 1810s, short, close-fitting knee breeches began to be replaced by full-length trousers. Among the first to try out the new style were Napoleon's soldiers, who wore them during military campaigns. Other Europeans were also quick to appreciate the advantages offered by longer styles. In England, full-length trousers began to be worn in the daytime, with the tighter knee breeches and stockings replacing them in the evenings. It is not uncommon, in the history of dress, for festive and evening wear to preserve older, even archaic styles, as was the case, for instance, with tailcoats and tuxedos.

The new, loose fitting trousers brought their own problems, however: due to the wider cut, they easily became creased. Brummell, naturally, could not endure wearing any garment that did not look fresh, and spent long hours with his tailors, discussing possible options. Finally, he came up with a solution: trousers with special buttons on the legs, and stirrups,[25] which were totally hidden inside high-Hessian boots. This ingenious invention caused Brummell to become known as the man whose trousers never creased, and for some time, no one could comprehend how the Beau pulled it off (Figure 5).

Besides enabling the wearer to avoid unsightly creases, Brummell's design also showed off gentlemen's legs to great advantage, the flawlessly smooth finish lending sex appeal

Figure 5 Prince Esterhazy, Lord Fife, Hughes Ball, Lord Winter (from left to right). All gentlemen are wearing stirrup trousers, one of Brummell's inventions. Source of illustration: Gronow R. H. Reminiscences of Captain Gronow, being anecdotes of the camp, the court and the clubs at the close of the last war with France. L.: Smith, Elder and Co, 1862.

and erotic charm: in this respect, the dandy innovation echoed the Empire style. With gentlemen in figure-hugging breeches accompanying beauties in flowing tunics, the simple, pure lines of their silhouettes put one in mind of neoclassical harmony.

Both with his ties, and with his trousers, Brummell essentially sought to resolve the same issues: eager to avoid unnecessary, unsightly bulk, he focused on the purely 'technical' details of his constructions. This minimalist strategy proved successful in every case. Ultimately, the stirrup trousers served the same purpose as the starched ties. Even though the starch accentuated the folds of the cloth, while the stirrups helped avoid them, both methods were used in order to achieve an effective silhouette. Worn together, the two created a pleasant contrast, the smooth, plain lower part of the body balanced by the structured, precise folds in the upper part.

Once Brummell's secret to perfect ties became known, men of fashion became obsessed with starch. The less-experienced dandies would often go too far, starching their ties so assiduously that it became impossible for them to turn their heads. Brummell himself, on the other hand, had discovered just the right amount of starch for the most pleasing, seemingly effortless, look.

His followers were not so fortunate. One young man took to wearing such highly starched ties that he could no longer turn around, and instead was forced to lean backwards. On one occasion, tipping his head back to call his man, he almost twisted his neck. Another made his cravat so stiff, he contrived to cut his ear on the starched fold. A third burned his chin, attempting to iron the corners of his cravat after it had been tied, so loath was he to waste the ideal knot he had painstakingly achieved.

Needless to say, these unfortunate incidents provided perfect material for caricaturists,[26] and Brummell himself was quick to offer cutting comments. The arbiter of fashion was merciless in decrying those who gave up their comfort in the senseless pursuit of vogue. The style introduced by Brummell, unusual and trendy at first, later became universally accepted precisely due to its practicality and lack of excess.

Renouncing external splendor, or perhaps rather, inventing new laws of good taste, the dandy created a system which was initially seen as an elitist esoteric code. The dandy's style must on no account be gaudy or overly eye-catching. Beau Brummell, according to Barbey D'Aurevilly, invented the great axiom of dress: 'To be well-dressed you must not be noticed'.[27] The true dandy aspires only to 'conspicuous inconspicuousness': his costume should not draw excessive attention from the unenlightened; within his own circle, however, it would be instantly noted and appreciated.

Another law of the dandy's elegance stated that against the general backdrop of 'conspicuous inconspicuousness', a single significant detail could stand out: a fastidiously tied cravat, for instance, a gadget cane, or an exquisite ring or superb gloves.[28]

Well-trained to notice 'conspicuous inconspicuousness', the fellow-dandy's shrewd gaze would instantly home in on such signs and symbols. The dandy's 'super vision' allows him to read these signals: members of one's circle could be immediately recognized thanks to small, yet telling details.

In this new urban everyday reality, the observer's gaze homes in on the micro-level, becoming accustomed to focusing on minute detail. The definitive function of detail becomes paramount. To this day, fashion uses such details as code: the workmanship around the buttonholes on a man's jacket, for instance, speaks volumes to the seasoned observer about the wearer's taste and financial status.

On Cravats

The cravat can be called the key element in early nineteenth-century dandy dress. Later evolving into the tie,[29] this item has continued to play an important decorative role in male attire, and is much loved by beaux to this day. Thanks to Beau Brummell, the art of tying the cravat came to be seen as a special dandy hobby. Even after Brummell, a well-tied cravat continued to be seen as a sign of good taste. The Beau, as we know, could spend hours on end, tying his cravat. Gathering up the discarded scarves from unsuccessful attempts, 'They are our failures,'[30] his valet would explain to guests. To fix his creations in place, Brummell devised a technique using starch, which held the meticulously tied cravat firmly in the desired position. The process of tying the cravat was in itself no mean feat.

> The collar, which was always fixed to his shirt, was so large that, before being folded down, it completely hid his head and face, and the white neckcloth was at least a foot in height. The first coup d'archet[31] was made with the shirt collar, which he folded down to its proper size; and Brummell then standing before the glass, with his chin poked up to the ceiling, by the gentle and gradual declension of his jaw, creased the cravat to reasonable dimensions, the form of each succeeding crease being perfected with the shirt which he had just discarded.[32]

For nineteenth-century dandies, the elegant starched folds of the cravat echoed the magnificent fluid lines of the drapes on antique male bodies. Sculptures of Greek gods and heroes tended to feature a chlamys slung casually over one arm: the classic nude figures of the Apollo Belvedere and Meleager are framed gracefully by the soft folds of their cloaks.[33]

The rhythm and direction of the creases in the dress of antique sculptures created an illusion of dynamic movement. Serving to accentuate the figure's pose or gesture, they drew attention to the rippling contours of the body. In Baroque sculpture and painting, on the contrary, the heavy layers of fabric concealed the body, obscuring it from view. The marble folds of the vestments of Bernini's sculptures and creased covers in Zurbarán's paintings take on a life of their own as indicators of the infinite and elevated: '…when marble seizes and bears to infinity folds that cannot be explained by the body, but a spiritual adventure that can set the body ablaze,' Gilles Deleuze writes of Bernini.[34]

In the French philosopher's opinion, the 'liberated' nature of Baroque folds is due to the elements at play in between the body and its clothing. Wind, air, water, and light, Deleuze suggests, soften the contours of the body, transporting it into the realm of more abstract and dynamic forces:

> Folds of clothing acquire an autonomy and a fullness that are not simply decorative effects. They convey the intensity of a spiritual force exerted on the body, either to turn it upside down or to stand or raise it up over and again, but in every event to turn it inside out and to mold its inner surfaces.[35]

The opulence of Baroque dress served to support Deleuze's observations: the flowing cloaks, full trousers, ruffle breeches, and puffed sleeves with lace cuffs created abundant folds which hid the contours of the body. The wearer's dress became a semantically laden emblem of power, sanctity or wealth, as the decorative, dynamic creases magnified the figure, lending it a monumental air.

This state of affairs is in marked contrast to the dandy's aesthetic code. From obfuscation and the full pleats of Baroque dress, dandies strove to create pure contours and clear outlines. Echoing classical antiquity in late eighteenth and early nineteenth-century art, neoclassicism brought closed, well-defined contours to every figure and detail.

> Winckelmann, criticising baroque sculpture, exclaims scornfully, "What a contour!" He regards the self-contained expressive contour line as an essential element of all sculpture and loses interest when the outline yields him nothing. Yet, beside sculpture with a stressed, significant outline, we can imagine sculpture with depreciated outline, where the expression is not formed in the line, and the baroque possessed such an art.[36]

In male dress, neoclassical culture produced a look which replicated the contours of the antique body, a clear silhouette with pure, flowing lines. The undulating play of the Baroque folds remained only in the cravat, which underwent significant change. The neoclassical canon could only allow for starched, static folds, frozen contours of a successful dynamic move. The play of elements we observed in Baroque dress was no longer part of the picture; neither did these folds carry a message of spiritual movement or élan.

Tamed and quieted, the elements were subjugated to the aesthetic will of the minimalist dandy taste. The rigid folds were arranged with infinite care: no fortunate coincidence, but a meticulous disposition requiring considerable technical skill. In neoclassical rationalism, the elements had no place: the wind would never toy with the ends of Beau Brummell's cravat. A flowing necktie belongs rather to the Romantic poet, like Byron, accentuating his dynamism and harmony with the elements.

Before Beau Brummell, the cravat often dangled loosely around the wearer's neck, with no fixed form or outline. The shape of the knot was not seen as possessing importance. Brummell, however, introduced a host of intricate knots and folds, giving rise to numerous imitations. Men strove to study his complex practices. Fashionable people tried to invent new styles of tying the neckcloths. Answering this demand, the satirical brochure 'Neckclothitania; or, Tietania, an essay on starchers, by one of the cloth', was published in 1818. Despite its playful title, it contained descriptions and instructions for fashioning a whole range of knots.[37] Later in 1827, a special treatise featuring 39 ways of tying the cravat appeared under the pseudonym H. Le Blanc (ascribed to the young Honoré de Balzac[38]).

The frontispiece of Neckclothitania depicted several basic ties: 'Oriental, Mathematical, Osbaldeston, Napoleon, American, Mail Coach, Trone d'Amour, Ball Room, Horse Collar, Irish, Hunting, Maharatta, Barrel Knot'.[39]

Each of the ties was designed with a particular fabric and colour in mind. The Oriental knot, for instance, was recommended 'with a very stiff and rigid cloth...

Care should be taken, that not a single indenture or crease should be visible in this tie… The Mathematical Tie (or Triangular Tie), is far less severe than the former. There are three creases in it… The colour best suited to it, is called couleur de la cuisse d'une nymphe émue'.[40]

Well-starched, the Trone d'Amour has a single horizontal fold in the centre, and best suits the colour 'yeux de fille en extase' ('the eyes of a girl in ecstasy') – it is difficult not to notice the ironic tone of the author! Combining the qualities of the Mathematical and Irish, the Ballroom Tie was made with 'virgin white'. The Mail Coach, 'worn by all stage-coachmen, guards, the swells of the fancy, and ruffians… was best made out of a cashmere shawl and had one end brought over the knot, spread out and tucked into the waist'.[41]

Meticulously arranged with a series of confident strokes, the neoclassical starched cravat lent to the dandy the air of a statue. Slowly lowering his jaw in order to produce natural-looking folds, Beau Brummell was, essentially, performing the actions of a sculptor. At the same time, of course, the overall effect was required to seem effortless: the carefully tied cravat was to appear donned almost as an afterthought. Paying tremendous attention to their looks and poses, some dandies, however, inevitably failed to achieve the required degree of casual nonchalance.

Lord Byron, despite his love of dandyism, did not approve of starched cravats, and is often portrayed with bare neck and unbuttoned collar. The Romantic poet better suited a raw, fresh look, baring his face to the elements, singing the praises of nature and powerful emotion. His poses and demeanour spoke of passion, reflecting the moods and anguish of his characters. His heroes are often seen in nature, the landscapes mirroring their state of mind, whereas the typical dandy, of course, was urban, inspired not by nature, but by art and artifice.

Among the artificial instruments used by dandies to achieve their desired look were special gadgets for fixing and tying the cravat such as 'col' in France. Nineteenth-century European beaux also favoured 'stocks', special supports of neckties which could be smooth or with fine fixed folds, and wrapped around the wearer's neck to help preserve the shape of his cravat.[42] Popular in the first decades of the nineteenth century, these helped the wearer fashion the sought-after knot. A good tie could also be produced with the use of a special wire frame. Of Russian beaux, the music expert Yuri Arnold wrote:

> But what gave the entire figure of the over-zealous beau its special importance and aplomb was the combination of the shirt collar, tie and haircut. The base of the tie was formed by a tiny 'machine' (I cannot think of another expression) composed of an infinite number of narrow coils of finest copper wire. Covered in calico, these were finished with thin goat or rabbit skin. Up to three *vershoks* [just over 13 cm] high, this construction could be carefully and tightly wrapped in a lightly starched, well-ironed fine cambric cravat, thus creating a tie to adorn the enthusiastic beau's neck. Holding the somewhat large scarf by the middle and pressing it to the front of his neck, which would be covered by a wide, well-starched cambric shirt collar reaching up to the wearer's very ears, the young man could wrap it around, tying it in the front in a wide bow. The ends would sometimes be adorned with elaborate embroidery. Sitting atop this construction, the wearer's head took on a lofty attitude, and his face appeared plump and healthy.[43]

European beaux, who adored inventing complex knots for their cravats, frequently resorted to such constructions. In Balzac's 'Lost Illusions', the aspiring poet Lucien Chardon is quite miserable without such a gadget (col): 'Instead of using flexible whalebone to keep his face well poised, he felt muffled up in his ugly shirt collar and his cravat was too lax to give support to his drooping head.'[44]

The frame's wire base may have been substituted with whalebone, yet its purpose remains the same: it is one of the modifications of stock. The action in Balzac's novel takes place in 1823. Known for his detailed passages on dress, the writer infuses his descriptions with symbolic meaning. A dandy able to hold his head up high exudes social confidence, whereas the unfortunate Lucien, new to Paris, feels like an awkward, poorly dressed provincial outsider.

With Brummell's introduction of starch, it became easier for fashion lovers to fix the folds of their cravats firmly in place. The frame, which remained popular among Russian dandies, offered extra support for those unable to engineer their own shape.[45]

Thus, with its rigid, carefully crafted folds, the starched cravat left no room for nature and the elements. Its immovable, immaculate appearance helped lend the dandy the air of a statue. A key element in the dandy's dress, it represented a localised focus of play which, at first glance, appeared carelessly casual, yet in reality constituted the result of meticulous planning, much like an intrigue in a classical drama.

The hours spent by the dandy tying his cravat and fashioning the perfect folds clearly demonstrate that this was the final stroke in the beau's ensemble, the culmination of his efforts, requiring discipline and control over the emotions. In situations of discomfort, indeed, it is perhaps no coincidence that men may begin to turn their head this way and that, attempting to ease their collar, or keep touching the knot of their tie, as if to give themselves more air. Closing the circle, the final knot in the cravat can be seen as a gesture of self-control and assurance. The fixed, starched folds of Brummell's cravats showed mastery over matter, while the skilfully achieved nonchalance of his knots appeared to hint at 'Je ne sais quoi', sparsely dosed emotion.

Styling Interiors

Let us examine an important aspect of the dandy's art of self-fashioning – the interior design. George Brummell furnished his London house with elegant boule furniture and collected rare snuff-boxes. Even in exile in France he continued to purchase boule furniture, bronze statuettes, and Sèvres china. His treasures included a rare service decorated with the portraits of the famous mistresses of Louis XIV and Louis XV. On display on a separate table were valuable knick-knacks – snuff-boxes specially ordered in Paris, a marble paperweight that once belonged to Napoleon, miniature paintings, albums, and knives.

Another famous dandy, Count d'Orsay (1801–1852) was also seriously interested in interior design. Each time he bought or rented a new house – Seymour Place, and then Gore House in London – he would take charge of the décor. His close friend Lady Blessington had acquired a large collection of antiquities during a trip to Italy, and they used these rarities to create a noble classical style. The living room and library were adorned with large Sèvres vases, magnificent chandeliers that had once belonged to Marie Antoinette, and corbels trimmed in plates of tortoise shell. Antique statues and busts adorned the niches of the living room, and lying on a table piled with books was a life-size marble copy of Lady Blessington's hand. Small individual cabinets contained a collection of knick-knacks and curiosities. This collection was displayed in the living room of the house on Seymour Place and not only served a decorative purpose but also was a conversation piece for guests. It included a golden needle case trimmed in agates and diamonds, a rock crystal vial that had belonged to Madame de Sévigné, and Madame Maintenon's pincushion in a frame in the shape of a heart made of gold and enamel. As Lady Blessington wrote in her diary when she bought this pincushion, 'it is stuck full of pins like the hearts of the Protestants with thorns after the revocation of the Edict of Nantes'.[46] The collection also contained scissors belonging to Madame du Deffand and a beauty spot box owned by Ninon de Lanclos. Through these treasured objects the Count d'Orsay and Lady Blessington not only expressed their aesthetic taste but also unambiguously declared their cultural identity. They thought of themselves as continuing the tradition of the royal court, heirs to famous beauties, courtesans, and influential figures in high society. Participation in the world of the French aristocracy is a semiotic trick that has been used more than once in European dandyism.

Dandy enthusiasm for interior design culminated towards the end of the nineteenth century with the appearance of the decadents. The famous dandy Robert de Montesquiou, the prototype of the Baron de Charlus in Marcel Proust's novel 'Remembrance of Things Past', was known not only for his elegant gray suits but also for the amazing décor of his homes. 'Décor is a state of the soul,' he was fond of saying. He arranged each residence as a special aesthetic space subordinated to the designer's conception. For example, he had a room dedicated to the moon imbued with the spirit of night and decorated in shades of azure and silver. Montesquiou himself describes it as follows in his memoirs:

> One wall of the room was dark blue in color, and in a shaded niche was a chair upholstered in fabric of the same shade; the opposite wall was covered in gray cloth with drawings of cameos, and the wall by the fireplace was done in silvery Morocco leather adorned with a branching pattern in light blue; finally, the fourth wall was covered in velvet of a charming gray shade that is usually known as 'Stevens', but in my opinion should more accurately be called 'mousy gray'. On the floor was a dark gray carpet on which played the shadows of semi-transparent gauze hung on the opposite side of the room, creating the illusion of streams of moonlight.[17]

In his analysis of the symbolism of décor, the French philosopher Jean Baudrillard argues that avoidance of vivid colours creates a special stylishness:

> Indeed, the bourgeois interior reduces it for the most part to discreet 'tints' and 'shades'. Grey, mauve, garnet, beige - all the shades assigned to velours, woollens and satins, to the profusion of fabrics, curtains, carpets and hangings, as also to heavier materials and 'period' forms, imply a moral refusal of both colour and space. But especially of colour,

which is deemed too spectacular, and a threat to inwardness. The world of colours is opposed to the world of values, and the 'chic' invariably implies the elimination of appearances in favour of being: black, white, grey - whatever registers zero on the colour scale - is correspondingly paradigmatic of dignity, repression, and moral standing.[48]

Thus, we see that Montesquiou displayed the same taste in both interior design and clothing. When he decorated a room, he not infrequently resorted to the language of allegory. Against a background of golden-green Morocco in the library, peacock feathers were meant to signify the hundred eyes of knowledge.[49] In the living room, which was stylized as a garden, he laid carpets of a grassy hue and placed on them bronze statuettes of animals. This is a manifestation of European decadence's typical penchant for the artificial. Not for nothing was the aquarium of Des Esseintes, the protagonist of Huysmans' novel Against the Grain (1884), filled with mechanical fishes. Incidentally, the prototype of Des Esseintes was, as it is not too difficult to guess, none other than Count Robert de Montesquiou. All of the decors described in the novel originated as direct copies of Montesquiou's style. Thus, on prominent display in the Count's room were special glass cases containing neckties in pastel shades and vests which served both as storage and for decorative purposes as reminders of his dandyism. The owner himself would remark not without aestheticism that from a distance such a case resembled a block of delicately veined marble.

Some of his devices were far ahead of their time. Experimenting with the dimensions of the room, he made very innovative use of illumination. Instead of tritely using bits of coloured glass to create the effect of rainbow patches of light, he arranged a collection of multi-coloured perfume bottles and goblets on the windowsill as refractors. In his opinion, this solution pleasantly stimulated not only sight but also taste and smell. On another occasion, he contrived to create the illusion of movement through an ornament of honeysuckle, whose vines climbed from one wall to another in a single pulsing rhythm. Dances of winding lines are characteristic of Art Nouveau, and Montesquiou's decors quite easily can be considered classics of the style.

One of the rooms in his home was dedicated to mysticism. At one time, he was seriously interested in spiritualism and fervently believed in the possibility of communicating with the dead. He used objects from churches, including an oaken choir bench and even a bell. It is this room that is described almost literally in Huysmans' novel as Des Esseintes' study. The ceiling there is covered in sky-blue fabric used for ecclesiastical garments, an old-chapel reading-desk of forged iron serves as a bookstand, and the windows are

> ...draped with curtains cut from old stoles of dark and reddish gold neutralized by an almost dead russet woven in the pattern. The mantel shelf was sumptuously draped with the remnant of a Florentine dalmatica. Between two gilded copper monstrances of Byzantine style, originally brought from the old Abbaye-au-Bois de Bièvre, stood a marvelous church canon divided into three separate compartments delicately wrought like lace work.[50]

Churchly objects similarly figure in Des Esseintes's bedroom, which is stylized as a monk's cell, with wax candles and an old-fashioned prayer bench serving as a night table. All of these attributes, of course, were not so much objects of religious contemplation as a decorative device, an occasion for aesthetic reflection. By all appearances, a similar attitude characterized Barbey d'Aurevilly's Catholicism. Thus, we see that the nineteenth-century dandy demonstrated his taste not only in clothing but also in structuring house decoration.

Notes

1 By the late eighteenth century, the vest had evolved into a long waistcoat.
2 Like modern-day hair gels and sprays, pomades were used in order to preserve the shape of one's wig.
3 The term "The Great Masculine Renunciation" was first used by J. C. Flügel. See J. C. Flügel, *Psychology of Clothes* (London: Hogarth Press, 1930).
4 Contemporary dress historians often see Flügel's ideas as somewhat abstract and oversimplified. Dress codes, they rightly argue, varied, and demand for male dress steadily grew. See Christopher Breward, *The Hidden Consumer. Masculinities, Fashion and City Life 1860–1914* (Manchester: Manchester University Press, 1999), 24–25. Nevertheless, Flügel's writing presents a useful overview of processes in late eighteenth – early nineteenth-century fashion.
5 *The Whole Art of Dress Or, The Road to Elegance and Fashion* (London: E. Wilson, 1830), 13.
6 In 1816, Lord Elgin's collection was purchased by the British Museum.
7 The term "Neoclassicism" has various meanings. We adhere to the tradition in Western scholarship which uses the term with reference to art of the second half of the eighteenth and first decades of the nineteenth century. In their work, the best-known Neoclassical artists such as architects Robert Smirke and Robert Adam, sculptors Antonio Canova, Jean-Antoine Houdon and Bertel Thorvaldsen, and painters Anton Raphael Mengs, Jean-Auguste-Dominique Ingres and Jacques-Louis David invoked the motifs of antiquity. In France, Neoclassicism underpinned trends such as the Louis XVI and Empire styles. In Russian art history, Neoclassicism is at times connected with a later period, the early twentieth century "second wave" of fascination with antiquity. See Viktor Vlasov, *Stili v iskusstve* [*Styles in Art*] (St. Petersburg: Kolna, 1995), vol. 1, 367–373 (in Russian); Valery Turchin, *Aleksandr I i stil neoklasssitsizma v Rossii* [*Alexander I and Neoclassical Style in Russia*] (Moscow: Zhiraf, 2001). See also Anne Hollander, *Seeing Through Clothes* (Berkeley: University of California Press, 1993), 117–128.
8 Johann Joachim Winckelmann, *On Art, Architecture, and Archaeology*. Trans. David Carter (Rochester: Camden House, 2013), 39.
9 Heinrich Wölfflin, *Principles of Art History: The Problem of the Development of Style in Later Art.* Trans. M. D. Hottinger (NewYork: Dover Publications, 2012), 54. As the context shows, this passage from Wölfflin discusses and develops the ideas of Winckelmann.
10 Dandy, 1910, no. 1, 23.
11 Ivan Goncharov, Pisma stolichnogo druga k provintsialnomu zhenikhu [Letters from a Friend in the Capital to a Bridegroom in the Country], in *Felietoni sorokovikh godov* [Feuilletons of the Forties] (Leningrad: Academia, 1930), 43–44.
12 Winckelmann, ibid., 138.
13 Winckelmann, ibid., 40.
14 The layered cut left curled tresses over the forehead, with hair cropped to the top of the neck at the back.

15 Nikolay Grech, *Puteviye pisma iz Anglii, Germanii i Frantsii* [Travel Letters from England, Germany and France], (St. Petersburg: 1839), part 1, 167–168 (in Russian). I would like to take this opportunity to thank Professor Igor Dobrodomov for bringing this material to my attention.
16 Winckelmann, ibid., 41.
17 Maria Edgeworth, *Belinda* (Oxford: Oxford University Press, 1994), 230–231.
18 Horace Raisson, *Code de la Toilette. Manuel Complet d'Elégance et d'Hygiène* (Paris: J.-P. Roret, 1829), 83.
19 William Jesse, *The Life of George Brummell, Esq*. In 2 volumes (London: Saunders and Otley, 1844), 1: 62.
20 Ibid., 2: 58.
21 At that time, country washing was considered by far the best, as clothes were washed in running streams of water. City washing, on the other hand, tended to involve limited water supply.
22 Quoted by Brent Shannon, *The Cut of His Coat: Men, Dress, and Consumer Culture in Britain, 1860–1914* (Ohio University Press: 2006), 28.
23 Max Beerbohm, *Dandies and Dandies*, accessed 20 March 2022, https://standardebooks.org/ebooks/max-beerbohm/the-works-of-max-beerbohm/text/dandies-and-dandies
24 See the section on 'Apollos in Double-Breasted Coats'.
25 In the eighteenth century, stirrup trousers had been used in military uniform; Brummell brought them into civilian dress.
26 See the catalogue of satirical prints: *Followers of Fashion. Graphic Satires from the Georgian Period*, prints from the British Museum, ed. Diana Donald (Newcastle: Hayward Gallery, 2002).
27 Jules Barbey D'Aurevilly, *On Dandyism and Georges Brummell*. Trans. George Walden. George Walden, *Who is a Dandy?* (London: Gibson Square Books, 2002), 108.
28 William Jesse, *The Life of George Brummell, Esq*. In 2 volumes (London: Saunders and Otley, 1844), 1: 54.
29 The vogue for narrow ties appeared in the middle of the nineteenth century, yet knotted kerchiefs were first thought to have been worn by the Romans. In Europe, they became popular in the seventeenth century, after Croatian soldiers appeared in Paris, wearing bright knotted silk neckties as part of their uniform.
30 William Jesse, *The Life of George Brummell, Esq*. In 2 volumes (London: Saunders and Otley, 1844), 1: 61.
31 Coup d'archet – stroke of the bow in violin playing (French).
32 Jesse, 1: 62.
33 An excellent analysis of the cultural significance of folds in dress can be found in: Anne Hollander, *Seeing Through Clothes* (Berkeley, Los Angeles, London: University of California Press, 1993), 1–83.
34 Gilles Deleuze, *The Fold: Leibniz and the Baroque* (London: The Athlone Press, 1993), 122.
35 Ibid., 122.
36 Heinrich Wölfflin, *Principles of Art History: The Problem of the Development of Style in Later Art*. Trans. M. D. Hottinger (New York: Dover Publications, 2012), 54.
37 *Neckclothitania; or Tietania: Being an Essay on Starchers, by One of the Cloth* (London: J.J. Stockdale, 1818). The title of the brochure parodied the style of popular contemporary novels.
38 Balzac has not been proved to be the author, yet most researchers ascribe the work to him. In England, the treatise was published in two editions under the pseudonym: H. Le Blanc, *The Art of Tying the Cravat* (London: 1827, 1828). Reprinted in: *Late Georgian Costume*, ed. R. L. Shep (Mendocino: R.L. Shep, 1991), 121–154.
39 Most of these names are no longer in use. The only knot whose name survives to this day is the Windsor.

40 *Neckclothitania or Tietania*, 21. The "couleur de la cuisse d'une nymphe émue" ("colour of the trembling thigh of a nymph") was a shade of pink, of which Raisa Kirsanova wrote extensively: Raisa Kirsanova, *Kostium v russkoy khudozhestvennoi kulture* [Dress in Russian Artistic Culture] (Moscow: Rossiyskaya Entzyklopedia, 1995), 35–36 (in Russian).
41 *Neckclothitania or Tietania*, 25.
42 https://www.metmuseum.org/art/collection/search/158752. Accessed 27 March 2022.
43 Yuri Arnold, *Vospominaniya (Memoirs)* (Moscow: Yu.Lissner and E.Roman, 1892), issue 1, 11 (in Russian).
44 Honoré Balzac, *Lost Illusions*. Trans. Herbert J. Hunt (London: Penguin Classics, 1976), 242.
45 The stock to shape one's cravat was but one of the gadgets used by nineteenth-century followers of fashion. Among men, folding top hats ('chapeau claque' or opera hat) and tricorns were popular, while ladies could make use of pads and wire to style their hair, and folding sleeves which could be adjusted to the desired degree of fullness. By the middle of the nineteenth century, the use of folding items and frames in women's dress became extremely widespread as Charles Worth popularised the crinoline.
46 Marguerite, Countess Blessington, *The Idler in France: A Sequel to The Idler in Italy* (London: H. Colburn, 1842), 252.
47 Quoted by Patrick Favardin, Laurent Bouëxière, *Le Dandysme* (Lyon: La Manufacture, 1988), 140.
48 Jean Baudrillard, *The System of Objects*, Trans. James Benedict (London, New York: Verso, 1996), 31.
49 The allusion is to the hundred-eyes Argus Panoptes, traditionally symbolising knowledge. There are ancient representations of Argus the astronomer constantly peering into a telescope. According to Ovid, Hera brought the eyes of Argus on peacock feathers, whence the semantics of hundred-eyed knowledge.
50 Joris Karl Huysmans, *Against the Grain*. Trans. John Howard (New York: Lieber & Lewis, 1922), 38.

Chapter Two
LITERATURE AND LEGENDS

Brummell: Constructing the Legend

The life of Beau Brummell remained a subject of unfailing interest to high-society gossips, memoirists, and biographers. Most writers tended to focus on the Beau's life in England, with its clear social triumphs and fame. His twenty-four-year stay in France, of course, was a different matter. If the English period was relatively straightforward and entertaining to document, the time in France, for most, was significantly more challenging to follow.

Brummell's main biographer, Captain William Jesse, on the other hand, knew the Beau only in France, and most of his two-volume work focuses on the French period. Jesse and Brummell met in February 1832 in Caen, where the Beau was serving as Consul. For his biography, Jesse attempted to gather additional information on Brummell's life in England, yet that period remained far more scantily covered than the subsequent years. Jesse's tone, in his book, might appear contradictory. A meticulous chronicler akin to Goethe's Eckermann, in recounting his hero's London triumphs with evident approbation, he seems careful to note every word and gesture. Describing the ageing dandy's failures, however, he shifts to a different register. Frankly critical, in the final chapter, Jesse attempts to draw a series of moralistic conclusions reminiscent of Victorian attacks on vanity. His hero, he supposes, will soon be forgotten: '…it is greatly to be dreaded, … that posterity will hardly accord to George Bryan Brummell one line in the annals of history'.[1]

Thanks to the French writer and dandy Barbey D'Aurevilly and Brummell's new Gallic admirers, however, in the middle of the nineteenth century the Beau was far from forgotten. His life was seen as the aesthetic manifesto of dandyism: he was venerated as a hero. In his 'Treatise on Elegant Living' of 1830, Balzac created a canonical image of Brummell as the teacher of all men of fashion. In 1845, Barbey D'Aurevilly used the Beau's biography to develop a philosophy of style. To this day, his treatise remains perhaps the most authoritative and well-written text on dandyism. Brummell's years in France are not well covered, Barbey clearly (and rightly) preferring to study dandyism by focusing on the period of its growth. Thanks to his treatise, the legend of George Brummell became part of European culture. Later, Barbey's study would be taken up by Baudelaire: in 1863, the poet mused on dandyism in his collection of essays 'The Painter of Modern Life'. The main focus of Baudelaire's book is dandyism as a phenomenon, rather than Brummell himself; nonetheless, he portrays the dandy as a hero of contemporary urban civilisation, a stoic, and a cynic.

Continuing the theme, in 1896, in his essay 'Dandies and Dandies', Max Beerbohm compared Brummell to the Count D'Orsay with typical entertaining wit. In the 1930s, Virginia Woolf returned to the subject of Brummell's biography in her essay 'Beau Brummell'.[2] Attempting to remain objective, she described both the Beau's English triumphs, and the 'process of disintegration' in France.

The twentieth century saw the first academic biographies of Brummell[3] appear, as well as two films. Harry Beaumont's 1924 picture 'Beau Brummell' starred John Barrymore. The second, a 1954 Hollywood film of the same name, 'Beau Brummell', was directed by Curtis Bernhardt, and featured Stewart Granger as the Beau, Peter Ustinov as the Prince of Wales, and Elizabeth Taylor as Lady Patricia. In 2006, Ian Kelly released the BBC television drama 'Beau Brummell: This Charming Man'. On screen, Brummell tended to be portrayed as a Romantic hero tortured by fatal passions, the tragic victim of treacherous intrigue: such was the interpretation of the dandy image in popular culture.

In pre-revolutionary Russia, Brummell was known from the translation of Barbey D'Aurevilly's treatise.[4] In Soviet years, the dandy's life continued to be a topic of discussion among the intelligentsia, and his biography became the subject of special interest. During the Soviet era, stories of the Beau's exploits were also recounted among the Leningrad Stilyagi, some of whom were, perhaps, familiar with the American films about Brummell. In the early 1960s, a popular romance was composed, featuring the 'famous fop' Zhora Bremel, who sported a leopardskin waistcoat, and knocked back Zubrovka with King George. Thus, Brummell entered Soviet urban folklore.

How, then, was the legend of Beau Brummell constructed? Despite the abundance of academic writing on the subject, romantic views of the Beau's life persist. The first author of this legend was, needless to say, Brummell himself. Ever aware of his audience, he knew full well how avidly his sayings were recounted in society. At times, he proved unable to stop the sharing of this or that incident, even when the story was evidently false. Such, it seems, was the famous anecdote about the Prince of Wales, whom Brummell allegedly bade summon his man with the words 'Wales, ring the bell!' Brummell himself consistently denied the episode ever took place; notwithstanding, the phrase became a nickname, sticking to him even long after he left England.

Comparing this incident with others involving the Beau, one may, indeed, notice a difference. Classic Brummell humour usually involved unexpected contrast, grotesque, and exaggeration. On one occasion, for instance, when someone enquired whether he could recall another summer so cold, the Beau replied: 'Yes, last winter.' Such quips were far more typical of Brummell than the 'Wales, ring the bell!' story.

In many of his best-known jokes, the humour was linked with renaming, or failing to acknowledge, certain objects. Recall, for instance, his early efforts with 'Do you call this thing a coat?' or, 'Shoes, are they? I thought they were slippers.' Such comments offered endless variations on recognition and acceptance, the key themes of his life. As arbiter of fashion, Brummell was confident in his privilege to 'name' items, acknowledge – or, fail to acknowledge – them, and to set cultural rules and categories.[5]

Many stories about Brummell also demonstrate that he was extremely skillful in the self-fashioning. The art of self-fashioning is largely a discursive strategy, the ability to fictionalize the trivialities of daily life and produce a narration out of ephemera. In Brummell's case, the effect was often achieved by revealing small secrets, the technology of his success. His pale primrose gloves were famous and when a friend asked him, who his glover was, he answered: '"Glover, my dear sir?" I have three, one of whom makes the glove, the second – the thumb, the third – the other fingers.'[6]

Now, what are we supposed to make of such stories? Perhaps, three glovers were indeed employed to make the gloves Brummell required. But yet one has to notice, that on the structural level these stories are all alike, forming a canon of urban folklore about the dandy as cultural type. They are all organized so as to elevate the principal character to the status of a heroic suffering consumer, for whom quality is everything. The narration of consumerism is caught here in its most poetic moment.

The Beau himself was constantly fighting to maintain his identity as a dandy. Everything which fell outside the boundaries of his personal fashion universe, was simply not acknowledged: such items were refused the very right to exist. In the same way, Brummell would refuse to accept events which did not sit well with the dandy legend. Coffee stains on the tablecloth, greetings from vulgar acquaintances, visits to inappropriate locations such as slums or hospitals – all this would be swept under the carpet as never having existed.

Despite the Beau's vigilant censorship, however, tales and anecdotes continued to spread. One publisher brought out an entire collection of apocryphal sayings, entitled 'The Book of Fashion; Being a Digest of the Axioms of the Celebrated Joseph Brummell'.[7] The quality of the book was evident from its very title, in which Brummell's name was cited incorrectly.

Legends, however, have a habit of forming, according to their own laws: the fashioning of these scenarios follows its own rigid poetics. Brummell's tragedy, indeed, lay in becoming trapped by this very poetics, his life playing out a script of prefigured composition.

These laws are well-studied. The folklore of this or that people can be described using typological formulae, and the legends of Brummell's jokes can also be seen as a special, albeit rather traditional, form of urban folklore. The structure of anecdotes frequently involves the collision of two worlds, the humour arising from the juxtaposition of the incompatible. Anecdotes about Brummell usually include his fans, simple souls who cannot grasp the Beau's vision, yet unquestioningly accept his superiority. Brummell himself habitually appears as the proponent of a new style, his eye, body, and mind far more sensitive than those of others. Responding to questions, he always demonstrates his exacting standards in dress, appearance, and personal hygiene.

Despite all the typological similarity between ordinary anecdotes and legends of George Brummell, however, one detail remains different: the viewpoint of the narrator. The effect of the legends is to elevate Brummell, rather than to ridicule his innocent admirers, as might be the case in traditional anecdotes. Filled with awe and veneration, the narrator sees himself as a pupil, a follower, a paparazzo attempting to capture and comprehend a novel and unexpected system of principles.

Brummell's approach can be seen as a precursor to the self-representation techniques of today's celebrities. Following their main motto, never to be forgotten, modern stars use a cunning mix of shock tactics and predictability to ensure they remain current. Living in an era when today's scale of social and mass media was all but impossible to imagine, Brummell, nonetheless, showed a good grasp of publicity. Whether the latest news shows you in a positive or negative light is far less important, he realized, than the simple fact of remaining in the headlines.

All in all, Brummell's behaviour could be seen as conforming to the laws of today's mass media. The stuff of legends, he welcomed the telling of tales about his originality, his scandals, and his mysteriousness. His audience, at first, was a wide circle of friends, admirers, and London high society. With time, however, the circle narrowed, leaving just one main spectator: Brummell's future biographer.

The Biographer's Gaze: Brummell in the Mirror

To this day, Captain William Jesse's biography of George Brummell remains the principal source for all writers interested in the Beau. Jesse's book could also be seen as establishing certain algorithms of the dandy legend: let us turn to one memorable episode, in which much is revealed about the way Brummell's first biographer saw his hero. Jesse observed the Beau at his toilet.

> In the morning visits that I sometimes paid him at his lodgings, the door of his bed-room being always left a little open to carry on the conversation, the secrets of his dressing-table were, much to my entertainment, revealed in the glass upon the mantel-piece of his *salon*. I think I see him now, standing without his wig, in his dressing trousers, before the glass, going through the manual exercise of the flesh-brush…[8]

In this intriguing situation, Brummell appears not unlike a monarch at his toilet, whilst Jesse assumes the role of the courtier. He is not, however, granted the favour of assisting his master directly, and instead carries on the conversation from the neighbouring room, through the half-open door.

In the past, we recall, Brummell had given the Prince of Wales a 'master class' in body care, during which the prince was admitted to the sanctum of the Beau's bedroom. Denied such access, Jesse resorts to indirect observation, following Brummell's toilet in the looking glass. At times, the captain was likely watching the double reflection of Brummell's likeness in his dressing table mirror, reflected in the mirror in the salon.

The use of multiple reflections was, of course, highly popular in Romantic aesthetics. Known as 'mise en abyme', in literature this technique allowed writers to insert infinite stories and novellas within their novels, playing with different viewpoints. In art, it made for striking optical illusions, enabling artists to create an impression of expanded space. The feature was much used by German Romantic painters, and, before them, by the Flemish School, and Velázquez (in 'Las Meninas', for instance).

Besides observing Brummell's likeness in a series of mirrors, Jesse also uses the technique of multiple reflections in the narration itself. His biography is filled with eyewitness accounts, stories from friends, and impressions of acquaintances, which, whilst reinforcing each other at times, more often than not offer contradictory views.

His own position of observer appears a sensitive one. Certain scenes, it seems, were not intended for anyone's eyes but the Beau's.

> Had Brummell known that I had ever caught a glimpse of him without his wig, he would, I think, have had a fit, and cut me the next time we met; for he did not like to be seen to disadvantage and "shorn of his beams;" but my curiosity, as well as my unwillingness to lose so amusing an acquaintance, entirely prevented me from disclosing the event to anyone.⁹

The game, it seems, was, however, even more complex. Both sides were, to some extent, following double standards: Jesse, who kept his observations to himself whilst Brummell was alive, appears to have had no qualms about publishing them, once the Beau had departed. Thus, he joined the 'tellers of dandy secrets', albeit in veiled form: rather than disclosing a sophisticated recipe for elegance, he merely shared half-hearted gossip about the tricks of an ageing, impoverished dandy.

Brummell himself was no fool, either, and that Jesse contrived to observe him, unobserved, would seem highly unlikely. Most probably, the Beau knew he was being watched, and secretly encouraged the process, as an exhibitionist might welcome a voyeur. The Beau was well-accustomed to being observed: in his favourite bow window seat at White's, he was regularly exposed to the gazes of passers-by. Furtive, admiring glances, it seems, fed his self-esteem, and his reputation:

> ...the dandy can only play a part by setting himself up in opposition. He can only be sure of his own existence by finding it in the expression of others' faces. Other people are his mirror. A mirror that quickly becomes clouded, it is true, since human capacity for attention is limited. It must be ceaselessly stimulated, spurred on by provocation.¹⁰

In this case, the system of multiple reflections included the added 'clouded mirror' of Jesse's gaze. For Brummell, his biographer's attention was, perhaps, the most significant: this was, after all, the man who would pave his way into eternity with his tale. Thus, Brummell sought to maintain Jesse's interest, ensuring he was kept intrigued and engaged at all times.

Stimulating the curiosity of his admirers was something at which the Beau was highly adept, for instance, by claiming to possess special 'secrets' of style. Upon closer examination, these 'secrets' were little more than basic maxims of dandy self-care, yet Brummell was careful to lend them a poetic air of mystery. An experienced consumerist, he never tired of promoting his 'secrets'. Traditionally associated with the female domain, flirtation, and efforts to please, in Brummell's case, the secrets were not coquetry, but rather ironic disclosures which made listeners somewhat uncomfortable. Did the Beau really polish his boots with champagne, admirers must have asked themselves, doubtfully. Could one really take on three tailors to make a single glove? Was it all really true? The era of department stores and Parisian 'grands magasins' had not yet arrived, and the individual approach still reigned, supreme, even in the most primitive everyday areas. All the 'secrets' boiled down to basic care for individual items: starching one's tie, wearing stirrup breeches. Every such find was poetic and unique, and could be easily transformed into legend.

The recognizable tone of admiration mingled with an element of doubt which this elicited, can also be found in Barbey D'Aurevilly's treatise on Brummell. Recall, for instance, the passage on the scraping of coats: the inside of a coat could, Barbey explains, be scraped, so as to make it almost semi-transparent.

The Romanticism of the first half of the nineteenth century was yet a period of personal taste. Heroic in its own way, this was a time of individual figures, whose chance 'inventions' are today seen as long-standing, established discoveries in the field of fashion.

The Poetics of Dandyism: Fashion and Fiction

A Dandy is… a Poet of Cloth.
Thomas Carlyle

In their writings on dandies, many researchers make frequent mention of literary characters, clearly stressing the special connections between dandyism and literature. The classical beau, indeed, may take pride in a rich lineage of nineteenth-century dandy writers such as Lord Byron, Edward Bulwer-Lytton, Benjamin Disraeli, the young Dickens, Oscar Wilde, and Sir Max Beerbohm in England; Honoré de Balzac, Stendhal, Barbey D'Aurevilly, Charles Baudelaire, Pierre Loti, Joris-Karl Huysmans, and Marcel Proust in France.[11] Their detailed descriptions of outfits, morals, and behaviour have served to build up a varied gallery of dandy portraits of the time. Dandyism is ever interacting with literature, feeding it, and, in turn, being enriched. These subtle energetic connections between culture and reality could be described as a constant process of self-fashioning.[12]

Let us then take a closer look at self-fashioning in the nineteenth century. At that time, fiction and conduct books offered infinite possibilities for improving one's spiritual and practical existence, from a ready-made Weltanschauung to practical behaviour strategies. When one's way of thinking and patterns of feeling are in tune with one's way of life, one could be said to have achieved a stable lifestyle. A single decision can bring meaning and purpose to one's actions, even those as small as mere gestures and intonation. This type of personality is open to interpretation and depiction in literature. The characters thus created take on a life of their own and begin to influence real people, which in turn inspires writers to take up the pen. In this way, life and literature are constantly interacting and nourishing each other.

In previous sections, we touched upon the construction of dandy self-fashioning, examining the life of George Brummell and the ways in which particular episodes and anecdotes from his life served to create the legend he became. Today, to build up a picture of the first dandy, researchers would consult not only memoirs of his contemporaries such as Captain William Jesse, Captain Rees Howell Gronow, and Harriette Wilson, and philosophical essays on dandyism from the likes of Barbey D'Aurevilly, Max Beerbohm, and Virginia Woolf, but also a multitude of works of fiction. In 'Childe Harold's Pilgrimage', we hear echoes of Byron's admiration for Brummell;

in Bulwer-Lytton's 'Pelham' (1828), the Beau inspired the character of Mr. Russelton, and in Thomas Henry Lister's 'Granby' (1826), we encounter him as Trebeck. As far as Brummell's own literary efforts are concerned, he left a multitude of gallant verses, and a work entitled 'Male and Female Costume'.

In many cases, the writer, romantic hero, and dandy are all one, a fine example, naturally, being Lord Byron. In his youth, the poet was friendly with many well-known beaux, and was even credited with pioneering a new, wide trouser cut. He was a member of Watier's, a club founded by eminent men of fashion such as William Arden, second baron Alvanley; George Brummell; Henry Mildmay and Henry Pierrepoint. After Byron dubbed it 'The Dandy Club', it became known by that name.

In his 'Detached Thoughts', Byron reminisces:

> I liked the Dandies; they were always very civil to me, though in general they disliked literary people, and persecuted and mystified Madame de Staël, Lewis, Horace Twiss, and the like, damnably... The truth is, that, though I gave up the business early, I had a tinge of Dandyism in my minority, and probably retained enough of it, to conciliate the great ones; at four and twenty, I had gamed, and drank, and taken my degrees in most dissipations; and having no pedantry, and not being overbearing, we ran quietly together. I knew them all more or less, and they made me a Member of Watier's (a superb Club at that time), being, I take it, the only literary man (except two others, both men of the world, M. and S.) in it.[13]

The literary tradition associated with the dandies essentially starts with Byron. Heavily influenced by the Romantic aesthetic, dandyism takes on the image of the lonely, disillusioned individualist burdened with the world's cares. Infused with the European pessimism we later encounter in the writings of Leopardi and Schopenhauer, dandyism exudes world-weariness and ennui. As Lord Byron's dramatic melancholy was adopted by thousands of young men in different countries, we note echoes for instance in Pushkin's Onegin. Recall Tatyana's disappointment when, having perused books from her beloved hero's study, she comes to the sad conclusion that he is no more than a parody.

> Which is he? Or an imitation,
> A bogy conjured up in joke,
> A Russian in Childe Harold's cloak,
> Of foreign whims the impersonation –
> Handbook of fashionable phrase
> Or parody of modern ways?[14]

Byron himself, of course, found lasting fame even during his lifetime. Known both for his writing and for his looks, he was depicted in countless works of art, from miniatures to grand sculptures. His particular type of appeal naturally prompted comparisons with ancient gods, most commonly the Apollo Belvedere, with Byron himself also favouring portraits which stressed this likeness.

Dispensing with the necktie, the poet frequently posed with unfastened collar, as in the celebrated portrait by Harlow. His shapely neck caused women to swoon; despite his club foot, thanks to vigorous exercise Byron succeeded in cutting an athletic figure.

His chosen sports were boxing, swimming, and horse-riding. When, finally, his weight did start to show, the poet subjected himself to a rigorous diet. Disciplined as the dandy should be, he was able to follow this religiously for many years.

Admirers saw Byron as flawlessly handsome, and he was able to live up to their expectations. In Romantic aesthetics, however, spirited beauty is frequently associated with imperfect proportions, and in the case of the poet, indeed, divine facial features were combined with a clubfoot. His reputation also was ambiguous: he was perceived both as hero and antihero, as demigod and demon.

After his death in Missolonghi, the poet's name became firmly associated with the struggle for freedom, with Byron seen as something of a martyr. Following his exile and divorce in 1816, he was perceived by many as a man of mystery and a libertine. After his death, the demonic aspect of his image appeared to fall away, leaving instead beauty and self-sacrifice. In Goethe's 'Faust', he appears as Euphorion, a spirited, brilliant boy.

The vogue for dandyism in the Romantic era was not, of course, purely down to Lord Byron: fashionable beaux can be found in the works of Jane Austen, William Hazlitt, Chateaubriand, Madame de Staël, and many others. With the advent of the silver fork novel, the dandy craze grew into a mass phenomenon.

The novel of fashionable highlife, or silver fork novel,[15] appeared in the 1820s, brought to the reading public by publisher Henry Colburn. The books could be deemed 'fashionable' in two senses: focusing heavily on dandies, their main characters were more often than not fashionable beaux always seen in high society. The novels' lively plots and colourful accounts of highlife served also to make them fashionable among readers.

Colburn's market assessment for his books was astute and accurate. By the mid-1820s, the wealthy, socially aspiring bourgeois middle class in England offered a large readership eager to be introduced to the secrets of high society. Many aristocrats disliked socialising with bankers and industrialists, deeming them vulgar and middle-class entrepreneurs were not accepted in London's elite gentlemen's clubs. A keen businessman, Colburn understood that the bourgeoisie, unable to access high society, had a huge desire to at least learn its ways. The 'information gap' between the aristocracy and the nouveaux riches created an ideal market for the fashionable novel.

Through Colburn's books, readers could discover clubs like Almack's, or listen in on conversations over high society dinners. The fashionable novel's formula inevitably included descriptions of balls, card-playing sessions with entire fortunes lost, romantic intrigue, horse races, and, of course, ladies and gentlemen's attire. At times, the authors even mentioned the real addresses of tailors offering their services to fashion-following readers.[16]

The principles behind silver fork novels were clearly thought through, and were often revealed in the texts themselves. In Bulwer-Lytton's 'Pelham', the aristocratic heroine offers the following advice to aspiring authors:

> There is only one rule necessary for a clever writer who wishes to delineate the beau monde. It is this: let him consider that 'dukes, and lords, and noble princes,' eat, drink, talk, move, exactly the same as any other class of civilized people—nay, the very subjects in conversation are, for the most part, the same in all sets—only, perhaps, they are somewhat more

familiarly and easily treated than among the lower orders, who fancy rank is distinguished by pomposity, and that state affairs are discussed with the solemnity of a tragedy—that we are always my lording and my ladying each other—that we ridicule commoners, and curl our hair with Debrett's Peerage.[17]

'Democratic' ploys such as this appeared to erase social boundaries, giving readers the much-desired impression of somehow communing with the upper classes, without experiencing any sense of inferiority.

A true master of public relations, besides publishing the novels, Colburn also ran an ingenious promotion campaign. The co-owner of a number of major literary magazines, he was in a perfect position to advertise his publications. Signing a contract with an author for a new book, he would immediately commission a positive review – not infrequently, from the very same author under a pseudonym. In order to offer readers, a stronger impression of authenticity, Colburn would deliberately spread rumours about the authors being extremely wealthy members of the nobility, who had wished to remain anonymous.

In this way, readers were drawn into lively debates, attempting to guess the 'true' authors. Furthermore, many of the characters were based on real figures from the aristocracy, with thinly veiled pseudonyms, offering more opportunities for guesswork. Some novels, indeed, even came with their own 'key' in the form of a table claiming to reveal the personages on whom the characters were based. Needless to say, such tables were often deliberately misleading.

Silver fork novels were read by members of the aristocracy, also. For them, the process of guessing the author was based on personal knowledge of the possible candidates. Studying the texts in detail, they strove to uncover which of their associates had chosen to present to the public this latest satirical view of high society. Overly mocking depiction of the aristocracy was, however, discouraged by Colburn, who wished to maintain readers' interest in the upper classes. Later, his strategy was completely reversed by Thackeray, who brought out his vitriolic 'The Yellowplush Papers' (1840) and 'The Book of Snobs' (1847).

The first fashionable novel to achieve real success was 'Tremaine, Or The Man of Refinement' by R. P. Ward. Published in 1825, this was the story of a dandy, which offered meticulously detailed descriptions of the beau's attire, lifestyle, and social success techniques. The main character was clearly based on George Brummell: Tremaine even picks the Beau's favourite spot to sit, the bow window of White's. Like Brummell, he makes sarcastic comments about the outfits of passers-by, and even rejects his fiancée for using a knife to eat peas.

His novel's unexpected resounding success took Robert Ward by surprise. At sixty, he was part of influential social and political circles, and did not want to risk endangering his career. Writing under a pseudonym, Ward was meticulously careful to avoid disclosing his identity. Even Colburn himself did not know the author's name, and his novel was copied out by his two daughters, so his handwriting could not be recognised. All contact with Colburn was handled by Ward's lawyer Ben Austen and his wife Sara, who also passed on all letters from readers, and fellow-writers' reviews. Among the authors to give praise to the novel were Henry Mackenzie and Robert Southey.

Once his novel had gained fame, Ward took delight in discussing it at social gatherings, putting forward all kinds of extraordinary conjectures as to the book's mysterious author. He also enjoyed taking part in debates, trying to 'guess' which high society figures had inspired the characters. Through these, he was able subtly to take revenge on those he disliked: to one lady, who had thought his book vulgar, he hinted indirectly that the most unpleasant character in the novel, Gertrude, was based on her.

The year after 'Tremaine', in 1826 Henry Colburn brought out Benjamin Disraeli's 'Vivian Grey'.[18] Published with the aid of Sara Austen, the book caused a sensation. The promotion involved the same deliberate rumour-spreading, commissioning of reviews, and a key to the characters. The author was anonymous, yet Disraeli's name was quickly uncovered. Having established that the writer was a little-known young Jewish man, journalists appeared mystified at his knowledge of fashionable highlife.

Some surmised that Disraeli had stolen Ward's diaries and copied from them his descriptions of well-known members of high society. Such suspicions can perhaps be better understood when one recalls that 'Tremaine' was, at that time, still the only well-known fashionable novel, and all subsequent efforts were inevitably compared to this trailblazer. In fact, Disraeli's text was his own, and Robert Ward even complimented the novel, stressing the young writer's clear talent. Little did anyone know that Disraeli's ambitions would eventually take him into a very different field.

Disraeli's protagonist Vivian Grey is a headstrong young man bent on going into politics. With the aid of intrigue, he aims to gain the support of influential lords to get into parliament. His trials and tribulations presage many of Disraeli's own: in 1867, he would become Prime Minister, and the moral cost of political success was a subject which occupied him profoundly.

A true dandy, Disraeli's character combines cold insolence with genteel manners. Late for a high-society dinner, he ignores the empty seats at the end of the table, pushing himself instead into the place next to the hostess, in the centre. That young lady looking favourably upon him, he brazenly has the servants shift guests' seats in order to occupy his chosen spot; the diners find their plates displaced as a result. Thus, instead of sampling her 'exquisite iced jelly', Miss Gusset takes instead a full spoon of fiery curry from the plate of an old colonel. Chaos reigns, yet Vivian is nonchalant: 'Now that is what I call a sensible arrangement; what could go off better?'[19]

Painting a portrait of a dandy, Disraeli was to some extent providing an autobiography: the author was famed for his extravagant dress. Henry Bulwer, brother of the writer Edward Bulwer-Lytton, recalled meeting him at a dinner:

> Disraeli wore green velvet trousers, a canary-coloured waistcoat, low shoes, silver buckles, lace at his wrists, and his hair in ringlets…[20]

Using exaggeratedly outrageous dandy style to make an impression, Disraeli hoped to stand out and make his mark. Being different was, of course, a tactic often employed by dandies, and the novelist used it throughout his life. Even as a high-ranking Tory politician, he still liked to sport purple trousers with gold trim, diamond rings on his white-gloved fingers, and gold chains. Thanks to a subscription from Lady Tankerville, Disraeli was a member of Almack's; he also frequented Lady Blessington's famous salon, and was friends with the Count D'Orsay, considered at that time to be the greatest of dandies.

Daniel Maclise's engraving 'Benjamin Disraeli as a Young Man' from 1833 shows the future Prime Minister in full dandy glory. Among his accessories one may note a cane with a monocle set into it – a fashionable novelty considered a sign of prestige, not unlike the latest smartphones of today (Figure 6).

In his behaviour, Disraeli also liked to stand out, honing his image of an elegant and rather effeminate beau. He had a passion for staging little scenes, mini performances to show off his idle refinement. On one occasion, Disraeli was watching a tennis match, when the ball landed right at his feet. Picking up the ball, he passed it to his neighbour to throw back to the players, explaining that he had never in his life had to throw a ball. The incident immediately became the talk of London.

The third novel in Colburn's series to gain impressive popularity was Bulwer-Lytton's 'Pelham; Or, The Adventures of A Gentleman'. Published in 1828, it became

Figure 6 Daniel Maclise. Disraeli as a young man. 1833–1834. The walking cane with a monocle in the handle lies on the sofa. Wikimedia Commons.

the best-known of the fashionable novels, and the only one to stand the test of time, entering the cultural tradition as a dandy bible.

The book's main character, the young aristocrat Henry Pelham is portrayed as a dedicated man of fashion who sports intricate hairstyles, uses creams for his skin, likes to admire his own rings, and, as befits a dandy, pays significant attention to personal hygiene. A typical awakening for the main character might look like this:

> I woke about two o'clock; dressed, sipped my chocolate, and was on the point of arranging my hat to the best advantage, when I received the following note…[21]

The protagonist's effete dandyism and obsession with appearance were a source of irritation for some of Bulwer-Lytton's contemporaries. The writer was accused of creating an overly effeminate, unhealthy character: Thomas Carlyle launched a satirical attack on dandies in his 'Sartor Resartus', and critics from Fraser's Magazine followed suit. Among them was William Thackeray, who, in his 1841 essay 'Men and Coats' made allusions to a writer who liked to work on his novels in a flowered damask dressing-gown, and Morocco slippers. In an ordinary jacket, Thackeray concluded, the novelist would doubtless produce something more direct, and 'manly'.

As a result of this onslaught, Bulwer-Lytton made significant changes to his text. In the second edition, many of the fascinating passages describing dandy lifestyles and sartorial practices have disappeared. The first edition, for instance, contains a beautiful description of a bathroom in Glanville's house:

> The decorations of this room were of delicate rose colour; the bath, which was of the most elaborate workmanship, represented, in the whitest marble, a shell, supported by two Tritons. There was, as Glanville afterwards explained to me, a machine in this room, which kept up a faint but perpetual breeze, and the light curtains waiving to and fro, scattered about perfumes of the most exquisite odour.[22]

Following savage criticism, Bulwer-Lytton replaced the pink bathroom with a drawing room decorated with paintings from the Old Masters. The initial description, though, was far more curious: such a passage would not have seemed out of place in the writings of late aesthetes such as Oscar Wilde or Huysmans, although 'Pelham' first appeared in 1828. Fortunately for followers of dandyism, however, Bulwer-Lytton did retain his famous Maxims, offering advice on the art of dressing (Figure 7). Let us turn to a select few:

MAXIMS

> 'The most graceful principle of dress is neatness – the most vulgar is preciseness.'
> 'Dress so that it may never be said of you "What a well-dressed man!" – but, "What a gentlemanlike man!"'
> 'Avoid many colours; and seek, by someone prevalent and quiet tint, to sober down the others. Apelles used only four colours, and always subdued those which were more florid, by a darkening varnish.'
> 'Inventions in dressing should resemble Addison's definition of fine writing, and consist of "refinements which are natural, without being obvious."'[23]

Figure 7 Edmund J. Sullivan. The Dandies' Holy of Holies. Illustration from Sartor Resartus by Thomas Carlyle. 1898. Wikimedia Commons.

In the final maxim, literary principles are used to illustrate good taste in dress, offering yet another gratifying instance of connection between dandyism and belles-lettres. At first glance, Bulwer-Lytton's Maxims may appear to be composed of elegant paradoxes. Upon closer study, however, one may discover a leitmotif: the principle of **conspicuous inconspicuousness**. This rule, which became a key underpinning concept in the contemporary aesthetic of male dress, was first formulated by none other than George Brummell.

A second principle, also put forward by Brummell, is that of **deliberate carelessness**. A gentleman might spend hours on his appearance, yet once in company, should behave with casual nonchalance, as if his outfit had been donned on a whim at the last minute. 'Pedantic preciseness' is vulgar, because it does not conceal deliberate effort. A newcomer who conspicuously devotes long hours to the laborious task of learning how to dress, will never impress. It was around this time that the art of tying an impeccable knot in one's cravat with casual elegance became highly prized.

When observed together, these two values create an overall effect of **naturalness**. This outcome rules out the many ploys in use at that time, which caused men to appear unnatural and somehow restricted. Ordering a coat, for instance, Pelham forbids the use of any form of padding, or anything that alters his natural shape, despite the tailor's plea:

> …we must have our chest thrown out, and have an additional inch across the shoulders; we must live for effect in this world, Mr. Pelham; a little tighter around the waist, eh?[24]

In describing those who succumb to the use of padding, Bulwer-Lytton is merciless:

> Sir Henry Millington was close by her, carefully packed up in his coat and waistcoat. Certainly, that man is the best padder in Europe… The fact was, that poor Sir Henry was not that evening made to sit down – he had only his standing up coat on![25]

Such awkwardness and constriction go against all the canons of dandy dress and behaviour. At that time, dandy fashion placed significant emphasis on personal freedom, promoting not merely a natural outline in dress, but also unrestricted behaviour. Excessive concern about spoiling one's dress, for instance, was not at all 'the thing'. At a deeper level, such attitudes were underpinned by a rigid social subtext, the aristocratic code of conduct, which dictated noble simplicity, and looked down upon excess of any kind.

In his frequent musings on social etiquette, we see Pelham attempt to formulate the connection between the art of dress and aristocratic tranquility:

> Keep your mind free from all violent affections at the hour of the toilet. A philosophical serenity is perfectly necessary to success. Helvetius says justly, that our errors arise from our passions.[26]

Aristocratic imperturbability combined with inner dignity and the stoical principles of British gentlemanly behaviour allowed dandies to perfect their celebrated composure. External self-possession also implies that one never shows surprise: dandies, in effect, were in a constant process of practising self-restraint. Concealing their own emotions allowed them to manipulate others by constantly assuming the position of power.

Even the ladies who become romantically involved with dandies are trained never to show their feelings: biting their lip, they are able to appear calm and collected, even through times of inner turmoil.

For the writers of fashionable novels, portraying inscrutable, imperturbable characters naturally raised certain difficulties. In order to describe them, authors of the first dandy novels frequently resorted to lengthy passages in the first person, which made the narration heavily laden with introspection. By the mid-nineteenth century, the heroes' own 'confessions' were often replaced with impersonal descriptions of their actions.

So how did the fashionable novel evolve after its initial success? Silver fork novels quickly became popular in other countries, also. In France, the first translations appeared almost instantly: 1830 saw the publication in French of Ward's 'Tremaine', Lister's 'Granby', 'Yes and No: A Tale of the Day' by Constantine Phipps, 1st Marquess of Normanby, as well as books by Theodore Hook and Benjamin Disraeli. Bulwer-Lytton's 'Pelham' appeared in English in France and England simultaneously in 1828, a French translation followed in 1832, and saw many subsequent editions.

French readers could also find silver fork novels in libraries. They were widely quoted in literary magazines, often discussed in cafes and salons. In the 1930s, the French language adopted a whole host of new English words, most of which are still in active usage. Even writers themselves noted this phenomenon: '*High life*: cette expression bien française se traduit en anglais par *fashionable people*' ('*High life*: this perfectly French expression is translated into English as *fashionable people*'), Apollinaire would later observe wryly.

For French dandies in the 1830s, English fashionable novels proved an invaluable source of information. Men of fashion saw them as manuals, devouring 'Pelham', Balzac's 1830 'Treatise on Elegant Living', and Barbey D'Aurevilly's 'The Anatomy of Dandyism, With Some Observations on Beau Brummell' (1845).

The Beau features in all three works, although in 'Pelham', the father of English dandyism appears as Mr. Russelton, a gentleman living in exile in France. In the essays of Balzac and Barbey D'Aurevilly, Brummell appears as himself; in all three works, he plays the role of arbiter of good taste, which he himself always exhibits.

Mr. Russelton's harsh treatment of friends who fail to meet his high standards in fashion, however, is shown in a sarcastic light. Brummell himself read 'Pelham' at an advanced age, and saw the book as a coarse caricature of himself. In his memoirs, Captain Jesse recalls the Beau's reaction when, on one occasion, Jesse wore a black coat with white shirt and waistcoat:

> My dear Jesse, I am sadly afraid you have been reading Pelham; but excuse me, you look very much like a magpie.[27]

Tensions such as these between the 'original' and his 'copies' were not uncommon, and serve to show the significant influence of literary works on fashion: Brummell is unhappy with a style copied by a friend from a book which, in this instance, has prevailed over his own advice.

In his attention to vestimentary detail in literature, Jesse was not alone: the interchange of ideas between fashion and fiction was constant. Many well-known male writers also became involved with women's fashion magazines: in 1874, Stéphane Mallarmé, for instance, published the women's periodical La Dernière Mode, unaided. Using a variety of colourful pseudonyms from all corners of the globe – Madame Marguerite de Ponti, a Creole Lady, Breton château proprietor, mulatto Zizi, Olympia la négresse, Lady from Alsace, – Mallarmé wrote countless articles on the latest ladies' fashion trends.[28]

Similarly, in 1887, Oscar Wilde became editor of The Woman's World magazine. Unlike Mallarmé, however, he did not do the job single-handedly. Writing for him were contributors such as the well-known authors Marie Corelli and Ouida, poet and critic Arthur Symons, and even Elisabeth of Wied, Queen of Romania. Queen Victoria declined his invitation to be involved, but Sarah Bernhardt wrote 'The History of My Tea Gown', and Wilde was perfectly happy to fill any gaps with his own texts.

What drew male writers to ladies' fashion? The allure was, doubtless, in part at least, of a sensual nature. A man well-versed in the intricacies of women's fashion gained deeper insight into female corporeality, literally and physically, 'the woman's world'. Knowledge of the intimate mysteries of the boudoir in the age of separate wardrobes was seen as linked with sexual prowess and experience in the bedroom, or, at least, with ease of access to the female sanctuary.

Focusing on ladies' fashion and outfits allowed writers to immerse themselves in a sensual world full of colours, scents, touch, and sound. In aesthetic dandy novels such as 'The Picture of Dorian Gray' and 'Against Nature', the meticulous descriptions of material objects of beauty play a vastly significant part. Recall the lovingly detailed passages devoted to collections of old instruments, Eastern carpets, clothes, jewels, and precious stones. Huysmans and Oscar Wilde both use what might appear a baroque literary technique, listing and describing objects, as if cataloguing accessible sources of pleasure:

> And so, for a whole year, he sought to accumulate the most exquisite specimens that he could find of textile and embroidered work, getting the dainty Delhi muslins, finely wrought with gold-thread palmatas and stitched over with iridescent beetles' wings; the Dacca gauzes, that from their transparency are known in the East as 'woven air', and 'running water', and 'evening dew'; strange figured cloths from Java; elaborate yellow Chinese hangings; books bound in tawny satins or fair blue silks and wrought with *fleurs-de-lis*, birds and images; veils of *lacis* worked in Hungary point; Sicilian brocades and stiff Spanish velvets; Georgian work, with its gilt coins, and Japanese *Foukousas*, with their green-toned golds and their marvellously plumaged birds.[29]

Conjuring up the full sensual richness of the textile world, the exotic names in passages such as this would excite the interest of any reader. Clothes are generally examined by touch, and the 'tactile' nature of these descriptions brought its own aesthetic effect, lending to the text the qualities of flowing, iridescent fabric.

Another writer who adored such literary experiments was Théophile Gautier. The French author's interest in fashion was well-known, as was the flamboyant red waistcoat, or pink doublet, he wore to the premiere of 'Hernani', and which produced such an impression. In his novels, the characters are clothed in extravagant costumes which stimulate the erotic imagination. In Gautier's celebrated 'Mademoiselle de Maupin' from 1835, the main heroine is a beautiful woman who chooses to wear men's dress – her admirer discovers her gender only when she plays the part of Rosalind in Shakespeare.

> Her dress was made of some material of changing color, azure in the light, golden in the shadow; a close-fitting buskin was tightly laced about a foot that needed not that to make it too small, and scarlet silk stockings clung amorously about the most perfectly moulded and most tempting of legs; her arms were bare to the elbows, where they emerged from a mass of lace, round and plump and white, gleaming like polished silver and of unimaginable fineness of texture; her hands, laden with rings, languorously waved a great fan of fantastically-colored feathers, like a little pocket rainbow.[30]

In this sensuous description, the lady's dress appears as a continuation of her body: deliciously fused, the two together create a striking image of beauty. The boundary between body and costume appears erased as they mutually complement each other. In Gautier's novels, ladies' clothing not only makes the woman desirable to men, but also brings her sensual pleasure.

In 1858, Gautier published 'On Fashion', a short essay highlighting his unique vision and understanding of costume. A proponent of 'art for art's sake', in this article, the writer examines dress and fabric as indicators of the crucial shifts taking place in the nineteenth century. Continuing the line of Balzac and Barbey D'Aurevilly, and, to some extent, presaging Baudelaire's essays on dandyism, Gautier muses on the capacity of fashionable dress at once to render wearers alike, and to differentiate them. As a late Romantic, Gautier deplored the abundance of black in contemporary male dress, perceiving the black coat as linked with gloom, mourning and monotony. Far more to his liking were the colours in vogue in previous years.

Turning to ladies' fashion, on the contrary, Gautier notes an abundance of aesthetic potential. For him, ladies décolleté evening gowns contained allusions to the ancient world, to classic Olympian etiquette, goddesses with bare shoulders and open necklines. Crinolines, Gautier suggested, could be viewed as pedestals of antique statues, framing the lady's bust. In his yearning for classical revival, the novelist harks back to early nineteenth-century style, with its fluid, flowing lines, and Romantic portrayal of corporeality. For Gautier, nudity is abstract and universal, yet the modern nude body speaks to him persistently of the clothing it has discarded.[31] 'L'habit est la forme visible de l'homme' ('clothing is the visible form of man'), Gautier claims. The writer, it seems, was able to perceive these 'visible forms' and elegantly convey them.

Aphorism as Dandy's Genre of Speech

Which literary genre, then, should be considered the closest and most appropriate to dandyism as a cultural tradition? We have examined Byron's poems, the fashionable novel, philosophical treatises, and writers' involvement with women's magazines. Let us now turn to another genre, one which may by right be considered best to reflect dandy culture: that of the aphorism. The brevity of the aphorism can be seen as directly reflecting simplicity in dress and the minimalist aesthetic. Oscar Wilde left a series of witty aphorisms on art, and Balzac's 'Treatise on Elegant Living' offers a multitude of aphorisms on the art of dressing.

Barbey D'Aurevilly's 'On Dandyism and George Brummell' and Baudelaire's 'The Painter of Modern Life' show similarly laconic style. All those writing on dandyism nowadays, indeed, find themselves obliged to consider this tradition, to play by these rules, or else to deliberately break them, since ignoring them altogether is simply not an option. The aggression of the dandy style has proved as appealing to modern authors as Byron's spleen was, for early nineteenth-century Romantics.

The minimalism of dandy gestures has its equivalent in the laconism of the dandy's speech. The true dandy used as few words as possible, never repeating himself or making lengthy flowery speeches. One could recall George Brummell's response when asked if he could recollect another summer's day as cold and rainy as the present one. 'Yes, last winter,' the Beau responded. The dandy's favored mode of expression was the short, witty retort, often directly linked to action. The father of one young man publicly accusing Brummell of ruining his son at the card tables, the Beau is said to have replied indignantly 'Why, I did much for your son, Sir – I once gave him my arm all the way from White's to Watier's'!'[32] This self-righteous retort not only highlighted the favour accorded to the young man – to be seen arm in arm with Beau Brummell was of course extremely prestigious – it also suggested that Brummell had taken the young man under his wing by leading him from the safety of one aristocratic club directly to another, rather than to the ruin of some ill-reputed gambling establishment.

Brummell's most laconic statement, however, was probably the note he left for his friends upon leaving England. Finally divulging the secret of his ever-perfect crisp white neckerchiefs, he is said to have written just a single word: 'Starch'.

At social events, dandies liked to speak in aphorisms (Figure 8). Robert De Montesquiou was famous for his aphoristic jokes. This terse, pithy form of expression was the perfect equivalent of the principle of economy in dress and, more generally, of the minimalist aesthetic.

Figure 8 Sem (Georges Goursat). Green album. From left to right: Jean Lorrain, Giovani Boldini, Kate Moore, Madeleine Lemaire, Robert de Montesquiou (in the centre), Jean-Louis Forain, Gabriel Yturri. 1905. Wikimedia Commons.

The same logic works in the specific tone of dandy's humour. According to William Hazlitt, Brummell

> has arrived at the very minimum of wit, and reduced it, 'by happiness or pains', to an almost invisible point. All his bons-mots turn upon a single circumstance, the exaggerating of the merest trifles into matters of importance, or treating everything else with the utmost nonchalance and indifference, as if whatever pretended to pass beyond those limits was a bore, and disturbed the serene air of high life.[33]

A lady once asked him if he never tasted vegetables and got the answer: 'Madam, I once ate a pea!'[34]

Notes

1. William Jesse, *The Life of George Brummell, Esq.* In 2 volumes (London: Saunders and Otley, 1844), vol. 2, 379.
2. Virginia Woolf, *Common Reader*, Second series (London: Hogarth Press, 1935), 148–156.
3. Lewis Melville, *Beau Brummell: His Life and Letters* (New York: G. H. Doran Co., 1925); Kathleen Campbell, *Beau Brummell: A Biographical Study* (London: Hammond, Hammond & Co, 1948); Ellen Moers, *The Dandy: Brummell to Beerbohm* (New York: The Viking Press, 1960); Hubert Cole, *Beau Brummell* (London: Granada Publishing, 1977).
4. Jules Barbey D'Aurevilly, *Dendizm i Georges Brummell*, Preface by Mikhail Kuzmin (Moscow: Al'ciona: 1912).
5. For more detailed analysis, see the section Visual Games and Optical Strategies.
6. Jesse, 1: 54–55.
7. Anon. (By one of the "Exclusives"), *The Book of Fashion; Being a Digest of the Axioms of the Celebrated Joseph Brummell* (London: W.Kidd, 1835).
8. William Jesse, ibid., vol. 2, 79.
9. William Jesse, ibid., vol. 2, 80.
10. Albert Camus, *The Rebel*. Translated from the French by Anthony Bower (New York: First Vintage International, 1991), 52.
11. On dandyism and French literature, see Rose Fortassier, *Les Écrivains Français et la Mode* (Paris: PUF, 1978).
12. For more detailed analysis in this area, see Stephen Greenblatt, *Renaissance Self-Fashioning: From More to Shakespeare* (Chicago: University of Chicago Press, 1980); Olga Vainshtein, "Zhiznetvorchestvo v culture evropeyskogo romantizma" [Self-Fashioning in European Romantic Culture], *Vestnik RGGU*, 1998, issue 2, (Moscow: Russian State University for the Humanities Press), 161–187.
13. George Gordon Byron, *Letters and Journals of Lord Byron: With Notices of His Life* (New York: J. & J. Harper, 1830), vol. 1, 477.
14. Aleksander Pushkin, *Evgeniy Onegin*. Translated from Russian by Henry Spalding (London: Macmillan and Co, 1881). Quoted from Project Gutenberg eBook 23997: https://www.gutenberg.org/files/23997/23997-h/23997-h.htm. Accessed 10.04.2022.
15. Diane Sadoff, 'The silver fork novel' in *The Oxford History of the Novel in English*, eds. John Kucich and Jenny Bourne Taylor (Oxford: Oxford University Press, 2012), vol. 3, 106–121.
16. For more on the fashionable novel, see Ellen Moers, *The Dandy: Brummell to Beerbohm* (New York: The Viking Press, 1960), 52–58.
17. Edward Bulwer-Lytton, *Pelham; Or, The Adventures of a Gentleman* (Leipzig: Bernhard Tauchnitz, 1842), 313.

18 Oscar Wilde's novel "The Picture of Dorian Gray", published in 1890, contains clear allusions to Disraeli's work, and both, of course, are novels about dandies.
19 Earl of Beaconsfield (Disraeli), *Vivian Grey* (London: Longman's, Green and Co. 1892), 61.
20 William Flavell Monypenny and George Earle Buckle, *Life of Benjamin Disraeli, Earl Beakonsfield*, in 6 volumes (New York: Macmillan, 1910–1920), vol. l, 124.
21 Edward Bulwer-Lytton, *Pelham; Or, The Adventures of a Gentleman* (Leipzig: Bernhard Tauchnitz, 1842), 167.
22 Quoted from Ellen Moers, *The Dandy: Brummell to Beerbohm* (New York: The Viking Press, 1960), 81.
23 Edward Bulwer-Lytton, Pelham; Or, The Adventures of a Gentleman (Leipzig: Bernhard Tauchnitz, 1842), 181–182.
24 Ibid., 178.
25 Ibid., 32–33.
26 Ibid., 181.
27 William Jesse, *The life of George Brummell, Esq.* In 2 volumes (London: Saunders and Otley, 1844), vol. 2, 77.
28 For more on Mallarmé and fashion, see Lecercle's thorough study: Jean-Pierre Lecercle. *Mallarmé et la Mode* (Paris: Librarie Seguire, 1989).
29 Oscar Wilde, *The Complete Works of Oscar Wilde* (Oxford: Oxford University Press, 2005), vol. 3, 117.
30 Théophile Gautier, *Mademoiselle de Maupin, A Romance of Love and Passion* (London: Gibbings & Co, 1899), 254.
31 This idea was consequently developed by Anne Hollander. See Anne Hollander, *Seeing Through Clothes* (Berkeley: University of California Press, 1993).
32 William Jesse, *The Life of George Brummell, Esq.* In 2 volumes (London: Saunders and Otley, 1844), vol. 1, 100–101.
33 William Hazlitt, *Brummelliana* (1828). http://www.dandyism.net/hazlitts-brummelliana/. Accessed 10 April 2022.
34 Ibid.

Chapter Three

CHARISMA AND CHAMELEONISM

Chameleonism

Dandyism is frequently manifested in the art of completely transforming external appearances, that is, the various means by which individuals change their personal style and ultimately their way of life. It is the art of the makeover in all its possible variations, the ability to change masks, poses and decors, to behave according to a given situation and desired scenario.

Thus, the late nineteenth-century aesthete and dandy Count Robert de Montesquiou-Fezensac (1855–1921) liked to arrange lavish masquerade balls at which the women could dress as Marie Antoinette's 'shepherdesses' and the host arrayed himself variously as Louis XIV, Louis of Bavaria, or Plato. Invitations were sent out on vellum paper, and the count personally saw to all the details of the menu, the house and garden decorations, the entertainment program, and the fireworks. Montesquiou's adeptness at making striking changes in appearance is also evident in photographs, where he appears now as the Sun King, now as an oriental sheikh, now as an automobile driver in a leather jacket. These were genuine metamorphoses, journeys in time and space through skillful reincarnations. The ideology of the dandy make-over is based on a very essential principle of nineteenth-century dandyism, namely complete 'chameleonism'. The chameleonic dandy transforms his life into a self-fashioning workshop, designing not only his outer appearance and roles, but also his scenarios, situations, and material surroundings. The dandy's chameleonic transformations are implemented through the principle of artificiality that is so characteristic of European decadence. For the aesthete, the artificial is always preferable to the natural – recall Oscar Wilde's aphorism:

> The first duty in life is to be as artificial as possible. What the second duty is no one has yet found out.[1]

Following this logic, the writers and dandies Théophile Gautier, Baudelaire, and later Sir Max Beerbohm wrote essays in praise of cosmetics. Cosmetics and outer looks function as a removable guise, a convenient mask, an occasion for an elegant theatricalized game. The experienced dandy uses the makeover to manipulate opinion, while laughing deep down at the gullible 'interpreters' of his appearance.

The notion of chameleonism in nineteenth-century culture is connected with Romantic irony. The insightful philosopher Friedrich Schlegel regarded Romantic irony as the highest manifestation of human freedom. As he writes in his famous 'Athenaeum Fragment 108':

> It is the freest of all freedoms, for it enables us to rise above ourselves, and at the same time it is the most natural, for it is absolutely necessary. It is an extremely good sign that harmonious banality does not know what to think of this constant self-parody, when again and again it is necessary to believe, then not to believe, until finally its head swims and it no longer takes jokes seriously and seriousness as jokes.[2]

The dandy does not except himself from irony. For him it is a necessary part of his constant inner training in the ability to switch. In the intellectual sense, it requires mastery of all registers of knowledge. As Schlegel observes:

> A genuinely free and well-educated man must be able at will to tune himself philosophically or a philologically, critically or poetically, historically or rhetorically, as an ancient or a contemporary, entirely arbitrarily, like a musical instrument—at any time and in any key to any tone.[3]

This ideal of self-control presumes at once both a kind of instrumentality or view of oneself as an object, and the haughty self-consciousness of a subject who personally invents and plays out life-roles. Romantic irony, while it notes the inescapable contradiction between the infinite creative intentions of the subject and his limited possibility of realizing them, nonetheless sometimes allows for a view from the outside or at least for the illusion of it:

> From the inside it is a mood regarding everything from above and rising infinitely above everything that is conditional, including one's own art, virtue, or genius.[4]

This 'transcendental buffoonery', as Schlegel calls it, presumes continuous self-control and organically implies a certain measure of cynicism, since in such an arrangement the ethical imperative is only one of the possible systems for the ironic chameleon. Following this logic to its conclusion the chameleonic dandy maintains a certain impersonality to guarantee future transformations and possible makeovers. Writing in the early nineteenth century, John Keats called this aesthetic principle of the 'poet-chameleon's' impersonality 'negative capability.' 'Negative capability' makes it possible to identify with any point of view and create any image. At first it may seem strange – what artist suddenly and voluntarily parts with his own presumed original view of things? A closer look, however, reveals that the principle of aesthetic chameleonism and impersonality is essentially very close to the notion of Romantic irony. It was not for nothing that Schlegel also wrote about the necessity of an 'empty place' ('Leerstelle') in the soul.

What are the practical possibilities for dandyism in today's field of chameleonic transformations and sophisticated makeover games? These included the performances of contemporary conceptualist artists, cross-dressing and gender-bending (recall Daniel Lismore) and risky plastic surgery dictated by the quest for the perfect body (culturally relative though it be). But for today's dandy, the possibilities for transformations are indeed limitless: it could be playing a nineteenth-century dandy for an evening out dressed in a tuxedo or tails and with careful attention to the entire ensemble (like a quotation from the classics in a postmodernist novel), or by demonstrating dandy erudition in collecting antiques. Other occasions for displaying such skills might include impudent wittiness at a dinner party or avant-garde design in a country house. Or, one could use the endless possibilities of self-fashioning through social media and become a dandy-blogger... Virtuoso chameleonism seems to facilitate getting into any role, but it is important not to lose sight of the historical tradition.

The Charisma of Count d'Orsay

Born in the family of a Napoleonic General in Paris in 1801, Count Alfred d'Orsay (1801–1852) spent most of his life in England. Having witnessed the reigns of George IV, William IV, and Queen Victoria, d'Orsay returned to France, where Napoleon III offered him the post of Superintendent of the Beaux Arts. The count's tenure in this position proved short, as he died the same year.

If George Brummell was known as England's Prime Minister of Elegance, d'Orsay was seen as the second most celebrated beau, with many calling him the Prince of Dandies.[5] Belonging to different periods, Brummell and d'Orsay were not in direct competition: the Beau left England in 1816, while d'Orsay's period of influence was the 1830s and 1840s.

An exceptionally striking man, the count never failed to impress with his athletic build, Greek profile and chestnut locks. Sporting a short curly beard, d'Orsay was the first to introduce this fashion in England. His well-proportioned features were, many noted, more typical of a female face. Unusually tall for his time at almost two metres, with eloquent blue eyes, he had but one less pleasing feature, teeth in poor condition, set wide apart.

For his eye-catching outfits, d'Orsay favoured the bold, vivid 'butterfly' dandy style (Figure 9). Like many Frenchmen, he adored intense colours, combining them fearlessly, and inventing new trends. Against the backdrop of sombre 1830s and 1840s male dress, his light blue coats and yellow waistcoats stood out as truly dazzling. In a letter to her mother, Jane Carlyle describes one of the count's outfits in detail, noting

> the fantastic finery of his dress: sky-blue satin cravat, yards of gold chain, white French gloves, light drab great-coat lined with velvet of the same color, invisible inexpressibles, skin-colored and fitting like a glove.[6]

Bedecked with gold chains and rings on his white gloves, d'Orsay wore figure-hugging skin-coloured breeches that left little to the imagination, shocking the puritanically minded public.

A true dandy, in matters of fashion d'Orsay was a clear arbiter. His extravagant tastes and innovative dress choices ensured him many followers. The bolder imitators strove to copy his open coats, brilliant waistcoats, tight breeches, and top hats, yet inevitably lacked d'Orsay's devil-may-care panache. An undisputed leader of London beaux,

Figure 9 Daniel Maclise. Portrait of Count Alfred D'Orsay. Middle of nineteenth century. Wikimedia Commons.

he frequently advised his friends on suitable styles. Once, he recommended the young Earl of Chesterfield to wear more blue, an instruction the Earl took so literally, he never wore anything else. Wishing to imitate the undisputed taste of d'Orsay, Benjamin Disraeli once also took to wearing rings on top of white gloves.

Copied by countless followers all over Europe, many of the count's trademark items became firmly associated with his name. His preferred type of coat, tall hat with curled brim, shoes with sides cut close to the sole, even his closed four-wheeled carriage with two doors: all these became known as d'Orsay.

Tremendously popular as a man of fashion, the count was in high demand for his advertising potential. Known as the face of a company producing highly popular items, he was constantly being approached by houses of fashion wishing to promote their wares. The mere assurance that an item was in his wardrobe was enough to send shoppers flocking to buy. Many clothes makers sent their pieces to the count free of charge, hoping he would show them off to advantage. On one occasion, d'Orsay received a dozen mustard-coloured gloves from Switzerland. Shortly after he appeared in them, a shower of orders for such gloves ensued. Not content with sending free clothing, some makers enclosed money as payment for d'Orsay's 'services', and tailors would often slip notes in the pockets of coats made for their illustrious client. Quite spoiled by the attention, d'Orsay was known to become peeved, and even send items back, when unaccompanied by such financial stimulus.

At times, however, the count made use of his formidable reputation for charitable causes. One day, out walking in Hyde Park, he met a boy selling matches. Purchasing a box, he started chatting to the young vendor, and, feeling a liking for him, decided to help. He told the boy to return the following day at noon, when he planned to go walking with his friends. The next day, when the boy duly approached, d'Orsay hastened to buy matches, declaring loudly that he never purchased them anywhere else, as these were 'the best in London'. Following his lead, the count's friends fell upon the boy, instantly buying up his entire supply.

So popular was d'Orsay, that many writers based their characters on him, including him in well-known works. Bulwer-Lytton's 'Godolphin' is dedicated to the count. Alcibiades de Mirabel in Benjamin Disraeli's 'Henrietta Temple' (note the antique name!); the dandy Henri de Marsay in Balzac's 'La Fille Aux Yeux D'or' ('The Girl with the Golden Eyes'), whose name, indeed, rhymes with that of d'Orsay: all of them were based on the count.

Known for his 'divine beauty', constantly compared to Apollo, d'Orsay was described by Lord Byron as 'un Cupidon déchaîné'. Equally appealing, it seems, to men and women, medallions with his likeness were bought by both sexes alike. In terms of universal popularity, a similar style icon was perhaps Georgiana Cavendish, Duchess of Devonshire, widely known for her looks and charisma.

The count's disposition, it seems, never failed to attract.

> Count d'Orsay was the model of all that could be conceived of novel demeanour and youthful candour, with a gaiety of heart and cheerfulness of mind that spread happiness on all around him.[7]

All those fortunate to spend time in his company appeared to hold him in the highest esteem as a pleasant and valuable companion. D'Orsay was known for his vigorous handshake, loud, infectious laugh, and relaxed, convivial manner. His enthusiastic greeting 'A-ha, mon ami!' always drew smiles. Even with those he knew little, he was gracious and warm, and those who were initially suspicious, inevitably succumbed to his good nature.

The count's charm appeared to act on everyone, regardless of class. Lord Lamington, for instance, recalled that 'commoners' tended to see him as a higher being, following his carriage with their gaze as he passed by. In Paris, during the July Revolution of 1830, the crowd surrounded d'Orsay, yet, upon recognising him, greeted him with enthusiastic shouts of 'Vive le Comte d'Orsay!' The count's charisma appeared to act on all. In this chapter, we take a closer look at this curious phenomenon. What was the secret of d'Orsay's unfailing appeal? And what, exactly, made up his charismatic charm?

Charisma, of course, is a key component of dandyism. At times, a word's etymology may offer fascinating clues to its meaning.[8] The Greek word 'charisma' means 'gift', and the Christian understanding of charisma linked it to God, defining it as 'God's gift': the gift of healing, for instance, or of language. The Eucharist, or Holy Communion, literally signifies thanksgiving. At a deeper level, 'charisma' is linked to the Ancient Indo-European root 'gher', associated with a whole host of meanings in different languages.

In English, it can be traced to words such as 'yearn', 'hungry', and 'greedy'. In German, it is connected with 'gern' (gladly). We may conclude that the overall sense is of 'desiring something specific, something sensually concrete'. Another version, 'ghr-ta', forms the root of the Latin verb 'hortari' (to encourage or motivate). Hence, English words such as 'hortative', or 'exhort'. This type of desire is more intellectual; a wish that connects one to others, motivating them to think or act. The Greek 'kharis' (charity, kindness) and 'khairein' (to enjoy) take us back to the initial meaning of universal joy and pleasure for oneself and others.

Thus, our etymological journey brings us to the field of 'gift – desire – motive – joy'. The desire may be of a direct sensual nature, or indirect, expressed through others, in the social realm. The charismatic subject lives through his desire, desiring others, and desired by them, in turn. Giving to others, he himself receives gifts. This initiates an intense energetic cycle, which gives rise to the warmth of life – joy, a sign that one is fully engaging with reality.

In the social culture of modernity, charisma retained this basic semantics. The charismatic person is seen as possessing an inner confidence, a unique faith in his or her own fate and gift. To others, such confidence acts as a magnetic charm, exercising a powerful pull. Musing on charismatic appeal, Max Weber wrote of 'milder forms of euphoria which may be experienced as either a dreamlike mystical illumination or a more active and ethical conversion'.[9]

Being in the company of Count d'Orsay, it seems, was sufficient to induce 'milder forms of euphoria'. How else does one account for the abundance of enthusiastic, even ecstatic, comments from such a wide variety of extremely different people?

Thackeray: 'Gracious and good natured beyond measure… He pleases by his unbounded good humour and generous sympathy with everybody'; Disraeli: 'a friend, and the best and kindest of men'. Macready: '…dear Count d'Orsay. No one who knew him and had affections could help loving him.'[10]

Considered a friend by the foremost Victorian writers and most opulent peers, d'Orsay was constantly invited to social gatherings, races, and hunting expeditions. A member of many prestigious clubs, he possessed a charismatic appeal that was truly universal.

At first glance, one was, perhaps, most likely to note the count's outstanding looks. Many of those who met d'Orsay, remarked on the intriguing element of femininity in his appearance. At times, his dress was held up as overly effeminate or daring, yet it seems it was precisely this womanly ingredient in his male charm that rendered him so irresistible. The element of 'otherness', at times, hard to put one's finger on or to describe, clearly stimulated the imagination.

In the dandy culture, a similar effect could be observed with elements of 'otherness' in the national context. In order to be seen as a true man of fashion in France, one had to be known as an Anglophile, whereas in England, it was crucial to be seen as adoring all that was French. As a Frenchman who had spent most of his life in England, the Count d'Orsay was ideally placed to shine.

D'Orsay's biography appears to confirm this pattern. His earliest successes in society followed his arrival in London in 1821 with his sister Ida, a rare beauty who married the Duke de Guiche. De Guiche's father, the Duke de Gramont, became the French ambassador to England, opening the doors to the best houses in London for the young d'Orsay. Received as an affluent, handsome foreigner, the count quickly made his mark with the London dandies. His knowledge of horses, riding prowess, magnificent outfits, and French courteousness never failed to impress.

At one gathering, d'Orsay found himself sitting next to Lady Holland, known for her demanding behaviour. Thinking to test the young newcomer, the lady dropped her napkin, which the count felt obliged to pick up. She then proceeded to drop her fan, her knife, and her fork. Picking up each object in turn, the young count smiled and continued the conversation, until the lady let fall her glass. Turning to one of the servants, the count ordered his plate and utensils to be placed on the floor. 'I shall finish my dinner there,' he explained. 'It will be much more convenient for my Lady Holland.'[11]

With his quick wit and easy, charming manners, d'Orsay made himself a wide circle of acquaintances among the aristocracy. His most important friendship was undoubtedly with the Blessington family. Twelve years older than d'Orsay, Lady Blessington was a famed society belle. Her portrait created by Thomas Lawrence in 1822 was said to have 'set all of London raving'. Well-educated, cultured, and open-minded, the couple quickly became attached to the young dandy, inviting him to join them in Europe. Becoming almost like a member of the family, between 1822 and 1828, Alfred accompanied the pair on their travels.

Much has been written of the relationship between the three, with many claiming the young d'Orsay was the lover of both husband and wife. Some critics, however, insist no proof exists.[12] In any case, Lord Blessington's will stated that d'Orsay should inherit half of the family fortune, if he married one of the couple's daughters. In 1827, d'Orsay, who possessed no other source of income, wed Harriet, Lord Blessington's daughter from a previous marriage. The couple had never spent any time together, and, as the union had been arranged for purely pecuniary reasons, it proved weak, dissolving altogether five years later.

During d'Orsay's time in Europe with the Blessingtons, the three spent a significant period in Paris, where they led an intense social life. Later, in Italy, they met Lord Byron in Genoa in 1823. Expecting a mournful, sombre figure, Lady Blessington was surprised to find a sociable, open, and witty host, who received them gladly, and did not appear to show signs of melancholia. The group rapidly developed a friendship, d'Orsay offering Byron his English journal to read on the second day of their acquaintance. Returning it later, the poet complimented the young man's astute observations on English society. 'The most singular thing is - how he should have penetrated not the facts, but the mystery of the English Ennui at two and twenty.'[13] Byron suggested that d'Orsay publish the text. Full of enthusiasm, the young count made a drawing of the poet. Later, Jean Cocteau referred to this episode, creating his own drawing of d'Orsay, captioned with the words: 'On the bank of Lake Geneva, the Count d'Orsay draws Lord Byron in profile. The aroma of that morning has reached us, also.'[14] Now, as in Borges's 'Coleridge's Dream', it remains for a present-day artist to create a portrait of Cocteau drawing d'Orsay.

Byron's letters from the spring of 1823 are filled with praise of his new friend, whom he describes as 'clever, original, unpretending; he affected to be nothing that he was not'. The compliments may be seen as a blessing from the ageing dandy poet to his younger protégé. When, two months later, the friends were forced to part, Byron, via Lady Blessington, gave d'Orsay a ring formed out of lava, 'adapted to the fire of his years and character'.[15]

Gifted with exquisite taste, d'Orsay liked to help Lady Blessington with her Ladies' Christmas annuals. The count himself had already published in America a book entitled 'Etiquette; Or, a Guide to the Usages of Society, With a Glance at Bad Habits' (1843). In general, such annuals and books on etiquette tended to find a significantly better market in America and the British colonies, than in England.

A special passion of the count's was perfume. Like a devoted alchemist, he could happily spend hours, experimenting with essences and alembic, creating new aromas. Perhaps his magnetic charm was, in some part, connected with his scents: his most famous perfume, Eau de Bouquet, was extremely popular among ladies. For Lady Blessington, d'Orsay created a special floral perfume (she disliked the odour of musk). After d'Orsay's death, his descendants established Parfums d'Orsay, a company said to use original formulas developed by the count.[16]

Following the death of Lord Blessington, in the 1830s, the home of Count d'Orsay and Lady Blessington became known as one of London's foremost literary salons. Among its frequent guests were Edward Bulwer-Lytton and his brother Henry, Walter Savage Landor, Charles Dickens, Edward Trelawny, Benjamin Disraeli, and William Thackeray. Foreign visitors included Alfred de Vigny, Franz Liszt, Hector Berlioz, Eugène Sue, Gustave Doré, and Paul Gavarni. The illustrious list even included Louis-Napoleon, who frequently visited d'Orsay, a staunch Bonapartist, whilst in exile in England.

How, then, did d'Orsay hold himself with such a formidable entourage of writers, artists, and intellectuals? Known for his excellent humour and wit, he was able to brighten any gathering with his particular blend of French charm and repartee. Furthermore, the count knew something of the arts, as he himself practised drawing, oil painting, and sculpture with considerable success. The Duke of Wellington, for instance, thought the bust made of him by d'Orsay to be the best likeness, and the count's bronze bust of Lamartine created in Paris also brought him wide acclaim. A number of his works survive, to this day.

As a high-society man and a dandy, d'Orsay's most striking feature was, perhaps, his remarkable capacity to enjoy life. When he was present, Lady Blessington's salon never descended into boredom or haughty pompousness. An enthusiastic organiser, d'Orsay was famed for his exuberant gatherings, spontaneous games and pranks. He was also adept at helping bring star-crossed lovers together: in this capacity, he features in Disraeli's 'Henrietta Temple' as a Deus ex machina, appearing near the end to untangle the complicated love-knot and magically reunite the loving couple.

> The Count stood before him, the best-dressed man in London, fresh and gay as a bird, with not a care on his sparkling visage, and his eye bright with bonhomie… Care he knew nothing about; Time he defied; Indisposition he could not comprehend. He had never

been ill in his life, even for five minutes. Ferdinand was really very glad to see him; there was something in Count Mirabel's very presence which put everybody in good spirits. His light-headedness was caught by all. Melancholy was a farce in the presence of his smile; and there was no possible combination of scrapes that could withstand his kind and brilliant raillery. At the present moment, Ferdinand was in a sufficiently good humour with his destiny, and he kept up the ball with effect; so that nearly an hour passed in amusing conversation.[17]

So, readers would have no doubt about the figure behind Count Mirabel, Disraeli even dedicated the novel to Count Alfred d'Orsay 'from his faithful friend'. A portrait of d'Orsay was included in the book as an illustration. The most striking trait of Disraeli's 'Alcibiades the Magnificent' is his sheer joie de vivre, a French hedonism that has him brand any form of melancholy, 'bêtise!'

'Fancy a man ever being in low spirits,' said the Count Mirabel. 'Life is too short for such bêtises. The most unfortunate wretch alive calculates unconsciously better to live than to die. Well then, he has something in his favour. Existence is a pleasure, and the greatest. The world cannot rob us of that; and if it is better to live than to die, it is better to live in a good humour than a bad one. If a man be convinced that existence is the greatest pleasure, his happiness may be increased by good fortune, but it will be essentially independent of it. He who feels that the greatest source of pleasure always remains to him ought never to be miserable. The sun shines on all: every man can go to sleep; if you cannot ride a fine horse, it is something to look upon one; if you have not a fine dinner, there is some amusement in a crust of bread and Gruyere. Feel slightly, think little, never plan, never brood. Everything depends upon the circulation; take care of it. Take the world as you find it; enjoy everything. Vive la bagatelle!'[18]

Albeit in exaggerated form, Count Mirabel's enthusiastic monologue sums up perfectly the sunny, epicurean aspect of dandyism. Bursting with life, 'passionné', in the words of d'Orsay's French biographer Pierre Lestringuez,[19] d'Orsay's experience of reality was constantly sensual, thriving on the pleasures of the dandy and gourmet.

A love of sensual pleasures was also characteristic of Beau Brummell. Ailing and destitute, in France he nevertheless continued to frequent the pâtisserie where he could still procure his favourite Rheims biscuits. D'Orsay's hedonism, however, was special: it was unusually infectious. His striking capacity to enjoy life in all its aspects from the simplest entertainment to the most complex situations, appeared to communicate itself instantly to others. In his company, food seemed more flavoursome, diversions, more stimulating. Whenever he appeared at a gambling gathering, the stakes leaped up. Like a catalyst for pleasure, d'Orsay unfailingly brought excitement and cheer, wherever he went.

On one occasion, an onlooker became a devoted admirer of the count after watching him consume a steak. So infectious was d'Orsay's enjoyment of the perfectly cooked meat, all those around him instantly felt a craving for beef. A true gourmet, d'Orsay possessed a well-developed, exceptionally fine palate. Even Thackeray, who regularly satirised dandies in his essays for Punch, could not resist d'Orsay's charisma. After his very first time in Lady Blessington's salon, he appeared to succumb to the count's good nature, becoming a frequent visitor. The critical tone of his writings softened, and, when Lady Blessington's fortunes changed, he even purchased several of her belongings at auction, and sent them to her in France.

Before long, Thackeray introduced d'Orsay to William Maginn, editor of Fraser's Magazine, the count becoming one of the 'Fraserians' depicted in Daniel Maclise's famous drawing from 1835. This particular development was all the more striking, given the magazine's war on dandyism: Bulwer-Lytton, for instance, had been all but obliterated by Fraser's. Yet, after just a couple of visits to the editor, d'Orsay was invited to contribute, had his portrait published, and came to be generally known as 'the beloved of all who knew him'! The force of individual personality, it seems, was capable of working wonders. Like Thackeray and Dickens, Maginn had repeatedly attacked the Regency dandies, and d'Orsay should, beyond a doubt, have been a prime target for his venom. The count's charisma, however, proved stronger.

Another well-known opponent of dandyism, Thomas Carlyle, is also known to have fallen under d'Orsay's spell. In her memoirs, Carlyle's wife Jane recalls a visit from the count:

> ...the sound of a whirlwind rushed through the street, and there stopped with a prancing of steeds and footman thunder at this door, an equipage, all resplendent with sky-blue and silver, discoverable thro' the blinds, like a piece of the Coronation Procession, from whence emanated Count d'Orsay! a sight it was to make one think the millennium actually at hand, when the lion and the lamb, and all incompatible things should consort together. Carlyle in his grey plaid suit, and his tub-chair, looking blandly at the Prince of Dandies; and the Prince of Dandies on an opposite chair, all resplendent as a diamond-beetle, looking blandly at him. D'Orsay is a really handsome man, after one has heard him speak and found that he has both wit and sense; but at first sight his beauty is of that rather disgusting sort which seems to be like genius, 'of no sex.'[20]

Jane Welsh Carlyle's colourful account suggests a reaction to d'Orsay that was not uncommon: contemporaries frequently described a first impression of mythological magnificence. The count's remarkable looks put many in mind of royalty, if not deity. His appearance was compared to an apocalyptic vision; a thunderbolt from above. Upon studying the dandy more closely, Jane Carlyle notes that he is the opposite of her husband. The dandy and the intellectual have not yet found comfortable shared ground, although their first meeting at Lady Blessington's was sufficient to inspire mutual feelings of interest.

A clever, shrewd, well-informed lady, Jane Carlyle can only give her approval to those who show intelligence and perspicacity. Once convinced of the count's intellectual discernment, she is prepared to appreciate his beauty, which, at first, she found unnerving. His erotic appeal as a dandy, it seems, troubled her puritanical conscience. After just one conversation, however, she succumbs to d'Orsay's charm. His innocent remark on a bust of Shelley is sufficient to win her regard: 'His manners are manly and unaffected and he convinces one, shortly, that in the face of all probability he is a devilish clever fellow.'[21] The count, it seems, had once again won over a convinced opponent.

The victories of d'Orsay commonly involved the gradual breaking down of stereotypes and preconceptions. A frequent reaction to his outstanding looks was an assumption of his stupidity: 'so handsome, he must not think much'. D'Orsay, however, was capable of shattering any such illusion with very little effort. Intelligent and well-informed, he was more than capable of holding his own, even with a celebrated philosopher such as Carlyle. Convinced of his intellect, his interlocutors often proceeded to assume that his morals, then, must be questionable. The count's polished, yet easy manner, however, soon convinced them of his total confidence and self-possession.

D'Orsay's relations with the nobility frequently followed a similar pattern. First meeting him, peers and aristocrats tended to assume that, as a foreigner, he knew little of English life: his accent, after all, was quite pronounced. Before long, they would be forced to concede that this 'outsider' knew more about horses than many an Englishman, that he had long been a member of the best clubs, and counts most of the wealthiest and finest families among his friends.

Such perfection could, of course, also have turned people away. After all, they had been proved wrong, their initial assessments had been inaccurate. Would he hold it against them? His perfection served merely to highlight their shortcomings. Clever, breathtakingly handsome, at home in the best circles – he had everything in far greater abundance than they. Yet d'Orsay's charm came to his rescue here, too. Like a generous demigod, he reached out to them, when they were all but ready to turn away. Showing those who had doubted him that he still considered them friends, d'Orsay turned all in his favour. That such a perfect creature should consider one his equal, indeed produced in people 'milder forms of euphoria'. Proud to be seen as his friends, they would attempt to imitate him in everything, seizing every opportunity to brag about him.

In this way, it seems, the Count d'Orsay made his impression. Besides his good-natured disposition, however, d'Orsay's special charisma stemmed from the aesthetic completeness of his appearance. He was like a work of art. After his first visit to Lady Blessington's salon, the American journalist Nathaniel Parker Willis described the count reclining on the ottoman, insouciant, as a picture of pure plasticity, a young tiger full of grace and poise. Many, encountering d'Orsay, were perfectly content to admire him from a distance: so strong was the impression, the aesthetic pleasure was heady enough, even from afar.

In Paris, the winter of 1829 brought abundant snow. Ordering a special sleigh, d'Orsay cut an imposing figure on his excursions. In her diary, Lady Blessington recalls:

> Count A. d'Orsay's sledge presented the form of a dragon, and the accoutrements and horse were beautiful; the harness was of red morocco, embroidered in gold…. The dragon of Comte A. d'Orsay looked strangely fantastic at night. In the mouth, as well as the eyes, was a brilliant red light; and to a tiger-skin covering, that nearly concealed the cream-coloured horse, revealing only the white mane and tail, was attached a double line of silver-gilt bells, the jingle of which was very musical and cheerful.[22]

Lady Blessington, of course, tended always to admire d'Orsay, yet, it seems, on this occasion he was gazed upon with veneration by the whole of Paris. In his memoirs, recalling a ride with the count, Lord Lamington also stresses the constant presence of d'Orsay's admirers:

> I have frequently ridden down to Richmond with Count d'Orsay. A striking figure he was in his blue coat with gilt buttons, thrown well back to show the wide expanse of snowy shirt-front and buff waistcoat; his tight leathers and polished boots; his well-curled whiskers and handsome countenance; a wide-brimmed, glossy hat, spotless white gloves. He was the very beau – ideal of a leader of fashion. As he rode through Kensington and Brompton, he excited general attention.[23]

D'Orsay's perfectly finished appearance could almost put one in mind of a beautiful object, gratifying to the gaze, displayed for general admiration. Such 'dandy-object' could serve an example of the wonderful in everyday life, a feature of the new economics and culture of modernity, in which the dandy's role was to take the exteriorisation and alienation of individuality to its logical conclusion. In this way, the dandy becomes a universal fetish, arousing everyone's curiosity and desire.[24] Here, we also see a fascinating example of dandyism's role in the emergence of the celebrity as an institution, a phenomenon clearly typical of late modernity.

Towards the end of his life, when d'Orsay struggled with pecuniary difficulties, his luck deserted him. A celebrity who was once admired by all, he gradually lost both his fame, and his charisma. In Bulwer-Lytton's 'Godolphin', Vernon, doubtless painted from d'Orsay, reflects thus:

> I became famous—and a ruined man! They could not dine without me; they could not sup without me; they could not get drunk without me; no pleasure was sweet but in my company. What mattered it that, while I ministered to their amusement, I was necessarily heaping debt upon debt—accumulating miseries for future years—laying up bankruptcy, and care, and shame, and a broken heart, and an early death? my life was reduced to two epochs—that of use to them—that not. During the first, I was honoured; during the last, I was left to starve—to rot![25]

Fortune deserts d'Orsay, and even the timing of everyday events falls out of sync. Things befall him at the wrong time, in the wrong places: his house arrest, Louis-Napoleon's tardy benevolence – everything is mistimed. Deep down, it seems, the count was out of step with himself: hence, the loss of his charismatic appeal.

Why, then, did d'Orsay's magnetic charm not come to the rescue sooner? What made his legendary charisma powerless to turn events in his favour? When money troubles came, his friends refused to help, many, turning away altogether. A dandy is not necessarily a man of means, as we know, and some well-known beaux even flaunted their lack of lucre. As Serge Moskovici writes, '…rejecting any compromise with everyday necessity and its benefits, charisma is "power of the anti-economic type."'[26] The sacral, romantic nature of charisma demands that it be constantly backed up with clear action: bold escapades, 'miracles', remarkable adventures. If these, for any reason, cease to be possible, charisma can turn sour, settling into the humdrum, the everyday. The emotional connection between the idol and his followers is broken; the leader loses his air of mystery and magnetic appeal. The loss of charismatic authority can trigger a collective return to rationality. The desire to follow and emulate the leader in everything, disappears.

Describing this process, Weber uses metaphors such as the cooling and hardening of liquid, or awaking from hypnosis. Such may be the reaction of the followers; yet, within the leader himself, there is also change. Charisma, as we saw earlier, tends to include an element of the alien: recall d'Orsay's 'Frenchness', the gender ambiguity of certain beaux, or the unusual physical traits demonstrated by some dandies. As Moscovici suggests, while their magic lasts, foreigners, or 'marked' individuals, are forgiven a multitude of sins. Allowed to bend the rules that bind other mortals, they are encouraged, praised, seen as special. Their peculiarities are considered amusing, wonderful, even. They may quickly become leaders, or jesters. Yet woe betide them when their fortune turns.

> These outsiders are tasked with leading the way out of the chaos that threatens existence. They are expected to show everyone what is to be done. In everyday terms, these people, who have nothing to lose, accept the risk of "sullying" themselves, when no one else is able to do so without damaging their own standing. Should they prove unsuccessful, the group can quickly cast them aside, turning them into scapegoats, far more easily than it could with an 'autochtone' [an "insider", a native – O.V.].[27]

Thus, the alien 'otherness' of the dandy, so appealing at first, may, when circumstances change, trigger a chain of destruction. An ideal victim, the dandy becomes an isolated object, a fetish. In the case of d'Orsay, the isolation was quite literal, as he spent seven years virtually under house arrest.

The 'objectification' of count d'Orsay was made easier, to some extent, by the aesthetic completeness of his image. As a dandy, his striking poise and grace were immediately evident, be it images of his sleighing jaunts, or Lord Lamington's descriptions. This jewel-like quality created an extra finish, ensuring him a special place outside traditional systems of criteria. Speaking of him, even very different people tended to use similar language, referring to the count as a butterfly, diamond-beetle, dragonfly, or hummingbird. Flitting hither and thither, all of these creatures enchant us with their vivid colours. Besides their bright appearance, however, they also share their small size and fragility. D'Orsay was a tall man, yet, on a more profound level, the comparison is a valid one. Delicate and vulnerable in a cruel, harsh world, all these creatures are doomed. Comparisons with insects are not uncommon in dandy culture, with d'Orsay frequently likened to a butterfly, dazzling, yet fragile.

Lady Blessington's fate is perhaps even more poignant. In her relationship with the count, she clearly sacrificed herself, keeping d'Orsay through her literary endeavours. His narcissistic egoism left its mark on her health, yet, despite all this, it was not the tireless, self-sacrificing woman writer who remained in history, but the Prince of Dandies. The count's fame likely owed much to the appealing legend which had formed around him: the dandy's biography as the cultural text proved the more convincing, durable construction.

Comparing the self-fashioning of d'Orsay and Brummell, we immediately become aware of marked differences. Bustling with anecdotes and bons mots, Beau's story is an epic tale of a great reformer of fashion. The count's biography, on the other hand, is largely reconstructed from the warm, less descriptive, yet more emotional memoirs of his friends, although John Mills's novel 'D'Horsay; or, the Follies of the Day' has more of a tabloid feel.[28] Although, in his lifetime, d'Orsay was no less known than Beau Brummell, his life did not engender dandy folklore. Surviving accounts stress the omnipotent magic of his name and charisma, fusing into a mythological legend of a devastatingly handsome demigod.

Both renowned leaders of fashion, the two men followed radically different principles. The radiant style of d'Orsay was all but the polar opposite of Brummell's minimalism. The count's passion for brilliant colours and gold accessories, his continental extravagance could not have been to Brummell's liking. Against the backdrop of sombre 1840s male style, shaped as it was by Beau's asceticism, d'Orsay exploded with colour like an effulgent butterfly. His experiments with style and colour left their mark on Aesthetic and bohemian dress of the late nineteenth century, as well as Parisian designs of the early twentieth. Later, this would, in turn, go on to influence the Sape movement in Africa.

Another interesting difference between the two dandies lay in their attitudes to corporeality and sport. Making a point of demonstrating his abhorrence of sports, Brummell despised virtually all traditional English outdoor pursuits. Strikingly athletic, well known as a connoisseur of horses and hunting, d'Orsay, on the other hand, although born a Frenchman, was the perfect English buck, a sporting dandy.

For Brummell, corporeality was largely a matter of order and almost narcissistic cleanliness. His relations with women appear generally to have been platonic. D'Orsay's erotic reputation, on the other hand, preceded him. Although many of the facts were never entirely clear, the count was widely seen as indulging in illicit amorous escapades, an image backed up by his flamboyant dress. Brummell and d'Orsay were both accused of being overly effeminate due to their obsessive attention to costume, yet Brummell was mostly perceived as a heterosexual, whereas d'Orsay had a more ambiguous reputation.

Hailed as a 'sublime demigod' (which no one ever said of Brummell), d'Orsay was seen as something of a divine being, superior to common mortals in every respect, from his height and eye-catching outfits, to his sensitive, effeminate features, athletic build, and flawless masculine figure. Like Brummell, d'Orsay was perceived as an arbiter of fashion, yet, unlike the Beau, he was not harsh in his comments. Well aware of his own uniqueness, he strove not to make others follow his tastes. A true French gallant, his manner was always courteous. On one occasion only is he said to have expressed criticism, albeit in a very mild form. His friend, the actor William Macready,[29] was playing in Bulwer-Lytton's 'Richelieu'. After the first performance, the actor enquired whether d'Orsay had any comments, whereupon the count responded that his cassock could perhaps be fuller:[30] a gentle hint that neither the play nor Macready's performance, merited further discussion.

The Beau, on the other hand, was a harsh judge, never content with anything but perfection. His shrewd gaze refused to even register anything not in keeping with the highest standards of dandy refinement. Should an item fail to measure up, it would no longer be deemed deserving of its name, as in his famous question 'Do you call this thing a coat?'

The energy and charisma of the two dandies were extremely different, also. If Brummell was respected and feared for his coldness and sharp tongue, d'Orsay, on the contrary, was warmly loved. His jovial amicability and sociable manners brought merriment to all around him. He appeared to make people feel more self-confident. In his presence, one felt inspired to live a better, more beautiful and full life. This, indeed, was the most appealing aspect of his dandyism. Everyone wanted to emulate him: talking to him, even the dullest soul felt engaged, motivated, and alive.

Initially experienced on a subconscious level, this desire to emulate was driven by the count's infectious hedonism. Intuitively, one wished to derive the same pleasure from life, to enjoy food, fine dress, and horses, to the same extent. D'Orsay's energy was overpowering: a surging tide of colossal force, an explosion of sensual delight. He awakened the pulse of desire in people who, be it due to age, ailments, or reticence, had long forgotten the taste of passion, pure sensual pleasure, and hedonistic pursuits. Thus, the first, and most basic, feature of d'Orsay's charisma was its infectiousness. Connecting followers to the energy and joy of collective sensual beings, he enabled them to reestablish their contact with physical reality.

Yet, d'Orsay's charisma went still further. It reassured those around him that their wishes could become reality. If other leaders of fashion were less jovial and gracious, D'Orsay's unique good humour and hearty conviviality raised the spirits of any gathering. Where others, including Brummell, came across as distant or critical, frequently alienating potential admirers, d'Orsay offered friendship and jolliness. Those meeting him were instantly won over: his warmth was interpreted as a sign of approval, confirmation that one was, indeed, truly worthy. In d'Orsay, many found a mirror, which showed them their best life. Raising their self-esteem, he prompted them to act from a place of optimism and self-worth. In his company, the wish to be a better person came naturally, and the goal appeared within reach. Coming to believe in themselves, people saw their dreams become reality: in imitating the count, they would begin to live their best life. His influence, though not deliberate or overt, served to transform lives.

Bearing this in mind, it may be easier to understand the emotional outpourings and vows of friendship offered to the count by so many very different people. Often, he contrived to win over those strongly prejudiced against him. The words 'my friend, the Count d'Orsay' opened doors and created opportunities, welcoming one into the world of the young, fashionable, beautiful, and carefree. The count's warmth recalled one to the lightness and joy of being, thus activating the original etymological semantic field of charisma: desire – motive – joy.

The magnetic appeal of d'Orsay may also have had its roots in his unfailing connection with childhood. Many noted the childlike aspect of his nature: on a number of occasions, he is said to have acted like a 'big baby'. His ardent desires, strong emotions and direct expression often put observers in minds of children. On one occasion, when Lady Blessington told him off for some oversight, he burst into tears. His behaviour, at times, was indeed quite puerile. In one establishment, he happened to notice an insult against him, scrawled on the windowpane. Picking up an orange, he flung it at the glass, knocking it into the Thames.

D'Orsay's infectious, boisterous gaiety, and his natural spontaneity which flouted convention, were precisely what made others love him. His childlike aspect, however, could border on infantilism. Where matters of finance were concerned, for instance, he preferred not to get involved, leaving these issues to the care of Lady Blessington. He often referred to her as his 'dear mother', another indication of puerility. In the final years of their lives, it seems, the pair's relations became increasingly like those of a mother and son.

This carefree juvenility is, perhaps, the 'downside' of ingenuousness, of the ability to desire vehemently, and to rejoice at the fulfilment of one's desires. This is the lighter, more hedonistic aspect of dandyism, quite distinct from the more sombre, 'grown-up' rationalism of the Regency era. Over time, this hedonistic aspect of dandyism would evolve into the Aesthetic sensuality of Oscar Wilde. In 'The Picture of Dorian Gray', a 'new Hedonism' is hailed as an inevitable development.

> Yes: there was to be, as Lord Henry had prophesied, a new Hedonism that was to recreate life and to save it from that harsh uncomely puritanism that is having, in our own day, its curious revival. It was to have its service of the intellect, certainly, yet it was never to accept any theory or system that would involve the sacrifice of any mode of passionate experience. Its aim, indeed, was to be experience itself, and not the fruits of experience, sweet or bitter as they might be. Of the asceticism that deadens the senses, as of the vulgar profligacy that dulls them, it was to know nothing. But it was to teach man to concentrate himself upon the moments of a life that is itself but a moment.[31]

Compared to d'Orsay's sheer joie de vivre, the 'new Hedonism' of Oscar Wilde is a more finished, conceptual phenomenon. If the count's charisma is warm and bright, Aesthetic hedonism favours the cold decadence of 'Les Fleurs du Mal'. Wilde's hedonism thrives on any sensual impression: for his 'passionate experience', source and moral nature are not important.

Until the very end, d'Orsay insisted on living life to the full. On his last day, he is said to have listened to his niece playing waltzes on the piano. 'Faster, faster!' the count murmured, his niece picking up the pace. 'Faster! Faster still!' he insisted, and when, after duly delivering several giddy pieces, the player turned round, she saw her uncle had passed away. The butterfly had flown to freedom.

Notes

1. Oscar Wilde, *Phrases and Philosophies for the Use of the Young* (London: 1903), 5.
2. Friedrich Schlegel, *Werke in zwei Bänden*. (Berlin und Weimar: Aufbau-Verlag, 1980), 1: 182 This quotation is translated by Sofia Horujaya-Cook.
3. Ibid., 283.
4. Ibid.
5. See Nick Foulkes, *Last of the Dandies: The Scandalous Life and Escapades of Count d'Orsay* (London: Little Brown, 2003).

6 Jane Welsh Carlyle, 'Count d'Orsay Calls on Mrs. Carlyle', Letter, April 7, 1830, in *The Portable Victorian Reader* (London: Penguin, 1977), 21.
7 Michael Sadleir, *Blessington-d'Orsay. A Masquerade* (London: Constable & Co., 1933), 98.
8 One could compare the idea of 'charisma' with a similar concept in ancient cultures. Partly corresponding to 'fate', it denoted one's 'personal lot, destiny, luck, and life force'. According to Aron Gurevich, the ancient Germans and Scandinavians, for example, used the term 'hamingja': 'this was both one's luck, and one's guardian spirit, which, in moments of crisis, could become visible to that person. When the person died, the spirit would either die, or leave, in order to join a descendant or relative of the deceased.' (Aron Gurevich, Dialektika sud'by u germantsev i drevnikh skandinavov [The Dialectics of Fate among Germans and Ancient Scandinavians] in *Poniatiye sudby v kontekste raznykh kultur* [The Concept of Fate in the Context of Different Cultures] (Moscow: Nauka, 1994), 152. Within this context, a contest or battle between people can be seen as the clash of their "fortunes" ('I fear your fortune will prove stronger than my poor fortune'), and, fascinatingly, personal good fortune is immediately apparent in the deeds, speech, and even the personal appearance of a hero – 'taking one look at Skarphéðinn, one of the characters in the Njáls saga, observers could instantly tell that he had poor fortune'. Thus, one's personal fortune created a powerful information field, which, like charisma, was immediately visible to observers.
9 Quoted from Serge Moscovici, *Mashina, tvoriashaya bogov* [*The Machine that Makes Gods*]. (Moscow: Tsentr psykhologii i psikhoterapii, 1998), 190. This quotation is translated by Sofia Horujaya-Cook.
10 Quoted from Ellen Moers, *The Dandy: Brummell to Beerbohm* (New York: The Viking Press, 1960), 155.
11 Michael Sadleir, *Blessington-d'Orsay. A Masquerade* (London: Constable & Co., 1933), 36.
12 See Horace de Viel-Castle, *Memoires de le regne de Napoleon III* (Paris: Chez tous les libraires, 1883), vol. 2, 91. A better argued, more balanced perspective may be found in: Michael Sadleir, *Blessington-d'Orsay*.
13 Michael Sadleir, *Blessington-d'Orsay*, 78.
14 Cocteau's account is not altogether accurate: the count in fact made the drawing of Byron in Genoa.
15 Quoted by William Teignmouth Shore, *D'Orsay or The Complete Dandy* (London: John Long, Limited, 1912), 51–52.
16 For a more detailed account, see Pierre Lestringuez, *Le chevalier d'Orsay* (Montrouge: Draeger, 1944), 31–32.
17 Benjamin Disraeli, *Henrietta Temple. A Love Story* (New York: P.F. Collier, n.d.), 342–343.
18 Ibid., 334–335.
19 Pierre Lestringuez, *Le chevalier d'Orsay* (Montrouge: Draeger, 1944). This edition has splendid illustrations by André Delfau.
20 Jane Welsh Carlyle, 'Count d'Orsay Calls on Mrs. Carlyle', in *The Portable Victorian Reader* (London: Penguin, 1977), 20–21.
21 Ibid., 21.
22 William Teignmouth Shore, *D'Orsay or The Complete Dandy* (London: John Long, Limited, 1912), 96.
23 Alexandre Baillie-Cochrane (Lord Lamington), *In the Days of the Dandies* (London, Edinburgh: William Blackwood and Sons, 1890), 12.
24 For a more detailed analysis, see Giorgio Agamben, *Stanzas: Word and Phantasm in Western Culture*. Trans Ronald L. Martinez (Minneapolis: University of Minnesota Press, 1993), 47–56.
25 Edward Bulwer-Lytton, *Godolphin* (London: George Routledge and Sons, n.d.), 14–15.
26 Serge Moscovici, *Mashina, tvoriashaya bogov* [*The Machine that Makes Gods*]. (Moscow: Tsentr psykhologii i psikhoterapii, 1998), 189. This quotation is translated by Sofia Horujaya-Cook.
27 Ibid., 295.

28. Jonn Mills [A man of fashion], *D'Horsay; or, the Follies of the Day* (London: William Strange, 1844).
29. William Charles Macready (1793–1873), a well-known actor, was best remembered as Richard III and King Lear. Between 1837 and 1839, Macready was manager of Covent Garden. Thackeray composed a sonnet about him leaving the stage in 1851.
30. Jane Welsh Carlyle, Count d'Orsay Calls on Mrs. Carlyle, in *The Portable Victorian Reader* (London: Penguin, 1977), 21.
31. Oscar Wilde, The Picture of Dorian Gray, the 1890 and 1891 text, in *The Complete Works of Oscar Wilde*, eds. Ian Small and John Bristow (Oxford: Oxford University Press, 2005), vol. 3, 109.

Chapter Four

MANNERS

Rules of Behaviour

From the very outset, dandies were at the forefront of fashion. Yet, their fashion encompassed not merely a style of dress, but a clear behavioural model which supposed that one's entire life was lived according to a certain code. Gradually, these norms turned into an element of social etiquette; a criterion which showed whether or not a man was a true dandy. The perfect dandy's manner was an exercise in ability to instantly and seamlessly change and adapt. Certain dryness with an element of affectation, haughtiness combined with deference: all this was to be exhibited with effortlessness and grace, yet in reality, the behavioural code was based on firm principles. For the true dandy, life was mercilessly governed by a complex system of norms. These could perhaps be reduced to three principal laws: 'Do not show surprise', 'Whilst maintaining an indifferent attitude, act in an unexpected manner', and 'In society stay as long as you need to make an impression; and as soon as you have made it – depart.'[1]

Let us examine these principles in more detail.

(1) **The first rule**, 'nil admirari', (let nothing astonish you) decrees that a dandy must, above all, maintain his composure. This norm prompted Baudelaire to compare dandies with the Stoics, and to see in dandyism something like a form of religion. The principle in fact derives from the ancient maxim 'nil mirari' ('do not be surprised at anything') or, in its fuller form, 'nil admirari' ('never show admiration'). A classical variant of this principle is to be found in the poetry of Horace:

> 'Nil admirari prope res et una, Numici,
> Solaque quae posit facere et servare beatum.'
> ('Not to admire, is of all means the best,
> The only means, to make and keep us blest.')[2]

According to Babichev and Borovsky,

> The maxim 'nil admirari' dictates that calm should be kept at all costs. Both schools of thought that defined Horace's worldview – Epicureanism and Stoicism – saw imperturbable emotional calm as the highest good. One should not seek superficial goods such as riches or awards: thus claimed many ancient philosophers, notably Pythagoras, Democritus, Epicurus, the Stoic Zeno.[3]

Antique minds saw astonishment as linked to admiration. The willingness to experience and to express surprise and admiration supposes openness to all of life's pleasures and temptations, and, consequently, a lack of self-sufficiency. The purist version of dandyism, however – that of Brummell and Baudelaire – supposes certain integrity, a selectivity of taste that protects the aesthete from the risk of being vulgar. Yet, it is perhaps Jules Barbey D'Aurevilly who comes the closest to the initial Romantic understanding of the maxim, seeing in the philosophy of dandyism an element of British Romantic spleen.

This requirement of inscrutability could also be linked to one of the well-known principles of gentlemanly behaviour. The dandy maxim 'nil admirari' recalls, and only slightly exaggerates, the gentleman's imperative of staying calm under any circumstances. Having assiduously trained his will, the true gentleman never shows his true feelings – especially confusion or surprise. Largely laconic, he is unlikely to launch into emotional speeches. 'Not bad,' would be his highest words of praise. Following a serious accident, he would most likely claim merely to have suffered 'a couple of scratches'. It is often thought that such self-possession is something of an English national trait, along with the accompanying speech habit of understatement. The English gentlemanly tradition, with its emphasis on composure and understatement, was of course close to home for Beau Brummell: 'He possessed an abundance of self-control and kept a close watch on himself.'[4]

The dandy code of conduct was also clearly influenced by the laws governing behaviour in the aristocracy. Among other things, these dictated contempt for all hyperbole, prescribing instead a noble simplicity of manner. Edward Bulwer-Lytton's hero Pelham makes frequent assessments of the demands of social etiquette, many of which became enshrined in the dandy code of conduct:

> I have observed that the distinguishing trait of people accustomed to good society is a calm, imperturbable quiet, which pervades all their actions and habits, from the greatest to the least, - they eat in quiet, move in quiet, live in quiet, and lose their wife, or even their money, in quiet; while low persons cannot take up either a spoon or an affront without making such an amazing noise about it.[5]

Among the nobility, a calm demeanour was linked to a firm sense of self-worth, further strengthened through the strict Stoic principles with which the British gentleman was raised. With the dandy maxim of 'nil admirari', self-control was taken even further and turned into a constant inner practice, a discipline that allows one to hide one's emotions and effectively manipulate people by assuming a position of power in one's communication.

Devoid of naivety or spontaneous emotion, this new type is more pragmatic and focused on social success. The heroes of dandy novels generally possessed perfect poise and self-control; it is hardly surprising, for instance, that both Pelham and Vivian Grey became involved in politics. 'Manage yourself and you will manage the world,' is their credo.

In a similar vein, Wilkie Collins in his early novel 'Basil' (1852) writes disapprovingly about

> that miserable modern dandyism of demeanour, which aims at repressing all betrayal of warmth of feeling; which abstains from displaying any sort of enthusiasm on any subject whatever; which, in short, labours to make the fashionable imperturbability of the face the faithful reflection of the fashionable imperturbability of the mind.[6]

Collins ascribes this imperturbability first and foremost to men – his position here is clearly gender-biased: he disapproves

> women of this exclusively modern order… who affect to ridicule those outward developments of feeling which pass under the general appellation of 'sentiment.' Nothing impresses, agitates, amuses, or delights them in a hearty, natural, womanly way.'[7]

This criticism was most likely a reaction to the women's emancipation of that time.

The theme of calm self-possession was further developed by mid-nineteenth-century French writers on dandyism. In his 1863 essay on dandies, Charles Baudelaire also dwells extensively on inscrutability, focusing in particular on the art of hiding one's emotions:

> The specific beauty of the dandy consists particularly in that cold exterior resulting from the unshakeable determination to remain unmoved; one is reminded of a latent fire, whose existence is merely suspected, and which, if it wanted to, but it does not, could burst forth in all its brightness.[8]

Quoting Ignatius Loyola's 'perinde ac cadaver' ('just as a corpse'), Baudelaire compares the discipline of dandyism to the spiritual practice of the Jesuits:

> …this doctrine of elegance and originality… imposes upon its ambitious and humble sectaries, men as often as not full of spirit, passion, courage, controlled energy, the terrible precept: Perinde ac cadaver![9]

It is worthy of note that of all the 'forbidden' feelings, astonishment is the top culprit: 'it is the pleasure of causing surprise in others, and the proud satisfaction of never showing any oneself.'[10] What is so terrible about showing surprise, one might ask?

In the dandy's world, astonishment is likened to the feminine, to the childlike, to the natural – and to the vulgar. It is connected with warmth and spontaneity, whereas the attributes most prized in this world are very different: the masculine, the adult, culture, aestheticism, the artificial, reserve, coldness, and closeness. Surprise and admiration are not, according to the dandy, positive states; at least, not according to Baudelaire, whose views were often based on the neoclassical minimalism of Brummell.

Baudelaire's dandy exhibits all the external signs of an aristocratic upbringing, without necessarily possessing social or pecuniary status. Indeed, dandyism could be seen as borrowing a portion of the aristocrat's code of conduct – with features such as coldness, arrogance, indolence, directness, and a passion for beauty – whilst removing the need for noble birth. The resulting stance is a somewhat ambivalent, forced self-assurance for 'a certain number of men, disenchanted and leisured "outsiders."'[11] Thus, in the writings of Baudelaire, the dandy becomes an aesthete, something of a 'virtual aristocrat'.

(2) **The second rule** of conduct, acting in logical continuation of the first, dictates: 'maintaining composure, shock with the unexpected'. Thus, whilst keeping his cool, the dandy reserves the right to make sudden striking gestures. Such an attitude might, at first glance, appear contradictory, yet it falls within the dialectic of mutually

complementary poles. We know of many recorded scenes which clearly show the dandy talent for producing a sudden and unexpected effect. Dandies were fond of practical jokes, frequently exhibiting considerable cruelty in their pranks and sarcastic put-downs.

One example is Beau Brummell's famous cutting comment about the Prince of Wales, although several versions of this story exist. Former friends, Brummell and the Prince were on worsening terms, especially following the latter's ascent to the Regency. Failing to acknowledge Brummell at a social event and thus 'cutting' him harshly, the Prince nonetheless pointedly greeted the Beau's companions. Not to be outdone, Beau Brummell turned to his neighbor and asked loudly, 'Who is your fat friend?' The Regent was, as Brummell knew only too well, most concerned about his corpulence, and this comment cost the Beau what remained of his friendship.

The second rule could be seen as promoting a dynamic, adventurist side of dandyism. The aim is 'always to produce the unexpected. For this the mind that toils under the yoke of logical rules is unprepared'.[12] Dandy ideologists recommended refraining from banal, predictable gestures; the primitive desire to please was not to be followed. In order to become truly memorable, they insisted, it was necessary to shock. If being shocked, in the dandy's world, was something to be avoided at all costs, shocking others, on the contrary, was something to be pursued.

A firm follower of this rule is Pelham. Appearing at social events, he was always quick to stun those present with his irreverent and unconventional comments:

> Pray, Mr. Pelham,' said Miss Paulding, turning to me, 'have you got one of Breguet's watches yet?' 'Watch!' said I. 'Do you think I could ever wear a watch? I know nothing so plebeian. What can anyone, but a man of business who has nine hours for his counting-house and one for his dinner, ever possibly want to know the time for? 'An assignation,' you will say, - true; but if a man is worth having, he is surely worth waiting for!'[13]

These comments kill several birds with one stone, putting down the self-satisfied owners of Breguet watches, demonstrating Pelham's own lack of need to work, the dandy's cult of slowness, and finally, asserting Pelham's right to arrive late – a privilege normally reserved for celebrities.

(3) Having succeeded in shocking his dinner mates, Pelham is the first to depart, thus observing **the third rule** of dandyism: 'Remain in society long enough to make an impression; once you have made it – leave!' The true dandy appears at a ball, enchants the crowd by casually dropping a few witty, cutting comments, then leaves. The dandy should never be 'de trop' (too much): such is the imperative of economy of presence. The dandy must never bore, seek attention or tire his company; he must not wait for anyone, continue speaking to an inattentive interlocutor, hail an acquaintance or be the last to leave a social event. On the contrary, having captured everyone's attention with some brief, striking word or gesture, he should be quick to depart: this way, people will be sure to remember his fleeting, yet vivid presence. Since economy of expression is the dandy's main stylistic principle, this third rule of behaviour is extremely important. The true dandy is a master of aphorism, laconic and quick to improvise. Adding a pinch of spice to the blandness of everyday life, he is most effective when taken in small doses.

So can one speak of any single unifying principle behind the three main rules of the dandy's behaviour? Our analysis shows that it would not be incorrect to say that these laws are brought together by a certain principle of conservation of energy, by an attempt at economy of expression. 'Nil admirari' supposes economy of emotion; 'maintaining composure, shock with the unexpected' sanctions a short burst of activity and 'once you have made your impression, leave' requires economy of one's very presence. What we observe here is a principle of minimalism that allows dandyism to function as a semiotic system by working on different levels.

Visual Games and the Optical Strategies

To see is only a language.
S. T. Coleridge.[14]

This section considers the culture of European dandyism of the nineteenth century in terms of strategies of visualization. Dandies tell us much about attitudes towards men's fashion, looking at men, and men looking at others. In focusing upon the Regency dandy Beau Brummell, I will argue that newly ordered visual games were part of social codes and models of representation introduced by the British dandies. By positing my own 'focus' upon newly developed technology, new lenses and glasses, and new fashionable accessories that enabled people to look more closely and with more flourish, I argue for a connection between men's fashion and a wider scopic regime.

As we have already seen, Beau Brummell, 'England's prime minister of taste', was recognized as 'arbiter elegantiarum' by all exquisites. The welcoming glance of the Beau had such value, that in some circumstances it appeared as a type of monetary equivalent. Once, one of his creditors reminded him of a debt, to which Brummell answered that he had already paid. 'When? – When I said to you, sitting at the window of the White's: "How are you, Jimmy?"'[15] To understand all of the implications of this episode one must know what the glance and the greeting at the window of White's meant among the dandies of that time. Brummell was a member of an old Tory club 'White's', one of the few closed and highly prestigious clubs with limited membership. The club was situated in St. James's Street, and in 1811 a bow window was installed and set into the middle of the club's façade, the front door being moved to the left. It was in this window that Beau Brummell sat and held court, passing judgments on passers-by, with his inner circle beside him. A company of friends gathered around Brummell, catching his retorts, as they flew by. In fact, the circle of participants in this spectacle was actually wider. Knowing that at a certain time Brummell took up his position at the club bow window, many London dandies went out to walk along St. James's Street in order to present their costume to the judgment of Brummell: they could thus indirectly discover his opinion. Because they themselves constituted an audience for the uncrowned king of fashion, even merciless criticism provided a moment of prestigious participation.

There was another feature to this spatial arrangement which was both amusing but also created a new dynamic. At the club, Brummell, sitting in the bow window, was himself very clearly visible from the street. He watched – but they also watched him, so he was, to use the Shakespearean phrase, 'the observed of all observers'. All of those passing by at an unhurried pace could glance at the details of his *toilette*, comparing his own attire with their appearance and evaluating the latest innovations in the costume of the recognized arbiter of elegance. Sharp-witted and sharp-eyed Brummell, sitting towards the centre of the bow window, appeared from the street as a type of doll or mannequin, although at the beginning of the nineteenth-century mannequins did not yet exist. They appeared somewhat later, with the rise of the store windows of the department store.[16] Brummell consciously presented himself to the studying glances, and played his role of a fashion-doll with professional pleasure. He shared this passion of being seen by and with many of his contemporaries. One of the dandy characters confesses, for instance, that he comes to the Hyde Park to see the ladies, but, even more, 'to show myself, to be admired'.[17]

In this way, a space was established in front of the club window that was full of lightning-quick glances, where the distinction between subject and object of contemplation, the observer and the observed, was instantly erased. There arose a completely unique visual tension, in which two impulses successfully interacted, voyeurism and exhibitionism. In this game of crossing glances there occurred what the philosopher M. Merleau-Ponty calls 'the vision… doubled with a complementary vision or with another vision: myself seen from without, such as another would see me, installed in the midst of the visible, occupied in considering it from a certain spot'.[18] The fashionable people of the Regency looked at one another as though looking in a mirror, having taken pleasure in and convinced themselves of the weight and reality of the body as a visible thing. The selectivity of vision automatically postulated its own system of criteria, imprisoning a whole series of things in veritable inverted commas, enlarging or shrinking them according to its scrutiny. The sophisticated gaze could easily perform the function of face control, scanning the appropriateness of a person by looks and dress:

> Lord Glenmorris … held out his hand with a stately air of kindly protection, and while he pressed mine surveyed me from head to foot, to see how far my appearance justified his condescension.[19]

The dandy's glance often concentrated on details, exaggerating trifles, and inspecting accessories. It is no accident that monocles, lorgnettes, and quizzing glasses (Figure 10) were often featured as amongst the most salient attributes of dandyism. Monocles and quizzing glasses were quite popular among the French incroyables – so in this aspect, the British dandies continued the earlier cultural tradition. As Peter McNeil has noted,[20] such devices had also characterized the pose of the English 'macaroni' in the period after 1760. The developing taste for such a range of optical accessories within the history of costume points to the principle of significant detail in dandies' fashion. Ulrich Lehmann concluded:

> Bodily movement, gesture, and facial expression become rigidly fragmented and mechanical, a representation in miniature of the increasing alienation between subject and object.

Figure 10 Quizzing glass to be held in the hand close to the eye in order to view distant objects, featuring a gold frame with a bevelled lens rim. The handle is comprised of two curving pieces and multiple oval loops and features a suspension ring at the end. French, c.1820. British Optical Association Museum, Catalogue number LDBOA1999.3776. © The College of Optometrists, London.

Therefore, it seems only natural that the 'invention' of the monocle in the first decade of the nineteenth century coincided with the rise of commodities and the objectification of modern society.[21]

That details become the leading semiotic code in men's costume of the Regency period is very important – hence the necessity of magnifying visual devices for scrutinizing those decisive details and judging the appropriateness of them. Thus, for instance, the collection of The College of Optometrists, London, preserves an incredible range of lorgnettes, some with a built-in watch; articulated quizzing glasses; rimless 'Waldstein' monocles; opera glasses, even a Wedgwood single-draw spyglass and a brass 'jealousy' glass for surreptitious sideways viewing (Figure 11). The use of the monocle demonstrated particular sophistication: it could be taken out for close inspection of a remarkable dress detail, for expression of interest or contempt – both by ladies and gentlemen, as seen in a bronze sculpture of an *Incroyable* of the 1790s, made a little later c1830. There existed, for instance, special walking canes with monocles fixed into the handle (Figure 12). One can see a man proudly raising such a cane before his eyes in the caricature entitled 'Monstrosities' (1822) by George Cruikshank. Here the cane with its attached monocle functions as the grotesque phallic eye of the flâneur, while the glance itself turned into the refined instrument of dandiacal power, his transparent 'sceptre'.

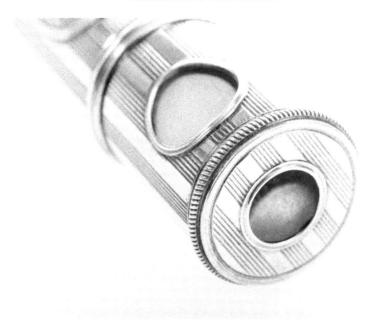

Figure 11 Brass jealousy glass for surreptitious sideways viewing. It incorporates a pill receptacle and scent bottle with brass stopper. Made by Bointaburet of Paris, early nineteenth century. British Optical Association Museum, catalogue number LDBOA1999.1916. © The College of Optometrists, London.

Figure 12 Ebony walking stick with an ivory and brass spyglass serving as the handle. The ultimate practical accessory for the gentleman around town. Early nineteenth century. British Optical Association Museum, LDBOA1999.1422. © The College of Optometrists, London.

If we seek another metaphor for the men's fashion and visual actions in this part of St. James's Street, we find something reminiscent of a duel, the instant exchange of shots, stinging remarks, or courtesies. Something of this verbal sting passed directly later in the nineteenth century to Oscar Wilde. The novels and memoirs of this period contain numerous detailed descriptions of such visual duels:

> My eyes were accidentally fixed on Glanville ... he looked up and coloured faintly as he met my look; but he did not withdraw his own – keenly and steadily we gazed upon each other, till Ellen, turning round suddenly, remarked the unwonted meaning of our looks, and placed her hand in her brother's, with a sort of fear.[22]

There was a famous episode of such a 'stand-off' concerning the relationship between the Prince of Wales and Beau Brummell after their quarrel.

> The Prince of Wales, who always came out rather before the performance concluded, was waiting for his carriage. Presently, Brummell came out, talking eagerly to some friends, and not seeing the prince or his party, he took up his position near the check-taker's bar. As the crowd flowed out, Brummell was gradually pressed backwards, until he was all but driven against the regent, who directly saw him, but of course would not move. In order to stop him, and prevent actual collision, one of the prince's escorts tapped him on the back, when Brummell immediately turned sharply around, and saw that there was not much more than a foot between his nose and the Prince of Wales's. His countenance did not change in the slightest degree, nor did his head move; they looked straight into each other's eyes; the Prince evidently amazed and annoyed. Brummell, however, did not quail or show the least embarrassment. He receded quite quietly, and backed slowly step by step, till the crowd closed between them, never once taking his eyes off those of the Prince. It is impossible to describe the impression made by this scene on the bystanders. There was in his manner nothing insolent, nothing offensive; by retiring with his face to the regent he recognized his rank, but he offered no apology for his inadvertence ... as man to man, his bearing was adverse and uncompromising.[23]

In such detailed descriptions, the exchange of glances functions as a test not only of social status but also of strength of personal character, in Brummell's case fortified by style and pose. It is important to notice that such optical duels also served for the affirmation of gender: the participants behaved 'as man to man'.

Similar optical games were also typical for the culture of macaroni – there is a famous description of a visual contest in Vauxhall Gardens between Bate, the clergyman and Fitz-Gerall, a macaroni. They argued 'whether any man had a right to look at a fine woman' – the actress Hartley being the object of their attention'. The exchange of meaningful glances followed: 'I ... turned around and looked them, in my turn, full in the face; in consequence of which, some distortion of features, I believe, passed on both sides'. During the verbal exchange Bate questioned Fitz-Gerall's gender: 'You judge of the fair sex as you do of your own doubtful gender which aims only to be looked at and admired'. Thus, it was the competition for the spectatorial authority but also the field for gender constructing.[24]

Contemporaries mythologized the power of the dandy's gaze. According to the descriptions, Brummell had a 'small gray scrutinizing eye, which instantly surveyed and summed up all the peculiarities of features, dress and manners of those who approached him, so that the weak point was immediately hit' – his gaze seemed to be a 'visible manifestation of intelligence'.[25] 'What a fine eye to discriminate',[26] Hazlitt noted enthusiastically, and Brummell's biographer Captain Jesse remarked, that his eyes were 'full of oddity' and 'could assume an expression that made the sincerity of his words very doubtful'.[27] In the novels of the period, such as *Tremaine* by R. Ward (1825), *Vivian Grey* by Disraeli (1826), *Pelham* by E. Bulwer-Lytton (1828), and *Cecil, or Adventures of a Coxcomb* by C. Gore (1841), one can find more detailed descriptions of the dandies' gaze. One of the most compelling comes from Lister's *Granby* (1826):

> That calm but wondering gaze, which veers, as if unconsciously, round the prescribed individual; neither fixing nor to be fixed; not looking on vacancy, nor on any object; neither occupied, nor abstracted, a look, which perhaps excuses you to the person cut, and, at any rate, prevents him from accosting you.[28]

As many texts of the period suggest, nearsightedness was almost fashionable among the dandies, so the glass lens was a necessary accessory. Going to the opera without a proper opera-glass (Figure 13) was impossible, and in Paris, there was a special

Figure 13 Pair of French opera glasses in brass and ivory, with painted enamel decoration depicting an early nineteenth-century ballroom scene, c.1850. British Optical Association Museum, LDBOA1999.2018. © The College of Optometrists, London.

Figure 14 Pair of early folding opera glasses, made of delicate tortoiseshell with four folding lenses, two of which are particularly wide and a very elaborate handle. French, c.1830. British Optical Association Museum, Catalogue number LDBOA1999.1342. © The College of Optometrists, London.

optician, Chevalier, who supplied opera-glasses magnifying thirty-two times. Chevalier binoculars were very finely crafted – the handles were typically made of mother of pearl or could be decorated with hunting scenes. The firm was established in 1765 by Louis Vincent Chevalier and continued as a family business throughout the nineteenth century. The French opera glasses were definitely considered to be the best (Figure 14). They were imported in England but often the eyecups were replaced with blank rings to cover French brand names, since people didn't admit to having bought foreign things.

The *lorgnette* – a pair of spectacles, mounted on a long handle – was worn popularly in the nineteenth century. Sometimes the *lorgnette* could be used as a piece of jewellery, rather than to enhance vision (Figure 15). *Lorgnettes* were also widely used by the dandies for contemplating the beauties of the ladies and commencing relationships. The essay 'Physiology of the Lion' (1841) remarks:

> You would like, I suppose, to show the lady that you have noticed her beauty … when you reach for your lorgnette, this movement informs the lady that her charms have produced a favourable impression. Her attention concentrates on your person. Then you give her a wink. Nothing can be better in creating the provocative look. It would be understood as if you had appreciated every detail and attentively scrutinized all the body lines under the dress.[29]

The *lorgnettes* and quizzing glasses provided not only the important element of visual games between the sexes, but they also functioned as a costume accessory,

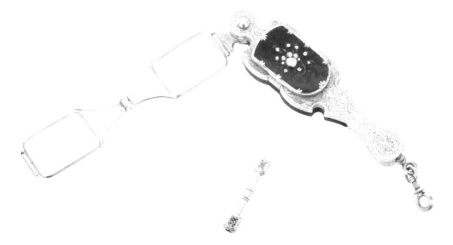

Figure 15 Spring lorgnette with in-built watch and with gold watch key and regulator, an 18ct gold case decorated with leaf and flower patterns. A rose-spray pattern featuring a diamond is depicted within the blue enamel case lid. Early–mid nineteenth century. British Optical Association Museum, Catalogue number LDBOA1999.900. © The College of Optometrists, London.

decorating the dress and defining the habitual system of the wearer's gestures. As we see from 'Physiology of the Lion', the aptly named text by Félix Deriège, the single gesture of lifting the *lorgnette* attracted the attention of a lady, thus serving as a strategic provocation. The variety of sophisticated lorgnettes was remarkable – they were frequently made in combination with other accessories, like a fan, a small musical instrument or a fob chain. Although the twentieth century considers the accessory to be very much the domain of women, in the early nineteenth century the mannered accessory was central to a gentleman's appearance. The survival of the monocle into the twentieth century for upper-class gentlemen as well as Sapphic ladies and women of great style can be noted here.

The famous monocle wearers were the British actor George Arliss, the architect Sir Patrick Abercrombie, and British politician and statesman Sir Austen Chamberlain. The monocle was a popular accessory among the bohemian women inhabiting Greenwich Village. In the 1920s, it was frequently depicted as a fashionable accessory in the portraits of artistic lesbian ladies (Romaine Brooks. *Una, Lady Trowbridge*, 1924; Otto Dix. *Portrait of a journalist, Sylvie von Harden*, 1926). Wallis Simpson, in her younger years, used to wear a monocle, as did the Russian poetess Zinaida Gippius. In these cases, a monocle functions as a symbol of dignity and power, but it also demonstrates the sustainability of the visual techniques originating in dandyism.

Observing society through a quizzing glass was a ritual moment in the behaviour of every respectable dandy. Lady Morgan describes the entry of the English dandy thus:

> I was one evening in the apartment of the Princesse de Volkonski when one of these 'fashion-mongering boys' newly arrived in Paris, appeared at the door of the salon, flushed with

the conscious pride of the toilette, and reconnoitering the company through his glass. I had the honor to be recognized by him; he approached, and half yawned, half articulated some enquiries, which he did not wait to be answered, but drawled on to somebody else, whom he distinguished with his notice.[30]

The surviving material culture of optical devices is incredible. Sometimes in the opera people used the 'jealousy glass' for surreptitious sideway viewing. But apart from the erotic dimension of looking at others, visual games involving judgment and scrutiny were also essentially connected with dandy fashion. Brummell was the first to invent a very important and modern principle of vestimentary behaviour, the principle of 'conspicuous inconspicuousness'. It meant the imperative of dressing elegantly, yet unobtrusively, without attracting undesirable attention. 'If John Bull turns round to look after you, you are not well dressed; but either too stiff, too tight, or too fashionable' – Brummell used to say.

The role of signifying detail as a decisive semiotic message also corresponded to the idea of 'conspicuous inconspicuousness'. A visual message could be encoded through the careful folds of starched neckcloth, a plain but stylish ring, or blackening the soles of the boots. That is why the role of magnifying optical devices was so important – they helped to concentrate on details.

In more general terms, this idea belongs to the broader concept of aesthetic minimalism, the principle of economy and refusal of superfluous. Within dandiacal visual discourse, the economy of minimalism worked to a considerable extent through rhetorical figures of intended blindness and selective insight, regulating one's visibility in appropriate contexts. Once, when a follower whom Brummell obviously did not consider very well, complimented him on the grooming and style of his outfit, Brummell famously replied: 'I cannot be elegant, since you noticed me'. To be well dressed, one should never be noticed. One of the stories about Brummell runs as follows. One day the Duke of Bedford met him in St. James's Street. 'Ah, Brummell, he said, how do you like my new coat?' The Beau eyed him up and down slowly, and then walked around him. 'My dear Bedford, he said, fingering the cloth, do you call this thing a coat?' The Duke, without a word, went home to change. William Hazlitt enthusiastically commented on this episode: 'A distinction … as nice as it is startling. It seems all at once a vulgar prejudice to suppose that a coat is a coat; the commonest of all common things, – it is here lifted into an ineffable essence, so that a coat is no longer a thing …'[31]

The principle of 'conspicuous inconspicuousness' also implied the blurring of class distinctions, since the new tactics erased the aristocratic pretensions to demonstrate wealth and noble origin through clothes and other trappings of status. 'When such solid values as wealth and birth are upset, ephemera such as style and pose are called upon to justify the stratification of society,' notes Ellen Moers.[32] But this principle did, nevertheless, signal an absolute dominance of persons with good taste. The dandies, these self-proclaimed arbiters of elegance, exercised their power by naming and categorizing, thus establishing the new order of things. They appropriated the privilege of culturally informed vision, reserving the right to recognize or ignore the existence of a certain person or object. These complicated visual games point to the detachment from the aristocratic life and style based on hierarchical and stable codes of representation.

Since the dandy's aim is to be recognized only by his peers, this recognition has to rely on discreet signs. That is why the details are so meaningful in men's costumes of the Regency period – hence the necessity of magnifying visual devices for scrutinizing the subtle details and judging the appropriateness of them. According to Richard Sennett,

> The clues the initiate reads are created through a process of miniaturization. Details of workmanship now show how "gentle" a man or woman is. The fastening of buttons on a coat, the quality of fabric counts when the fabric itself is subdued in colour or hue. Boot leather becomes another sign. The tying of cravats becomes a intricate business. How they are tied reveals whether a man has 'stuffing' or not, what is tied is nondescript material. As watches became simpler in appearance, the materials used in their making are the mark of the owner's social standing. It was, in all details, a matter of subtly marking yourself; anyone who proclaims himself a gent obviously isn't.[33]

The optical strategies cultivated by the dandies indicate the deep shifts in the discourse of visuality in the nineteenth century – the rise of a new art of sign-reading, the interpreting of clues. Carlo Ginzburg appropriately calls this new frame 'conjectural paradigm', implying that apparently negligible details can reveal deep and significant phenomena.[34]

And indeed, 'conjectural paradigm' in the second half of the nineteenth century had a predictable success. The deductive method of Sherlock Holmes, the fictional character of Conan Doyle, had numerous parallels in real life. F. Galton made a crucial contribution to the analysis of fingerprints; A. Bertillon invented a criminal identification system known as anthropometry; at the beginning of the twentieth century, S. Freud founded the discipline of psychoanalysis on the theory that marginal details can be analyzed as symptoms pointing to the hidden cause of illness or unresolved conflict. In male fashion the job of the 'detail', relying on the process of miniaturization allowed the dandy to escape the masses due to the sophisticated techniques of representation.

Dandies' sartorial experiments did not immediately catch on during the Regency period, and yet they mark certain important tendencies. We might detect some of the mannerisms in the pose of contemporary fashion culture, which eschews the 'neat' and the 'tidy' as intrinsically 'uncool'. For instance, dandies tried to make their coats as thin as possible to reach a perfect clinging fit. For this purpose, according to Barbey D'Aurevilly, they used a sharp fragment of broken glass, scraping the inside of the coat so as to make it almost semi-transparent.[35] They also obviously wanted their clothes to look worn out to distance themselves from the rich. Some of them ended up making holes in their coats, thus achieving a rather modern look of conspicuous outrage, which could remind us, for instance, of the contemporary fashion for ragged or stonewashed jeans.

When Barbey D'Aurevilly commented on the dandies' attempts to scrape their frock-coats with a fragment of glass, he added an aesthetic dimension and motive, noting, 'These Gods wanted to walk in the clouds'.[36] But allusions to antique culture in men's fashions were often indirect, quite subtle, yet recognizable to the trained eye.

This visual model can be explained through the dominance of 'nude fashion', providing the new convenient frame for the fashionable body. So, the textiles had to be as thin as possible in order to accentuate the silhouette of the body. In a similar way, Brummell invented a strap reaching under the foot to achieve the perfect clinging fit of the pantaloons. As Anne Hollander puts it, the male Regency costume offered

> a complete envelope for the body that is nevertheless made in separate, layered, detached pieces ... The separate elements of the costume overlap, rather than attaching to each other, so that the great physical mobility is possible without creating awkward gaps in the composition.[37]

This smooth envelope presented the ideal package for visual consumption. It once again connects to aesthetic modernism, like the plates of a streamlined car or a modern enamel stove.

In the context of the early nineteenth-century culture, these persistent efforts to refine the fabric also point to the romantic preoccupation with the ideal of transparency, their permanent efforts to transcend the material things and play with the effects of translucent layers. Images of transparent things – thin veils, glass, windows, shadows, and mirror reflections – can be found practically in every important romantic literary text. The stories of the German romantic writer E. T. A. Hoffmann provided a rich variety of such motifs, including crystals, microscopes, and magnifying lenses. In this period, the favourite entertainment was the magic lantern – *laterna magica*. The most famous 'phantasmagoria' showman was the Belgian E. G. Robertson. He placed his projector behind a translucent screen, out of the view of the audience. His lantern, the 'phantascope', was mounted on wheels. By moving the projector back and forward, he could rapidly alter the size of the images on the screen, much like a modern zoom lens. The range of reactions to its use in the beginning of the nineteenth century varied from fear and disbelief to amazement, reverence, and admiration. People were fascinated with penetrating vision – the capacity to expand human vision beyond its natural confines. The wide use of the microscope easily produced confusion in unprepared minds. In the caricature by William Heath entitled 'Monster soup commonly called Thames water' (1828), the reaction of a lady observing through a microscope the bacteria in river water carries the joke. This specific interest in visual effects was further supported by the production of optical toys, including stereoscopes, phantascopes, zootropes, and kaleidoscopes, and the installations of large dioramas in Paris and London.[38] As Jonathan Crary remarks,

> What takes place from around 1810 to 1840 is an uprooting of vision from the stable and fixed relations incarnated in camera obscura ... In a sense, what occurs is a new valuation of visual experience: it is given an unprecedented mobility and exchangeability, abstracted from any founding site or referent.[39]

Disrobing, unmasking, laying bare was a fixation the dandified fashion shared with uncanny fantasies of S. T. Coleridge and E. T. A. Hoffmann. Coleridge's

Figure 16 Lover's eye portrait miniature in watercolor on ivory of a woman's left eye and face with brown curling hair and nose. Face is set into sky and clouds symbolizing a person is deceased. Set into a round brooch with inset of woven hair border terminating in snake head biting its own tail and red stone eye. Circa 1810–1820. British in origin. Courtesy of The Three Graces. www.thethreegraces.com, www.georgianjewelry.com

romantic symbolism implied optical fetishism: 'O! What a life is the eye! What a strange and inscrutable essence!'[40] Yet he constantly tried in his thinking to lift the visible surface of matter, displacing the signs. The final line to 'Hexameters' has a startlingly modern conclusion: 'to see is only a language'.[41] William Wordsworth also wrote about 'the bodily eye, in every stage of life the most despotic of senses'.[42] This tantalizing fixation on visual experience can be also traced in the popular elite accessory of the period – the painted miniatures set in jewelled brooches, often designed as an intertwined serpent tail (Figure 16). Called the 'lover's eye', and made famous by the example of the Prince of Wales's mistress, they featured a perfectly painted miniature of an eye, generally with eyebrow. They represented the eyes of real people as if watching every movement of a person, absent or not. It was a popular variation of sentimental or mourning jewellery from the end of the eighteenth century. Both men's and women's eyes were portrayed in eye brooches.

Thus, the new discourse of seeing and exploring differences was a cultural experience on all levels: body/vision/dress/style of behaviour. In this regime of representation, practised and promoted by the dandies, the transgressive vision functioned as a correlate to transgressive behaviour.[43] I have argued, however, that the key strategy of representation in dandyism is connected with a special visual experience: a dandy knows how to look at others and to stand up under their looks. He is even especially attuned to these objectifying looks, creating the 'to be looked at' situations when out on a stroll, at a ball, in the parlour, sitting by the window of a club. An unhurried gait and immobile face are evidence of self-control, signaling the art of provocative subversion.

The dandies explored the possibilities offered by the new paradigm of vision, being profoundly mapped into a network of visual relations characteristic of urban modernity. This new paradigm of vision operated through optical accessories creating the new scopic regime for male fashion, in which the principle of 'conspicuous inconspicuousness' implied the art of visible detail. The sophisticated reading of signs became possible due to the cognitive resources of 'conjectural paradigm'. Dandyism also made an art of commodifying personality, and so contributed to the formation of the modern subject. At the same time, the subversive visual strategies of dandies had opened up a space for the rise of the new bourgeois elite. It was experimental ground on which the demand for changes in male fashion, indeed male lifestyle, could be made.

Dandyism and the Disdain for Vulgarity: A History of Meanings

"It's worse than wicked, my dear, it's vulgar"
Punch, 1876

'A dandy,' Charles Baudelaire famously wrote, 'can never be a vulgar man'.[44] The antinomy between dandyism and vulgarity appears so well understood, so often quoted, so totally accepted. Yet how should we define vulgarity? As a concept, despite, at first glance, appearing obvious, it remains somewhat elusive, the difficulty springing in part from the evolution of meaning throughout history. A glance at Roget's Thesaurus will inform us that vulgarity is akin to 'plebeianism, ill-breeding, indelicacy, mauvais ton (Fr.), bad taste, mauvais goût (Fr.), Philistinism, barbarity, provincialism, ostentation'. Synonyms of 'vulgar' are 'unrefined, coarse, gaudy, inelegant, rough'.[45]

As we see, the connotations are almost exclusively negative.

Initially, however, vulgarity was a concept most closely linked with accessibility. The Latin adjective 'vulgaris' meant 'ordinary, everyday, accessible, common, simple', whilst the noun 'vulgus' referred to the people: the masses, the public, the herd, the crowd, and the commoners. The literal meaning of 'vulgaris' was, accessible to the masses. The 'accessible' Latin translation of the Bible, completed by Jerome in 404, which became the official Latin version promulgated by the Catholic Church in the sixteenth century (1592–1605), was known as the Vulgate. Vulgar Latin, used from ancient times into the Middle Ages, was also known as Popular, or Colloquial Latin. The original connotations of the vulgar, thus, were far from negative, referring more to the public and the popular. In Shakespeare's 'Hamlet', Polonius's advice to Laertes yields an interesting illustration of contemporary usage of the word 'vulgar': 'Be thou familiar, but by no means vulgar',[46] (Act I, Scene 3).

In Shakespeare's time, 'vulgar' did not necessarily imply 'tasteless' or 'crude'. The C.T. Onions Shakespeare Glossary, for instance, suggests it rather meant 'of the common people', 'commonly known or experienced', 'ordinary', and 'public'.[47]

The negative connotations to which we have today become accustomed began to appear in the eighteenth century. Upheaval and revolution saw the aristocracy in Europe surrender its dominant role, giving way to figures from the bourgeoisie and common people. As yet unversed in the art of social etiquette, the new leaders nonetheless wished to appear well-mannered and refined. Hence, the pejorative association with vulgarity, as members of the nobility came to use the term derogatively when referring to their unwanted competition. Thus, the complex semantic contrast between the aristocratic and bourgeois codes of behaviour came into being. To some extent, this can also indirectly be observed in the opposition of worldly and vulgar manners, albeit this difference does not necessarily imply noble or humble birth.

The basic concept of 'vulgarity' which established itself in eighteenth-century culture can be found in a whole range of writings on poor manners. In his celebrated Maxims, Lord Chesterfield offers detailed thoughts on vulgar behaviour. Vulgarity, for him, is the product of poor upbringing; yet noble birth in itself cannot guarantee a lack of vulgarity, which young people may 'catch' from their fellow pupils, or the servants.

A vulgar person, according to Lord Chesterfield, exhibits a certain style of behaviour:

– "…a vulgar man is captious and jealous; eager and impetuous about trifles". The well-bred man, on the contrary, rises above trivialities: "He…thinks, but never seems to think himself slighted, undervalued, or laughed at in company, unless where it is so plainly marked out, that his honour obliges him to resent it in a proper manner".[48]

– The vulgar man "…suspects himself to be slighted, and thinks everything that is said meant at him: if the company happens to laugh, he is persuaded they laugh at him".

– Focused entirely on his own person, his conversation "…turns chiefly upon his domestic affairs, his servants, the excellent order he keeps in his own family, and the little anecdotes of the neighbourhood; all which he relates with emphasis, as interesting matters. He is a man-gossip".[49]

– Vulgarism in language is a certain characteristic of bad company, and a bad education. Proverbial expressions, and trite sayings, are the flowers of the rhetoric of a vulgar man. Would he say, that men differ in their tastes; he both supports and adorns that opinion, by the good old saying, as he respectfully calls it, 'What is one man's meat, is another man's poison'.… He has always some favourite word for the time being; which for the sake of using often, he commonly abuses: such as *vastly* angry, *vastly* kind, *vastly* handsome, and *vastly* ugly.[50]

 The vulgar man adores foreign words, never missing an opportunity to demonstrate his learnedness, yet more often than not confusing the meaning, and floundering hopelessly.

– The vulgar man does not know how to behave in good company, and gets into all manner of scrapes with the most common objects, his cane, hat, or cup of coffee. Even his own suit floors him: 'he does not wear his clothes, and in short, does nothing like other people'.[51]

Thus, the main traits of the vulgar man, Chesterfield claims, are:

1) testiness, irritability, intractability even over trifling matters;
2) egocentrism, a strong focus on his own person, and a habit of talking about his own affairs with undue emphasis;
3) a passion for trite sayings, clichés and borrowed words;
4) awkwardness, clumsiness, and an inability to wear clothes well.

All in all, one could say that such people always try to make a favourable impression using overly direct, coarse, common means. Hence, their love of borrowed wisdom in the form of sayings, and their pompous accounts of domestic life. The vulgar man lacks a sense of appropriate distance; he is incapable of indirect, understated expression. This aspect of etiquette is perhaps, for him, the most challenging, as it requires discipline of thought and feeling. Bigoted, the vulgar person knows not the meaning of self-restraint, always giving sway to his emotions. In this, he goes against the classic dandy requirement to keep one's cool, to remain unperturbed – an element, indeed, of the gentleman's code of honour.

The theologian John Henry Newman famously wrote that a gentleman 'is one who never inflicts pain'.[52] For a gentleman, the ability to put oneself in another's shoes is a key quality. The vulgar man, however, is unable to sense the finer nuances of interaction. Incapable of observing ethical boundaries, he fares no better with the physical world. Unable properly to position his body in space, he is constantly waging war with his clothing and objects.

In 'The Mysteries of Paris' (1842–1843), the French novelist Eugène Sue paints a wonderful portrait of a vulgar man, the Duke de Lucenay.

> I know nothing in the world more insupportable than this man; he is such bad company; he laughs so loud at his own jokes; he is so noisy that he almost deafens one; if you have any affection for your smelling bottle or your fan, keep them from him; for he has the inconvenient fashion of breaking everything he touches, and that with the most frolicsome and satisfied air in the world.[53]

This type of excessive behaviour at the corporeal level fits into Balzac's disdainful description of haste and fuss implied by the verb 'virvoucher'. De Lucenay's behaviour at the ball fully confirms this unflattering description. In no time at all, he contrives to commit an array of unspeakable deeds, beating his hat 'after the fashion of a tambourine', falling over the back of a divan and tumbling a decorative tree, demolishing the stopper of a lady's perfume bottle, and paying a devastating 'compliment': 'You have to-night a turban, which, allow me to tell you, on my word of honour, resembles an old turtle eaten up with verdigris.'[54]

Onlookers tend to humour De Lucenay, who comes from an old noble family. His lineage affords him the freedom to appear eccentric and unconventional; it cannot, however, save him from accusations of vulgarity. His actions are not merely breaches of social etiquette, which dandies, indeed, often break: the graver fault here lies with his style. A dandy might also criticise an ugly hat, but in so doing, charm his audience with daring humour and wit. The Duke's physical clumsiness, which mirrors an inner awkwardness, is a good illustration of Lord Chesterfield's observations on the vulgar man's uneasy relationship with objects. Furthermore, De Lucenay's jokes appear repetitive, shallow and laboured. He is 'too much': again, unthinkable for the true dandy, who is always sparing with his bon mots and, indeed, with his presence.

Duke de Lucenay is vulgar due to his awkward nature and disagreeable temperament, which can be seen as subjective. At times, however, vulgar behaviour can be linked to objective reasons. We have already discussed the tensions between the aristocracy and the bourgeoisie, and the shifts taking place in society. In the nineteenth century, tensions receded as the two elites began to merge. 'Vulgarity' came to be associated with the behaviour of bourgeois parvenus who breached social etiquette.

The aristocracy saw the newcomers as vulgar upstarts seeking to raise their social status. Having accessed new circles, the bourgeois did their best to imitate high society manners, yet in so doing, were doomed to failure. Their very attempts to become something they were not; their overly zealous efforts and exaggerated gestures caused their behaviour to stand out as unnatural and forced. In 1821, the English essayist William Hazlitt defined vulgarity thus:

> its essence, I imagine, consists in taking manners, actions, words, opinions on trust from others, without examining one's own feelings or weighing the merits of the case.[55]

In his novel 'Pelham', published in 1828, Edward Bulwer-Lytton expresses the same idea, almost word for word. His heroine likewise associates vulgarity with imitation and unnatural behaviour:

> This is the chief reason why our manners are betters than low persons: ours are more natural, because they imitate no one else; theirs are affected, because they think to imitate ours, and whatever is evidently borrowed becomes vulgar. Original affectation is sometimes good *ton* – imitated affectation, always bad.[56]

Upon her son's return from Paris, Lady Pelham warns the young man not to use too many French expressions. Recall Lord Chesterfield's disdain for popular sayings and foreign words. A passion for euphemisms, long-winded chatter, and overly complex figures of speech can be seen as a similar failing.

Affected speech is often accompanied by inappropriate dress. The vulgar man commonly adorns himself with over-the-top accessories and excessive trappings, piling all his best things on at once and failing to notice the overall absurd effect.[57] He always strives to be wearing the latest fashions – as he, at least, perceives them – and points this out to all that will listen. The vulgar beau favours garish, bright colours and gaudy, showily expensive accessories. Behind this ostentatious façade lies a deep insecurity, as he is ever unsure of his standing with the very people, he is trying so hard to impress.

More than confident of his prowess as a social leader, the true dandy, on the other hand, favours understated style. His dress is elegant, laconic, serving to reinforce the impression of conspicuous inconspicuousness. With him, everything is the very opposite of vulgar.

Brash imitation is commonly associated with vulgarity where behaviour is concerned, also. Extravagant gestures, exaggerated facial expressions, excessive surprise, horror and admiration have long been the target of satirists – let us recall the caricatures of George Cruikshank. William Hazlitt, with his sharp, venomous wit, was quick to link vulgarity with affectation, artifice, pretence, and insincerity.[58]

In Pushkin's 'Eugene Onegin', Tatyana offers an example of a heroine entirely free of affectation and vulgarity:

> Calm, her gestures unobtrusive,
> Not cold at all, yet not effusive,
> No pride, and no chilly glance,
> No pretension in her advance,
> No breath at all of haughtiness,
> No affected coquetry…
> Only serene simplicity.
> She seems the image, to excess,
> Of *comme il faut*…
> Yet she'd not a single trace
> In all her person, form or face,
> Of what the fashionable view,
> In London sets especially,
> Considers *vulgar*[59]

The 'comme il faut' described by Pushkin has, it would seem, a paradoxical quality. In fully observing social etiquette, the 'comme il faut' person appears the most natural. Hence, a complete lack of vulgarity, although certain allowances should nevertheless be made for the evolution of cultural norms through the ages.

On what, then, does the degree of naturalness seen as 'correct' in this or that circle, depend? After the works of Norbert Elias, we can no longer talk of any fixed norms of etiquette, even with regard to basic bodily functions.[60] Let us assume, then, that 'naturalness' implies reacting in the manner appropriate in a given setting, at a given time. Appropriate behaviour appeals to onlookers, who benevolently deem it 'free of affectation'. In reality, however, most likely the person has simply complied with the rules of etiquette accepted within that particular social group. Sensing the norms of behaviour required in a given context is a matter of cultural experience.

Marcel Proust, who wrote much on matters of good breeding, suggests that the well-bred person has about him a certain natural air:

> A certainty of taste in the region not of beauty but manners, which when he was faced by a novel combination of circumstances enabled the man of breeding to grasp at once – like a musician who has been asked to play a piece he has never seen – the feeling, the motions that were required, and to apply the appropriate mechanism and technique, which then allowed this taste to display itself without the constraint of any other consideration, by which the average young man of the middle class would have been paralysed, from fear as well of making himself ridiculous in the eyes of strangers by his disregard of convention as of appearing too deferential in the eyes of his friends…[61]

Thus, we see that in social terms, vulgarity is connected with ignorance of the behavioural norms of a certain circle. Mastery of these norms lends ease and grace, allowing one instinctively to sense the boundaries of accepted behaviour – a feature cherished by dandies. Ignorance in these matters, however, dooms the unfortunate parvenu to shallow imitation, artifice, awkwardness, and constant excess, bringing upon him accusations of vulgarity.

Let us now turn to two further aspects of vulgarity, the ethical and the aesthetic. These, as John Ruskin brilliantly demonstrated, can be surprisingly closely connected. In 'Sesame and Lilies' (1865), for instance, Ruskin wrote:

> … the essence of all vulgarity lies in want of sensation. Simple and innocent vulgarity is merely an untrained and undeveloped bluntness of body and mind; but in true inbred vulgarity, there is a deathful callousness, which, in extremity, becomes capable of every sort of bestial habit and crime, without fear, without pleasure, without horror, and without pity. It is in the blunt hand and the dead heart, in the diseased habit, in the hardened conscience, that men become vulgar; they are forever vulgar, precisely in proportion as they are incapable of sympathy — of quick understanding — of all that, in deep insistence on the common, but most accurate term, may be called the 'tact' or 'touch — faculty' of body and soul…[62]

The sensitive woman, Ruskin suggests, possesses that faculty of tact more than anyone else.

Continuing Lord Chesterfield and John Henry Newman's thoughts on the capacity to ethically 'sense' other people, Ruskin's definition of vulgarity also breaks new ground. A key influence for the Pre-Raphaelites, Ruskin paid tremendous attention to 'fineness and fulness of sensation'. This ability, is, for him, universally positive: in intellectual matters it is accompanied by quick wit, in ethical questions it enables tact, and in the aesthetic realm it offers access to all the nuances of Beauty.

In late nineteenth-century culture, the third feature was perhaps the most prized. The challenge, indeed, lay in bringing together all three aspects of 'fineness and fulness of sensation'. Aesthetically sensitive, Huysmans's Des Esseintes and Oscar Wilde's Dorian Gray are both portrayed as 'ideal' dandies who abhor vulgar, common tastes. Yet Dorian Gray, as Ruskin astutely observed, also belongs to a type that takes pleasure in crime and cruelty. The gentlemen in his club begin to shun him when rumours reach them of his activities: his lack of moral sensitivity does not match the gentleman's code of honour. A dandy, yet not a gentleman – such is the nature of Dorian Gray.

All this may lead us to draw some interesting conclusions concerning more general cultural and historic patterns. The vulgar person, essentially, is constantly committing the same mistake on different levels by offering a direct message instead of oblique reference. Metaphorically, vulgarity could be defined as a highly uneconomical way of working with one's personal energy. In English culture, we have frequently seen 'vulgarity' paired with 'affectation', or, more recently, with 'ostentation'. Both are seen as fake, forced display of certain actions or qualities: an uneconomical model of personal energy use, an uncontrolled emission unbacked by inner resources and, hence, at constant risk of exposure and ridicule.

The opposite paradigm, economy of energy, is closely linked to the dandy maxim of reserve, understatement and inner discipline in the expression of feeling. The same minimalist model of energy use underpins the gentleman's code of honour, the social etiquette of the aristocracy, and the dandy style of dress. Through mastery of this culture of economic energy use, the dandy manages to create a unique impression of pleasant and reassuring appropriateness.

The Fine Art of Scandal

It is, perhaps, impossible to understand dandies, without appreciating the risqué games they played with social norms in the nineteenth century. Although the essentially normative codes of self-presentation originally structured the world of 'high society' in the Regency period, the dandies dared to violate the existing etiquette. Why, where and in what form were these social subversions staged? Young beaux, as we have already seen, had developed three main rules: 'Never show surprise', 'Maintaining composure, shock with the unexpected', and 'Having made your impression, withdraw'. The second principle, naturally, offered ample possibilities for improvisation and disruption of social etiquette. Maintaining a sense of measure was crucial: in challenging the norm, one had always to feel just how far one could go.

So, what were the necessary ingredients of a juicy, truly shocking scandal? First and foremost, the fine art of noble scandal required strict rules of behaviour – precisely so they could be broken! Those involved had also to belong to different groups (elderly/young, insiders/outsiders), or to perform different roles (instigators/observers). In the absence of different groups, any outburst could be quickly extinguished. Let us examine some examples of potential rows which went nowhere due to the absence of 'outsiders' or fixed rules.

In the nineteenth century, young men's gatherings could frequently take a wild turn; far less restrained than balls, these soirees brimmed over with unbridled abandon. The key figures at such events were seldom the relatively reserved dandies; these raucous dinners were presided over by rowdier, more boisterous characters. One famous friend of George Brummell and Lord Byron, Scrope Berdmore Davies[63] was especially known for his wanton exuberance and love of extravagant entertainment.

More complex and nuanced 'scandalous' behaviour could be observed on the part of dandies who challenged social norms, whilst at the same time playing according to the social rules. Barbey d'Aurevilly wrote:

> Dandyism, while still respecting the conventionalities, plays with them. While admitting their power, it suffers from and revenges itself upon them, and pleads them as an excuse against themselves; dominates and is dominated by them in turn. To play this twofold and changing game requires complete control of all the suppleness which goes to the making of elegance, in the same way as by their union all shades of the prism go to the making of the opal.[64]

Happily, Beau Brummell possessed such suppleness, and contrived successfully to play a dangerous game in the most recherché circles. As Barbey d'Aurevilly remarked,

'Where cleverer men would have perished, he escaped. His audacity was accurate. He could caress the axe-edge with impunity.'[65]

An important element of any beau's social life was hospitality.[66] A key activity from the point of view of social etiquette, it possesses a series of traditional rituals ideally suited for close study and analysis. Frequent guests at balls and dinners, dandies also often received guests at home. So how did beaux entertain their visitors?

George Brummell, as we well know, liked to take advantage of the hospitality of his aristocratic friends.

> At Belvoir he was *l'ami de la famille*, and at Cheveley, another seat of the Duke of Rutland's, his rooms were as sacred as the Duke of York's, who was a frequent visitor there; and if any gentleman happened to be occupying them when he arrived unexpectedly, he was obliged to turn out.[67]

Ever present at balls and social gatherings, Beau Brummell was always the first gentleman of non-noble descent to be invited. The famous dandy also held magnificent dinners for select groups of friends at his own lodgings in Chesterfield Street. One of his frequent guests was the Prince of Wales, the future King George IV. Always the centre of attention, Brummell entertained his guests with witty anecdotes, provoking peals of laughter.

But Brummell's special talent was to break social conventions, skillfully violating the rules of politeness and hospitality.

His jokes were often risqué, pushing the boundaries of convention, going against social etiquette and accepted rules of hospitality. At one ball, having engaged the most handsome lady to dance, he presently enquired of her

> who the ugly man near the chimney-piece might be? 'Why surely, my good fellow, you know him,' said his acquaintance; 'that is the master of the house!' 'No,' replied the unconscious cornet, 'how should I? I was never invited'.[68]

With his sarcastic turn of mind, Brummell, it seems, was capable of keeping calm throughout his precarious pranks. His striking ability to maintain composure ('nil admirari' principle), was, perhaps, precisely what kept his highbred hosts from showing him the door.

On another occasion, when he again came uninvited to the reception of Mrs. Thompson, where he was an undesirable guest, the hostess demanded the invitation card. Brummell searched in his pockets and finally took out the card of another lady, Mrs. Johnson. When his mistake was pointed out, he coolly replied:

> Dear me, how very unfortunate! Really, Mrs. Johns – Thompson, I mean, I am very sorry for this mistake, but you know, Johnson and Thompson – and Thompson and Johnson – are so much the same kind of thing. – Mrs. Thompson, I wish you a very good evening;' and making a profound bow, he slowly retired from the room amidst the suppressed anger of intimates, the titter of his own friends, and the undisguised wrath of the lady.[69]

Such conspicuous outrage was based on his wish to irritate his former friend, the Prince of Wales, who was expected at that ball and everybody knew he did not want to appear publicly in the same places with Brummell after their quarrel. But Brummell also managed to humiliate a hostess by playing with her 'common' name. Such multivalent jokes were a regular pattern with Brummell, displaying a typical variant of the dandy's insolence. Naturally, such behaviour goes against accepted social etiquette for guests. A deliberate, planned provocation by Brummell, it was perfectly carried off thanks to his admirable cool composure: calm insolence was, indeed, a common feature of dandy behaviour.

Given their penchant for scandal and impertinence both as hosts and guests, can we really talk about genuine hospitality on the part of dandies? In order to answer this complex question, let us turn to the writings of contemporary French philosopher Jacques Derrida, who, indeed, stressed the particular aporia[70] of hospitality. On the one hand, a generally acknowledged Law of hospitality exists, implying that

> absolute hospitality requires that I open up my home and that I give not only to the foreigner (provided with a family name, with the social status of being a foreigner, etc.), but to the absolute, unknown, anonymous other, and that I give place to them, that I let them come, that I let them arrive, and take place in the place I offer them, without asking of them either reciprocity (entering into a pact) or even their names.[71]

On the other hand, this 'categorical imperative of hospitality' is realized through individual, abstract laws, constituting an infinite empirical diversity of specific forms. The aporia is due to the fact that 'the two antagonistic terms of this antinomy are not symmetrical. There is a strange hierarchy in this. The Law is above the laws.' The Law allows for forms which contradict, threaten and even altogether disprove it – this multitude of diverse variants serving only to confirm and stress the Law's uniqueness and perfection.[72]

If we accept the logic of Derrida, the dandies breaking the main Law of hospitality fall into a special metaphysical space which sanctions the possibility of an infinite number of 'jokes', 'impudent pranks', etc. These provocative gestures are precisely the very attempts to undermine the main Law, dialectically necessary for its execution. 'For this pervertibility is essential, irreducible, necessary too. The perfectibility of laws is at this cost. And therefore, their historicity.'[73] A closer look at the time periods corresponding to particular forms of hospitality as well as to specific ways of subverting it, shows the historicity of individual laws; and dandy scandals, without doubt, were closely connected to the particular nature of their time.

What were the reasons for the unprecedented tolerance towards such scandalous behaviour? During the period of Regency England, high society, having been shaken by the events in France, adopted a peculiar masochistic attitude towards self-confident individuals from lower classes, allowing them to play the role of sadistic dictators. They all wanted to know the latest jokes of Brummell: 'Did you hear what Buck Brummell said – or did?' Caught in the pattern of a sado-masochistic relationship, they often involuntarily provoked his double-edged practical jokes or invited direct criticism, exposing their own insecurity. Yet, it is worth noting that the majority of

Brummell's victims are the assuming *parvenus* who were very anxious to be well placed among the exquisites. Brummell himself did not belong to the aristocratic families – his grandfather was a valet to a baronet, Sir John Monson. He mixed mainly with young aristocrats, not necessarily wealthy ones, and the rich bourgeois bankers, who were eager to manoeuvre themselves into higher society. In this sense, some of his behaviour relates to the *Incroyables* across the Channel, who were also partly drawn from a financial speculative group called *agioteurs*.

On another occasion a wealthy young gentleman then commencing life in society, invited Brummell and a large party to dine. After the party the Beau enquired, who could take him to Lady Jersey that evening? and the host offered him his carriage, hoping thus to accompany him and be introduced to Lady Jersey. 'Pray how are you to go? – said Brummell – you surely would not like to get up behind? No, that would not be right and yet it will scarcely do for me to be seen in the same carriage with you.'[74] This is a classic case of Brummell's cutting, and, what is most interesting, the host laughs good-naturedly with everybody: the conspiracy of players, sharing the same sado-masochistic relationship, is proved again, although the pretensions of *nouveau-riche* aspiration are dismantled. A similar story provides the object of sarcasm in a more material format: it revolves around champagne.

> When Brummell was dining at a gentleman's house, where the champagne was very far from being good, he waited for a pause in the conversation and then condemned it by raising his glass, and saying loud enough to be heard by everyone at the table, 'John, give me some more of that cider.'[75]

The public condemnation of wine serves, surely, to condemning the host, but also points to the normative force of Brummell's judgment.

In the fine art of noble scandal, Brummell, indeed, specialized in sarcastic japes about people's outfits. Generally recognized as the ultimate arbiter in matters of elegance, the Beau used his position to publicly criticize others' dress sense. One of these incidents, as we recall, was the fuss over the unfortunate coat of the Duke of Bedford. Another topic for Brummell's sharp tongue was social status: once, when calling Mrs. Fitzherbert's carriage, he substituted the word 'Mistress' for the usual 'Mrs', thus stressing the lady's connection with the Prince of Wales.[76]

Brummell's sharp comments are quite typical of the dandy insolence.

> His wit crucified; but his impertinence was too spacious to be condensed and imprisoned in epigrams. He distilled the wit which expressed him into his actions, his gestures, his attitude, the tone of his voice. And above all he practised it with that incontestable superiority which it demands from men of breeding who would employ it; for it leans towards rudeness as the sublime leans towards the ridiculous, and if it loses its exact tone it is lost.[77]

Brummell, as his friends testify,

> had a happy facility in placing the most ordinary circumstances in a ridiculous point of view.[78]

This type of behaviour is sometimes called, in the tradition of the Russian semiotic school, 'anti-povedenie'[79], the reversal of conventional conduct.

The specific form of 'anti-povedenie' is what would later be called the art of 'cutting', a strategy which became particularly associated with the nineteenth- and twentieth-century English *salonniers*. The dandies elevated a cool cutting to the rank of high-society rhetorical games. Brummell's jokes were directed also at his aristocratic friends and he acted as the severe arbiter of elegance, correcting the public taste in costume. When the rear view of the Duchess of Rutland offended him, he simply ordered her to leave the ballroom, but – moving backwards ... His patronizing habits with regard to the Prince of Wales became the talk of London.

Brummell's sharp tongue spared neither those of humble birth, nor the nobility. The Beau himself was not from the aristocracy, yet, having been to Eton, he had long enjoyed highborn company. At that time, many wealthy men of affairs and bourgeois bankers were keen to enter high society to increase their prestige, yet they were not welcomed by the nobility, which saw them as cheap, vulgar upstarts.[80] The rules of gentlemen's clubs were often made up precisely in such a way as to exclude the nouveaux riches, and the Beau's sharp flicks of the tongue in their direction were always vastly reassuring for his highborn friends.

Dandyism mastered the strategy of objectifying personality and transforming the individual style into marketable goods. Brummell could fully exploit the potential of his authority for manipulating the public opinion to his own commercial profit. Similar tricks were practised later by Count D'Orsay. At times, Beau Brummell was known to use his fame for material gain. Criticizing the best tobacco from a particular vendor, he thus forced him to lower his prices, subsequently buying up a large amount at vastly reduced cost. The tobacconist then put up the price, citing Brummell's purchase as proof of high quality.[81]

Brummell was also quick to turn to his advantage the opportunities offered by hospitality. When serving in the army, he was once late for a parade in which his troop was taking part. His commander was furious, yet Brummell quickly appeased him, telling him that the Duke of Rutland had invited him to dine. The general was pleased, and the conflict extinguished; yet Brummell had to exert himself to warn the Duke of the general's impending visit, as the invitation had, of course, been entirely his own invention.[82]

In this example, hospitality is used not unlike a bargaining chip, an invitation to lunch being exchanged for lenience in military service. Such exchanges were in fact more typical of pragmatic bourgeois-style relations, in which everything, including prestigious ties with aristocratic families, has its value, and can be used for social advancement. In some cases, such symbolic capital may even serve as direct payment: Beau Brummell frequently used his reputation in order to avoid having to pay off his debts, as in the joke 'How are you, Jimmy?'.

Thus, prestigious invitations, personal views, compliments, recommendations, and all manner of other non-material resources served as units of exchange, denoting prestige in the new system of bourgeois society. This process was indicative of the key shifts taking place, as a new urban culture began to govern etiquette and hospitality.

The dandy art of elegant subversion can be seen as a sign of these social changes. The gradual legitimization of scandalous behaviour meant the blurring of class distinctions; the expansion of the new bohemian values often signaled the weakness of the accepted aristocratic codes. Thus, the world of dandyism contained the germs of oppositional style, both in clothes and in the models of social self-presentation.

Be Insolent!

Be insolent – it is the only chance!
Maurice Blanchot

As a deliberate behavioural practice, insolence is often seen as being connected with a wide range of cultural factors. In 'On Insolence Considered as One of the Fine Arts', Maurice Blanchot writes:

> Insolence is not an art without value. It is a way to be equal to oneself and superior to others in all the circumstances in which others seem to have the advantage of you. It is also the desire to reject the conventional, the customary, the habitual.[83]

The dandy principle of 'shocking with the unexpected', linked as it was with challenging stereotypes, created ample ground for practising all shades of insolence. As leaders in fashion, dandies vied with each other to show off the most acerbic wit, calmly playing Russian roulette with social convention.

The dandy manner typically combined gentlemanly courteousness with withering impertinence. A master of this style, George Brummell skilfully fused seeming graciousness with scorn and disdain. Balancing on the knife edge of the permissible, the Beau regularly put down his interlocutors, making them blush and bite their tongue. All his best-known witticisms we have already discussed follow this pattern. 'I cannot be elegant since you have noticed me,' he tells a gentleman who compliments him.

Naturally, in Brummell's companions such comments could produce considerable unease and self-doubt. The dandy's exaggerated politeness combined with cold irony left many puzzled, unsure whether they were being complimented, or ridiculed. Knowing how to respond to such a mixed message was perhaps more challenging than reacting to obvious rudeness, so veiled and unexpected was the taunt.

Take, for example, Pelham's conversation with one somewhat unrefined lady in Edward Bulwer-Lytton's classic novel.

> 'Were you at Bath last winter, Mr. Pelham?' continued the countess, whose thoughts wandered from subject to subject in the most rudderless manner.
> 'No, Lady Babbleton, I was unfortunately at a less distinguished place'.
> 'What was that?'
> 'Paris!'
> 'Oh, indeed! I've never been abroad; I don't think persons of a certain rank should leave England; they should stay at home and encourage their own manufactories'.

'Ah!' cried I, taking hold of Lady Babbleton's shawl, 'what a pretty Manchester pattern this is'.

'Manchester pattern!' exclaimed the petrified peeress; 'why it is real cachemere: you don't think I wear anything English, Mr. Pelham?'

'I beg your ladyship ten thousand pardons. I am no judge of dress; but to return—I am quite of your opinion, that we ought to encourage our own manufactories, and not go abroad…'[84]

During this apparently cordial exchange, Lady Babbleton twice falls into the trap of the dandy's irony: when discussing the 'less distinguished' location of Paris, and her 'unpatriotic' cashmere shawl. Pelham's sarcasm is, in both cases, veiled by genteel politeness, and an innocent observer might indeed believe that he is 'no judge of dress' and genuinely bent on supporting English manufacturers. Lady Babbleton, perhaps fortunately, does not understand the sarcasm, and remains oblivious to Pelham's digs.

The insulting undertones of the dandies' seeming politeness were further exaggerated by their cold indifference. Following the maxim 'never show surprise', the beaux fused insolence with apathy, creating an impression of effortless, even lazy superiority. Their studied carelessness can be likened to the nonchalance of 'La Sprezzatura'. An inscrutable expression completed their powerful stance, conveying total control over the situation. Peering at their interlocutors through a lorgnette, or failing to notice them whatsoever, dandies used deliberate visual tactics to assert their superiority.

Writing of Brummell, Jules Barbey D'Aurevilly repeatedly stresses the Beau's particular brand of impertinence, also a form of dandy insolence:

> When it exists it is the greatest possible guarantee of respect against the so-often hostile vanity of other, as it is also the most elegant cloak with which one may conceal one's own infirmities.[85]

True dandy insolence, Barbey D'Aurevilly continues, is always accompanied by graceful, genteel manners. The two complement each other,

> mutually embellished by contrast; and indeed would not Grace without Impertinence appear a somewhat washed-out blonde? Would not Impertinence without Grace appear a too-pungent brunette?[86]

Brummell, of course, was a master of calculated wit and meticulous impertinence. 'He distributed terror and charm in exactly equal measure, compounding from both the magic philtre of his influence,' Barbey D'Aurevilly writes, likening the Beau's approach to a chemical formula. Should the magical balance be upset, however, what is left is mere rudeness, since wit 'leans towards rudeness as the sublime leans towards the ridiculous, and if it loses its exact tone, it is lost'.[87]

This is an important nuance, as rudeness was not unknown in high society. Let us take a closer look at Bulwer-Lytton's 'Godolphin' (1834), which offers a frank portrayal of contemporary social interaction. The novel's heroine Constance is described as a leader of fashion.

> The power of fashion! This mysterious and subtle engine she was eminently skilled to move according to her will. Her intuitive penetration into character, her tact, and her grace, were exactly the talents Fashion most demands; and they were at present devoted only to that sphere. The rudeness that she mingled, at times, with the bewitching softness and ease of manner she could command at others, increased the effect of her power. It is much to intimidate as well as to win. And her rudeness in a very little while grew popular; for it was never exercised but on those whom the world loves to see humbled. Modest merit in any rank; and even insolence, if accompanied with merit, were always safe from her satire. It was the hauteur of foolish duchesses or purse-proud roturiers that she loved, and scrupled not, to abase.[88]

Bulwer-Lytton's apparent approval of Constance's rudeness may appear strange, yet he is careful to stress that her sharp comments were reserved for 'haughty duchesses and purse-proud roturiers'. Such characters, he seems to suggest, deserve no better. Importantly, Constance herself is not of noble birth. Arming herself with 'plebeian' rudeness, she flouts a key rule of aristocratic upbringing: to behave with equal politeness towards everyone, irrespective of social background.

Turning to a particular instance of Constance's rudeness, we see the heroine at a ball, approached by the Duchess of Winstoun.

> "How do you do, Miss Vernon? I am happy to see you looking so well. What truth in the report, eh?" And the duchess showed her teeth – videlicet, smiled.
> "What report does your grace allude to?"
> "Nay, nay; I am sure Lord Erpingham has heard it as well as myself; and I wish for your sake (a slight emphasis), indeed, for both your sakes, that it may be true."
> "To wait till the Duchess of Winstoun speaks intelligibly would be a waste of her time and my own," said the haughty Constance, with the rudeness in which she then delighted, and for which she has since become known." [89]

Undaunted, the duchess continues to share a rumour she claims to have heard concerning Constance's forthcoming marriage. The heroine's response is sharper still: "I thought till now," said Constance, with grave composure, "that no person could be more contemptible than one who collects idle reports: I now find I was wrong: a person infinitely more contemptible is one who invents them."

Such episodes were not uncommon in high society. Quickly turning into its polar opposite, politeness would fall by the wayside as the more confident opponent resorted to ill manners or blatant cynicism. In the episode above, despite her clear intention of roiling Constance, the duchess nonetheless sticks to social etiquette, whereas the heroine herself speaks with undisguised hostility. Despite this, she justifies her behaviour with the need to avenge her late father, whose highborn friends failed him, and readers find themselves sympathetic to her cause.

Coarse sarcasm stemming from pure misanthropy and bad nature, however, tends to provoke a different reaction. In Eugène Sue's 'Mysteries of Paris' (1842–1843), for instance, the behaviour of the Duke de Lucenay is seen by all as vulgar. A favourite pastime of his is to ascribe to others some bizarre illness or outlandish injury, and offer them his sympathies. On one occasion, he enquires of his companion:

God bless me! Why, what is the matter with you? Ah! I suppose that confounded plaguy cough still sticks to you.[90]

These gibes form but a small element of the Duke's antisocial manner. His comportment is constantly at odds with social etiquette governing physical behaviour: 'by way of terminating his discourse, M. de Lucenay threw himself almost on his back beside the two ladies, crossed his left leg over his right thigh, and held his foot in his hand'. 'Beating the crown of his hat after the fashion of a tambourine,' he tears off the 'floating wreaths' of decorative plants at a ball, and ruins ladies' fans and essence bottles. His voice is 'loud and harsh', and he does not hold back – following a fraught exchange with a lady sporting a questionable turban, he swears: '… if I don't take devilish good care, I shall let fly at that stupid old prude and pull her old stew-pan off her head.'[91]

So, what is it that sets the dandy's taunts and deliberately provoked scandals apart from De Lucenay's ridiculous capers? An accomplished actor, the dandy is able to switch roles at the drop of a hat, fusing sarcastic impudence with cold politeness, seasoning everyday gallant manners with mockery. De Lucenay, on the other hand, is simply unable to behave differently: incapable of changing, he only ever plays a single role – that of himself. His companions see him as an obnoxious clown, a disagreeable character from some second-rate comedy.

This type of behaviour could, perhaps, be traced back to the jesters' tradition, in which the fool was granted special licence to behave in an outrageous or distasteful manner. In the Middle Ages, events such as the toppling of figures of authority or social hierarchies were frequently accompanied by the wit of jesters. The fool was able to address even the highest-ranking officials with comical jeers and taunting insults. Let us be mindful, though, that this kind of provocative insolence and sanctioned flouting of convention on the part of the jester belonged in the realm of specifically traditional culture.

After the Middle Ages, such rudeness ceased to be tolerated, and any members of society behaving thus found their reputation ruined. Let us turn to Maria Edgeworth's 1801 novel 'Belinda', in which Harriet Freke, an outspoken feminist with a love of daring pranks, is portrayed in a negative light. 'Harriet Freke had, without comparison, more assurance than any man or woman I ever saw; she was downright brass, but of the finest kind – Corinthian brass. She was one of the first who brought what I call *harum scarum* manners into fashion.'[92] Harriet's bold manner is disconcerting for the more positive characters; always getting into awkward scrapes, she attempts to engineer complex intrigues, yet often falls victim to her own machinations. The more sensible and enlightened characters tend to make fun of her: her unsophisticated, coarse rudeness is nothing like the dandy's cool insolence. The two, indeed, are worlds apart, and one may even imagine them as polar opposites of 'nature' and 'artifice'.

On occasion, of course, dandies too resorted to pure, unrefined rudeness, yet in their case, it is used as a deliberate device. Often directed at an unpleasant character or member of the 'vulgar class', it was always meticulously polished and served up with a good measure of impudent politeness. If we attempt to trace the dandies' predecessors in terms of insolence, the closest influence would likely be the particular brand of aristocratic impudence known as 'l'art de plaire en déplaisant'. A system of sophisticated behavioural tactics for communication, the 'art of pleasing by displeasing' formed within French court culture in the late seventeenth – early eighteenth century.

In this model, the boundaries between pleasing and displeasing were deliberately erased. Those who mastered this art created complex interdependent relationships with their admirers, with both partners drawn into a secret game. The mysterious tension present in such situations sharpened the mutual interest, attracting and repulsing at the same time.

One famed master of the art of pleasing by displeasing was Antoine Nompar de Caumont, duc de Lauzun.[93] The story of his relationship with Mademoiselle,[94] the cousin of Louis XIV and one of the richest heiresses in Europe, features in the memoirs of Saint-Simon. Known as La Grande Mademoiselle, Anne Marie Louise d'Orléans fell in love with the duc de Lauzun in her middle age. He treated her coldly, and even after she had declared her feelings for him, showed her no more than gallant politeness.

Barbey D'Aurevilly found Lauzun's tactics most admirable, and described his behaviour in detail.

> It is here that the most delicious comedy, the Love Comedy, begins. She intends to be understood, and he – who understands very well – will not understand. Having cracked the ice, she hands it to him to break it finally. It is nothing more than a thin, transparent film, but he does not break it. He does not even lay on it the finger-tip which could have broken it at a touch. Lauzun becomes the most graceful, profound, and irritatingly respectful Tarfufe who ever existed. The man's conduct is a masterpiece. One can draw from it general maxims and axioms for gaining a princess's love.[95]

Today, Lauzun's behaviour might have been described as 'negative control'; in the language of late seventeenth – early eighteenth court culture, it was known as the refusal of love.[96]

Lauzun's approach bears fruit. Mademoiselle applies to Louis XIV for permission to marry, yet the wedding must be delayed: as a true dandy, Lauzun puts off 'his marriage with her (to which the King had consented), in order to have fine liveries, and get the marriage celebrated at the King's mass'.[97] Even finally married, Lauzun maintains his distance and insolent approach, yet Mademoiselle, it seems, develops ways of dealing with this. On one occasion, learning of Lauzun's infidelity, she sets a condition for forgiveness: the duke has to traverse the length of an entire gallery on his knees to reach her.

An influential figure at the court, Lauzun was known to treat his enemies harshly. Women were not exempt. Displeased at the behaviour of Madame de Monaco, the duke treats her with sadistic brutality:

> one summer's afternoon he went to Saint-Cloud, and found Madame and her Court seated upon the ground, enjoying the air, and Madame de Monaco half lying down, one of her hands open and outstretched. Lauzun played the gallant with the ladies, and turned round so neatly that he placed his heel in the palm of Madame de Monaco, made a pirouette there, and departed. Madame de Monaco had strength enough to utter no cry, no word![98]

In this episode, two details are worthy of note: the duke's extra pirouette, executed with the aim of causing deeper pain, and the lady's silence. Madame de Monaco's refusal to cry out shows an effort of will equal to Lauzun's deliberate effort to hurt.

Cruel, almost sadistic insolence towards women is often encountered in later dandies. Recall Brummell's sharp comments about unfortunate outfits, or Baudelaire's sarcastic misogyny. All in all, cold insolence as a means of attracting attention would remain a key tool in the dandy's arsenal for many years.

Sugared Wigs and Luminous Rabbits: Practical Jokes in Dandyism

Beau Brummell, contemporaries noted,

> never refrained, when opportunity offered, from indulging his taste for exciting the risible muscles even of those who, very probably, thought but little of his talent in this way.[99]

The Beau's talent for provoking laughter and merriment was, indeed, one of the qualities which often prompted hosts to invite him to their dinners.

Among dandies, very particular forms of humour were popular. The dandy culture espoused the tradition of practical jokes and 'cutting': the victims of these cold, insolent gibes were often those too quick to assume that they had been accepted in dandy circles.

On one occasion, wishing to please him, a certain Mr. R-s invited George Brummell to lunch, and even bade him bring his friends to make up the party. The dinner, the Beau remarked later, was exceptionally good, with 'every delicacy in, or out of season'; indeed, everything was to his liking, apart from the fact that 'Mr. R-s had the assurance to sit down, and dine with us!'[100] The roles of host and guest are hereby confused, as the visitor claims superior rights, chastising the host as undeserving of his company.

The incident bears a certain similarity to a well-known episode involving Alcibiades, the striking Athenian statesman. Notorious for his eccentric and, at times, harsh behaviour towards his many admirers, Alcibiades was said to treat Anytus, son of Anthemion, with marked insolence.

> This man was a lover of his, who, entertaining some friends, asked Alcibiades also to the dinner. Alcibiades declined the invitation, but after having drunk deep at home with some friends, went in revel rout to the house of Anytus, took his stand at the door of the men's chamber, and, observing the tables full of gold and silver beakers, ordered his slaves to take half of them and carry them home for him. He did not design to go in, but played this prank and was off. The guests were naturally indignant, and declared that Alcibiades had treated Anytus with gross and overweening insolence. 'Not so,' said Anytus, 'but with moderation and kindness; he might have taken all there were: he has left us half.'[101]

Having received a good education, Brummell was, of course, aware of these stories of Alcibiades. In the nineteenth century, indeed, the flamboyant Athenian was a popular figure, with Lord Byron, among others, praising him as a superior ancient hero. Naturally, we cannot assume that Brummell's prank involving Mr. R-s was a deliberate variation on the Alcibiades theme; yet the resemblance in their behavioural patterns is striking.[102] Both men behave insolently: Brummell, with cold refinement, Alcibiades, with brutal directness. Unlike the dandy, he wastes no time masking his intentions with sarcastic politeness, but simply claims the tableware as the stronger, wealthier party. Anytus, as we see, acknowledges Alcibiades' superior status. Brummell could be described as imitating this aristocratic arrogance, trying it on, playfully, lightly, without excessive involvement. In the words of Barbey D'Aurevilly,

> Every Dandy is endowed with audacity, but his boldness is combined with tact, so that he will always and unerringly home to the point famously identified by Pascal, where originality and eccentricity intersect.[103]

These beaux think nothing of flouting social convention. The behaviour of Alcibiades, in particular, can be temperamental in the extreme:

> Once, as he was getting on past boyhood, he accosted a school-teacher, and asked him for a book of Homer. The teacher replied that he had nothing of Homer's, whereupon Alcibiades fetched him a blow with his fist, and went his way.[104]

Alcibiades thinks nothing of hurting a man or wounding his feelings, simply to demonstrate his own superiority.

> He once gave Hipponicus a blow with his fist—Hipponicus, the father of Callias, a man of great reputation and influence owing to his wealth and family—not that he had any quarrel with him, or was a prey to anger, but simply for the joke of the thing, on a wager with some companions.[105]

In this case, the victim is a man of considerable standing, offering Alcibiades an even greater triumph. Unlike the scene with Anytus, in which the admirer of Alcibiades meekly submits to the theft of his precious tableware, the incident with Hipponicus takes an about-turn. The following day, Alcibiades comes to present his apologies, doing so with great gusto:

> Early the next morning Alcibiades went to the house of Hipponicus, knocked at his door, and on being shown into his presence, laid off the cloak he wore and bade Hipponicus scourge and chastise him as he would. But Hipponicus put away his wrath and forgave him, and afterwards gave him his daughter Hipparete to wife.[106]

Besides great insolence, Alcibiades here shows himself also capable of great remorse; his actions, on the whole, can still be considered as conforming to the aristocrat's code of conduct. Hipponicus not only forgives him, but even welcomes him into his family.

Let us now compare this incident with another escapade of George Brummell's. One morning, the Beau felt moved to play a prank on a learned man of some repute: one

Mr. Snodgrass, a Fellow of the Royal Society. Accompanied by several friends, he once knocked up this *savant*, at three o'clock on a fine, frosty morning; and when, under the impression of his house being on fire, he protruded his body *en chemise*, and his head in a nightcap, from the window, the Beau put the following very interesting question to him:

> 'Pray, sir, is your name Snodgrass?' 'Yes, sir,' said he, very anxiously, 'my name is Snodgrass.' 'Snodgrass – Snodgrass,' repeated Brummell, 'a very odd name that, upon my soul, a very odd name indeed! But sir, is your name *really* Snodgrass?' Here the philosopher, with the thermometer below freezing point, naturally got into a towering passion, and threatened to call the watch; whereupon Brummell walked off, with – 'Good morning to you, Mr. Snodgrass'.[107]

Brummell's pranks[108] are, on the whole, more humane than the escapades of Alcibiades. It is, after all, safer to lean out of the window at three in the morning, than to receive a blow from a feisty man's fist. The pranks played by the Beau damaged victims' reputation and pride, rather than their bodies. Making them a laughing stock, he dealt a hefty blow to their self-confidence, yet the entire affair would be playfully, expertly staged, at times even grandiose, and carried off in keeping with a long-standing cultural tradition.

In England, practical jokes were a well-established form of humour. Let us turn to one classic example, in which Beau Brummell pokes fun at a French émigré marquis. Contriving to sprinkle his wig with sugar instead of the usual powder, the Beau and his friends observed the proceedings with glee. At breakfast, the poor marquis was plagued by flies. Shaking his head vigorously, he attempted to wave them off; yet even as he did so, the sugar melted, trickling down his face in sticky streams. Finally, covered in flies, he leaped up and rushed out of the room, holding his head. Why on earth was the poor fellow so plagued by flies, Brummell enquired whimsically.[109]

What, then, is the difference between practical jokes, and 'cutting'? If practical jokes have an element of performance and involve activity, 'cutting' is mainly based on verbal wit. The Snodgrass incident is a practical joke; yet Brummell bidding the savant good morning has also the effect of cutting.

Frequently targeting haughtiness and obsequiousness, cutting was often directed at those with social aspirations above their station. Practical jokes, much of the time, were just that: a bit of fun. Witty and clever, at times, they could also be quite coarse or even cruel, causing the victim physical pain.

Popular among English dandies, practical jokes were in vogue both before and during the times of Beau Brummell. George Selwyn, whom Brummell much admired, was extremely partial to them. Around the turn of the century, however, the nature of these pranks began to change. In the eighteenth century, practical jokes were frequently educational and possessed allegorical undertones. Like skilled directors, the instigators strove to give participants and audiences alike a moral or educational message. By the nineteenth century, the clear didactic tone had vanished; more often than not, jokes were merely eccentric pranks played for pure fun. Some jokes, of course, possessed elements of both types, yet on the whole, this trend was clear.

Writing in The Spectator in 1712, Joseph Addison describes a series of gatherings hosted in Bath by 'one of the wits of the last age, who was a man of a good estate, though he never laid out his money better than in a jest'. This gentleman, it seems, took it upon himself to bring together guests suffering from a common shortcoming. On one occasion, he invited exceptionally loquacious friends, who all had the unfortunate habit of inserting superfluous expressions in their speech, such as 'd'ye hear me, d'ye see, that is, and so Sir'. When the party began to converse, the guests became aware of each other's frustrating tendency.

Soon, they realized that this habit was shared by all, including themselves, and, upon becoming aware of this, immediately dropped the redundant expressions. Before long, they succeeded in ridding themselves of the habit altogether.[110]

Another time, the host invited friends who liked to pepper their speech with abundant swearing. After the second bottle, the guests gave free reign to their habit, and the host bade his servant take down the whole exchange in writing. Ten sheets were produced, of which a good eight were 'sonorous but unnecessary words'. Upon hearing this record of their conversation read out to them, 'every one trembled at himself'. What a tax, the host concluded, would have been raised for the Poor, had the habit of swearing been subject to taxation![111]

In the same way, storytellers addicted to telling dull, long anecdotes, 'awakened out of that Lethargy with which each of them had been seized for several Years'. Upon being forced to listen to one another, they became aware of their inconvenient habit. Such, indeed, was the host's intention: subjecting his guests to the company of others with the same tendency, he encouraged them to become aware of their own shortcomings. This accomplished, enlightenment, and general improvement could follow.

The underlying principle, of course, was perfectly typical of that era. By creating favourable circumstances, it was thought, one could stimulate the intelligence inherent in every human being, and doing this with humour was considered a bonus. Realizing that they belong to a certain type, people will, it was assumed, find it easier to change their ways. In the eighteenth century, the study of moral and physiological 'types' was widespread, as were classifications according to facial features and character. One need only recall the physiognomic studies of William Hogarth[112] in England, Charles Le Brun in France, and Johann Kaspar Lavater in Switzerland.

Bearing in mind this context, let us turn to another incident described in The Spectator. The host gathered, on this occasion, a number of people with long chins, who all 'had their mouths in the middle of their faces'. At first, the guests were unable to imagine what had brought them together, but eventually 'grew sensible of the jest, and came into it with so much good-humour, that they lived in strict friendship and alliance from that day forward'. The host's idea can be seen as an enquiry into the diversity of human nature, an act of curiosity not dissimilar to the collection of rarities (recall the Kunstkameras of that period). The incident is not devoid of humour, as the company is deliberately selected to have 'something of burlesque and ridicule in its appearance'.[113]

Eighteenth and early nineteenth-century aesthetic theories specifically stated that humour entails a somewhat abstract view of humans as examples of collective being. 'It recognizes no individual foolishness, no fools, but only folly and a mad world,' Jean Paul Richter writes in his 'Preschool of Aesthetics'.[114]

But let us now look at practical jokes from a different perspective – that of the victims. How were they made to feel? Not always able to 'come into it with so much good humour', victims were often offended or enraged. One such example is a gathering organized by the same 'wit of the last age', which brought together guests that stammered. The host bade his servant record the proceedings, and established that during the first course, there were not above twenty words spoken. During the second, one gentleman took a quarter of an hour to note that 'the ducklings and asparagus were very good', and another guest spent the same amount of time voicing agreement. Realizing how the company had been selected, one of the guests became offended and left, subsequently challenging the host to a duel. The tension was eventually defused with the aid of friends.[115] In most cases, however, such pranks were looked upon with tolerance by their participants. The guests with long chins, after all, 'lived in strict friendship and alliance from that day forward'. In nineteenth-century England, humorous pranks were common, their purely fun side increasingly taking precedence over the didactic aspect.

During the Regency period, members of the Society of Eccentrics became known for their practical jokes. The club brought together members such as Charles James Fox, Richard Brinsley Sheridan, Lord Petersham, Henry Peter Brougham (Baron Brougham and Vaux), and Theodore Hook.

Known for works such as 'The School for Scandal', the playwright Sheridan was partial to practical jokes. On one occasion, he convinced his friend Richard Tickell to follow him down a dark corridor, on the floor of which he had spread a large number of plates and dishes. Leaving a clear path for himself, he positioned them in such a way that Tickell was bound to crash into them. Running through the crockery, Tickell kept falling, and was cut in many places. The following day, Lord John Townshend visited him and found him in bed. Complaining of Sheridan, Tickell vowed to get his revenge. 'But,' added he, his admiration at the trick entirely subduing his indignation, 'how amazingly well it was managed!'[116]

One of the best-known practical jokers of the Regency was Theodore Hook (1788–1841). Generally known as 'much more entertaining', Hook was famous as a society wit capable of brilliant improvization, sparkling quips, and impromptu singing and piano playing. Visitors such as Hook, Sydney Smith, Samuel Rogers, and Henry Luttrell were often invited to society dinners for their wit alone, rather than their wealth or social standing. Hosts valued their conversational powers and ability to amuse and entertain. Like dandies, who were valued for their taste and elegance, they were welcome at social functions, irrespective of descent. Some, indeed, were able to combine the talents of dandy and society wit: George Brummell, for instance, was known both for his appearance, and for his witticisms. The same went for his friend Lord Alvanley. Theodore Hook, however, was famed for his wit, yet was not a dandy (Figure 17).

On one occasion, chancing upon an ostentatiously dressed stranger, Hook enquired: 'Excuse me, Sir, but are you anyone in particular?' His remark, of course, recalls Brummell's equally dry treatment of showily overdressed beaux.

Fond of word play, about the funeral of a theatre-going friend, Hook observed with typical British black humour 'I met him in his private box going to the pit.'

THEODORE HOOK.

Figure 17 Daniel Maclise. Portrait of Theodore Hook. 1834. Source of illustration: Lewis Melville. The Beaux of the Regency, London: Hutchinson, 1908, vol. II, p. 228.

A man of letters, Hook was editor of the John Bull Sunday newspaper and The Monthly Magazine. In 1812, he was appointed Account-General of Mauritius. The post did not last long, however, and upon coming back to England, he returned to his role of society wit. Hook's eccentric nature was of interest to many writers. In 'Vanity Fair', he inspired William Thackeray to create the character of Mr. Wagg. In Benjamin Disraeli's 'Vivian Grey', Stanislaus Hoax is based on Hook, and in 'Coningsby', he figures as Lucian Gay.

Like many lovers of practical jokes, Theodore Hook boasted a unique collection of signs,[117] knockers, and bellpulls, which even included a figure of an eagle, drawn down from a hotel roof using a noose, and a number of wooden gnomes purloined from pub entrances. A favourite pastime of Hook's was paying visits. On one occasion, he and a friend spent so long at one gentleman's house that the host eventually went to bed. The following morning, when he enquired of his servant what time the guests had left, the man responded with 'oh, they are not gone yet, sir, they've just rung for coffee!'

Many of Hook's practical jokes are still remembered today; in some, he figures in his favourite role of high-society guest. On one occasion, Hook was walking with his friend, the actor Daniel Terry, and passed a house where a fine dinner was being prepared. Betting his friend that he would make one of the party, he bade him call back for him at ten. Calmly entering the house as the servants took him for one of the invited guests, he proceeded to make himself at home and entertain the assembled company with his jokes. Upon the host cautiously asking his name, claiming the servants had most likely confused the matter, 'Smith, sir, Smith', replied the unblushing Theodore, 'don't apologise; you are quite right, sir, servants are great blockheads: I remember a most remarkable instance of their mistakes.' 'But really, sir', interrupted the host mildly, 'I did not anticipate the pleasure of Mr. Smith's company to dinner. Whom do you suppose you are addressing?' 'Mr. Thompson[118], of course', answered Hook, 'an old friend of my father's'. Upon the host replying that his name was not Thompson, Hook claimed to be much embarrassed. He had been counting on remaining there until ten, he explained, thinking it to be the home of his father's friend. Offering to depart straightaway, he clearly touched his host, who furthermore had noted the guest's talent for entertaining. Upon the host begging him to stay, he finally accepted.

> Everybody was delighted with him, all the evening he kept up a constant fire of wit and repartee, and ultimately sat down to the piano, and sang extempore verses on every one present. In the midst of these the door opened and, true to his appointment, in walked Terry, at the sight of whom, striking a new key, he sang:
>
> I'm very much pleased with your fare,
> Your cellar's as fine as your cook;
> My friend's Mr. Terry, the player,
> And I'm Mr. Theodore Hook.[119]

Upon hearing these verses, the generous host and friendly guests immediately realized that the entire incident was a hoax. But should it be seen as a rude, thoughtless escapade? Was Hook breaking all the rules of hospitality to make fun of his host? He entered the house under a false name, gained permission to stay thanks to a ruse, and enjoyed his host's food and drink for an entire evening before publicly showing him up. On the other hand, in many ways he fulfilled his role as a guest admirably, putting effort into keeping the party entertained at all times as everyone laughed at his jokes. Even as he admitted the hoax, he also praised his host's cook and cellar. All in all, he pulled the incident off well thanks to his wit and skill. No one, most likely, was seriously offended, even the host: after all, practical jokes, and especially bets, were already a long-standing tradition.

Incidents such as this were but trivial, however, compared to some of the better known – and, at times, far more cruel – practical jokes instigated by Hook. Let us take a look, for instance, at the famous Berners Street Hoax.

The Berners Street Hoax

Strolling with a friend one day, Hook bet his friend that he could make an ordinary London home the focus of the entire city's attention in just a week. Together with a lady and another gentleman as accomplices, Theodore Hook sent out some four thousand letters, summoning hordes of tradesmen and officials to one Mrs. Tottenham's home at number 54, Berners Street, at different times on the same day.

Early that momentous morning, a crowd of chimney sweeps assembled at the house, claiming to have been specially summoned. The first arrived around five o'clock, waking the neighbourhood with his cries of 'Sweep! Sweep!' As the irate maid attempted to send the sweeps away, explaining that their services were not required, a number of heavy carts laden with coal appeared. Blocking the street, they impeded each others' progress, causing the coal merchants to swear in frustration. Picking their way gingerly through the obstruction, a line of cake-makers approached next, bearing wedding cakes they claimed had been ordered for number 54.

These were followed in rapid succession by tailors, shoemakers, upholsterers, and carmen with barrels of beer. No sooner had the heavy carts departed, than a dozen festive wedding coaches appeared, the drivers all enquiring 'where the happy couple was'. These were followed by surgeons with scalpels expecting to amputate limbs, lawyers summoned to work on an inheritance case, priests coming to conduct special services, and painters commissioned to produce portraits. By midday, some forty fishmongers had arrived, bearing cod and crabs; hot on their heels were butchers carrying forty legs of lamb. The area was brought to a complete standstill, as carts, tradesmen, and onlookers became caught up in the chaos. Just as the commotion reached its peak, with poor Mrs. Tottenham at her wits' end, the Lord Mayor of London arrived in a sumptuous carriage with liverymen in silk stockings, plumed hats, and wigs.

Not content with this, however, Hook had also involved even higher-ranking personages. The Lord Mayor was followed by the Governor of the Bank of England, who had received a letter stating that Mrs. Tottenham was ready to disclose to him some vital information on fraud by clerks from Threadneedle Street.[120] A similar letter had summoned the chairman of the East India Company.[121] Finally, the Duke of Gloucester himself arrived. The nephew of King George III, he had been informed that a former lady-in-waiting to His Majesty's mother wished to share with him on her deathbed some secrets of the royal family.

The chaos resulting from the hoax was such that police offered a reward for the apprehension of the perpetrator. The tradesmen who had brought their wares to Berners Street suffered huge losses. Despite many suspecting that the prank was instigated by Hook, he was never formally accused. After observing the incident, Hook left the country for some time, and only decades later alluded to it in his semi-autobiographical novel 'Gilbert Gurney'. The hoax, he claimed in what is seen as an indirect confession, was something of a masterpiece: 'for originality of thought and design, I *do* think that was perfect.'[122]

The entire grotesque escapade, indeed, is constructed not unlike a literary work. An urban legend, it follows a text of its own, with its four thousand letters, forty fishmongers, and forty legs of lamb. Humble Berners Street becomes the very epicentre of universal chaos – the scene of carnival, the topos of upheaval. The entire world is turned upside down, with 54 Berners Street in the eye of the storm. The order of the unwanted guests' appearance is in itself highly symbolic. The first ones on the scene are the chimney sweeps.

The first to cross the boundaries of the house, in mythological terms they can be seen as envoys of the underworld.[123] The sweeps are followed by heavy carts packed with coal: chaos reigns, curses break out, the victim is on the way to a symbolic 'hell'.

Like Gargantua or Robin O'Bobin, the victim of the hoax devours tonnes of provisions, and downs beer by the barrel. Her grotesque, bloated 'carnival' body requires an entire legion of apothecaries. The pranksters turn Mrs. Tottenham into a hyperbolised consumer of all nature of services, from weddings to inheritance, deathbed confession and last rites, with all of life's major stages covered. She is said to require lawyers, priests, and doctors; she confers with officials, bankers, and royals.

The participation of such high-ranking figures naturally raises the profile of the entire affair. The elderly lady at the centre of the hoax has a multitude of social roles forced upon her: cast in the parts of portrait commissioner, surgeon's patient, and queen's maid of honour, with each new arrival she is obliged to turn down a new set of functions.

The common factor in all the roles foisted upon Mrs. Tottenham is that she always ends up playing the inhospitable hostess. Guests knock on her door, but she refuses to receive them, thus going against the ancient tradition that bids the host offer even uninvited guests a warm welcome. In myths, failure to properly welcome one's guests is often punished with tragedy of cosmic proportions.[124] The events which unravelled around 54 Berners Street can indeed be seen as catastrophic.

Hook's harsh treatment of his victim has the effect, paradoxically, of elevating her in the eyes of others, making her a part of the overall Game. Due to its epic proportions, admittedly, this particular incident is perhaps not entirely typical. The traditional practical joke involves participants who are more or less 'equal', and part of the same enclosed group. Under the unspoken 'rules' of practical jokes, the victim must not take offence. Should victims become offended, they are seen as demeaning themselves and failing to play the game, which supposes equal parties. The ideal response from a victim is either a fresh prank, or perfect calm and equanimity. A good practical joke tested one's ability to respond in the proper manner, and admitting that one was upset was tantamount to admitting defeat. For this reason, pranks did not give rise to gentlemen's duels, the victims preferring instead to 'believe' in the hoax.

An example of this can be seen in a famous incident involving the Pre-Raphaelite artist Sir Edward Burne-Jones. In his 'Autobiography', Bertrand Russell talks of a time when his grandmother stayed at Naworth Castle.

> Burne-Jones, who was also staying there, had a tobacco pouch which was made to look like a tortoise. There was also a real tortoise, which strayed one day by mistake into the library. This suggested a prank to the younger generation. During dinner, Burne-Jones's tobacco pouch was placed near the drawing-room fire, and when the ladies returned from dinner it was dramatically discovered that this time the tortoise had got into the drawing room. On its being picked up, somebody exclaimed with astonishment that its back had grown soft. Lord Carlisle fetched from the library the appropriate volume of the Encyclopaedia, and read out a pretended passage saying that great heat sometimes had this effect. My grandmother expressed the greatest interest in this fact of natural history, and frequently alluded to it on subsequent occasions. Many years later, when she was quarrelling with Lady Carlisle about

Home Rule, her daughter maliciously told her the truth of this incident. My grandmother retorted: 'I may be many things, but I am not a fool, and I refuse to believe you.'[125]

The best milieus for practical jokes were groups of people of means, free, with spare time on their hands, and a good sense of humour. Naturally, pranks were played among the less wealthy also – recall talented wits such as Mullah Nasruddin. There was, however, a special type of prank, understood more as pure art, performance without material interest. Practical jokes are most successful when played in a closed group governed by its own clearly defined rules. They can be described as rituals that go against ritual; socially acceptable and safe means of defusing social tension. Being rude in social situations, deliberately provoking scandal, and exhibiting various forms of shocking behaviour (such as wearing outlandish or provocative dress) can be seen as similar behavioural techniques. In the twentieth century, methods such as these were adopted by artists and poets, who staged performances and flash mobs to attract attention.

In England, practical jokes were especially widespread due to the existing national comic tradition: English black humour, limericks, comedy series such as 'Monty Python's Flying Circus', the caricatures and cartoon strips targeting politicians.[126] The British culture of practical jokes carried on in the twentieth century, with a prime example in the wonderfully memorable characters of P. G. Wodehouse. Recall, for instance, the occasion when Bertie Wooster muses about revenge on his friend Tuppy Glossop, who has played a practical joke on him.

> He was the fellow, if you remember, who, ignoring a lifelong friendship in the course of which he had frequently eaten my bread and salt, betted me one night at the Drones that I wouldn't swing myself across the swimming-bath by the ropes and rings, and then, with almost inconceivable treachery, went and looped back the last ring, causing me to drop into the fluid and ruin one of the nattiest suits of dress-clothes in London.[127]

In this incident, many prime ingredients of a practical joke are present: 'disregard' for friendship and hospitality, a bet, and treachery. Having been forced to drop into the water in full evening dress, Bertie vows to exact revenge, and prepares a water pistol called The Giant Squirt. This way, Tuppy will also be subjected to a dousing. Bertie's main weapon, however, is a Luminous Rabbit.

> I hear excellent reports of it on all sides. You wind it up and put it in somebody's room in the night watches, and it shines in the dark and jumps about, making odd, squeaking noises the while. The whole performance being, I should imagine, well calculated to scare young Tuppy into a decline.[128]

The instruments and, indeed, the entire scenario for Bertie's revenge may appear at first glance terribly childish. Yet make no mistake: a practical joke's childishly innocent aspects in no way preclude real cruelty.

Another interesting aspect of this incident is Bertie's behaviour as a stereotypical dandy. After dropping in the pool, he mainly regrets ruining 'one of the nattiest suits of dress-clothes in London'. His taste, however, leaves much to be desired: the wise Jeeves is forced to burn a hole in a certain white jacket of his master's, in order to stop him from wearing it. Thus, in a comical exchange, the servant, like a true dandy, shows better taste than his master, and is capable of finer irony. One might recall the colourful and ingenious Sam Weller in 'The Pickwick Papers'.

When discussing features of the English gentleman, one notes that both the dandy, and the gentleman are fond of play – a tendence not unconnected with aristocratic models of behaviour. The philosopher José Ortega y Gasset, for instance, clearly states that 'games are a luxury not to be indulged in before the lower zones of existence are well taken care of.'[129] The gentleman can allow himself to become involved in games and practical jokes, because he feels 'safe regarding the elemental needs of life'.[130]

A gentleman is open to becoming involved in a game as an element of an aristocratic way of life. Practical jokes, indeed, can be seen as indulging in luxury, in a culture of free play by free people. Noble birth is not a prerequisite.

When indulging in games, the gentleman must observe an extra principle: he must keep his composure. A calm exterior is crucial in the dandy canon. As a true gentleman, the dandy always remains calm, his reactions are understated, and he keeps his cool. For the instigator, a practical joke is a chance to show off creative inventiveness; for the victim, it is an exercise in self-control. This equanimity relies upon, and indeed balances, the energy of play.

Another important gentleman's principle – that of fair play – does not always appear to be observed in practical jokes. Often, they appear unfair, unjust: readers will recall the innocent Snodgrass, and the poor French marquis with his sugared wig. Such incidents, however, are perhaps dwarfed by the broader paradigm of gentlemen's games: they are the exceptions which prove the rule.[131] Such small-scale incidents of injustice may even serve to switch the register, indicating a transition from solemnity to play: the trickster is in the house, they announce. Convention being flouted at the very outset forms part of the joke itself; the participants see it as a necessary signal bidding the fun to begin. In his role as trickster, a gentleman may instigate such injustice, which may then grow from a trivial incident into a local catastrophe, such as the Berners Street event.

For a practical joke to be successful, however, certain conditions must be met. What, then, are the features of the classic prank?

1. The participants must be part of the same group or circle, or at least belong to the same social group: this will ensure friendly understanding. *The ideal practical joke is played within a closed group governed by its own clearly defined rules.* Should the joke extend beyond the closed group, the risk of causing conflict and hurt increases.
2. Practical jokes require proper planning, even if this involves a lot of work. The Berners Street Hoax is, in this regard, perfection itself; yet even the path cleared among the plates is a fine example of proper preparation.[132]
3. Practical jokes should not affect anyone's key life interests, or significantly damage any person's health. At times, it may be a question of a very fine line, and the instigators of practical jokes had to rely on their best judgement in planning their pranks.

If these lines are not crossed, the energy of the prank is fully able to be felt without impediment in the field of etiquette. The energy is also fed by the constructive contradiction between the two mutually complementary principles of 'equanimity' and 'play'. Mindful of the gentleman's code of conduct, the dandy is able to excel at practical jokes, indirectly confirming the code's value as a cultural paradigm of significant authority.

Notes

1. Jules Barbey d'Aurevilly, *On Dandyism and George Brummell*. Trans. George Walden; George Walden, *Who is a Dandy?* (London: Gibson Square book, 2002), 103.
2. Horace, *The Works of Horace: Consisting of His Odes, Satires, Epistles, and Art of Poetry*. Trans. P. Francis and P. Griffin (London: Doig and Sterling, Edinburgh; Tabernacle-Walk, 1815), 247.
3. Nikolay Babichev, Yakov Borovsky, *Slovar latinskik krylatikh slov* [Dictionary of Commonly Used Latin Expressions] (Moscow: Russky Yazyk, 1988), 497–498.
4. D'Aurevilly, *On Dandyism*, 114.
5. Edward Bulwer-Lytton, *Pelham; Or, the Adventures of a Gentleman* (London: Chapman and Hall, 1849), 27–28.
6. Wilkie Collins, *Basil* (Oxford: Oxford University Press, 2008), 21.
7. Ibid.
8. Charles Baudelaire, The Painter of Modern Life, in *Selected Writings on Art and Artists*. Trans P. E. Charvet (Cambridge, London: Cambridge University Press, 1981), 422.
9. Ibid., 421.
10. Ibid., 420.
11. Ibid., 421.
12. D'Aurevilly, *On Dandyism*, 80.
13. Bulwer-Lytton, *Pelham*, 67–68.
14. Samuel Taylor Coleridge, Hexameters, in *The Portable Coleridge*, ed. I. A. Richards (New York: Viking, 1950), 161.
15. William Jesse, *The Life of George Brummell, Esq*. In 2 volumes (London: Saunders and Otley, 1844), 1: 323.
16. Mark Sandberg, *Living Pictures, Missing Persons: Mannequins, Museums and Modernity* (Princeton: Princeton University Press, 2003).
17. Anon. *The Exclusives* (London: Henry Colburn and Richard Bentley, 1830), 1: 62–63. The authorship of the novel is attributed to Lady Charlotte Bury.
18. Maurice Merleau-Ponty, *Basic Writings*, ed. Thomas Baldwin (London: Routledge, 2004), 252. ['Une vision complémentaire ou une autre vision: moi-même vu du dehors, tel qu'un autre me verrait, installé au milieu du visible, en train de le considerer d'un certain lieu'. Maurice Merleau-Ponty *Le Visible et l'invisible* (Paris: Gallimard, 1964), 177].
19. Edward Bulwer-Lytton, *Pelham or the Adventures of a Gentleman* (New York: John Lovell Company, n.d.), 118.
20. Peter McNeil, Macaroni Masculinities, in *The Men's Fashion Reader*, eds. Peter Mc Neil and Vicki Karaminas (Oxford, New York: Berg, 2009), 59.
21. Ulrich Lehmann, *Tigersprung: Fashion in Modernity* (Cambridge, MA: MIT Press, 2000), 367.
22. Bulwer-Lytton, *Pelham*, 280.
23. William Jesse, *The Life of George Brummell*, 2: 388–389.
24. See *The Vauxhall Affray: or, the Macaroni Defeated* (1773), as quoted by Peter de Bolla, The visibility of visuality, in *Vision in Context*. eds. T. Brennan and M. Jay (New York: Routledge, 1996), 77–78. See also: Peter McNeil, '"That doubtful gender": macaroni dress and male sexualities', *Fashion Theory* 3, no. 4 (1999): 411–449.

25 Quoted from Ellen Moers, *The Dandy* (New York: The Viking Press, 1960), 37.
26 William Hazlitt, Brummelliana, in *The Complete Works in 22 Volumes*, ed. P. Howe, (London: J. M. Dent, 1934), 20: 153.
27 Jesse, 1: 53.
28 Quoted by W. Jesse from the novel *Granby* by Th. H. Lister: Jesse, *The Life of George Brummell*, 1: 104.
29 'Vous voulez, je suppose, témoigner à une femme que vous la trouvez jolie ...; le mouvement que vous faites pour saisir votre lorgnon avertit la dame de l'impression favorable que ses charmes ont produit. Son attention se concentre sur votre individu. Alors vous clignez les paupières. Rien qui donne l'air aussi provocateur. On dirait que vous appréciez chaque détail et que vous suivez attentivement la ligne sous le vêtement'. Félix Deriège, *Physiologie du Lion* (Paris: Delahaye, 1841), 10–11.
30 Lady Morgan, *France in 1829–1830* (London: Saunders & Otley, 1831), 12–13.
31 Hazlitt, *Brummelliana*, 153.
32 Moers, *The Dandy*, 12.
33 Richard Sennett, *The Fall of Public Man* (Cambridge: Cambridge University Press, 1977), 165.
34 Carlo Ginzburg, Morelli, Freud, and Sherlock Holmes: clues and scientific method, in *The Sign of Three: Dupin, Holmes, Peirce*, eds. Umberto Eco and Thomas A. Sebeok (Bloomington: Indiana University Press, 1984), 81–118.
35 Other texts mention the use of sand for this purpose, but there are no documentary sources to prove such practices.
36 Jules Barbey d'Aurevilly, *On Dandyism and George Brummell*. Trans. George Walden (London: Gibson Square book, 2002), 36.
37 Anne Hollander, *Sex and Suits* (New York: A. Knopf, 1995), 8.
38 See Barbara Stafford, *Artful Science* (Cambridge, MA: MIT Press, 1994).
39 Jonathan Crary, *Techniques of the Observer: On Vision and Modernity in the Nineteenth Century* (Cambridge, London: MIT Press, 1996), 14.
40 *The Portable Coleridge* (1950), 160.
41 Ibid., 161.
42 William Wordsworth, *The Prelude*, eds. Ernest de Sélincourt and Helen Darbishire (Oxford: Oxford University Press, 1959), 127.
43 See the chapters on insolence and scandals in this book.
44 Charles Baudelaire, The Painter of Modern Life, in *Selected Writings on Art and Artists*. Trans. P. E. Charvet (Cambridge: Cambridge University Press, 1981), 421.
45 *The New Roget's Thesaurus in dictionary form*, revised by Norman Lewis (New York: Putnam, 1978), 475.
46 *The Complete Works of William Shakespeare* (London: Odhams Press, n.d.), 1132.
47 Charles Talbut Onions, *A Shakespeare Glossary*, enlarged by R. D. Eagleson (Oxford: Clarendon Press, 1986), 310.
48 Philip Dormer Stanhope Chesterfield, *Advice to His Son, on Men and Manners: Or, A New System of Education* (London, Philadelphia: T. Bradford and P. Hall., 1781; Ann Arbor: Text Creation Partnership, 2011), accessed 17.04.2022, http://name.umdl.umich.edu/N13748.0001.001
49 Chesterfield, ibid.
50 Chesterfield, ibid.
51 Chesterfield, ibid.
52 John Henry Newman, *The Definition of a Gentleman*, in The Portable Victorian Reader, ed. G. S. Haight (London: Penguin, 1977), 466.
53 Eugène Sue, *The Mysteries of Paris*. Trans. Charles H. Town (New York: Harper and Brothers, 1843), 91.
54 Ibid., 92.
55 William Hazlitt, *Table-Talk* (London, Toronto: W. Dent, 1908), 161.
56 Edward Bulwer-Lytton, *Pelham* (Boston: Estes and Lauriat, 1891), 106.

57 'When worn by rich, yet insufficiently cultured merchant's wives, the expensive outfits ordered from the best firms in Paris, London, or Vienna, simply lost their elegance. The ladies did not know how to wear them, pairing them with excessively lavish decorations, or adding some entirely unnecessary detail to ensure a "stunning" effect: a diamond brooch, or strings of large pearls with a simple day dress, a light summer dress, even… With no thought for their own style or colouring, these ladies would always make a beeline for the most fashionable and complex looks. Their sole aim was to appear better, more lavishly dressed than anyone else. Ordering their tailors to use the most expensive trimmings, they adored guipure, lace, beads, and fringes. Their dress, often incongruous in cut, colour, and trimming, would generally be paired with the very latest style of shoe. Some merchant's wives, preferring comfort, however, would opt for prunella or Morocco leather shoes with a small heel and elasticated sides or ties in the style worn by housemaids. These shoes did not stop the wearer from choosing a hat heaped high with ornaments, a fashionable cape, a garish silk umbrella with frills and bows, a gold lorgnette for a cultured look, and of course her favourite beaded reticule…' Elizaveta Berman, Elena Kurbatova, *Russky Kostyum 1750–1917* ["Russian Dress 1750–1917"], in 5 vols, ed. Vadim Ryndin, vol. 5 (Moscow: VTO, 1972), 38–39.
58 Hazlitt, ibid., 156–168.
59 Alexander Pushkin, *Eugene Onegin*. Trans. A. S. Kline, 2009, chapter 6, accessed 17 April 2022, https://www.poetryintranslation.com/PITBR/Russian/Onegin8.php#highlightonegin
60 Norbert Elias, *The Civilizing Process: The History of Manners* (New York: Pantheon, 1982).
61 Marcel Proust, *The Guermantes Way* (Germany: Books on Demand, 2019). Quoted from The Guermantes Way - Marcel Proust - Google Books, accessed 17 April 2022.
62 John Ruskin, *Sesame and Lilies* (London: Smith, Elder & Co, 1865), 60.
63 Scrope Berdmore Davies (1783–1852) was a well-known Regency dandy and friend of Lord Byron. Byron, indeed, considered him the most witty and eloquent of all his acquaintances, dedicating to him his 1816 poem 'Parisina'. Byron's 'Detached Thoughts' contains some interesting episodes featuring Scrope Davies.
64 Jules Barbey D'Aurevilly, *The Anatomy of Dandyism: With Some Observations on Beau Brummell*. Translated from the French by D. B. Wyndham Lewis (London: Peter Davies, 1928), 10.
65 Barbey D'Aurevilly, ibid., 11.
66 For more on dandies flouting the rituals of hospitality, see Olga Vainchtein, La subversion de l'hospitalité et les jeux visuels dans le dandysme, in *Mythes et représentations de l'hospitalité*, ed. Alain Montandon (Clermont-Ferrand: Presses Universitaires Blaise Pascal, 1999), 267–281.
67 William Jesse, *The Life of George Brummell, Esq.* In 2 volumes (London: Saunders and Otley, 1844), 1: 84–85.
68 Jesse, ibid., 1:44.
69 Jesse, 1:106–107.
70 In philosophy, an aporia is seen as a logical conundrum, a 'state of puzzlement'. Aporias were particularly associated with Zeno of Elea (5th century BC).
71 *Of Hospitality. Anne Dufourmantelle Invites Jacques Derrida to Respond* (Bloomington: Stanford University Press, 2000), 25.
72 Ibid., 79.
73 Ibid.
74 Jesse, 1: 109–110.
75 Jesse, 1: 108.
76 Jesse, 1: 272.
77 Barbey D'Aurevilly, ibid., 34–35.
78 Jesse, 1: 116.
79 See Boris Uspensky, Antipovedenie v kulture drevnej Rusi [Counter-conduct in the culture of ancient Russia], in *Izbrannie trydi* [Selected Works] (Moscow: Gnozis, 1994), 320–333.

80 For an accurate analysis of the social aspects of aristocratic conduct see Domna Stanton, *The Aristocrat as Art* (New York: Columbia University Press, 1980).
81 Jesse, 1: 102.
82 Ibid., 92.
83 Maurice Blanchot, *Faux Pas*. Trans. Charlotte Mandell (Stanford: Stanford University Press, 2001), 306.
84 Edward Bulwer-Lytton, *Pelham, Or the Adventures of a Gentleman* (London: Henry Colburn, 1828), 26–27.
85 Jules Barbey D'Aurevilly, *The Anatomy of Dandyism: With Some Observations on Beau Brummell*. Translated from the French by D. B. Wyndham Lewis (London: Peter Davies, 1928), 35.
86 Ibid.
87 Ibid., 34–35.
88 Edward Bulwer-Lytton, *Godolphin* (London, n.d.), 120.
89 Bulwer-Lytton, ibid., 80.
90 Eugène Sue, *The Mysteries of Paris*. Project Gutenberg e-book 33801, 2010, vol. 2:18. https://www.gutenberg.org/ebooks/33801. Accessed 21.04.2022.
91 Sue, ibid., 13–16.
92 Referring to 'Corinthian brass', Edgeworth plays on the different meanings of both words. 'Brass' – (1) a copper-zinc alloy or (2) brazenness. 'Corinthian' could mean: (1) of or relating to ancient Corinth or its people or culture or (2) given to licentious and profligate luxury. Corinthian brass was a valuable alloy in classical antiquity. Maria Edgeworth, *Belinda* (Oxford, Oxford University Press, 1994), 43.
93 Antoine Nompar de Caumont, duc de Lauzun (1632–1723) was a French courtier and marshal, who was the lover and supposedly, morganatic husband, of Anne Marie Louise d'Orléans.
94 Anne Marie Louise d'Orléans (1627–1693), Duchess of Montpensier, was the cousin of Louis XIV. Known as La Grande Mademoiselle, she is largely remembered for her memoirs and influence in the Fronde civil wars. Mademoiselle's life story has been the focus of many researchers; among her biographers was Vita Sackville-West.
95 Jules Barbey D'Aurevilly, *The Anatomy of Dandyism: With Some Observations on Beau Brummell*. Translated from the French by D. B. Wyndham Lewis (London: Peter Davies, 1928), 73–74.
96 A detailed study of one refusal of love can be found in Madame de La Fayette's 'The Princess of Cleves'.
97 Duc de Louis de Rouvroy Saint-Simon, *The Memoirs of Louis XIV, His Court and of the Regency*. Project Gutenberg e-book 3875, 2004. https://www.gutenberg.org/ebooks/3875. Accessed 21.04.2022.
98 Saint-Simon, ibid.
99 William Jesse, *The Life of George Brummell, Esq.* In 2 volumes (London: Saunders and Otley, 1844), 1: 116.
100 Jesse, ibid., 1: 108–109.
101 Plutarch. *Plutarch's Lives*. Trans. Bernadotte Perrin (Cambridge, MA: Harvard University Press; London: William Heinemann Ltd., 1916), 4:5.
102 Yuri Lotman looked at classical antique patterns in the behaviour of the Russian nobility in his essay: Dekabrist v Povsednevnoi Zhizni [The Decembrist in Everyday Life], in *Literaturnoe Nasledie Dekabristov* [Literary Heritage of Decemberists] (Leningrad: Nauka, 1975), 25–74.
103 Jules Barbey D'Aurevilly, *On Dandyism and George Brummell*. Trans. George Walden (London: Gibson Square books, 2002), 106–107.
104 Plutarch, ibid., 7: 1.
105 Plutarch, ibid., 8: 1.
106 Ibid.

107 Jesse, ibid., I: 115–116.
108 For more on Brummell's language in pranks, see Dita Svelte, "Do You Call this Thing a Coat?": Wit, the Epigram and the Detail in the Figure of the Ultimate Dandy, Beau Brummell, *Fashion Theory*, 22, no. 3 (2018): 255–282, DOI: 10.1080/1362704X.2017.1354436
109 Jesse, ibid., I: 114–115.
110 Joseph Addison. *Selections from Addison's Papers Contributed to The Spectator*. Ed. with Introduction and Notes by Thomas Arnold (Oxford: Clarendon Press, 1925), 290. My sincere gratitude goes to Liudmila Aliabieva for sending me this text.
111 Ibid., 290.
112 William Hogarth, *The Analysis of Beauty: Written with a View of Fixing the Fluctuating Ideas of Taste* (London: J. Reeves, 1753). See in particular Chapter XV 'Of the Face'. http://name.umdl.umich.edu/004798055.0001.000. Accessed 23.04.2022.
113 Addison, ibid., 288.
114 Jean Paul Richter, *Horn of Oberon: Jean Paul Richter's School of Aesthetics*. Introduction and Translation by Margaret R. Hale (Detroit: Wayne State University Press, 1973), 88.
115 Addison, ibid., 289.
116 Jesse, ibid., 1: 113–114.
117 Collecting entertaining signs was also a favourite hobby of Soviet times. The author's father Boris Vainshtein, a physicist and crystallographer, had a sign from a building site in his study, which read 'Do not walk on the wall'.
118 Beau Brummell also played upon the common names of Johnsons and Thompsons when he turned up to a dinner at a Mrs. Thompson's house, uninvited. The two incidents share many similarities, although Hook's prank is, of course, on a grander scale.
119 Anecdote of Theodore Hook, *Nelson Evening Mail*, Vol. XIII, Issue 58, 8 March (1878), 4.
120 The City of London's Threadneedle Street was home to a number of banks, including the Bank of England. Hence, its nickname, The Old Lady of Threadneedle Street, which hinted at the bank's conservative stance.
121 The East India Company was a large commercial enterprise founded in 1600. In the nineteenth century, it exerted significant influence on the British Empire's policy in India. The well-known essayist Charles Lamb worked for the company between 1792 and 1825. It ceased to exist in 1958.
122 This account of the Berners Street Hoax is drawn chiefly from Lewis Melville, *The Beaux of the Regency*, in 2 volumes (London: Hutchinson & Co, 1908) 2: 235–237.
123 The mythological image of the chimney sweep as mediator, go-between from both worlds, a devil, or, indeed, a fallen angel, is a familiar one in English culture. Recall William Blake's poem 'The Chimney Sweeper', Charles Lamb's well-known text 'The Praise of Chimney Sweepers' in 'Essays of Elia', Charles Kingsley's 'The Water-Babies', and 'The Three Sleeping Boys of Warwickshire' by Walter de la Mare.
124 Alain Montandon, Préface, in *Mythes et représentations de l'hospitalité*, ed. Alain Montandon (Clermont Ferrand: Université Blaise Pascal, 1999), 11–21.
125 Bertrand Russell, *Autobiography* (London and New York: Routledge, 1998), 29.
126 In France, by comparison, the cultural tradition of practical jokes is not so salient.
127 Pelham G. Wodehouse, *Very Good, Jeeves* (London: Random House-Penguin, 2005), 23.
128 Ibid.
129 José Ortega y Gasset, *Toward a Philosophy of History* (Urbana: University of Illinois Press, 2002), 130.
130 Ibid.
131 See Jacques Derrida, *De l'hospitalité*. Anne Dufourmantelle invite Jacques Derrida à répondre sur l'hospitalité (Paris: Calmann Levy, 1997), 73.
132 In another incident, the employees of a certain company created a special website which stated that the boss of the enterprise was being sought by police. The site caused quite a stir. Eventually, it was discovered that it was only available within the office.

Chapter Five

THE BODY

The Dandy's Body

> *True dandyism is the result of an artistic temperament working upon a fine body within the wide limits of fashion.*
> Sir Max Beerbohm

In his 1821 essay 'On the Look of a Gentleman', the English essayist and critic William Hazlitt offers a fascinating description of the true gentleman:

> Ease, grace, dignity have been given as the exponents and expressive symbols of this look; but I would rather say, that a habitual self-possession determines the appearance of a gentleman. He should have the complete command, not only over his countenance, but over his limbs and motions. In other words, he should discover in his air and manner a voluntary power over his whole body, which with every inflection of it, should be under the control of his will. It must be evident that he looks and does as he likes, without any restraint, confusion, or awkwardness. He is, in fact, master of his person, as the professor of any art or science is of a particular instrument; he directs it to what use he pleases and intends. Wherever this power and facility appear, we recognize the look and deportment of the gentleman, – that is, of a person who by his habits and situation in life, and in his ordinary intercourse with society, has had little else to do than to study those movements, and that carriage of the body, which were accompanied with most satisfaction to himself, and were calculated to excite the approbation of the beholder.[1]

This description fully works for the corporeality of a dandy. Of huge value both from a cultural and an anthropological perspective, Hazlitt's canon describes the nineteenth-century ideal: a gentleman able to use and control his body as one would a precise and sophisticated instrument. At ease and free, he is adept at showcasing his body to pleasing effect. Following this somewhat general introduction, Hazlitt proceeds to go into more detail:

> Ease, it might be observed, is not enough; dignity is too much. There must be a certain retenu,[2] a conscious decorum, added to the first, – and a certain 'familiarity of regard, quenching the austere countenance of control,' in the other, to answer to our conception of this character.[3]

From these aphoristic descriptions, we may deduce how Hazlitt perceived the distinction between a dandy and a gentleman. For him, the dandy was 'the fine gentleman', one who exhibits particular elegance. 'Perhaps propriety is as near a word as any to denote the manners of the gentleman; elegance is necessary to the fine gentleman.'[4]

One man who, in Hazlitt's eyes, habitually possessed such elegance was Richard Colley Wellesley. 'Elegance is something more than ease; it is more than a freedom from awkwardness or restraint. It implies, I conceive, a precision, a polish, a sparkling effect, spirited yet delicate, which is perfectly exemplified in Lord Wellesley's face and figure,'[5] the essayist writes. According to Hazlitt, the impression produced by a gentleman is always connected with his manner, dress, and deportment.

Elegance and Movement

Beauty and the body are all but impossible to discuss, without alluding to the historical and cultural context. Throughout history, elegance in dress has always in no small measure been linked to the specific properties of costume. Movement, after all, is largely determined by the possibilities offered by dress. Throughout the ages, attire has been designed with particular activities and gestures in mind: limiting certain movements, clothing was made to ease others. Eighteenth-century panniers,[6] for instance, did not allow ladies' arms to hang by their sides, which came to be regarded as normal. Not until the late nineteenth century did ladies' attire evolve to offer greater freedom, allowing women to ride bicycles. Even in the 1920s, Coco Chanel had difficulty convincing male couturiers of the need for generous armholes for women: why, after all, would a lady ever need to lift her arms, they would shrug.

The degree of freedom offered by a garment depended on factors such as its tightness and elasticity. In the early seventeenth century, English dress shifted from old rigid outlines to more elastic materials, the changes bringing about a different manner in comportment.

> In conversing with his companions, the nobleman was now able not only to stand, stiff as a pillar, but to lean forward, stepping out a little with his right foot. Holding himself with a new lightness, he was able, without bringing the conversation to a standstill, to exchange a few words with those around him. This new, simple and casual image of the English aristocrat emerged thanks to… industrial development, which was so advanced that many fabrics were produced with a greater degree of elasticity.[7]

Maria Mertsalova's meticulous description reveals a striking detail: male elegance was beginning to be associated with a highly mobile body. The ideal social person, it seems, was agile, self-possessed, and able to maintain elegance of movement in any situation.

In 'The Guermantes Way', Marcel Proust introduces us to the young dandy and aristocrat Robert de Saint-Loup. On one memorable occasion, Saint-Loup vaults over tables and makes his way along the back of a bench in a restaurant to pass a coat to his friend Marcel. Diners gaze on enrapt as he leaps over wires, moving gracefully across the space; Marcel sees the escapade as a demonstration of aristocratic corporeality. For him, natural physical grace is a sign of noble origin. Saint-Loup's easy agility makes his body appear 'significant and limpid', rendering

> the movements of that light-footed course that Robert had pursued along the wall as intelligible and charming as those of horsemen on a marble frieze.[8]

For Proust, physical agility and 'certainty of taste' is the equivalent of aristocratic 'naturalness', an intuitive second-by-second sensing of the correct way to behave in given circumstances.

The body of Saint-Loup, which Marcel sees as quintessentially aristocratic, is perhaps of greater importance to him than his friend's moral qualities. Saint-Loup's manner, Marcel muses, displays the nature 'that by birth and upbringing he had inherited from his race': innate simplicity, ease of deportment, and a noble liberality. 'The leaping Saint-Loup is a spiritualised figure embodying the concept of the aristocrat, if we take that concept to imply a limpid body,' Merab Mamardashvili suggests in his lectures on Proust.[9] What we see here is not merely a beautiful body, but the beautiful body of the nobility: in a class of its own, this is a mystical phantom of good-looking, noble aristocracy.

Despite Marcel's impressions, the elegance and grace of Saint-Loup were not, of course, entirely innate; not so much 'born with them', he cultivated them through rigorous training. A soldier, Saint-Loup had been taught to ride, and in his youth he certainly took dance lessons.

Among the social skills, dance occupied a special spot. A happy fusion of physical exercise, musical sensitivity, and sense of rhythm, it was taught to both boys and girls without fail (Figure 18). For many, it laid important foundations for good posture and graceful movement. As Raisa Kirsanova rightly notes, the poses adopted by sitters in old portraits were often connected with dance. Upright bearing, head

Figure 18 The first quadrille at Almacks. From left to right: Marquis of Worcester, Lady Jersey, Clanronald Macdonald, Lady Worcester. Source of illustration: Gronow R. H. Reminiscences of Captain Gronow, being anecdotes of the camp, the court and the clubs at the close of the last war with France. L.: Smith, Elder and Co, 1862.

held high, elbows out to the sides, good turnout – all these elements of posture were taught as part of dance.

A basic requirement for children, upright posture was often seen as synonymous with goodness and strength of character. A straight back not merely implied moral rectitude, but furthermore served as a sign of noble birth: for this reason, portraits of aristocrats from the same era tend to share a subtle resemblance. 'Elegance of posture in everyday life became an indicator of class, a more accurate sign of "genuineness" than dress or hairstyle,' Raisa Kirsanova writes.[10]

Social discipline required the mastering of certain skills, the most significant physical characteristic being posture. Besides holding the back straight, however, the fashionable socialite also had to learn to handle canes, hats, snuffboxes, and coffee cups, to wear a suit well, and to move elegantly.

> Mme. de Guermantes advanced upon me, that I might lead her to the table, and without my feeling the least shadow of the timidity that I might have feared, for, like a huntress to whom her great muscular prowess has made graceful motion an easy thing, observing no doubt that I had placed myself on the wrong side of her, she pivoted with such accuracy round me that I found her arm resting on mine and attuned in the most natural way to a rhythm of precise and noble movements. I yielded to these with all the more readiness in that the Guermantes attached no more importance to them than does to learning a truly learned man in whose company one is less alarmed than in that of a dunce…[11]

The 'inconspicuous' grace of the duchess recalls the dandy principle of 'conspicuous inconspicuousness' in dress.

A typical list of aristocratic talents may be found in Balzac's 'The Girl with the Golden Eyes'. Recall the writer's description of the dandy Henri de Marsay, based on the Count D'Orsay:

> Underneath this fresh young life, and in spite of the limpid springs in his eyes, Henri had a lion's courage, a monkey's agility. He could cut a ball in half at ten paces on the blade of a knife; he rode his horse in a way that made you realize the fable of the Centaur; drove a four-in-hand with grace; was as light as a cherub and quiet as a lamb, but knew how to beat a townsman at the terrible game of *savate* or cudgels; moreover, he played the piano in a fashion which would have enabled him to become an artist should he fall on calamity, and owned a voice which would have been worth to Barbaja fifty thousand francs a season.[12]

Henri de Marsay is portrayed as an aristocratic dandy with exceptionally striking looks. In the first decades of the nineteenth century, dandy self-possession and composure were honed through rigorous sporting activity. Many dandies had been through military service, learning, at the very least, to hold themselves upright, wear their uniform with style, and ride a horse. Beau Brummell himself, of course, had served with the Tenth Royal Hussars, and his close friend, the well-known society wit Lord Alvanley, had even taken part in the unsuccessful Walcheren Campaign launched to seize Antwerp from the French in 1809.

In the early nineteenth century, an extremely popular form of physical activity was racing, as young bloods vied with each other in walking, running, and riding. Bets were common, with hefty sums gained and lost. In 1808, Alvanley ran a mile along the Edgware Road in under six minutes, winning fifty guineas. In September 1807, another officer won a thousand guineas in a bet for riding from Ipswich to London, a distance of seventy miles, in four hours and fifty minutes.

A renowned sportsman of Regency London was 'Gentleman' John Jackson. A bare-knuckle boxing champion, his academy in Old Bond Street was celebrated among young bloods, and Lord Byron was among the many fashion-conscious men who took lessons from 'Gentleman' John. Besides pugilism, Jackson excelled in sprinting, jumping, and other sports. Walking around London, he was said to cover five and a half miles an hour. Among his most striking feats, allegedly, was writing his name with an eighty-four-pound weight suspended from his little finger.

The formidable sportsman boasted an exceptional physique. Contemporaries referred to him as the 'finest formed man in Europe': six feet tall, he weighed fourteen stone, and possessed ' "noble shoulders", a narrow waist; beautiful calves, delicate ankles and small, fine hands' (Figure 19).[13]

Well aware of his handsome looks, 'Gentleman' John chose flamboyant, eye-catching clothing to complete the effect. Favouring bright colours, he could be seen in a scarlet coat with gold trim, frills of fine lace, pale blue satin waistcoat decorated with white, buff knee breeches, striped white silk stockings, and pumps with

Figure 19 Sir Henry Smyth. John Jackson at his boxing academy. Source of illustration: Pierce Egan. Boxiana; Or, Sketches of Ancient and Modern Pugilism. (1830). Wikimedia Commons.

paste buckles. His striking outfits caught the eye not merely with their vivid hues and bold design, but also with their deliberate, exaggerated eighteenth-century archaism. The message was, clearly, that the wearer was unique, unconventional, quite unlike anyone else. Abhorring the ordinary, Jackson presented himself as a gentleman of times gone by, a Gulliver-like giant among Lilliputhians.

The Sporting Dandy

Among the dandies there existed two distinct trends: the bucks and the beaux. The bucks were sporting types, lovers of physical activity, and the beaux, from the French word meaning 'handsome', more effete, men of fashion.

Although the two types were frequently in close contact, they were markedly different. Beaux were not known for their love of athletic activities, and were often disdainful of sporting enthusiasts. Preferring to spend their time on fashion and self-care, the beaux liked always to be preened from head to toe. Flâneurs, for them, the best pastime was a casual stroll through the town, a visit to their favourite antique shop, or to their tailor. Despising 'coarse' village pursuits such as fox hunting and racing, they made no secret of their contempt. At one time, Beau Brummell even attempted to change the rules of Watier's to bar village squires who smelled of the stables.

The bucks, however, were happy with their horses, hunting, and boxing. Many noblemen at that time sponsored boxers, who fought under their patronage and gave them lessons. Lord Byron was a keen boxer, relying on the activity to stop the dreaded weight from piling on. One of the best-known boxing clubs in London was, of course, the academy in Old Bond Street owned by 'Gentleman' John Jackson.

In his novel 'Rodney Stone', Sir Arthur Conan Doyle describes a typical social event centred around boxing.

> It was at the end of my first week in London that my uncle gave a supper to the fancy, as was usual for gentlemen of that time if they wished to figure before the public as Corinthians and patrons of sport. He had invited not only the chief fighting-men of the day, but also those men of fashion who were most interested in the ring... The rumour that the Prince was to be present had already spread through the clubs, and invitations were eagerly sought after.[14]

Besides such suppers, as Pierce Egan shows us in his renowned novel 'Life in London',[15] young bucks enjoyed socialising at balls, in gambling houses, parks, boxing clubs, and horse auctions. Some of their pursuits might, to the modern reader, appear outlandish: a popular early nineteenth-century pastime, for instance, was coaching. Young men established teams which raced against each other; for many, this was not merely a prestigious hobby, but a way of life. Known as whips, for their coaching sorties these bucks favoured not merely the fashionable West End, but most of the growing metropolis. Lovers of thoroughbred horses and high-quality carriages, they embraced the skills of country squires, even when based in the city. A thorough knowledge of horse and dog breeding, excellent coach-driving skills, and the ability to put up a good fight were the main attributes valued in these circles.

Christian Goede describes a typical buck's day thus:

> Of such a one, a single day describes the whole life: he thinks of rising about eleven in the morning and, having taken a slight breakfast, puts on his riding coat and repairs to the stables. Having inspected his horses, asked a hundred questions of his coachmen and grooms, and given as many orders, he either rides on a horseback, or in his curricle, attended by two grooms, dashing through all the fashionable streets of Hyde Park... visits the shops of the most noted coachmakers and saddlers... After bespeaking something or other there, he repairs to Tattersall's[16] where he meets all his friends seriously engaged in studying the pedigree or merits of the horses... or in discussing the invaluable properties of a pointer... drives from one exhibition to the other, stops at the caricature shops and, about three, drives to a fashionable hotel. Here he takes his lunch... and at five strolls home. His toilet he finds prepared and his valet waiting for him... by seven he is dressed and goes to dinner... At nine he goes to the play, not to see it... but to flirt from box to box, to look at ladies... and to show himself... he then proceeds to one or two routs... about four in the morning, exhausted... he returns home.[17]

Manoeuvring their coaches through the narrow streets of London, the young men showed off their driving skills and prowess. Among their firm favourites were the Tilbury and Dennett gigs, much used for everyday trips around town. For special occasions, carriages with four horses were preferred; the carriage of the Prince of Wales was usually drawn by six.

Many young bucks strove not only to drive their carriages like seasoned coachmen, but to imitate their manners. Cursing and spitting, some went so far as to remove one of their front teeth, in order to spit more authentically. One Mr. Ackers not only had a tooth pulled out, but paid fifty guineas to the famous Cambridge coach driver Richard Vaughan, known as Hell-Fire-Dick, who taught him to spit tobacco. Another prized skill was knowledge of Cockney rhyming slang, with young men who could speak the dialect held in particular esteem.

The bucks had their own clubs: the Four Horses, the Defiance Club, and the Tandem Club. The ever-popular Four Horses was known by a variety of names such as the Four-in-Hand, the Barouche Club, or the Whip Club. Members wore special uniforms with single-breasted dark-green coats with long waist and yellow buttons, waistcoats with yellow or blue stripes, white breeches, short boots, and deep, wide-brimmed hats. Many wore sprigs of myrtle or geranium in their buttonhole.[18]

Occasionally, the whips liked their dress to match the horses' trappings, forming a complete ensemble with their equipage. John Timbs describes the carriages of the best-known driving club, the Four-in-Hand.

> The vehicles of the Club which were formerly used are described as of a hybrid class, quite as elegant as private carriages and lighter than even the mails. They were horsed with the finest animals that money could secure. In general, the whole four in each carriage were admirably matched... The master generally drove the team, often a nobleman of high rank,

who commonly copied the dress of a mail coachman. The company usually rode outside, but two footmen in rich liveries were indispensable on the back seat, nor was it at all uncommon to see some splendidly attired female on the box. A rule of the Club was that all members should turn out three times a week; and the start was made at mid-day, from the neighbourhood of Piccadilly, through which they passed to the Windsor-road,—the attendants of each carriage playing on their silver bugles. From twelve to twenty of these handsome vehicles often left London together.[19]

Wealthy aristocrats did their utmost to be taken for professional coachmen, imitating their speech, manners, and habits. How does one explain so seemingly strange a phenomenon? 'With their studied transgression of class roles – and with horses impacting nearly every aspect of British life – clubs like the Four-in-Hand cut daringly across the boundaries of sporting, dandy, and military cultures, attracting aristocrats, officers, and other young professionals,' Michael Gamer notes.[20]

In many ways, this obsession with speed and 'lowly' pursuits can be seen as similar to the later biker craze, and the races of the Hell's Angels. For many, speed, of course, offers a devil-may-care allure, an aura of danger and attraction. At that time, coaching at breakneck speeds was perhaps the only available form of extreme urban sport.

Another likely factor was the enduring popularity of equestrian sports in England. The eighteenth century was precisely the period when skilled horsemanship became the subject of public gatherings, turning into a mass attraction. In 1768, Philip Astley, a Sergeant Major with a passion for riding, established the first modern circus in London. This traced its beginnings to Astley's Amphitheatre, a riding school ran by Astley with his wife.[21] In 1780, Astley's competitor Charles Dibdin opened the rival Royal Circus in London, turning this form of entertainment into a regular favourite. In theatres, acts with horses never failed. When a special scene involving twenty horses was included in the Covent Garden production of 'Blue Beard' in 1811, audience numbers leapt up.

None of this, however, fully explains why affluent noblemen went against the class hierarchy by imitating the manners and dress of coachmen. A better insight can be gained by taking a closer look at the relations between different social groups in Regency England. Wealthy peers were not well-disposed towards bourgeois circles, with bankers and financiers barred from gentlemen's clubs and aristocratic salons. At the same time, noblemen were not above conversing with simple folk, like country squires, who knew all the workers and servants on their estate. 'Ordinary people' were, of course, also frequently the heroes of Romantic-era verse. Their appealing skills such as athleticism, the ability to drive a carriage, and good knowledge of horse and dog breeds meant that light-hearted appropriation of their style became a commonplace form of social bravado.

Besides coachmen, in the early nineteenth century, aristocrats, as we mentioned earlier, also 'adopted' boxers. The supper for pugilists described by Conan Doyle takes place in a modest public house.

> The Waggon and Horses was a well-known sporting house, with an old prize-fighter for landlord. And the arrangements were as primitive as the most Bohemian could wish. It was one of the many curious fashions which have now died out, that men who were *blasé* from luxury and high living seemed to find a fresh piquancy in life by descending

to the lowest resorts, so that the night-houses and gambling-dens in Covent Garden or the Haymarket often gathered illustrious company under their smoke-blackened ceilings. It was a change for them to turn their backs upon the cooking of Weltjie and of Ude, or the chambertin of old Q., and to dine upon a porter-house steak washed down by a pint of ale from a pewter pot.[22]

The novel describes the rivalry between two wealthy noblemen-turned-coachmen. One of them, Sir John Lade,

with his many-caped coat, his white hat, and his rough, weather-beaten face, might have taken his seat with a line of professionals upon any ale-house bench without any one being able to pick him out as one of the wealthiest landowners in England.[23]

Taking his 'peculiarities' to great lengths in another example of socialist morals, Sir John marries the sweetheart of a highwayman who had been executed. Lady Letty proves to be his match in her ability both to curse, and to drive a carriage. Sir John's rival, Sir Charles Tregellis, is a well-known dandy who owns a magnificent equipage drawn by two horses. Unlike Sir John, Sir Charles does not attempt to imitate coachmen: immaculately turned out, he pays great attention to his appearance, does not curse, and can compete with George Brummell in matters of fashion. Sir Charles wins his race against Sir John, all the time observing the gentleman's code of honour. Lady Letty, however, is not so compliant: risking a suspect manoeuvre, she puts her horse in danger. Gentlemen's honour was, indeed, at times a factor which distinguished aristocratic whips from lovers of speed of more humble origins.

Further fascinating examples of this kind may be found throughout the history of the prestigious Jockey Club. In Newmarket, horseracing is recorded to have taken place from the days of James I in the seventeenth century.[24] The popular races were accompanied by bets, which were placed not only by the wealthy, but also by the poor. Moneyed aristocrats were known to bet fortunes on the horses, yet the entire system was corrupt and poorly organized. Lawmakers sought in vain to bring the situation under control with the aid of special Bills, as the seemingly indomitable fraudsters continued to thrive. Finally, in 1750, the Jockey Club was established and soon set up premises in Newmarket. Among its founders were some of the most influential figures in society, whose horses regularly took part in the races. At that time, it was usual for the horses to be ridden by the owners themselves, the practice of hiring jockeys emerging somewhat later. Thanks to this powerful new body, a set of rules governing the races was established, encompassing all aspects from the weighing of jockeys to the betting procedure. The success of the wealthy horseracing lobby, Paul Johnson claims, demonstrated an important trend:

What the Jockey club established was that even in a sport like horseracing, which was peculiarly susceptible to corruption, the most effective mode of control was not legislation and police, but the arbitrary rulings of an unelected body whose verdicts were unchallenged because the social status and wealth of its members made them disinterested.[25]

The most effective means of change, Johnson concludes, proves to be unofficial control by a lobby of leading figures.

The rules established by this group of aristocrats came to be treated as something of a sporting code of honour for gentlemen. For many years, the Jockey Club refused to publish any names, yet its prestigious membership was well-known. Made up of some of the wealthiest and most influential figures in society, including members of the Royal Family, the club saw horseracing take its place as a leading form of entertainment. In 1780, the Twelfth Earl of Derby first hosted the race which took his name and turned into a world-famous yearly event.

By the late eighteenth century, aristocrats commonly employed professional jockeys to take part in races. This, Johnson points out, made for another important principle of the sport.

> Racing was the first sport to professionalize itself and attract mass-following. The notion that its professionals should be closely supervised by eminent amateurs became the model for the regulation of all sport, first national, then international.[26]

The aristocratic members of the Jockey Club presided over racing in the same way as the patronesses of Almack's managed the famous Assembly Rooms.[27] Anyone caught cheating, or failing to observe the rules, was immediately banished. Thus, in 1791, the Prince of Wales was told to stop using his jockey Sam Chifney, who was suspected of deliberately finishing late in order to ensure better winnings in the next race. Outraged, the Prince sold all his horses, and terminated his connection with racing.

The Jockey Club's acclaim continued to rise. After its members purchased the Newmarket racecourse, the body's informal authority received a solid economic boost. At the beginning of the nineteenth century, the Two Thousand Guineas Stakes and One Thousand Guineas Stakes were established, and became prestigious yearly fixtures. The Jockey Club also brought out the Racing Calendar and General Stud Book, popular publications which were carefully studied in every high-society home.

By the end of the eighteenth century, the role and status of racing in English life were such, that the Jockey Club was seen as a cultural emblem of the country. Riding dress had a vast impact on fashion, the English-riding coat evolving into the universal French redingote. Riding boots and light breeches became staple ingredients of men's fashion not only in England but also in France. In the mid-1790s, French fashion went through a phase of Anglomania. The outfit of Pierre Sériziat in Jacques-Louis David's well-known portrait from 1795, for instance, clearly shows British influence: clothed in a dark green riding coat and light suede breeches, the sitter is holding a riding crop.

Several decades later, in the 1830s, France saw a fresh wave of Anglomania, which, this time around, led to the opening of the Jockey Club de Paris. Among its founders was the eminent racing expert Lord Henry Seymour, who came to be known as the father of French racing. Largely thanks to Seymour, the 1830s saw the revival of the vogue for all things English, and knowledge of horses and racing came to be seen as highly chic.

According to Anne Martin-Fugier,

To be seen as a 'lion' or a dandy, one must, among other things, become a member of the Jockey Club, and break a rib or two in a steeplechase. In practice, however, many members of the club had never taken part in any races, and merely made a huge fuss of horses... in their conversation.[28]

Thus, the English passion for sports did not, seemingly, entirely communicate itself to French dandies: in France, bucks were far fewer.

In nineteenth-century England, the two types of dandies continued distinctly separate, although both trends evolved over time. The beaux looked down on sports, seeing horses as fashion accessories, rather than sporting companions. The closest they came to coaching would be a slow ride through the London streets in a comfortable, compact vis-à-vis phaeton, or placing a bet on the horses. Any activity which risked spoiling their immaculate looks was frowned upon. Stemming from the seventeenth and eighteenth centuries, by the end of the nineteenth, the tradition of the beaux led to the emergence of Aesthetic dandies.

A notable few men could be said to have combined the features of beaux, and bucks. One of these exceptions was the Count D'Orsay: a handsome, immaculately turned out man, he was also an active lover of sports.

Corporeality: Poses and Gestures

The true dandy's posture and gestures were always aimed at demonstrating his worth. Each movement had to be precise, brief, and elegant. The chiastic pose with one leg drawn slightly back produced an impression of perfect stability and self-sufficiency. Contemporary writings on style and elegance insisted that readers should on no account make excessive gestures with the hands, waving the arms or raising them above their head. The hands were to be kept out of one's pockets[29] (Figure 20) and preferably occupied by holding some elegant accessory such as a cane, snuffbox or monocle. Thus, the bodily canon of dandyism revolved around forming a smooth protective shell of elegant motions, forming the frame of sparse self-expression.

Although the gestures of a true dandy are minimal, yet beneath this economy lies a wealth of meaning. Just a glance and nod from Brummell could be regarded as financial transaction. In the episode I have already discussed, one of dandy's creditors reminded him of a debt, to which Brummell answered that he had already paid by greeting him from the window of White's.'[30] Sitting by the bow window in White's club in London, George Brummell would nod graciously to acquaintances, with this simple acknowledgement bestowing upon them more prestige than any flowery, effusive utterance could ever do.

The dandy's laconic yet potent signals can, in their expediency, be compared to those of a fearsome gangster, whose slight click of the fingers can decide a man's fate. Analysing the poetics of gangster 'cool', Roland Barthes observed that such crisp gestures are in fact based on a myriad of cultural traditions, 'from the numen of the old gods, whose nod of the head would topple the destiny of mortals, to the touch of the fairy's

Figure 20 Dandies of 1831. A rare picture of breaking the rules: a dandy holds his hands in the pockets probably because it is cold – he is wearing a warm redingote. Journal des Dames et des Modes. 1831. Wikimedia Commons.

(or the magician's) wand'.[31] The depth of meaning of the gangster's curt signals can be attributed to the fact that in bypassing words, they are directly connected to action.

But this gesture, in order to signify that it is identical with action, must refine any extravagance, compress itself to the perceptual sill of its existence; it must have no more than the density of a liaison between cause and effect.[32]

The dandy's slick movements operate under the same laws. His sangfroid can indeed be seen as a manifestation of 'conspicuous inconspicuousness'. All necessary information concerning the dandy's persona can be gleaned from a series of minute yet telling signs. Attention to detail in dress, as in the corporeal, ensures that minimalist movements will not go unnoticed. A dandy's demonstrative gestures might include, for instance, opening one's snuffbox with a series of precise, practiced moves. For Beau Brummell, taking snuff involved something of a performance. Standing in a special pose and holding the snuffbox in his left hand, he would give onlookers a good view of his impeccably tailored waistcoat. Next, snapping the box open with a deft click of the thumb, he would take a pinch of snuff with his right hand in such a way as to simultaneously show off his elegant gold ring, exquisitely embroidered cambric handkerchief peeping tastefully from his coat sleeve, and just the right length of pristine shirt cuff.

Accordingly, the dandy's gestures were the ideal embodiment of the principle of economy and deliberate minimalism in the corporeal.

Corporeality: Inscrutable Face

William Hazlitt has made some striking and meticulous observations on the facial expression of the man of the world:

> Instead of an intense unity of purpose, wound up to some great occasion, it is dissipated and frittered down into a number of evanescent expressions, fitted for every variety of unimportant occurrences: instead of the expansion of general thought or intellect, you trace chiefly the little, trite, cautious, movable lines of conscious but concealed self-complacency.[33]

Hazlitt likewise noted the gentleman's 'familiarity of regard, quenching the austere countenance of control'. The facial expression of the man of the world is constantly shifting, metamorphosing, as fleeting, frequently contradictory moods take hold of his features. Hazlitt himself referred to this flux as the 'telegraphic machinery of polite expression'.[34]

Thus, the overall impression produced by such a face is one of *inscrutability*. Whilst dynamic, it remains closed to any attempts at interpretation. By concealing the wearer's true motives, an expression of inscrutability allows him to assume a position of power and social advantage. In providing a base of calm neutrality, it offers an opportunity to respond in a multitude of ways to any given situation. Beau Brummell was a master of inscrutable gaze.

At the same time complete inscrutability is, according to the founder of transactional analysis Eric Berne, a sheer physical impossibility. Using the name Jeder to refer to the 'typical human being',[35] Berne writes:

> The human nervous system is so constructed that the visual impact on the onlooker of small movements of the facial muscles is greater than the kinesthetic impact on the subject. A two-millimetre movement of one of the small muscles around the mouth may be quite imperceptible to Jeder but quite obvious to his companions.[36]

Human facial muscles are extremely mobile, and most of us aren't always aware of how much our facial expression betrays what we are feeling. During the first few seconds of an encounter, our interlocutors can glean much more information about us than we think. Children, with their unashamed staring, may often gain an especially accurate picture of our moods and intentions. Furthermore, Berne suggests, our facial expression involuntarily conveys a wealth of basic information concerning our life path, strength of character and personality.

> He [Jeder] is continually giving out script signals without being aware of it. Others respond ultimately to these signals, instead of to Jeder's persona or presentation of himself. In this way the script is kept going without Jeder having to take the responsibility for it.[37]

Our first impression of an interlocutor depends largely on his or her facial expression. A frank, open expression throws open the doors, spontaneously revealing a person's character and preferred mode of communication. A face that appears hard to control is often associated with a rebellious nature, whereas an inscrutable expression, gained through experience and hours of perseverance, is linked with culture. With his love of artifice and his preference for art over nature, the dandy, of course, always aims to wear an expression of inscrutability. Edward Bulwer-Lytton thus describes one brief, yet highly typical social duel: 'again Thornton looked pryingly into my countenance. Poor fool! It was not for a penetration like his to read the *cor inscrutabile*[38] of a man born and bred like me, in the consummate dissimilation of *bon ton*'.[39] Here Pelham is, of course, referring to the high-society taboo on showing emotion, which can be seen as the visible expression of the dictum *nil admirari*.

Referring both to the expression of emotion, and to the stance of the body, the dandy canon of inscrutability covers both the inner and the outer worlds. Should a dandy's face happen to betray feeling, this was seen as defeat. A man whose expressions could be 'read' would instantly attract critical or coldly appraising stares, becoming a ready target for cutting comments and gossip. The true dandy's expression, on the other hand, put him in a position of power. Now sharp, now somewhat distrait, it never allowed the man's 'inner child' to emerge, always concealing true feeling beneath an invisible mask of inscrutability.

An inscrutable face could be achieved through other means also. In the middle of the nineteenth century, women used rice powder, which made their faces resemble those of antique statues. Softening their features, the powder created something of an abstraction – an archetype. 'The use of rice-powder […] is successfully designed […] to create an abstract unity in texture and color of the skin, a unity […] like that produced by the tights of a dancer,' wrote Baudelaire.[40] The virtues of cosmetics were also sung by the likes of Théophile Gautier and, later, Max Beerbohm – in keeping with the overall philosophy and with its emphasis on artifice and self-possession.

Optical devices such as the lorgnette, monocle, glasses, and binoculars could likewise be used to create an air of inscrutability. Whilst allowing the user to scrutinize those around at his leisure, they partially concealed his own face, giving him an advantage and something of a fashionable disguise. Furthermore, the use of certain optical devices, most notably, the monocle, demanded of the wearer some considerable skill. Holding the monocle in place required a certain effort and training of the facial muscles. Use of the lorgnette also entailed particular facial expressions: a derisive squint, a raising of the eyebrow. These in themselves were quick to become attributes of the fashionable gentleman, metonymies for observation. In his *Arcades Project*, Walter Benjamin quotes Taxile Delord, the man who proudly claims to have started facial tics:

> It is I who invented tics. At present, the lorgnon has replaced them…. The tic involves closing the eye with a certain movement of the mouth and a certain movement of the coat… The face of an elegant man should always have … something irritated and convulsive about it. One can attribute these facial agitations either to a natural satanism, to the fever of the passions, or finally to anything one likes.[41]

The facial tic can be seen as creating an inscrutable mask of its own, although in its mobility this dynamic face of course differs from the traditional dandy composure.

Yet both extremes – deliberate tic and Stoical composure – are the result of artifice, and a testament to the power of individual will.

The twentieth century brought with it a new fashionable device of concealment and inscrutability – dark glasses. Sunglasses have long been associated with the likes of spies, detectives – and dandies. Contemporary lovers of dark glasses continue to contribute to the iconic cool associated with this image, successfully combining the mysterious air of a spy with the nonchalant elegance of the dandy.

The Quest for Cleanliness: Dandy's Hygiene

All that is elegant is ephemeral, sterile and transient.
Jean Paul Sartre

Buying shampoo or taking a shower nowadays, we are unlikely to ponder on the origin of norms of hygiene. Our habits appear so natural, we may find it difficult to believe that the culture of the body to which we are so accustomed, did not emerge until the early nineteenth century. At that time, English dandies began to introduce 'amusing trifles' in their toilet such as daily bathing, shaving, washing the hair, and elaborate skincare routines.

In those days, urban hygiene was far from what we know today. Nineteenth-century Paris shocked visitors with its stench and cesspools. Even decades earlier, Louis-Sébastien Mercier deplored the putrid air of the French capital,[42] and Balzac, the tireless chronicler of Parisian life, concurred: 'There is a narrow staircase clinging to the wall… each landing being indicated by a stink, one of the most odious peculiarities of Paris.'[43] Angry at the 'moral degradation' of the authorities, which failed to clean up the city's rotting mess, the writer made no secret of his disgust.

> If the air of the houses in which the greater proportion of the middle classes live is noxious, if the atmosphere of the streets belches out cruel miasmas into stuffy back-kitchens where there is little air, realize that, apart from this pestilence, the forty thousand houses of this great city have their foundations in filth, which the powers that be have not yet seriously attempted to enclose with mortar walls solid enough to prevent even the most fetid mud from filtering through the soil, poisoning the wells, and maintaining subterraneously to Lutetia[44] the tradition of her celebrated name. Half of Paris sleeps amidst the putrid exhalations of courts and streets and sewers.[45]

As historians such as Georges Vigarello[46] and Alain Corbin[47] have shown, seventeenth- and eighteenth-century Europeans commonly resorted to 'dry cleaning'. Courtiers of Louis XIV, for instance, would wipe their faces and hands with perfumed serviettes, leaving the rest of the body as it was. The air at balls and social gatherings would be heavy with sweat, absorbing the smell of unwashed bodies.

Even in the first half of the nineteenth century, washing was a complicated business. The practical side was far from simple, requiring the heating of large tanks of water. Most families of average means could only afford a shared bath once a week at best, usually on Saturdays, when the bathing would become something of a ceremonial ritual.

The poor were unable to afford anything of the kind. The laundry posed another problem. Wealthier households hired washerwomen, who heated huge vats of water and scrubbed, bleached, starched, and ironed clothes by hand.[48] Less fortunate families simply washed their clothes in the river, or any nearby stretch of water.

The English, it seems, were clearly ahead of European standards in hygiene.

> Their attitude to washing already cut them off from most Continental nations… The stress placed on cleanliness and constant bathing by dandies like Beau Brummell and Lord Byron was an important factor.[49]

London's drains, furthermore, were in a far better state than those of Paris. In the early nineteenth century, wooden pipes made of elm were laid, which in the early 1840s were substituted with metal.

The English attentiveness towards the body had its roots in the dandy tradition. For the gentleman, indeed, self-respect began with the ennoblement of his most basic corporeal needs. English dandies not only accepted, but perfected standards of hygiene: the reputation of Englishmen as Europe's champions in cleanliness in the nineteenth century was largely due to dandyism.

George Brummell, whose influence in the early nineteenth century was considerable, is chiefly known as the creator of the modern canon of male elegance. Besides matters of sartorial taste, however, this canon also introduced a new model of corporeality, which included personal hygiene. Famed for his neatness, Brummell also stood out due to his unusual body care habits. According to captain Jesse,

> There was in fact nothing extreme about Brummell's personal appearance but his extreme cleanliness and neatness, and whatever time and attention he devoted to is dress, the result was perfect. No perfumes, he used to say, but very fine linen, plenty of it, and country washing.[50]

The dandy changed his shirt three times a day and, if he noticed the tiniest of blemishes, immediately sent the shirt back to the washerwoman.[51] The Beau's laundry, indeed, accounted for a not inconsiderable portion of his spending.

Changing his undergarments every day, Brummell turned morning baths into a daily routine. His outlandish habits were much discussed, frequently giving rise to gossip and anecdotes. Most of Brummell's friends would bathe extremely seldom, preferring to use scent to mask the smell of sweat. The Beau took a stance in rejecting the constant use of scent: he simply had no such need of it.

Brummell's morning ritual involved a number of stages. His morning shave was famous: thanks to him, it became fashionable for dandies to be clean-shaven. Among the Beau's accessories were a silver shaving bowl and sets of cut-throat razors. After shaving, he would commence his lengthy ablutions, which lasted around two hours. The final stage would see Brummell bathing in milk, not unlike Cleopatra.[52] More often than not, the milk would subsequently be resold: many Londoners, indeed, feared to purchase milk, afraid that the dandy might already have used it for his own purposes.

Brummell took his toilet extremely seriously. In the words of his biographer Captain William Jesse, a military man, the Beau possessed an entire 'batterie de toilette'.

Among his favourite accessories were a striking water jug of blue glass, decorated with exotic birds, a silver spitting bowl (Brummell liked to joke that one 'could not spit into clay'), and a large basin, which accompanied the Beau on his trips.

After bathing, Brummell would perform a series of cosmetic procedures, scrubbing his back and chest with a hard brush until the skin glowed bright red. Arming himself with a long-handled mirror, the type used by dentists, he would seek out and remove any stray hairs from his face with the aid of tweezers.

The entire morning routine took around three hours, and was faithfully performed every single day, much to the amazement of Brummell's contemporaries.[53] Even the Beau's chronicler Captain Jesse struggled to comprehend the practice:

> Be it remembered, that these farcical details were daily repeated when he was upwards of fifty years of age, and in the full possession of all his faculties![54]

After being forced to emigrate to France, the Beau found himself in jail for debt, yet even in prison, he contrived to remain faithful to his routine. In a letter to Charles Armstrong, he requested that his friend send him three clean towels a day, and bade him look after his favourite washing accessories, which he had been forced to leave in his hotel: 'Let the large basin and water-jug be taken great care of.'[55]

Eventually, Brummell was able to find a way to get all these beloved objects sent on to his cell. Finally reunited with his basin, jug, mirror, tweezers, silver shaving bowl, and spitting bowl, he even reclaimed his 'comestibles', soaps, pomades, cologne, and a travel necessaire with an abundance of small jars and bottles. With the benevolent protection of the jail's warden, the Beau was able to recommence his three-hour sessions in all their glory. Every morning, twelve to fourteen litres of water and two litres of milk would be delivered to him for bathing, his servant musing regretfully that for the price of the milk, an entire glass of spirits might have been purchased.[56] Nonetheless, upon hearing of Brummell's death sometime later, the servant was said to have been genuinely distraught, and wept.

So striking and unusual appeared Brummell's quest for cleanliness,[57] that it could not fail to be picked up by writers and thinkers of the era. Soon, it became associated with dandyism in general, with novelists depicting narcissistic heroes, much given to long, self-indulgent bathing sprees. Bulwer-Lytton's Pelham presents a perfect example:

> I was a luxurious personage in those days. I had had a bath made from my own design; across it were constructed two small frames – one for the journal of the day, and another to hold my breakfast apparatus; in this manner I was accustomed to lie for about an hour, engaging the triple happiness of reading, feeding, and bathing.[58]

For many puritanical English readers, such decadence might have been off-putting; in France though, such passages were studied with great delight by aspiring dandies. By the middle of the century, a philosophical version of French dandyism had formed. The Gallic followers of Brummell and Pelham liked to imitate their aesthetic and hygienic habits, changing their clothes frequently, and taking long baths. Balzac's hero Henri de Marsay takes his lead from Brummell in everything.

Laurent had set before his master such a quantity of utensils, so many different articles of such elegance, that Paul could not refrain from saying:
"But you will take a couple of hours over that?"
"No!" said Henri, "two hours and a half."[59]

Henri, it seems, is determined to take as long at his toilet as does Brummell. His friend Paul, more ignorant in the matters of dandy elegance, is genuinely bemused:

Why spend two hours and a half in adorning yourself, when it is sufficient to spend a quarter of an hour in your bath, to do your hair in two minutes, and to dress![60]

Henri, 'who was at that moment having his feet rubbed with a soft brush lathered with English soap,' explains that the true dandy is, above all, a fop, and that a man's success with the ladies is largely dependent on his self-care routine.

Women love fops... Do you know of any woman who has had a passion for a sloven, even if he were a remarkable man? ...I have seen most remarkable people left in the lurch because of their carelessness.[61]

In this example, one clearly sees the difference between French and English men of fashion. For a Frenchman, the erotic function of hygiene is paramount. One must be able to undress with confidence, without concern about one's body. The body is cared for as the true final focus of attention: clothes are but a temporary covering. Later, similarly meticulous self-care routines will be observed among the famous Paris courtesans, who can in many ways be seen as following the dandies' trend.

If French beaux took care of their bodies in order to please women, English dandies made the most of their appearance primarily to please themselves. A clean body delights the beau's ego, lending him an air of unassailability and supreme confidence. George Brummell, we should note, was no womanizer, even though he counted many wealthy and fashionable ladies among his acquaintances. His lengthy bathing sessions were rather connected with his personal dignity and pride, which, in turn, allowed him to exude confidence when around others, and, indeed, to perform the role of social dictator.

The Beau's opinion was well-respected and feared by lovers of fashion of both sexes. In pronouncing his verdict, Brummell took cleanliness and neatness to be the key virtues. Once, when asked for his impressions after staying the night with friends in their country home, he answered his host thus: 'Don't ask me, my good fellow, you may imagine, when I tell you, that I actually found a cobweb in my -----!'[62] The Spartan simplicity which had oftentimes sat comfortably with the traditions of the English aristocracy was, by then, quite unacceptable to Brummell, accustomed to urban luxury.

A member of Watier's, the Beau battled to have village squires barred from the exclusive club, so unpalatable did he find the smells of stables and horses. In his youth, Brummell had served in the army and ridden frequently, yet his distaste for the horsey stench was well-known. Living in the city, he preferred to make trips in his equipage, and on rainy days often stayed at home. He disliked his boots getting soiled: Brummell's manservant was instructed to polish even the soles of his footwear.

Receiving this instruction for the first time, the man had been at a loss, whereupon the Beau himself had taken up the brush to demonstrate how this should be done.

In France, Brummell had been forced to contend with dirtier streets. With no carriage, he had no choice but to make his way everywhere on foot. To protect his shoes from the dirt and rain, the Beau developed a special tactic.

> In muddy weather, as there were no *trottoirs*, he was too much occupied with his lower extremities to think of noticing anything but the unequal paving-stones, on the highest of which he always placed his foot, and, so cleverly did he pick his way on the points of his toes, that I have seen him travel the whole length of the street, without contracting one speck of dirt on his boots.[63]

In those days, the dirty streets forced many to wear wooden soles; the Beau, however, refused to ruin his style. Never wearing wooden soles in the day, he allowed himself to resort to them only when returning home at night, safe from view. This was the biggest compromise on style that the dandy was capable of making.

For warding off the rain, Brummell carried an umbrella which folded into a neat, compact silken case. The handle featured a handsome carving of the head of King George IV, and Brummell, it seems, was pleased by its remarkable resemblance. Walking with a friend in wet weather, the Beau would always instruct his companion to keep his distance, to prevent stray splashes from ruining his clothes.

Another novelty introduced by Beau Brummell was his hairstyle. Refusing to wear a wig, the dandy was among the first to sport a short cut. In those days, this gesture had clear Liberal connotations. Wigs in England were firmly linked with Conservatism: all Tory figures wore abundantly powdered hairpieces.[64] In 1795, under Prime Minister William Pitt the Younger, an Act of Parliament introduced a tax on the powder used for wigs. In those days, the powder was made from flour. Later, when wheat was in short supply due to poor harvests, horse chestnuts were used. One of the first public protests against the new tax flared up at Woburn Abbey, as 'a general cropping, washing, and combing out of hair took place'[65] among a group of young noblemen led by the Duke of Bedford. For men accustomed to powdering their hair, the combing out likely entailed removing insects, as well as tangles.

The so-called Crop Clubs, which sprung up in protest at Pitt's powder tax were, however, insufficient to completely turn the tide of European vogue. Only several years later, when the arbiter of fashion Beau Brummell took a clear stance against wigs and long hair, did the trend for crops finally settle.

The change was, in fact, a considerable one, wigs having formed a key element of both male and female fashion for some time. Some owners wore the same hairpiece for decades: wigs were seldom changed. In cases where their use involved a complex, lengthy procedure, the owner would frequently keep the wig on at night. In his 'New Picture of Paris', published in 1781, Louis-Sébastien Mercier vividly describes the inconvenience caused by French women's love of wigs:

> Women would rather suffer unpleasant itching, than renounce their fashionable hairdos. The itching would be alleviated with the aid of a special scraper. The blood would rush to their head, their eyes redden, yet they would persist in erecting their beloved constructions

on their heads. Besides false hair, these also contained large cushions stuffed with horse hair, long pins, which would dig into the scalp, powder, and pomade. The aromatic essences they contained would irritate the skin; the wearer could no longer sweat freely, which posed significant danger. The wearing of such hairpieces wrecked women's health as they consciously shortened their own lifespan, losing the little real hair they possessed, and risking toothache, ear and skin infections, and abscesses.[66]

Besides such lugubrious issues, the attachment to wigs could, at times, quite literally prove fatal, as hairpieces could be the vehicles for transmitting deadly disease. The wig of a noblewoman could, for instance, have been made with the hair of a fatally ill man. Wigs were also often created using hair from corpses, a practice which became especially problematic during outbreaks of the plague. In one notorious case, a doctor treating smallpox patients infected his own daughter through his wig. In another case from 1778, smallpox travelled from London to Plymouth on a doctor's wig.[67]

Wigs, all in all, were far from being safe. If, for doctors and judges, they represented a traditional element of their professional image, for most aristocrats (and their imitators), wigs were all about fashion, and, it seems, most wearers were quite happy to suffer the risks and inconveniences in return for prestige.

Let us take a closer look, then, at the social distribution of 'clean' and 'dirty'. Early eighteenth-century sources offer an interesting example: a young Quaker woman and a wealthy, slovenly fop, travelling in the same carriage. Turned out with 'all the elegance of cleanliness', the young woman wears a neat dark dress, which frames her white hands. Her travelling companion, on the other hand, wears a tangled, greasy wig and old coat, the shoulders of which are covered in hair-powder.[68] The two people are juxtaposed in many ways, through their sex, age, faith, social status, and, finally, their degree of neatness.

The semiotic contrast between clean and dirty is, indeed, clearer when examined through juxtaposition. Within the confines of people's own social groups, these distinctions are less obvious, and personal hygiene habits tend to be more uniform. An outside observer, however, will instantly note the situation – especially if that observer is also an arbiter of fashion. In this case, cleanliness and slovenliness will be seen as carrying additional semiotic weight.

George Brummell developed his innovative code of the dandy toilet reforming eighteenth-century high-society fashion, which was favoured by the Prince of Wales and his circle. In advocating his principles of uncompromising cleanliness, Brummell attempted to introduce this group to a more bourgeois, puritanical style, with reserved understatement in dress and rigorous corporeal self-care routines. Coming from Brummell at that time, the epithet 'dirty' usually applied to the Conservative elite.

A number of interesting parallels may be drawn between Brummell and another great reformer, Coco Chanel, whose impact on twentieth-century women's fashion was truly revolutionary. From a humble bourgeois family, Chanel had never admired the aristocracy. She felt no desire to emulate the 'dirty' noblewomen whom she frequently criticized, her attacks strikingly similar to Brummell's comments about the English lords. Chanel had no qualms about publicly chastising the wealthy women 'with birds in their hair, false hair everywhere, and dresses that dragged on the ground and gathered mud'.[69] Cocottes, on the contrary, were much admired by Chanel: 'I liked the *cocottes*: they were clean.'[70]

> I didn't think the *cocottes* were all that bad. I thought they were pretty with their hats broader than their shoulders, and their big, heavily made-up eyes. They were sumptuous. I admired them far more than the society women. The *cocottes* were clean and well turned out. The others were filthy.[71]

Chanel's preference of the cocottes over wealthier society ladies was chiefly based on her appreciation of their personal hygiene. In the late nineteenth century, cocottes were among the first to adopt significant changes in self-care. Following in the footsteps of the dandies and fops, cocottes were well turned out and clean. Their aim was to please: spending significant sums of money on the best body care products and accessories, they would often install baths of the latest design in their homes. In 'Scenes from a Courtesan's Life', Balzac stresses that his heroine Esther spends more time on her ablutions than the majority of women:

> She then bathed and went through an elaborate toilet which is unknown to most women, for it takes up too much time, and is rarely carried out by any but courtesans, women of the town, or fine ladies who have the day before them. She was only just ready when Lucien came, and appeared before him as a newly opened flower.[72]

Emile Zola's famous courtesan Nana from his 1883 novel despises bourgeois women for their slovenly habits. Sitting naked by the fireside with her lover, she vents her indignation.

> But they're not even clean, your respectable women! No, they're not even clean! I defy you to find one who would dare show herself as I am here. Really, you make me laugh, with your respectable women![73]

In Nana's luxurious dwelling, the dressing room provides a focal point, and it was not uncommon for her to receive visitors immediately after bathing.

> And by a door almost always open, one caught sight of the dressing-room, all in marble and mirrors, with the white basin of its bath, its silver bowls and ewers, its furnishings of crystal and ivory.[74]

The cocotte's main appeal is her sensuous body, of which she takes such good care.

> And cuddling herself up, drawing round her the unfastened dressing-gown she had slipped on, Nana appeared as though she had been surprised at her toilet, her skin scarcely dried, looking smiling though startled in the midst of her laces.[75]

The eroticism of damp skin was seen as a prime element of female beauty: suffice to recall the nude bathers in the 1880s paintings of Edgar Degas.

This notwithstanding, in the nineteenth century, regular bathing was certainly not a common habit. The effects of hot water, on the contrary, were viewed with considerable suspicion: warm baths were said to lead to excessive relaxation, loss of muscle tone and nervous conditions. Overall, frequent bathing was seen as linked with feebleness and frailty: 'One should not take a bath more frequently than once a month,' educators recommended. 'Sitting in the bath for long periods causes indolence and sloth, most inappropriate for a young lady.'[76] Frequent hot baths, doctors warned, may make one less productive. For all his dandy regard for cleanliness, during periods of intense creative activity, Balzac would cease to bathe, fearing he might lose his concentration.

In the nineteenth century, advances in positivism and biology brought about a change in attitudes towards personal hygiene. In the 1860s, the work of Pasteur and Lister enabled clearer understanding of viruses and microbes, and in the 1880s, typhoid, cholera, and tuberculosis bacilli were discovered and identified. Disproving the theory of spontaneous generation which claimed that life arose from non-living matter,[77] Pasteur also greatly aided the development of aseptic and antiseptic techniques. His contribution was not immediately acknowledged: visitors to the Pasteur Museum in Paris may get a glimpse of the fierce debates that raged on these subjects in Pasteur's day. In 1888, finally, the scientist was able to establish his own institute of microbiology.

The revolution in medicine also brought about a gradual shift in attitudes towards personal and social hygiene. By the end of the century, city churches, libraries, and drinking fountains were being regularly treated with disinfectant. Attitudes towards washing and bathing were changing. A new concept, that of unseen threat of infection, was emerging: no longer purely concerned with obvious soiling and dirt, people also began to worry about 'invisible' microbes. Tests were conducted to compare the number of microbes on a person's body prior to, and directly after washing. Following the tests, Remlinger concluded that washing significantly lowers the quantity of bacteria on the skin. Henceforward, water came to be seen as an ally in the fight against disease. Regular bathing began to be recommended as a healthy prophylactic measure: this was a cardinal shift in the history of European hygiene.

Everyday approaches to the body were rethought in the light of the latest discoveries. The battle against microbes, the 'invisible enemies', required new personal hygiene practices.[78] Keeping one's body clean, one was now told, would increase protection against disease. Areas of the body, which had previously seldom come into focus, were now constantly being written about. Special instructions on cleaning one's teeth so as not to leave particles of food stuck in the gaps appeared alongside advice on cleaning one's nails. Removing the dirt from under one's nails came to be seen as a key element of fighting the microbial threat. Parents began to instruct their children to wash their hands often, and their intimate areas every day. At school, pupils were discouraged from putting their finger in their mouth before turning the pages of books.

Before long, however, this triumph of positivist knowledge came to be appropriated for the purposes of specific social groups. Following Pasteur's discoveries, the public eye turned to potential sources of infection. Hygiene propaganda was quick to come up with an enemy image, identifying manual labourers as possible carriers of disease. The homes of the poor, researchers were quick to claim, contained fifty times more microbes, than did drainpipes. The filthy hands of the poor came to instil terror: dreading infection, bourgeois families avoided the 'putrid' slums and their inhabitants.[79]

Adrian Forty sees this kind of behaviour as bourgeois class prejudice. One could assume, he writes, that the middle class was establishing new standards of cleanliness, in order to avoid social coups and gain psychological security. Besides the general humane impulse, the middle class had a material interest in the hygiene of the proletariat. After all, a drop in diseases and deaths among the workers would allow them to work even harder, thereby increasing the wealth of the bourgeoisie.[80] While Forty's argument may appear a little simplistic, the social aspect of the drive for hygiene is clear. The educational efforts were mainly aimed at poorer circles, with numerous pamphlets being published with the aim of improving their personal hygiene habits. Technological inventions were also frequently geared to this purpose.

In the mid-nineteenth century, the more deprived social groups such as the poor, soldiers, and students, would wash in the communal baths. The water usage was very high, even given the relatively small number of people involved, and new techniques to cut down the volume of water were sought. Experiments with targeted jets eventually led to the development of showering – a form of washing the body which remains highly popular to this day. The first organized showers were recorded as having been instituted in the French army and prisons.

In 1857, the Thirty Third Marseille Regiment tested a new way of bathing. The process was described by Vigarello: after undressing, the soldiers entered the showering space in groups of three, each armed with his own soap. For three minutes, the trio would wash using the vertical stream of water, after which time the next group would come in.[81] The experiment proved successful and well-suited to the army spirit of discipline, although the short time allocated to each group meant that soldiers would often shove each other out of the way in their attempts to finish in time.

Following the first experiments, two features of showering changed. A shower head to diffuse the water more effectively was developed, and shower cabins introduced, which at times were formed using curtains. The water pressure was regulated by an army officer, who stood above the bathers, directing the jet.

The system of communal showering was subsequently taken on by prisons. In 1876, prisoners in Rouen washed in eight cabins, which they queued to enter, the water supply controlled by the warden. This method proved extremely economical, with ninety-six to a hundred and twenty prisoners able to shower each hour, and water use varying between a thousand and a half to a thousand eight hundred litres – the equivalent of just six to eight baths.[82]

The possibility of controlling the jet of water also meant that it could be used for repressive purposes. Cold water jets came to be used in mental hospitals in order to subdue unruly patients. Michel Foucault summed up the practice in Philippe Pinel's Parisian hospital thus: 'With Pinel, the use of the shower became frankly juridical; the shower was the habitual punishment of the ordinary police tribunal that sat permanently at the asylum.'[83] Later, similar practices were used at the huge Salpêtrière hospital by Charcot.[84]

The somewhat harsh, communal nature of showering practices was very much at odds with the privacy and comfort of bathing. By the 1880s, the bathroom had become a space of quiet, luxurious seclusion, although traditionally, servants had assisted their masters and mistresses throughout their toilet. As dressing rooms became more associated with solitary preening, only wealthier bourgeois families could allow themselves the luxury of such a separate room. In working-class English homes, bathrooms did not become commonplace until the 1920s.

Initially, bathrooms were not much different in design to other rooms, and contained sofas, carpets, armchairs, and tables. The cast-iron bath tended to be covered with neat wooden panelling, making it look like an ordinary piece of furniture. Bathrooms were seen as places of intimate ritual and private self-care, not unlike secluded studies or small dressing-rooms. In his painting 'The Bath' from 1873, the Belgian artist Alfred Stevens shows a woman reclining in the bath. Her expression pensive, she holds a flower in her hand; a book lies nearby. From a luxury indulged in by dandies and cocottes, unhurried, solitary bathing had become a pleasure accessible to the middle class.

Advances in scientific knowledge and better understanding of the nature of dirt and infection brought about a complete transformation of the bathroom. No longer encased in wood, baths acquired feet, allowing for the floor underneath to be cleaned. The walls began to be tiled, brown shades giving way to brilliant white. Traditional furniture was no longer used; instead, shelved niches and functional accessories such as soap dishes, sponge holders, and towel hangers appeared. The entire bathroom formed a single gleaming white ensemble, dazzlingly clean, the light tiled floor immediately showing the slightest speck of dirt. Homes began to be designed with the bathroom next door to the master bedroom, thereby 'widening the private sphere in the bourgeois way of life'.[85]

From the late-nineteenth century onwards, cleanliness came to be seen as one of the central attributes of the attractive bourgeois home. Hygiene was virtually synonymous with health. Science-conscious designers began to recommend simple furniture and furnishings to allow the air to circulate more freely, facilitate cleaning, and prevent dust from accumulating. Families began to move away from the heavy decorative curtains and canopies, so popular in the Victoran era. For middle-class Victorians, no surface was complete, unless covered with a decorative napkin or rug, and no empty corner was to be left without a screen or dresser. The bourgeois interior resembled a comfortable, well-padded labyrinth. Enshrouding its inhabitants, it has been interpreted as a manifestation of the womb complex, Otto Rank's birth trauma, a desire to return to the soft, warm, well-rounded safety of the mother's belly.

In gender terms, the later, more minimalist aesthetic could be viewed as a more masculine approach to structuring space. Bare surfaces, sharp lines, glass, metal, and starker tones – all these features were later integrated in the new technocratic styles of the twentieth century. In the early 1920s, the Constructivist movement inspired by Le Corbusier strove to create functional, well-lit, transparent, and open spaces that were easy to look after and clean.

As cleanliness became one of the features of the minimalist aesthetic, hygiene came to be associated with ideal order. Taking this association one step further, we can imagine it linked with ideologies of power, totalitarianism, and state control. The hint of totalitarianism present in the semantics of communal showering may easily find itself amplified on a metaphorical scale from the individual body to the collective, and from physical cleanliness to moral rectitude. In the late-nineteenth century, such motifs could already be found in utopian/dystopian fiction. In Jules Verne's utopian town of Frankville, children are

> accustomed to such strict cleanliness, that they consider a spot on their simple clothes quite a disgrace. Individual and collective cleanliness is the great idea of the founders of Frankville. To clean, clean unceasingly, so as to destroy the miasmas constantly emanating from a large community, such is the principal work of the central government.[86]

Similar passages may be found in many classic utopias and dystopias of the last century.[87]

Thus, the 1880s and 1890s witnessed a key shift in social perception of cleanliness and dirtiness, which in many ways determined today's attitudes. The contemporary model of corporeality, and basic gender stereotypes were also formed around that time. A crucial detail to bear in mind is that the foundations of this process were laid even earlier, through the dandy tradition of personal hygiene. The cultural type of the scrupulously clean dandy was a key factor in this fascinating process, and one which altered the structures of everyday experience in a number of ways.

Festina Lente: Slowness in Dandy Culture

> *Impatience is a luxury. Don't worry.*
> *I will slowly gather speed.*
> *With a cold step, we'll hit the path.*
> *I have kept my distance.*
> Osip Mandelstam

Discussing Baudelaire as flaneur, Walter Benjamin mentions the fashionable ritual among the Parisian dandies: walking the turtles on a leash.[88] This act, typical for dandies' culture of the 1840s, may seem quite eccentric. Today it can be easily interpreted as a performance of 'slow living', a protest against the increasing speed of everyday life. And indeed, certain aspects of dandyism could be seen as precursors of the contemporary 'slow-living' trend. Yet if we trace its origin to the lifestyle typical for Flaneur and Dandy, it could be inscribed in the system of meaningful gestures and be read as part of the semiotic structure of dandyism.

So, what was essentially this new eccentric ritual among the dandies of Paris? Strolling unhurriedly in the Jardin du Luxembourg, they could be seen taking their pet turtles for some air. This leisurely task demanded that the dandy conquer truly new heights of Stoical implacability and noble self-possession. The ritual can also be seen as a form of training in order to perfect a slow, deliberate, and self-assured stroll. Dandyism was habitually associated with noble immobility and statuary stasis. For many dandies, leisurely, languid gestures were an important means to create an impression. For instance, Osborne Hamley in Elizabeth Gaskell's 'Wives and Daughters': is depicted as a dandy with slow movements '…Osborne came in dressed in full evening dress. He always moved slowly; and this, to begin with, irritated the squire.'[89] We can imagine how Osborne's father the squire saw his son's languor as deliberate, perceiving it as something of a challenge, an attempt by Osborne to distance himself and to show his superiority.

Even dancing had to be slow for the perfect dandy. The dandies tried to avoid the quick dances, like polka, mazurka, or gallop. They preferred the position of observer or – in case they danced – they opted for slow dances, allowing them to keep dignity. But their dance manners signalled tediousness. According to Yuri Lotman, in Russia during the 1820s, the French graceful manners of rapid mazurka give way to the slow style of dancing under the influence of British dandyism. But even if dandies danced, they did not talk, which was considered rude by many ladies, who got used to the light conversation during the dance. Russian poet and dandy Pushkin were particularly known for his 'lazy and silent manner of dancing'.[90]

Languid, unhurried movements were of course especially important for flâneur.[91] In his treatise 'The Theory of Walking', Honoré de Balzac dwells extensively on slow gait: 'All our body participates in movement, but no part should predominate', 'when the body is in movement, the face is immobile', and 'all unwarranted movement is extremely wasteful'.[92] The perfect gait, Balzac suggests, supposes practical coordination and economy of movement. An important element of the ideal gait is smoothness: 'slow movement is essentially majestic', 'economy of movement is the means to render a noble and gracious walk'.[93] Thus, the gait of flâneur can never be hurried; its grace is largely based on physiological economy of movement.

The fine art of dandy flâneuring certainly supposes a leisurely, smooth gait. Unhurried movement was, according to writers on dandyism, graceful in itself. The facial equivalent of a slow gait – a composed expression – also went to demonstrate the noble self-possession of the flâneur. Enabling detached contemplation, leisurely flâneuring with an inscrutable face could be seen as a form of aestheticism in action, a programme for body and living. It gave a perfect chance for urban spectatorship.

Thus, the beauty of the dandy's gait is largely due to its constructive principle of economy of movement. Besides the aesthetic aspect, this also has a purely physiological side. Balzac holds that a slow gait befits wise men, philosophers, and men of the world: 'gentleness in the gait is what simplicity is in the dress'.[94] Economy of expression in dress here finds its direct correlation in the economy of laconic gesture and in the stasis of the poised stance. The chiastic pose of antique statues signifying the idea of perfect balance were interpreted, as we have already seen, in a similar frame of neoclassical aesthetics. Smooth movements also recall the clear, flowing outlines of the dandy's dress.

In direct opposition to the dandy's calmly poised aplomb is the frantic, anxious scurrying that Balzac refers to by the old French verb *virvoucher*: '*Virvoucher* suggests rushing backwards and forwards, getting in everyone's way, grabbing at everything, leaping up, then sitting down again, fretting, meddling, being in constant aimless movement, buzzing around like a fly' (Balzac 1833). The writer also criticizes another type: the person who walks quickly, whose movements are mechanical, reminiscent of clockwork and whose facial expression is always anxious. Such unprepossessing characters are, Balzac suggests, worthy of nothing but disdain:

His gait resembles that of a soldier on his march. He likes to talk; his voice is loud, and he loves the sound of it. He may even become indignant, as if debating with an invisible adversary, offering his arguments, gesticulating, becoming upset, then brightening up again.⁹⁵

Needless to say, the cool, collected dandy's behaviour lies at the opposite end of the spectrum: his are the aplomb of the observer, the self-possession of the gentleman.

Behind the dandy's legendary unflappable exterior and unruffled languor often lies a basic refusal to accept the ever-quickening pulse of city life. Filled with aesthetic nostalgia for bucolic times gone by, the dandy often resists industrial progress. The leisurely strolls with tortoises point very clearly at the fundamentally idle, self-sufficient nature of flâneuring. The dandy does not merely avoid haste; he avoids hurrying about any business or applying himself to any mechanical job (Figure 21). The flâneur's idleness is akin to the carefree nonchalance of the aristocrat, who knows he will never have to worry about where his next meal is coming from. Work, or even any serious and demanding occupation, is simply not for him. He would not be seen dead running down the street. 'Running!' cried I, 'just like common people - when were you or I ever seen running?' the young Pelham inquires indignantly of his friend.⁹⁶

In his speech, the true dandy was likewise unhurried and calm, many dandies deliberately cultivating a languid drawl. The first generation of English dandies, followers of Beau Brummell, spoke slowly and somewhat lazily, thus, adhering to the principle of economy of effort. Waiting for a pause in the conversation, they would then make their

Figure 21 Paul Gavarni. Dolce Far Niente. 1831.

comments in a slow, deliberate, pithy drawl. Brummell's cutting comments were often all the more poisonous for the contrast between his initial polite, unhurried 'Excuse me, Sir' and the ensuing laconic, deadly barb.

Even in the situation of conflict, Brummell preserved slow movements. Thus, after his 'Thomson-Johnson' episode, when he came to the ball uninvited and had to leave, 'he *slowly* retired from the room amid the suppressed anger from the bevy of intimates, the titter of his own friends and the undisguised wrath of the lady.'[97]

The dandy's signature languor is directly connected with his love for contemplation and attention to detail. A calm, unrushed manner is key in the sensual practices he favours, from tasting food to contemplating a landscape. He believes that a fruit is best savoured when eaten slowly, not wolfed down in hasty mouthfuls. In taking one's time, one is better able to appreciate small details. Many dandies would likely have agreed with the ancient maxim *festina lente* – 'make haste slowly'. Lack of haste was, indeed, a crucial attribute of their very unhurried way of life.

Notes

1 William Hazlitt, *Essays*, selected and edited by Frank Carr (London: Walter Scott, 1889), 182–183.
2 From the French, retenue – self-possession, restraint.
3 Hazlitt, ibid., 183.
4 Ibid.
5 Ibid., 189–190.
6 In the eighteenth century, panniers, or side hoops, provided a carcass of willow or whalebone, which extended ladies' skirts at the sides.
7 Maria Mertsalova, *Kostium raznykh vremen i narodov* (Moscow: Akademiya Mody, 1996), vol. 2: 116 [The Costume of Different Times and Peoples].
8 Marcel Proust, *The Guermantes Way*. Trans. C. K. Scott Moncrieff, edited and annotated by William C. Carter (New Haven and London: Yale University Press, 2018), 456.
9 Merab Mamardashvili, *Lektsii o Pruste* [Lectures on Proust]. (Moscow: Ad Marginem, 1995): 539.
10 Kirsanova R. Chelovek v Zerkale Mira, *Russkaya Galereya*, 2: 49 (1998). [Man in the Mirror of the World, in Russian].
11 Proust, ibid., 477.
12 Honoré de Balzac, *The Girl with the Golden Eyes*, trans. Ernest Dowson (London: Leonard Smithers, 1896), 28.
13 Paul Johnson, *The Birth of the Modern: World Society 1815–1830* (New York, Weidenfeld and Nicolson, 1992), 710.
14 Arthur Conan Doyle, *Rodney Stone* (London: Eveleigh Nash & Grayson, 1921), 153.
15 Pierce Egan, *Life in London, or Days and Nights of Jerry Hawthorne and His Elegant Friend Corinthian Tom, Accompanied by Bob Logic, the Oxonian, in Their Rambles and Sprees through the Metropolis* (London: Sherwood, Neeley and Jones, 1821).
Besides '*Life in London*', Egan also wrote about boxing: Pierce Egan, *Boxiana; Or, Sketches of Ancient and Modern Pugilism, From the Days of the Renowned Broughton and Slack, To the Championship of Cribb*, vol. 1–3 (London: Sherwood, Jones and Co, 1811–1830).
16 Tattersall's is an eminent auctioneer of racehorses founded by Richard Tattersall (1724–1795). The first premises were situated near Hyde Park.
17 Christian Goede, *The Stranger in England* (London: Mathews and Leigh, 1807). Quoted from: Colin McDowell, *The Man of Fashion* (London: Thames and Hudson, 1997), 51.

18 Lewis Melville, *The Beaux of the Regency*, in 2 vols (London: Hutchinson & Co., 1908), 1: 204–206.
19 John Timbs, *Club Life in London with Anecdotes of the Clubs, Coffee-houses and Taverns of the Metropolis*, in 2 volumes (London: Richard Bentley, 1866), 1: 291–292.
20 Michael Gamer, 'A Matter of Turf: Romanticism, Hippodrama, and Legitimate Satire', *Nineteenth-Century Contexts*, 28, no. 4, (2006): 305–334 (309).
21 The diameter of Astley's circular arena became fixed at 13 metres, the size used by circuses ever since.
22 Arthur Conan Doyle, *Rodney Stone* (London: Eveleigh Nash & Grayson, 1921), 153.
23 Conan Doyle, ibid., 122.
24 Since 1711, horse races have also been held at Ascot. The racecourse there was founded by Queen Anne.
25 Johnson, ibid., 712.
26 Johnson, ibid., 712–713.
27 One might recall the similar occasion, when Lady Jersey refused to admit the Duke of Wellington to Almack's, after he arrived seven minutes late.
28 For more details see: Anne Martin-Fugier, *La Vie élégante, ou La Formation du Tout-Paris 1815–1848* (Paris: Perrin, 1990).
29 Cavalry Officer, *The Whole Art of Dress or, the Road to Elegance and Fashion* (London: E. Wilson, 1830), 73.
30 Jules Barbey D'Aurevilly, *On Dandyism and George Brummell*. Trans George Walden (London: Gibson Square Books, 2002), 129.
31 Roland Barthes, *Mythologies*, Trans. R. Howard and A. Lavers (London: Jonathan Cape, Ltd. 1972), 76.
32 Barthes, ibid., 78
33 William Hazlitt, *Essays*. Selected and edited by Frank Carr (London: Walter Scott, 1889), 191.
34 Hazlitt, ibid., 192.
35 Eric Berne, *What Do You Say after You Say Hello? The Psychology of Human Destiny* (New York: Bantam Books, 1973), 65. Open Library, https://archive.org/details/whatdoyousayafte00bern. Accessed 25.04.2022.
36 Berne, ibid., 245.
37 Berne, ibid., 246.
38 'Inscrutable heart' (Latin).
39 Edward Bulwer-Lytton, *Pelham; Or, the Adventures of a Gentleman* (London: Chapman and Hall, 1849), 147.
40 Charles Baudelaire: *Selected Writings on Art and Artists*. Trans P. E. Charvet (Cambridge, London: Cambridge University Press, 1981), 427.
41 Taxile Delord quoted by Walter Benjamin, *Selected Writings*, vol. 1–4, eds. Howard Eiland and Michael Jennings (Cambridge, MA: Belknap Press, 2002), 4: 76.
42 Louis-Sebastien Mercier, *New Picture of Paris* (Dublin: Gale Ecco, 2018).
43 Honoré de Balzac, *Scenes from a Courtesan's Life*. Trans. James Waring, Project Gutenberg e-book 1660, https://www.gutenberg.org/ebooks/1660. Accessed 26.04.2022.
44 Lutetia, the predecessor of Paris, was a Roman city whose name likely originated in words meaning 'swamp' or 'mud'. Lutetia was home to the Parisii, a Gallic tribe, who lived on an island in the Sequana River (today's Seine).
45 Honoré de Balzac, *The Girl with the Golden Eyes*. Trans. Ellen Marriage (Auckland: The Floating Press, 2011), 10.
46 Georges Vigarello, *Concepts of Cleanliness: Changing Attitudes in France Since the Middle Ages*. Trans. J. Birrell (Cambridge: Cambridge University Press, 1988).
47 Alain Corbin, *The Foul and the Fragrant: Odor and the French Social Imagination*. Trans. M. Kochan, R. Porter, and C. Prendergast (Cambridge, MA: Harvard University Press, 1986).
48 For a more detailed description, see Daniel Pool, *What Jane Austen Ate and Charles Dickens Knew* (New York: Touchstone, 1994), 201–203.

49 Paul Johnson, *The Birth of the Modern: World Society 1815–1830* (New York: Weidenfeld and Nicolson, 1992), 754.
50 William Jesse, *The Life of George Brummell, Esq.* In 2 volumes (London: Saunders and Otley, 1844), 1: 69.
51 Certain Russian dandies were also known for their obsessive cleanliness. Pyliayev, for instance, describes an incident involving the Count Arakcheyev. Notorious for his ruthlessness, especially among the liberal intelligentsia, the count was also famed for his extraordinary care in dress. 'One night, His Majesty sent for him, so as they might travel together. Leaping up from his bed, Arakcheyev began to dress in haste, yet at the last moment, his manservant dripped some wax from a candle onto his light-coloured breeches. Despite the rush, Arakcheyev took off the breeches and got changed, even though the new pair had to be fetched from a faraway room. His decision meant that the Tsar was kept waiting for an extra five minutes – such was his obsession with cleanliness'. See Mikhail Pyliayev, *Zamechateniye chudaki i originally* [Memorable eccentrics and originals] (Moscow: Interbuk, 1990), 109. In this extract, the author's condemnation of Arakcheyev is clear: he should not, Pyliayev implies, have kept the monarch waiting. The count's determination to appear before the Tsar, impeccably dressed, could perhaps, however, be interpreted differently: as the rigour of a dedicated disciplinarian, who will not allow himself to appear slovenly. In the Soviet time the poet Vladimir Mayakovsky, also famous as an ambitious dandy, was known for his strict hygienic habits.
52 Besides Cleopatra, donkey milk baths were a daily favourite of Poppaea, wife of the Roman Emperor Nero. In the eighteenth century, milk baths were also favoured by William Douglas, Duke of Queensberry.
53 William Jesse, *The Life of George Brummell, Esq.* In 2 volumes (London: Saunders and Otley, 1844), 2: 202–203.
54 Ibid., 2: 80.
55 Ibid., 2: 198–200.
56 Ibid., 2: 204.
57 Heightened awareness of cleanliness was also interesting to Freud. Together with parsimony and obstinacy, excessive orderliness was considered by the father of psychoanalysis to be a feature of the anal personality. See Sigmund Freud, in *The Standard Edition of the Complete Psychological Works of Sigmund*, vol. 9 (London: Hogarth Press, 1959), 167–176.
58 Edward Bulwer-Lytton, *Pelham, or the Adventures of a Gentleman*, in three volumes (London: Henry Colburn, 1828), 1: 266.
59 Honoré de Balzac, *The Girl with the Golden Eyes*. Trans. Ellen Marriage (Auckland: The Floating Press, 2011), 41–42.
60 Balzac, ibid., 42.
61 Ibid.
62 Jesse, ibid., 1: 70.
63 Jesse, ibid., 1: 81–82.
64 On the symbolism of wigs, see Marcia Pointon, 'The Case of the Dirty Beau: Symmetry, Disorder and the Politics of Masculinity', in *The Body Imaged*, eds. K. Adler and M. Pointon (Cambridge: Cambridge University Press, 1993), 175–189.
65 Jesse, ibid., 1: 48.
66 Louis-Sebastien Mercier, *New Picture of Paris* (Dublin: Gale Ecco, 2018).
67 Pointon, ibid., 181.
68 The Spectator, № 631, 10 December 1714. Quoted from Pointon, ibid., 181.
69 Marcel Haedrich, *Coco Chanel; Her Life, Her Secrets*. Trans. Charles Lam Markmann (Boston: Little Brown, 1972), 68.
70 Ibid., 84.
71 Ibid., 69.
72 Honoré de Balzac, *Scenes from a Courtesan's Life*. Trans. James Waring, Project Gutenberg e-book 1660, https://www.gutenberg.org/ebooks/1660. Accessed 26.04.2022.

73 Émile Zola, *Nana*. Trans. Burton Rascoe (New York: Dover Publications Inc, 2007), 156.
74 Zola, ibid., 219.
75 Zola, ibid., 37.
76 Philippe Perrot, *Les dessus et les dessous de la borgeoisie* (Paris: Librairie Artheme Fayard, 1981), 228–229.
77 By that time, scientists had already observed basic microorganisms. The inventor of the microscope Antonie van Leeuwenhoek began to publish drawings of his findings in 1673, yet no consistent theory on bacteria yet existed. For more detailed analysis, see Nancy Tomes, *The Gospel of Germs: Men, Women and the Microbe in American Life* (Cambridge, MA: Harvard University Press, 1998).
78 In an English pamphlet on hygiene from the time of the First World War, the quest for cleanliness is portrayed as a military battle, with microbes wearing German soldiers' uniforms.
79 For a more detailed account, see Alain Corbin, *The Foul and the Fragrant: Odor and the French Social Imagination*. Trans. M. Kochan, R. Porter, and C. Prendergast (Cambridge, MA: Harvard University Press, 1986), 226–227.
80 Adrian Forty, *Objects of Desire. Design and Society Since 1750* (London: Thames and Hudson, Cameron Books, 1992), 159–160.
81 Georges Vigarello, *Concepts of Cleanliness: Changing Attitudes in France Since the Middle Ages*, Trans. J. Birrell (Cambridge: Cambridge University Press, 1988), 236.
82 Ibid., p. 237.
83 Michel Foucault, *Madness and Civilization: A History of Insanity in the Age of Reason* (London: Routledge, 2006), 253.
84 Jean-Martin Charcot (1825–1893) – a French physician who established the first neurological clinic at the Salpêtrière hospital in Paris. Among those he taught was Sigmund Freud.
85 Vigarello, ibid., 233.
86 Quoted from Philippe Perrot, *Les dessus et les dessous de la borgeoisie* (Paris: Librairie Artheme Fayard, 1981), 230.
87 Recall, for instance, this passage from Zamytin's 'We': 'Amid our walls, transparent, as though woven from gleaming air, we are living always in plain sight, always bathed by the light…' Evgeny Zamyatin, *Mi* [We], Aldous Huxley, *Prekrasniy Novyi Mir* [The Brave New World] (Moscow: Khudozhestvennaya Literatura, 1989), 20.
88 Walter Benjamin, The Paris of the Second Empire in Baudelaire, in *Selected Writings*, eds. H. Eiland and M. Jennings (Cambridge, MA: Belknap Press, 2006) 4: 30–31.
89 Elizabeth Gaskell, *Wives and Daughters* (London: Harper and Brothers, 1864), 335.
90 Yuri Lotman, *Besedi o russkoy culture* [Talks on Russian Culture, in Russian] (St. Petersburg: Iskusstvo, 1994), 97.
91 See Keith Tester (ed.), *The Flaneur* (London, New York: Routledge, 1994); Alain Montandon, *Sociopoétique de la promenade* (Clermont-Ferrand: Presses Universitaires Blaise Pascal, 2000); Montandon 2000; Edmund White, *The Flaneur: A Stroll through the Paradoxes of Paris* (London: Bloomsbury Publishing, 2001).
92 Honoré de Balzac, *Théorie de la démarche* (1833), http://www.ebooksgratuits.com/ebookslib/balzac1318.pdf. Accessed 27 April 2021.
93 Balzac, ibid.
94 Ibid.
95 Ibid.
96 Edward Bulwer-Lytton, *Pelham; Or, the Adventures of a Gentleman* (London: Chapman and Hall, 1849), 67–68.
97 William Jesse, *The Life of George Brummell, Esq*. In 2 volumes (London: Saunders and Otley, 1844), 1: 107.

Chapter Six

OSCAR WILDE

Oscar Wilde: The Dandy-Aesthete

'A really well-made buttonhole is the only link between Art and Nature.'
'The first duty of life is to be as artificial as possible. What the second duty is no one as yet discovered.'
'Nothing that actually occurs is of the smallest importance.'
'The only way to atone for being occasionally a little overdressed is by being always absolutely over-educated.'
'No crime is vulgar, but all vulgarity is crime.'
'One should either be a work of art, or wear a work of art.'
'Wickedness is a myth invented by good people to account for the curious attractiveness of others.'
'To love oneself is the beginning of a life-long romance.'
'In all unimportant matters, style, not sincerity, is the essential. In all important matters, style, not sincerity, is the essential.'[1]

Penning his provocative aphorisms, Oscar Wilde set out to shock bourgeois society with his manifesto of a self-confident Aesthete. Perhaps unexpectedly for him, however, long-standing associations with the genre came into play, with readers seeing the aphorisms as stemming from a solid cultural tradition. British humour had long sanctioned light-hearted sarcasm even on the gravest of topics, and the witticisms of high-society eccentrics were accepted as a necessary rhetorical accompaniment to the ceremonial rituals of salon conversation.

Aphorisms concerning fashion, naturally, also possessed their own associations: through George Brummell and his undying fame, they were commonly linked with early nineteenth-century dandyism. In fashionable novels and treatises, large collections of maxims on good taste and the art of dress did not appear out of place. With its laconic form, which suited the dandy principle of minimal energy expenditure, the aphorism was seen as the perfect dandy genre. Wilde, furthermore, contrived to lend dandy aphorisms a new air of conceptual elegance and philosophical paradox. Inspired by the works of Walter Pater and John Ruskin, he attempted to render their ideas on pure art through more accessible expressions, thought-provoking, yet entertaining. Encountering his maxims, even the poorly educated paused to think. The amusing nature of his paradoxes caused readers' attention to focus, whilst relaxing at the same time.

In any paradox, one encounters a counterpoint, a meeting of conflicting interpretations. As many of Wilde's aphorisms are uttered by his characters, the possibility of multi-layered readings is infinitely multiplied. Creating a deliberate distance between himself and the speaker, Wild plants his paradoxes in ambiguous style. The characters with the most quotable maxims are, of course, Lord Henry from 'The Picture of Dorian Gray', and Lord Goring from 'An Ideal Husband'.

Turning to Wilde's famed first-person mottos, one immediately notes their resemblance to those of George Brummell. As with the Beau, Wilde's witticisms and critical observations express a fashionable man's demonstrative disdain for vulgarity. Of Rudyard Kipling's 'Captains Courageous', Wilde remarked: 'It seems very odd to me that a man should write a whole novel about cod-fishing - but I suppose that is because I do not like cod.'[2] Recall Brummell's explanation concerning the termination of his engagement: 'I discovered that Lady Mary actually ate cabbage!' With Oscar Wilde, the highest compliments are accorded for lack of vulgarity: his laconic praise of Herbert Beerbohm Tree's 'Hamlet' is a fine example, as he called the production 'funny without being vulgar'.[3] Wilde's exaggerated contempt for vulgarity may in part have arisen from terror and vulnerability in the face of quickly developing bourgeois culture of 'the inartistic age'.

Wilde on Fashion: Reform and Ideal

The final decades of the nineteenth century saw Victorian conservatism in England give way to the more liberal Regency mood. Reviving the traditions of lavish aristocratic lunches and country jaunts, Albert Edward Prince of Wales was a frequent guest at the estates of his protégés. Recalling the leisure and pursuits of King George IV and his entourage of flawlessly turned-out dandies, society once more turned to the image of Beau Brummell. Everything French was back in vogue, the frivolous elegance of the continental style appealing to the likes of Aubrey Beardsley, Max Beerbohm, James Whistler, and, of course, Oscar Wilde. Devouring novels by Flaubert, Zola and the Goncourt brothers, writers and artists worshipped the poetry of Théophile Gautier and Stéphane Mallarmé.

Together, this French influence and the English Aesthetic movement formed the foundations of European decadence. In 1894, the famed 'Yellow Book' first appeared, considered by many the decadent manifesto. The flavour of the time could be felt even earlier, however, in the clash between Aesthetes and pragmatists. 'Pure art' was having to assert itself with vigour, artists being forced to operate within the market economy of firmly established middle-class modernity. All this combined to make Oscar Wilde's aphorisms against bourgeois vulgarity all the more pithy.[4]

> Indeed, the dominant note of the decade appears to be its commercialism: the *tragic* spectacle of literature and personality thrown open on the market place, the great *experiment* of selling talent by advertising, publicity and showmanship.[5]

Writers began to adopt a deliberately imposing manner, ensuring the press got to know of their amusing escapades, cutting quips, and dramatic debates. Many wrote open letters to newspaper editors, exchanged telegrams, and got involved in litigation. High-profile cases never failed to capture the public's attention. Among the best-known legal wrangles were those of the artist James Whistler, who sued first John Ruskin, then Oscar Wilde.

Wilde's extravagant manners and appearance were clearly designed to attract attention. His dress always drew comments, just as his observations often courted scandal. He liked to be mysterious, with statements such as 'I am finding it harder and harder to live up to my blue china'. Showering her with lilies in honour of her name, he demonstratively courted the actress Lillie Langtry, his attentions earning a mention in Gilbert and Sullivan's comic opera 'Patience'. You could be considered an Aesthete, the verses claimed, 'if you walk down Piccadilly with a poppy or a lily in your medieval hand'. Well-known cartoonist George du Maurier regularly produced caricatures of Wilde for 'Punch', yet, far from being irked, the writer tended to welcome the attention, seeing it as boosting his fame.

One of Wilde's main areas of interest was clothing. Seen as an arbiter of fashion, he played an active part in contemporary debate on the evolution of modern dress. At that time, women wishing to ride bicycles and practise sports were insisting on new forms of dress, with blazing discussions flaring up at public gatherings and in the press. Traditional costume, many argued, did not allow sufficient freedom of movement for women to engage in modern activities.

An active supporter of dress reform, Wilde was outspoken in his ideas. In the 1880s, the movement was gathering momentum as advocates of rational dress spoke out against the use of corsets, crinolines, pointed shoes, and high heels. Dress reform supporters suggested wearing culottes and divided skirts, which allowed women to practise sports and, importantly, to ride bicycles.

New forms of rational dress were created in artistic circles. Some of the first designs emerged from the Pre-Raphaelites and William Morris. In the 1870s, a group of artists and writers headed by the novelist Mrs. Humphry Ward promoted Aesthetic dress: loose garments with wide armholes and sleeves, and high waist, to be worn without a corset. The Aesthetes being against artificial aniline dyes,[6] the colours suggested were deep, intense, natural hues: dark greens, indigos, and earthy browns. Popular accessories for such garments included amber jewellery.

On 1 October 1884, Oscar Wilde gave a lecture on dress, in which he put forward his ideas on modern attire. The key point was, that one's clothing should fall freely from the shoulders, not the waist, which made the wearing of corsets unnecessary. Citing ancient Greek styles as examples, Wilde praised their comfortable feel, and the beauty of their folds, so dearly loved by sculptors and painters. Divided skirts, Wilde stressed, offered 'lightness and freedom' of movement, whilst corsets, crinolines, and other constricting items met with his disapproval. High heels, the writer insisted, should also be consigned to history.

Following the lecture, which was covered in the papers, Wilde began to receive indignant letters from female readers. How could British women possibly wear Greek robes, frustrated ladies enquired, when the climate clearly does not allow them to do so? Wilde's response was to suggest the use of warm woollen undergarments, which, at that time, were promoted by Dr. Gustav Jaeger as healthy and hygienic.[7] High heels, the ladies continued, were necessary in order to raise the hem of one's dress, and to keep it from becoming soiled in the street. Wilde's response was to suggest clogs: that way, he claimed, the body would be raised up evenly, not at the unhealthy angle created by high heels.[8] The ideal costume, Wilde concluded, should combine 'Greek principles of beauty with German principles of health'.[9]

Oscar Wilde's ideas could frequently be seen, put into practice, in the outfits of his wife Constance. At Wilde's behest, she rejected the bustles and corsets favoured by the majority of fashionable women, opting instead for freely flowing, loose Aesthetic dresses of patterned Liberty silks. Her wedding ring was designed by Wilde himself.

Contemporary descriptions of Constance paint a picture in line with Wilde's ideals. 'Constance was wearing a Greek costume of cowslip yellow and apple-leaf green.'[10] On another occasion, Wilde's wife is described as wearing a wide brim Gainsborough hat: the writer often stressed that broad-brimmed hats were not only aesthetically pleasing but also practical, protecting the wearer from the elements.

An active supporter of dress reform, Constance spoke at several gatherings of the Rational Dress Society.

> She attended a meeting on Rational Dress in the Westminster Town Hall in March 1886, and when she rose to propose a motion, showed herself to be clad in cinnamon-colored cashmere trousers and a cape with the ends turned under to form sleeves.[11]

Naturally, Wilde's creative ideas did not stop at female dress reform. At that time, men's fashion columns had begun to appear in magazines, and the possibility of changes in male costume was a much-discussed topic. Like many Aesthetes, Wilde felt frustrated by the limitations of the traditional black suit. Finding it drab and lifeless, he proposed to broaden the range of possible colours. 'Freedom in such selection of colour is a necessary condition of variety and individualism of costume.'[12] The colour of a man's coat, Wilde suggested, possesses 'great psychological value', as it reveals the wearer's personal traits and outlook on life. In his famous letter to the editor of the Daily Telegraph, Wilde shared some ideas concerning fashion trends of the future:

> The colour of the coat will be symbolic. The imagination will concentrate itself on the waistcoat. Waistcoats will show whether a man can admire poetry or not. That will be very valuable. Over the shirt-front Fancy will preside. By a single glance one will be able to detect the tedious.[13]

This ironic Utopia possesses an important creative aspect, with freedom of individual expression within a society that looks favourably upon the fashionable innovations of people with good taste. It also offers optimal conditions for the fashion observer, one who analyses dress. After all, the dandy comes to life not only in front of the mirror but also in society, in the roles of hero and author, combined. In 1891, the sole milieu in which Wilde's fashionable ambitions could be realised was the stage: in the costumes of Sir Charles Wyndham, he saw fashion of the future.

In the past, Wilde held, there was a brief period, when male dress was both aesthetically pleasing, and comfortable: this was the reign of Charles I. At that time, men had worn breeches and stockings, doublets with full, slashed sleeves, lace collars, and wide brim hats. In the portraits of Anthony van Dyck, English aristocrats can be seen sporting such outfits.

Male dress of his own era was seen by Wilde as utterly boring and hopeless. Stone and bronze sculptures and statues, he found, showed its total lack of aesthetic appeal particularly eloquently. Unexpectedly though, the writer discovered an example of attractive male dress during his trip to America. Observing the miners of Colorado, Wilde was struck by details of their dress such as the broad-brimmed hats (quite reminiscent of van Dyck), loose-fitting capes (with all the folds his Aesthetic soul could want), and thick-soled shoes. 'They only wore what was comfortable, and therefore beautiful,' Wilde quickly concluded.[14] Whether or not the Aesthete was aware of jeans when he visited America, we do not know. Thanks to Levi Strauss, Gold Rush miners began wearing them in California in the 1850s. One might suppose that their practical nature would have pleased Wilde.

An Aesthete's Wardrobe

Through his own dress choices, Wilde attempted at least in part to promote change, and to carry out his desired reforms. Opting for more unusual colours, he could choose dazzlingly vivid waistcoats, or a flamboyant purple coat. Paying tremendous attention to detail, the Aesthete writer would sport elaborately decorated gilded or enamel buttons, unusual ruffled shirts, rings with precious stones. His favourite fabric was grey or brown velvet. The most useful outdoor clothing for a man, he held, was a loose, sleeveless coat or cape, which not only protected the wearer from the elements but also offered a pleasing sight with its countless folds and 'play of light and lines'. The practical dark colour of such a coat was always to be offset by a bright lining for aesthetic balance.

Wilde loved accessories, and often chose flowers for his buttonhole. His favourites were lilies, and the sunflowers used as symbols of the Aesthetic movement. For the premiere of 'Lady Windermere's Fan', Wilde is reported to have urged his supporters to wear green carnations, as he, apparently, did himself. Among his other favourite accessories were amethyst tie-pins, lemon-coloured gloves, and an ivory-handled walking cane.

Besides his extravagant appearance, Wilde drew attention by his inherent talent in standing out. His unusual witticisms and cold dandy insolence helped him dominate any conversation. The ultimate impression noted by all those who knew him, however, was of a unique personal energy, a euphoric intensity of existence. As one of Wilde's contemporaries recalled,

> That evening he was dressed with elaborate dandyism and a sort of florid sobriety. His coat had a black velvet collar. He held white gloves in his small pointed hands. On one finger he wore a large scarab ring. A green carnation – echo in colour of the ring – bloomed

savagely in his buttonhole, and a large bunch of seals on a black moiré ribbon watch chain hung from his white waistcoat. This costume, which on another man might have appeared perilously like fancy dress, and on his imitators was nothing less, seemed perfectly to suit him; he seemed at ease and to have a great look of the first gentleman in Europe.[15]

In London, Wilde's fame led Gilbert and Sullivan to feature him in their comic opera 'Patience', which premiered in the capital in 1881: the aesthete Bunthorne was thought to have been inspired by Wilde.[16] If mildly vexed by the caricature to start with, the writer quickly realised that this association with the popular musical would only augment his fame.

Before long, 'Patience' was staged in America, and the producer suggested that Wilde give a series of lectures there. The project was to bring him not only good money, but transatlantic fame, also, the opera serving to promote the lectures, and the lectures, the opera. Approving of the idea, Wilde prepared a series of talks on the 'English Renaissance', with essays on the Aesthetic movement in England, and on interior design.

For his upcoming trip, he had made a fur-trimmed green coat, and fur hat. Wearing the coat at his first meeting with American reporters, Wilde ensured that his arrival instantly featured in all the papers. 'I have nothing to declare except my genius,' he is said to have stated at Customs Control in New York.

For his lectures, Wilde wore special Aesthetic dress, which he designed himself. Fully aware of the scale of public attention, and of the associations with 'Patience', he gave the theatrical costumier detailed instructions.

> They should be beautiful; tight velvet doublet, with large flowered sleeves and little ruffs of cambric coming up from under the collar... Any good costumier would know what I want – sort of Francis I dress: only knee-breeches instead of long hose. Also get me two pair of grey silk stockings to suit grey mouse-coloured velvet. The sleeves are to be flowered – if not velvet then plush – stamped with a large pattern. They will excite a great sensation... They were dreadfully disappointed at Cincinnati at my not wearing knee-breeches.[17]

Wilde's breeches, indeed, provoked a sensation. The deliberately theatrical nature of his dress made no less an impression on audiences than the lectures themselves. One listener recorded her observations:

> Costume. - A dark purple sack coat, and knee-breeches; black hose, low shoes with bright buckles; coat lined with lavender satin, a frill of rich lace at the wrists and for tie-ends over a low turn-down collar, hair long, and parted in the middle, or all combed over. Enter with a circular cavalier cloak over the shoulder. The voice is clear, easy, and not forced. Change pose now and then, the head inclining toward the strong foot, and keep a general appearance of repose.[18]

The outfits chosen by Wilde for his lectures were designed to promote his image as an Aesthete, whilst drawing maximum attention. With their exaggerated theatricality, some everyday functions of dress were no longer present: one could not, for instance, guess Wilde's social status, or whether he was a gentleman. One could not assess his personal qualities, his temperament, or his political views. One could, however, be certain that the lecturer was conducting an aggressive promotional campaign, and that his appearance was a form of protest against drab nineteenth-century male dress. Wilde's costume possessed echoes of courtiers' dress, sending audiences back to times gone by, preserving vestimentary traits of the past.

Wilde's Aesthetic outfits made such an impression, that before long, he acquired crowds of transatlantic imitators. Some took the task to parodic lengths: at one of his lectures, some hundred and fifty students turned up in knee-breeches, stockings, and with sunflowers in their buttonholes. Seeing the crowd of would-be Wildes in the first row, far from panicking, the writer entered into discussion with them. Thanks to his famed sarcasm, he quickly gained the upper hand. Wilde's ability to sense the mood of his audience was almost telepathic: he was always able to choose the right tone for any gathering, be it a group of miners, or a high-society luncheon.

Upon his return from America, the writer went to Paris, where he once again took the look of a contemporary European man of fashion. The extravagant 'Aesthetics Professor' outfit was dropped in favour of more reserved dress. In the 1890s, when his plays were enjoying resounding success, he habitually chose formal, almost stern outfits, livened by a single detail such as an exquisite buttonhole, brightly coloured waistcoat, or turquoise cufflinks.

His experiments with Aesthetic dress, however, had not ceased to produce unexpected results. In the late 1880s, Wilde's costume gave rise to an entire new trend in children's fashion. In 1886, Frances Hodgson Burnett's 'Little Lord Fauntleroy' appeared, instantly becoming a classic of children's literature. The main hero, Cedric, was clothed in a dark blue or black velvet suit, knee-breeches with silk stockings, a white shirt with Vandyke lace collar, and a silk sash. He wore his hair long. His outfit was finished with a soft velvet beret and buckled shoes.

The first edition of 'Little Lord Fauntleroy' was illustrated by Reginald Birch, whose iconic drawings proved so popular that parents immediately rushed to dress their boys in Fauntleroy suits. The sons themselves were not, most likely, overjoyed at their new outfits: teased for their long hair and effeminate looks, they were invariably seen as spoiled and mollycoddled.

Little Lord Fauntleroy's costume bore a marked resemblance to Wilde's Aesthetic dress, the only significant difference being the writer's cravat. Wilde's American tour took place in 1882, Burnett's book appearing four years later. Burnett had emigrated to America, and during his tour, Wilde paid her a visit. It appears likely that his outfit played a key part in Burnett's subsequent clothing choices both for her sons, and for her literary character.[19]

Wilde's contribution to fashion made a significant impact. He had many followers and imitators, with tailors even naming a particular style of collar after him. Crucially, though, his American tour showed that English dandyism and Aestheticism could be sold as a commercial product, and exported to other countries. Wilde's theatrical dress, and his lectures, with their Aesthetic principles and cult of pure beauty, can be seen

Dandyism in 'The Picture of Dorian Gray'

Wilde's novel 'The Picture of Dorian Gray' combines the features of at least three genres. An excellent example of a fashionable novel, it follows the tradition started in the late 1820s by the publisher Henry Colburn. The main hero, a dandy, plays the role of arbiter of fashion.

> Fashion, by which what is really fantastic becomes for a moment universal, and dandyism, which, in its own way, is an attempt to assert the absolute modernity of beauty, had, of course, their fascination for him. His mode of dressing, and the particular styles that from time to time he affected, had their marked influence on the young exquisites of the Mayfair balls and Pall Mall club windows, who copied him in everything that he did, and tried to reproduce the accidental charm of his graceful, though to him only half-serious, fopperies.[20]

Modernizing the customary adventures of a young man of fashion, in 'The Picture of Dorian Gray' Wilde introduces a pair of dandies: the world-weary cynic Lord Henry, and the 'golden boy' himself, Dorian. Similar roles are to be found in the author's other works, 'An Ideal Husband', where Lord Goring is the older of the pair, or 'Lady Windermere's Fan', in which this role is played by Lord Darlington. 'Golden boys' appear in Wilde's fairy tales: recall his Young King, and Star-Child.

Besides fitting in the genre of the 'fashionable novel', 'The Picture of Dorian Gray' also combines features of the Gothic novel built on the mystery of the portrait, and of French-inspired decadent Aesthetic novel.

A passionate admirer of Théophile Gautier and Stéphane Mallarmé, Wilde was influenced most of all by Joris-Karl Huysmans. The French writer's 'Against Nature' ('À Rebours') appeared in 1884, and 'The Picture of Dorian Gray', in 1890. Wilde borrowed much from Huysmans: the poetics of the Aesthetic novel, with its Baroque cataloguing of beautiful objects, and listing of exotic sensations.[21] The hero becomes a connoisseur of rare pleasures, a collector of experiences, whose love of the bizarre takes him from works of art to sensual experiments. Hence, the themes of temptation and seduction, present in the works of both writers.

Fascinated by the 'poisonous' yellow book in his novel, readers begged Wilde to reveal its author. Although 'Against Nature' is not mentioned in the novel, its influence is clear.

> It was a novel without a plot and with only one character, being, indeed, simply a psychological study of a certain young Parisian who spent his life trying to realize in the nineteenth century all the passions and modes of thought that belonged to every century except his own, and to sum up, as it were, in himself the various moods through which the world-spirit had ever passed…[22]

In his letters, Wilde gave differing accounts of the book. To Ralph Paine, he claimed that in reality, the book did not exist, that was wholly the product of his imagination.[23] To another reader, however, he wrote:

> The book in 'Dorian Gray' is one of many books I have never written, but it is partly suggested by Huysmans's 'À Rebours'… It is a fantastic variation of Huysmans's over-realistic study of the artistic temperament in our inartistic age.[24]

In 'The Picture of Dorian Gray', Wilde's 'artistic nature' is spread across three characters. 'Basil Hallward is what I think I am; Lord Henry, what the world thinks me; Dorian is what I would like to be - in other ages, perhaps.'[25] The character of Dorian Gray was not, as some have suggested, based on Lord Alfred Douglas, whom Wilde met in 1891, a year after his novel was published. The resemblance, however, has been stressed by many, and might be seen almost as an example of art influencing life. The plot created by Wilde proved so strong, that it developed a 'mind of its own', unravelling quite independently of the participants. 'The Picture of Dorian Gray' could even be seen as foretelling its author's fate: after meeting Dorian Gray, the artist Basil Hallward ('what I think I am') has a presentiment of his own death.

> A curious sensation of terror came over me. I knew that I had come face to face with someone whose mere personality was so fascinating that, if I allowed it to do so, it would absorb my whole nature, my whole soul, my very art itself… Something seemed to tell me that I was on the verge of a terrible crisis in my life. I had a strange feeling that fate had in store for me exquisite joys and exquisite sorrows.[26]

A painter, Basil Hallward is a keeper of an Aesthetic tradition. Sensitive and vulnerable, he seeks love and justice. He appears to have much in common with Wilde, the author of children's tales in the spirit of Hans Christian Andersen, lost in the new 'iron age'. It is no coincidence that Basil loses Dorian to a more experienced dandy.

Lord Henry, however, is not merely an Aesthete who utters coldly cynical quips. He also offers Dorian an introduction to the world of art by encouraging his collection of rare objects: Dorian's love of old fabrics, for instance, is inspired by none other than Lord Henry. Late for one of their first meetings, Lord Henry admits he 'went to look after a piece of old brocade in Wardour Street and had to bargain for hours for it'.[27]

Lord Henry appears as a superior authority perhaps also as he is an illustration of Wilde's paradigm of the 'critic as artist'. In Wilde's view, the critic is the ideal expert in pure art.

> From the high tower of Thought we can look out at the world. Calm, and self-centred, and complete, the aesthetic critic contemplates life, and no arrow drawn at a venture can pierce between the joints of his harness. He at least is safe. He has discovered how to live.[28]

For Wilde, the new dandy is a refined, elegant Aesthete, who contemplates beauty whilst perfecting his own lifestyle: in this, Wilde saw the manifesto of creative hedonism. This vision was significantly different to that of Baudelaire, for whom the dandy was far closer to the artist. This is an important difference: for Wilde, the contemplative, reflective critic is closer to the truth than the artist himself. From his bird's eye view, at a remove from the battlefield of everyday life, maintaining a safe distance, the critic, Wilde holds, is better able to be wise. Thus, in the decadent tradition, the dandy's obsession with style, his coldness and remove from the hustle and bustle of everyday life, are filled with a different meaning.

Wilde's Dandyism and Camp

> In every generation Society has its favourites, who lead and follow it at the same time, occupy themselves largely or exclusively with trivialities, and yet remain men of real ability and character. Brummell, Lytton, and D'Orsay are examples. But Wilde carried the pose much further than any of his forerunners and made explicit what they had implied. Those who knew him well were made to realize that over-careful dress was almost the least of his dandyisms. He appeared to have subdued his existence into a pattern, a formula of elegance lacking at no point in dignity of style. He was never off parade; not even when he laughed at himself, as he constantly did; even his handwriting displayed a conscious beauty of form.[29]

Arthur Symons's view of Wilde was not uncommon, although his thoughts on Wilde's elegant dress may, at first glance, appear paradoxical. Appearance, he claims, was not the most important thing for Wilde. What mattered far more, he insists, was Wilde's conscious Aesthetic self-fashioning as an individual, his tone of freedom, his determination never to be 'off parade'. Wilde's first, and most successful, role in society was that of the classical Aesthetic dandy. In his style of dress, ironic remarks, and general comportment, he can be seen as continuing the tradition of dandyism. He also brought a new tendency to look at his own mask of a dandy in a detached manner, as an observer. Thanks to this, he was able to produce his memorable plays, in which dandies are often portrayed. Present in virtually all of Wilde's plays, dandies are frequently among the main characters. In his directions, Wilde describes their traits with cutting precision. Lord Goring, in 'An Ideal Husband', is said to be

> …thirty-four, but always says he is younger. A well-bred, expressionless face. He is clever, but would not like to be thought so. A flawless dandy, he would be annoyed if he were considered romantic. He plays with life, and is on perfectly good terms with the world. He is fond of being misunderstood. It gives him a post of vantage.[30]

Wilde's lapidary description, whilst painting a picture of a familiar literary type, also conveys the author's sarcastic, deliberate remove from his character. Goring proves key in resolving the muddles in which the characters find themselves: at the crucial moment, Wilde stresses, he shows 'the philosopher that underlies the dandy'.[31] Upon more careful scrutiny, however, Goring's dandyism appears tinged with parody.

> Enter Lord Goring in evening dress with a buttonhole. He is wearing a silk hat and Inverness cape. White-gloved, he carries a Louis Seize cane. His are all the delicate fopperies of Fashion. One sees that he stands in immediate relation to modern life, makes it indeed, and so masters it. He is the first well-dressed philosopher in the history of thought.[32]

At first glance, one might think one is genuinely reading a description of an elegant, finely dressed arbiter of fashion. The final sentence, however, trips one up: Wilde's irony is beyond doubt, and all the more effective for being unexpected. This intriguing overture continues with a wonderful exchange between Goring and his man Phipps.

LORD GORING. Got my second buttonhole for me, Phipps?
PHIPPS. Yes, my lord. [Takes his hat, cane, and cape, and presents new buttonhole on salver.]
LORD GORING. Rather distinguished thing, Phipps. I am the only person of the smallest importance in London at present who wears a buttonhole.
PHIPPS. Yes, my lord. I have observed that,
LORD GORING. [Taking out old buttonhole.] You see, Phipps, Fashion is what one wears oneself. What is unfashionable is what other people wear.
PHIPPS. Yes, my lord.
LORD GORING. Just as vulgarity is simply the conduct of other people.
PHIPPS. Yes, my lord.
LORD GORING. [Putting in a new buttonhole.] And falsehoods the truths of other people.
PHIPPS. Yes, my lord.
LORD GORING. Other people are quite dreadful. The only possible society is oneself.
PHIPPS. Yes, my lord.
LORD GORING. To love oneself is the beginning of a lifelong romance, Phipps.[33]

Goring's musings, essentially a monologue, are a chain of aphorisms, the vigour of parody is increasing with each utterance. This 'manifesto' of dandyism is presented to the acquiescent Phipps with exemplary self-irony: many of these sayings were already attributed to Wilde himself, and had appeared in his earlier writings. In 'The Picture of Dorian Gray', for instance, some of them are uttered by Lord Henry.

Thus, Wilde's method of narration offers a number of striking traits. Firstly, the author presents ideas which lie close to his heart in the form of a caricature. Secondly, simplifying these ideas, he renders them accessible to a mass readership. Thirdly, through his tone of irony, the author maintains a degree of remove, even though his intimate knowledge of the subject is clear.

It was not until the twentieth century that this method of narration began to be recognised and described as 'Camp'. The term 'Camp' became widely used by critics following Susan Sontag's 1964 essay 'Notes on "Camp"'.[34] Sontag defined Camp as an aesthetic perspective characterized by a love of the unnatural, artifice, and exaggeration. For Sontag, Camp is a sensibility closely connected with the theatrical and carnival aspects of urban culture, cross-dressing, and gay parades.

An esoteric code, Camp is not for the many, but for the few. A private affair, it revels in theatricality: those wearing masks must be able to recognise their own kind. Secret games, provocations, flirting, the tantalising promise of mysteries unveiled – all these form elements of Camp.

Camp largely overlaps with queer culture, yet, aesthetically, it is broader. Camp welcomes the androgynous in any form. 'What is most beautiful in virile men is something feminine; what is most beautiful in feminine women is something masculine,'[35] Sontag wrote. Such, for instance, were the ideal 'archetypical' faces of Greta Garbo or Marlene Dietrich.

Very early on, attempts were made to classify Camp. In his 1954 novel 'The World in the Evening', Christopher Isherwood drew the distinction between High and Low Camp. In our view, from a critical perspective, these categories remain relevant. In contemporary Russian culture, for instance, High Camp is represented by figures such as Andrey Bartenev. Wilde's Aethetic dress worn for his American tour is another example of High Camp.

Susan Sontag also distinguished between naïve and deliberate Camp, where naïve, 'pure' Camp is a genuine attempt to create beauty. The result may be kitsch, like the extravagantly ostentatious costumes of cabaret dancers. Deliberate Camp is self-aware and reflective, though no less expressive. Wilde's most memorable characters are deliberately 'camping'. A true master of deliberate Camp was Salvador Dalí, who, of course, also loved to play the dandy.

Of the delicate balance between naïve and deliberate Camp, the intonation of self-parody is born. 'Being natural is simply a pose, and the most irritating pose I know,'[36] Lord Henry laments ironically. Sontag takes this paradox further:

> the whole point of Camp is to dethrone the serious… Camp involves a new, more complex relation to 'the serious. One can be serious about the frivolous, frivolous about the serious.[37]

Camp, for Sontag, was a strategy of 'aggressive self-defence', a contemporary modification of romantic irony which brings new principles of theatricality and artifice as ideal. Camp is comedy, which always supposes a degree of remove (where tragedy, on the contrary, implies total engagement).

At this point, Sontag brings dandyism into her line of reasoning.

> Detachment is the prerogative of an elite; and as the dandy is the 19th century's surrogate for the aristocrat in matters of culture, so Camp is the modern dandyism. Camp is the answer to the problem: how to be a dandy in the age of mass culture.[38]

The dandies of previous generations, Sontag muses, valued rare objects and good taste, yet the

> connoisseur of Camp has found more ingenious pleasures. Not in Latin poetry and rare wines and velvet jackets, but in the coarsest, commonest pleasures, in the arts of the masses. Mere use does not defile the objects of his pleasure, since he learns to possess them in a rare way. Camp – Dandyism in the age of mass culture – makes no distinction between the unique object and the mass-produced object. Camp taste transcends the nausea of the replica.[39]

Once they have left behind the limitations of traditional 'good taste', lovers of Camp are free to discover all the pleasures of what Sontag terms the 'good taste of bad taste'. This, she claims, is an exhilaratingly liberating experience, which opens the door to a whole host of new opportunities and bold stylistic experiments one may mix and match at will. Camp, Sontag suggests, may even allow the new-style dandy to accept vulgarity: 'Where the dandy would be continually offended or bored, the connoisseur of Camp is continually amused, delighted.'

In this, Oscar Wilde was a traditional dandy, rather than a lover of Camp: vulgarity in any form, he could not stomach. His biting quips targeted narrow-minded bourgeois morals and petty norms of decorum. Sontag sees Wilde as a 'transitional' figure: in art, he supports high Aestheticism. His main contribution to Camp sensibility, Sontag claims, was his formulation of the equivalence of all objects. His demonstrative delight at blue china, neckties, and boutonnieres is, Sontag suggests, a precursor to the 'democratic esprit' of Camp. In this spirit of aestheticization, however, Wilde was already following the ideology of William Morris, the Pre-Raphaelites, and the Arts and Crafts movement. One of his American lectures, as we recall, was devoted to interior design.

Adopting Wilde's 'new hedonism', present-day lovers of Camp delight in seeking untapped sources of creativity in the 'good taste of bad taste'. Mixing styles with courage and wit, they feel liberated and inspired. Visiting a flea market, a camper may purchase some Gavarni prints, together with a purple feather boa for good measure.

Camp, Sontag continues, is closely connected with queer culture: its unique, heady mix of decadence, travesty, irony, and aestheticism appeals to the queer community. Thus, after Wilde, the flavour of dandyism came to include notes of gay and queer. If, previously, men of fashion could show their passion for exquisite dress without arousing suspicion around their sexual orientation, after Wilde, dandies came to be seen as closely linked to a sexual minority. Decadent dandyism was viewed as playing with fire in search of forbidden erotic pleasure.

Following Wilde's trial, and his outspoken speech on 'the love that dare not speak its name', his relationship with Lord Alfred Douglas turned into a chapter of cultural history, a living legend with no less influence on contemporary minds than 'The Picture of Dorian Gray'. Indeed, the legal proceedings may have made more of an impact on social consciousness, than did Wilde's novel. Young men began to associate themselves with the writer and his characters. In his famous book, Havelock Ellis recounts the stories of several young men who realized their sexual identity as the topic was publicly discussed for the first time during the trial.

Despite warnings from friends, Wilde did not flee the country, deciding instead to walk his chosen path to the end. His arrest was widely anticipated. He was sentenced to two years in prison: an experience which ruined his health, as well as his relationship with Alfred Douglas. Writing his poignant text 'De Profundis' in jail, Wilde bids farewell to his lover, and to his dandy days.

> I let myself be lured into long spells of senseless and sensual ease. I amused myself with being a flâneur, a dandy, a man of fashion. I surrounded myself with the smaller natures and the meaner minds. I became the spendthrift of my own genius, and to waste an eternal youth gave me a curious joy. Tired of being on the heights, I deliberately went to the depths in the search for new sensation. What the paradox was to me in the sphere of thought, perversity became to me in the sphere of passion.[40]

Recounting his 'sins', Wilde remains strikingly eloquent and candid. Even in these grim, heavy days, he remains himself.

Wilde's fate sounded a dreadful warning to other members of gender minorities. Many opted to leave England, hoping to find refuge in more liberal France. French high society, however, proved barely more tolerant: after all, Robert de Montesquiou never made public his homosexual tendencies, and Marcel Proust in his novel deemed it safest to portray his young male lover as the charming Albertine.

In England, the trial of Oscar Wilde was much discussed, its outcome likely instrumental in keeping queer and gay themes out of social and literary life for decades. At his own request, for instance, E. M. Forster's 1912 novel 'Maurice' was only published in 1971, after the writer's death.

Wilde's lifelong process of self-fashioning fully brought out the hint of tragedy, ever present in dandy stories. This clearly manifested itself with George Brummell also, especially during his French period, which ended with the Beau, destitute and demented. Never far off in Baudelaire's life, tragedy closely followed even the ostensibly contented Count D'Orsay. 'The desire for beauty is merely a heightened form of the desire for life,'[41] Wilde wrote. After his term in prison, the writer admitted he had lost the joie de vivre necessary for writing.

How, then, might we sum up Oscar Wilde's contribution to dandyism? Thanks to Wilde, European dandyism accepted the challenge of mass culture, developing the Camp aesthetic. From elitist dandyism, Wilde himself shifted towards playful Camp. His trip to America became the first instance of the commodification of dandyism. With the aid of Wilde's eclectic outfit, designed as it was to make a striking impression, and his lectures, which brought together the main ideas of Aestheticism, dandyism was turned into a commercial product of mass demand. In his talks, Wilde contrived to fuse the formal clarity of French treatises on dandyism with the depth of Pater and Ruskin. His American tour became the first successful experiment in the popularisation of dandyism, which came to be widely seen as a collection of familiar poses and ironic aphorisms. The new version of dandyism was enhanced with its own advertising campaign, ready to enter mass culture. Thanks to Oscar Wilde, decadent dandyism became a successful brand. The commodification of dandyism was complete.

Dandyism after Oscar Wilde

How did dandyism evolve after Oscar Wilde? Over time, the velvet coats, sophisticated accessories, purple, mustard, and blue berets of bohemian Aesthetes were taken up by Russia's Mir Iskusstva (World of Art) movement, and, later, by the likes of Cecil Beaton, Stephen Tennant, and Harold Acton. By the turn of the century, the image of the refined Dandy-Aesthete, so strikingly presented by James McNeill Whistler and Robert de Montesquiou, was seeing its fullest development in England.

In 1896, Sir Max Beerbohm's essay 'Dandies and Dandies' appeared. At first glance, this famed text appeared a natural continuation of the tradition of dandy treatises. Upon closer examination, however, one becomes aware that its entire fabric contains a multitude of microscopic mirrors of ironic reflection.

The dandy described by Beerbohm is said throughout his life to have kept a diary of his outfits. Every year, the author explains, he would begin a fresh Journal de Toilette, and, by the time of their meeting, some fifty volumes had been produced. An entire collected works, Beerbohm enthuses with affected admiration.

> The first page of each volume of the Journal de Toilette bears the signature of Mr. Le V. and of his two valets. Of the other pages each is given up, as in other diaries, to one day of the year. In ruled spaces are recorded there the cut and texture of the suit, the colour of the tie, the form of jewellery that was worn on the day the page records. No detail is omitted and a separate space is set aside for 'Remarks'.[42]

Whether or not such a journal really existed, we cannot be certain. Most likely, it is a product of Beerbohm's ironic imagination, yet, even as such, the notion is both pleasing and plausible. In the eighteenth century, albums with fabric samples and descriptions of entire ensembles did exist,[43] albeit without remarks from the authors, and can still be found in museum collections.

A fictional character, Mr. Le V. is so strikingly and colourfully described, one has no doubt he was based on a real figure. A Dandy-Aesthete, he follows the traditions of true men of fashion, devoting the first part of his day to the rituals of his toilet. Like George Brummell, during these procedures he receives visitors and admirers: for his devoted followers, being present at his petit lever is a sign of good taste, and a lesson in self-care.

The way in which Le V. structures his time and space is described by Beerbohm in intriguing detail. Based in St. James's Street, Le V. is next door to London's main clubs.

> In the first room the Master sleeps. He is called by one of his valets, at seven o'clock, to the second room, where he bathes, is shampooed, is manicured and, at length, is enveloped in a dressing gown of white wool. In the third room is his breakfast upon a little table and his letters and some newspapers. Leisurely he sips his chocolate, leisurely learns all that need be known. With a cigarette he allows his temper, as informed by the news and the weather and what not, to develop itself for the day. At length, his mood suggests, imperceptibly, what colour, what form of clothes he shall wear. He rings for his valet – 'I will wear such and such a coat, such and such a tie; my trousers shall be of this or that tone; this or that jewel shall be radiant in the folds of my tie.' It is generally near noon that he reaches the fourth room, the dressing-room. The uninitiate can hardly realise how impressive is the ceremonial there enacted. As I write, I can see, in memory, the whole scene – the room, severely simple, with its lemon walls and deep wardrobes of white wood, the young fops, philomathestatoi ton neaniskon, ranged upon a long bench, rapt in wonder, and, in the middle, now sitting, now standing, negligently, before a long mirror, with a valet at either elbow, Mr. Le V., our cynosure. There is no haste, no faltering, when once the scheme of the day's toilet has been set. It is a calm toilet. A flower does not grow more calmly.[44]

By the end of this passage, Beerbohm's famed tongue in cheek can be clearly felt, the ironic intonation rising as the panegyric develops. Regardless of the sarcasm, his description of fin-de-siècle dandy habits is most valuable. A particularly striking detail is Mr. Le V.'s approach to selecting his outfits: he allows his 'temper to develop', taking time to 'feel into' his mood and desired image of the day. Focusing on his state of mind, he gives priority to his 'inner atmosphere'. His method is not dissimilar to that of contemporary Impressionist literary criticism. Anatole France, for instance, insisted that whilst reading, the critic must tap into his feelings, taking note of the most fleeting thoughts and sensations in order to pass on his impressions to the reader.

With decadent lemon wallpaper in his dressing room, Mr. Le V. can be seen as a 'close relative' of Des Esseintes and Dorian Gray. If these illustrious Aesthetes pursued their experiments with sensations with the aid of art, however, Le V. is quite happy with a newspaper, letters, and the weather report. Where Des Esseintes plans his abode as an Aesthete's heaven, choosing every detail with the greatest care, Le V. moves between rooms in strict order, in accordance with his daily routine. His 'royal' petit lever can be seen as an ironic version of Brummell's midday receptions.

In the first decades of the twentieth century, the tradition of dandy Aestheticism was continued by Ronald Firbank.[45] One of those men, who are 'naturally artificial, and sincerely paradoxical', the writer adored extravagant dress. For a social visit, he might choose dark pink trousers with black stripes, and a silk hat, although his usual favourite was a strikingly positioned bowler.

Firbank was often compared to a butterfly, an image linked to the dandy style and temperament. Adoring strawberries, peaches, champagne, and Monte Fiascone wine, he strove always for sensual perfection. Even in the library, the writer would choose books for their beautiful covers, or satisfying dimensions of the pages. For many years, he composed his works on blue postcards, expertly conjuring up an atmosphere of spicy fin-de-siècle decadence. In his final letter, he apologizes to a friend for not being able to receive him in his hotel, not because of any illness, but because the wallpaper in his bedroom was so terrible. Even after Firbank's death, contemporaries would often recall his unusually abrupt, raucous, and irrepressible laugh. His novel 'The Artificial Princess' has been republished several times.[46] In life, as in his art, this late decadent writer mastered the Camp style of Oscar Wilde brilliantly.

The Aesthetes, of course, borrowed much from the English macaronis of the second half of the eighteenth century. Favouring French and Italian trends, these men of fashion chose bizarre, eye-catching outfits, often eliciting public suspicion and bemusement. The late-nineteenth-century Aesthetes developed an invisible defence against social attitudes, however, with the self-irony of Camp: ridiculing someone already ridiculed by the narrator is, after all, far more difficult. Paradoxically, in twentieth-century literature, the continued existence of the Aesthete was due to Camp discourse: through this, the dandy was able to survive as a cultural hero.

Notes

1 Oscar Wilde, *Phrases and Philosophy for the Use of the Young* (London: 1903), https://www.sas.upenn.edu/~cavitch/pdf-library/Wilde_Phrases_and_Philosophies.pdf. Accessed 29.04.2022.
2 Oscar Wilde, *Interviews and Recollections*, vols. 1–2 (London: Macmillan, 1979), 1: 395.
3 Oscar Wilde, ibid., 1: 394.

4 For more detailed analysis, see Regenia Gagnier, *Idylls of the Marketplace: Oscar Wilde and the Victorian Public* (Stanford: Stanford University Press, 1986).
5 Ellen Moers, *The Dandy: Brummell to Beerbohm* (New York: The Viking Press, 1960), 292.
6 The first aniline dyes were low-quality products, which tended to produce somewhat unpleasant, 'poisonous' shades. In carpet-making, the use of aniline dyes caused a marked deterioration in quality, with carpets that were less visually pleasing, faded quickly in the sun, and ran during cleaning.
7 Dr. Gustav Jaeger (1832–1917) was a German scientist, hygienist and physiologist. In 1884, Jaeger published his book 'Sanitary Woollen System', in which he defended the advantages of woollen undergarments and clothing. Among his followers was George Bernard Shaw. Lewis Tomalin translated the book into English, and opened a Jaeger shop selling woollen clothing in London in 1884.
8 Oscar Wilde, *Selected Letters of Oscar Wilde*, ed. Rupert Hart-Davis (Oxford: Oxford University Press, 1979), 55–56.
9 *Selected Letters of Oscar Wilde*, 57.
10 Richard Ellmann, *Oscar Wilde* (New York: Vintage, 1988), 259.
11 Ibid.
12 *Selected Letters of Oscar Wilde*, 91.
13 Ibid., 92.
14 Oscar Wilde, *Essays and Lectures* (London: Methuen and Co, 1913), 164.
15 Oscar Wilde, *Interviews and Recollections*, vols. 1–2 (London: Macmillan, 1979), 1: 270.
16 Many critics insist that Bunthorne was modelled on a number of figures including Whistler, Rossetti, Swinburne, and Ruskin.
17 Oscar Wilde, *The Complete Letters of Oscar Wilde*, eds. Merlin Holland and Rupert Hart-Davis (New York: Henry Holt, 2000), 141.
18 Ellmann, 245.
19 Olga Vainshtein, "The Latest Thing for Boys": Little Lord Fauntleroy and Children's Fashion, *Archivist Addendum*, 2021, 42–69.
20 Oscar Wilde, *The Collected Works of Oscar Wilde* (Herts: Wordsworth Editions Ltd., 2007), 91.
21 Similar themes had already been developed by Flaubert in 'Salammbô'. For more detailed analysis, see the chapter on dandyism and literature in this book.
22 The Collected Works of Oscar Wilde, 88.
23 *Selected Letters of Oscar Wilde*, 116.
24 Ibid., footnote 3. A quote from Wilde's letter to E. Pratt of 15 April 1892.
25 *Selected Letters of Oscar Wilde*, 116.
26 The Collected Works of Oscar Wilde, 8.
27 Ibid., 35.
28 Ibid., 999.
29 Arthur Symons, The Diner out, in *Interviews and Recollections*, vols. 1–2 (London: Macmillan, 1979), 1: 175.
30 The Collected Works of Oscar Wilde, 598–599.
31 Ibid., 659.
32 Ibid., 633.
33 Ibid.
34 Susan Sontag, Notes on Camp, in *Against Interpretation and Other Essays* (New York: Noonday, 1966), 275–293.
35 Sontag, 280.
36 The Collected Works of Oscar Wilde, 7.
37 Sontag, 279.
38 Ibid., 280.
39 Ibid., 281.
40 Selected Letters of Oscar Wilde, 194.

41 Wilde, *Interviews and Recollections*, 1:41.
42 Sir Max Beerbohm, Dandies and Dandies, in *The Works of Max Beerbohm* (London: Charles Scribner's Sons, 1896), 27–28.
43 *A Lady of Fashion: Barbara Johnson's Album of Styles and Fabrics*, ed. Natalie Rothstein (New York: Thames and Hudson, 1987). One might also recall a similar album by Prince Kurakin (see the chapter on Russian 'petit maître' in this book).
44 Beerbohm, 26–27.
45 Arthur Annesley Ronald Firbank (1886–1926) was a British writer and dandy. Among his best-known works are 'Inclinations' (1916), 'Caprice' (1917), and 'Sorrow in Sunlight' (1925).
46 Ronald Firbank, *The Artificial Princess* (London: Duckworth, 1934).

Chapter Seven

RUSSIAN DANDYISM

Russian 'Petit Maître': Occupational Hazards

Dandies, petits maîtres, muscadins: Russia's men of fashion were known by many names. Historically, there were different words in Russian denoting the man of fashion. The first words in use included 'shchegol' (fop), 'petimetr' (petit maître), and 'fert' (coxcomb). Times changed, new words appeared, yet beaux always strove to look their best, arousing distrust in some, and admiration, in others.[1]

The origins of Russian dandyism can be traced back to the eighteenth century. Let us begin by taking a closer look at Russian dandies of this period. Here is the typical portrait of the man of fashion – Prince Kurakin, who had a nickname 'diamond Prince', so fond was he of luxurious costumes, richly decorated with diamonds and precious stones.

> Kurakin was a great pedant about clothes. Every morning when he awoke his servant handed him a book, like an album, where there were samples of the materials from which his amazing suits were sewn and pictures of outfits. For every outfit there was a particular sword, buckles, ring, and a snuffbox. Once, playing cards with the Empress the Prince suddenly felt something amiss; opening his snuff-box, he saw that the ring which was on his finger did not go at all with the box, and the box did not match the rest of his outfit. His displeasure was so great, that even though he had a very strong hand he still lost the game, but fortunately nobody except himself noticed the dreadful carelessness of his servant.[2]

All of Kurakin's actions were highly typical of the eighteenth-century man of fashion. For him the harmony of the details of his costume was the basis of his spiritual tranquillity and feeling in control. One might remember here the ironic saying of R.W. Emerson, who once declared that the sense of being perfectly well-dressed gives a feeling of inner tranquillity which even religion is powerless to bestow. His album is not unlike Journal de Toilette of Mr.Le.V. Kurakin behaved like a classic aristocrat, using fashion as a sign of his high status, wealth, and economic ability to manage his personal property to the greatest effect. Thus, an involuntary neglect of trifles equalled for him for a symbolic loss of status that left him feeling exposed, almost naked.

In this story there is also something else curious – the tone of the narrator. For Mikhail Pyliayev, writing about this event in 1898, classified it as an eccentricity that betrays peculiarities of character. Such anecdotes were quite commonplace in European biographies of the dandy. By the end of the nineteenth century in Russia, aristocratic dandy culture was already fairly incomprehensible, since even at court a standard of dark frock coats and black tails reigned.[3]

Pyliayev's intonation here contains inevitable irony, but note that there is a nuance of respectful admiration. When he says further with obvious sympathy 'Prince Kurakin never in his entire life insulted anyone', he explains everything.[4] This ethical criterion is decisive, even though it is mentioned in passing. We will return to this important factor later.

The luxurious costume of Kurakin would have been impossible outside the context of an existing vestimentary tradition. Peter the Great established the beginnings of a culture of foppishness in Russia by issuing in 1700 his famous decrees ordering 'all ranks of persons' to shave their beards, wear German and Hungarian dress on workdays and French costume on holidays. These decrees were aimed at all social classes except the clergy, coachmen, and peasants engaged in agriculture. The appropriate examples of costume were displayed on mannequins and fines were set for failure to observe the new norms.

One might be tempted to think here about the Foucaldian 'discipline and punish' policy, the effort of the power to write its message on the docile bodies of people, but I would like to stress another aspect: this dress reform made possible the appearance in Russia of a new European style of daily and formal apparel and finally later resulted in the adoption of dandyism by some members of Russian gentry as a specific cultural method of self-presentation.

What kind of dress was brought in by the Petrine reforms? According to J. Laver, in Europe the fashionable outfit took shape under Louis XIV and consisted of a coat, vest, and knee-length pants.[5] It had rather complex trimmings – round frills on the shirt front (called 'jabots') and sleeves decorated with buttons (of which there could be over a hundred) and sewn with gold or silver thread and braid. In the first half of the eighteenth-century women's and men's costumes were made from the same materials – brocade, velvet, patterned silk – while for men's coats, sequins, gold and silver thread, coloured mirror glass, and foil insets were used too. Bright colours – pinks, yellows, and greens – were also thought appropriate for men's clothing. They were considered normal for a masculine style and no one accused the aristocratic dandy of the eighteenth century of exaggerated devotion to decoration and colour, later considered the attributes of feminine dress, since these were the universal language of fashion at that time.

The importation of this aristocratic fashion with a European accent resulted in the adoption of foppish behaviour by some members of the Russian gentry as a specific cultural form of self-expression. This was an example of successful modernization not only in dress but also in lifestyle, an indicator that Russia was participating in European historical development. During the eighteenth century Russian fashion changed several times,[6] culminating in the male wardrobe of the 1780s becoming simpler under the mediating influence of English clothing. Yet these changes all took place within the European framework laid down by Peter the Great at the start of the century.

In the eighteenth-century Russia, fashionable men were chiefly found among the aristocracy nearest to the court, but in Catherine the Great's time (1762–1796) there appeared a kind of fop from the middling sort, imitating (sometimes in quite caricatured form) noble fashion. These men of fashion were called in the French manner 'petits maîtres', that is, fops. The patriarchal structure of Russian society dictated a reserved attitude to finery among most members of the middle class: excessive attention to one's toilet was judged to be evidence of conceit and vanity, and there was widespread moralistic condemnation of fashionable men. Despite this disapproval, some people from the middle ranks of society did aspire to dress according to the latest fashion.

In his second satire, the Russian poet Antioch Kantemir offers a detailed description of Evgeny, an ardent follower of fashion. A true expert in the latest male dress, Evgeny muses at length on the texture of coattails, the shape of sleeves, and the precise positioning of pockets. In any season, be it spring, autumn, summer, or winter, he can offer the best tips on impeccable costume.

The charitable Filaret, while critical of Evgeny's profligacy, nonetheless gives him wise advice on choosing fabric. In summer, he explains, rich velvet would only weigh down the body, whilst in winter, taffeta appears brazenly out of place. Fabric, he concludes, should be chosen in accordance with one's age, means, station, and conditions.[7]

The patriarchal structure of Russian society dictated a reserved attitude to finery among most members of the middle class: excessive attention to one's toilet was judged to be evidence of conceit and vanity, and there was widespread moralistic condemnation of fashionable men. Despite this disapproval, some people from the middle ranks of society did aspire to dress according to the latest fashion.

Literary luminaries such as N. Novikov, A. A. Maikov, N. I. Strakhov, and I. A. Krylov frequently satirized the petits maîtres. Krylov, the wellknown author of fables, actively mocked the inclination to French fashion of young fops in the journal 'Pochta Dukhov' and in his short stories entitled 'Nochi' [Nights]. One petit maître in his satires was called Pripryzhkin (from the verb 'to hop, skip'), another Vertushkin ('to whirl, spin'). In the pamphlet 'Thoughts of a Philosopher on Fashion', Krylov gave ironic advice to the petit maître just starting out on 'how to look sensible with having a jot of sense'. One should speak about everything a little bit, prattle using the words of others, joke about important things, forget about modesty, get used to being a 'lucky stiff' who is not obliged to work, and so on. The society man of fashion in this ironic light became a very useless and odious creation. But it was notable that Krylov's attacks on petits maîtres were based primarily on gendered arguments, comparing the fops to women and children, unmasking their claims to masculinity.[8]

It is somewhat unexpected that Krylov did not mock the dress of the petit maître. He concentrated his analysis on discourse and manners. According to Krylov, fops spoke with voices resembling women's.

> There is another way to speak amusingly without sense, only make your tongue as flexible and agile as a chatterbox's; but this is a difficult art, that can only be learned from women. Strive to imitate them, strain so that your words have no connection nor sense, so that your conversation switches topics five times in a minute, so that abuse, praise, laughter, pity and simple tales, all of it just mixed together, fly past the ears of those who listen to you.[9]

In the paradoxical logic of Krylov, the fop appealed to women the more he spoke as they did. Symbolically denying the man of fashion masculinity in speech, Krylov nevertheless linked him with women, offering disparaging caricatures of their likeness to one another.

An analogous attitude was used in comparing the fop with children, although the pamphleteer's tone was outwardly less aggressive: he rather 'forgives' his unsuccessful hero, as though he were an innocent child.

> You just play quietly with your toys; you are kept quiet with your catkins, carriages, dogs, caftans, women; you often get into scraps, but then children fight over their trifles. Your quarrels are no more important than theirs, and so like theirs are just as innocent.[10]

The two lines of comparison, with childishness and femininity, hinted at a likening of the petit maître to a girl. Krylov wrote that the fop 'in his deliberations about important things was so funny and simple, like a little girl with her dolls'.[11] Thus the fop in his scheme was denied those substantial signs of 'real' men, the ability to reason properly about politics and science. Similar motifs of infantilism and femininity can be heard in the satirical invective against fops from Novikov and Strakhov.

The attraction to European fashion in Russian mentalities was automatically tied to western ideologies, so that those who prized foreign fashion were assumed to prize foreign ideas as well. When relations with the West soured, therefore, men of fashion were forced to endure various indignities. Plainly, in Russia much more than in other countries, attempts to regulate fashion had come from above for purely political reasons, so it was more likely that the fashionable man could become a 'fashion victim' in not only a figurative but literal sense.

Paul I in the first days of his reign in 1796 published special decrees against European dress, which for him symbolized the liberal ideas of the French Revolution. As F. F. Vigel' noted,

> Paul took up arms against round hats, tails, waistcoats, pantaloons, boots and shoes with cuffs. He strictly prohibited wearing them and ordered they be replaced with single-breasted jackets with standing collars, tri-cornered hats, shirts, short undergarments and Hessian boots.[12]

Attempting to influence fashion with purely police methods, Paul sent special detachments of soldiers into city streets to tear offending garments off their wearers, forcing unhappy fashion plates to find their way home half-dressed.

Ironically, the offending fashion was English in origin, having appeared in France before the Revolution. The top hat was worn instead of the popular tri-cornered hat by British country gentlemen, as were boots instead of shoes, and so too with the tail-coat, originally a riding-coat, and the short waistcoat instead of the long nobleman's vest. They eschewed lace on sleeves and jabots and luxurious embroideries, since these attributes of aristocratic linery were ill-suited to the active life in the open air and to British traditional pursuits like fox-hunting.[13]

Attempts to contradict the course of history (in this case, the internal logic of the evolution of men's costume) were always doomed to failure, so it is unsurprising that after the death of Paul in 1801 his clothing reform was spontaneously annulled.

> The first use to which young people put their newly obtained freedom was the alteration of their clothing; not two days after the news of Paul's death top hats appeared in the streets, and after about four days tails, trousers and waistcoats, although previously forbidden as an ensemble, began to appear worn together. Everything changed in St Petersburg in a few days. By the end of April, only the poorest people were still to be found wearing the old single-breasted coats and vests.[14]

These descriptions are interesting not only for the details of the rapid return of the previous style of dress, but for the social geography of these fashions. First, the vestimentary revolution proceeded faster in Moscow, for it was farther from the enforcers of power in the capital, St Petersburg, and men of fashion there had less to fear from them. Second, the most affluent were the first to express themselves in this way, as poorer people simply could not permit themselves to change their wardrobes rapidly, given the significant costs involved.

During this time, the streets of Moscow and St. Petersburg offered a curious sight, with wildly different styles mingling. The ageing beaux of Catherine's time, loyal to the look of their youth, now appeared absurdly overdressed.

> In the main streets of St. Petersburg, one could see men dressed as if for a carnival. In the first years of the reign of Nicholas I, some grandees of Catherine's time were still living, and liked to promenade with full regalia, stars, coats, and golden camisoles with gold keys on the back. One encountered old brigadiers with their white-plumed hats, aristocrats who, like in 'mother Catherine's' times, would take their stroll down Nevsky on their red heels, muffs in hand, this most aristocratic habit going back to the French kings.[15]

Typical examples of 'fossilized' fashion, these sights clearly harked back to olden days. Red heels were brought into vogue by French beaux in the first half of the eighteenth century, whilst a golden key on a camisole denoted a courtly chamberlain. In the eighteenth century, this was positioned on the left side of the back, later, in the nineteenth, on the tails of court coat.[16] The brigadiers' white plumes, of course, were also mementos of a time gone by, the rank of brigadier having been abolished in 1799. Pilyayev also gives another example of 'fossilized' eighteenth-century fashion: that even in the 1830s, a certain landowner was known for 'dressing like the Incroyables of the French Revolution, constantly wearing the same blue coat with gold buttons'.[17]

'Fashion's Loyal Devotee': Russian Dandies of the Nineteenth Century

After the repeal of Paul's decrees, men's fashion began to develop more naturally, within European lines but with Russia's usual time delays. Male dress of the beginning of the nineteenth century can be seen as marking a phase of transition. Still vivid in colour and finished with accessories, it nonetheless reflected the new trends of minimalism and simplification. The memoirs of composer and music critic Yuri Arnold offer a detailed description of a man of fashion from 1812. He still uses the old term 'muscadin', reminding about the fashions of the French Revolution:

> The main items in the wardrobe of the muscadin were his coats, and only they were deemed worthy of being known as 'habits'. At that time overcoats, in the current sense of the word, did not exist. The item known as the 'surtout' was indeed worn over all others, thus fulfilling the functions of the coat. The petit maître had to possess no fewer than three coats. The first, for morning errands or visits, was his 'habit pour aller en ville'. The accepted colour for this was green, the exact shade determined by the wearer's age. Older gentlemen wore 'vert foncé de bouteille', men of middle age, 'vert gris', whilst very young men had 'vert de pomme'. For a dîner en ville, the only acceptable options were indigo, or azur de Naples. Balls (and funerals) called for black, the difference lying in the material used for the lining and lapels: if a ball demanded satin, a burial called for merino. Two types of hauts-de-chausses were worn. The first, pantalons, were ankle-length, and the second, culottes, shorter, just below the knee, where they fastened with a gold or silver buckle, sometimes decorated with precious stones. Culottes were always made of thick black satin, considered obligatory for balls. Two types of pantalons were in use. The first, from Manchester velvet, were used for going about one's daily business. The second, from a fine black material not unlike satin, known as drap à la francaise, were donned for visits, although they could also be worn with everyday clothing.[18]

The fashionable outfits described by Arnold are virtually the same as those worn by European fops of the time.[19] In 1810s, in England and France, brightly coloured coats were also popular, although the exact shade might vary with time of day, and according to the age and social standing of the wearer. In St. Petersburg, just as in Paris or London, most men's tailors and shoemakers were of German origin. In Russia, as in other countries, tailors would commonly recommend particular styles or material to their clients.

The sign of a well-dressed beau was not only an impeccable coat, but properly selected accessories, also. With black pantalons, one chose patterned black silk stockings and closed shoes with small buckles. With the shorter culottes, however, beaux had to don long black silk stockings, and more open shoes, with large metal buckles.

In the decades following the costume changes of the French revolutionary epoch, the minimalist style of the British dandy gradually became more popular. In England the word 'dandy' was already in use around 1810, and it was adopted in France between 1815 and 1820. In Russia, the word 'dandy' appeared in 1820–1823, first used by Pushkin in 'Eugene Onegin': 'kak dandy londonskiy odet' (dressed like a London dandy).[20] Characteristically, Pushkin, being a dandy himself,[21] spelled it in English, as it was still a new word, and explained its meaning in a special note. The Russian spelling of the word 'dandy' varied throughout the nineteenth century and there existed other words in this semantic field (frant, shematon, and lev) but gradually 'dandy' became the most generally accepted term.[22]

The dandy style in Russia, as in Europe, entailed a simplicity of contours and economy of expressive forms, yet with a significant emphasis on the eroticism of the male body. Neoclassic 'nude fashion' was primarily achieved through very tight pants.

> Trousers were closefitting; such that 'avoir la jambe bien faite' (to have nicely shaped legs) was considered among the prime external qualities of the petit maître. This quality was far less marked in other trouser forms then becoming fashionable, such as long and wide 'à la marinière' or 'Jacobin' pants.[23]

This small example of French terminology describes a style and also demonstrates the use of foreign fashion jargon among dandies. In nineteenth-century Russia this was extremely prevalent, and many dandies subscribed to French fashion journals. Meanwhile in Paris, London, St Petersburg, and elsewhere in Europe, most tailors and bootmakers were German. Tailors frequently suggested the appropriate types of materials and fashions. Not for nothing did Pushkin complain: 'But pantaloons, tailcoat, vest / In Russian such words don't exist.'[24]

The lively debates in the nineteenth century over foreign influences often linked the borrowing of fashion ideas and of West European words. As O. A. Proskurin convincingly demonstrated, partisans of French fashion were perceived to be promoters of a 'freethinking cosmopolitanism', of destructive liberal ideas and of the defiling of the native language.[25] The 'language – dress' parallel is often drawn in the debate on 'Old and New Language'. Even power institutions have been shown to acknowledge the close links between fashion and political freedom. 'In your conversations with Bestuzhev, in what sense, and with what aim, did you passionately advocate Russian dress and freedom of publication?' – investigators in the Decembrists' case enquired of Alexander Griboyedov.[26]

In a polemic against the followers of historian N. M. Karamzin, traditionalist thinker A. S. Shishkov created the image of the literary dandy, the bearer of a 'fashionable-urbane consciousness', for whom the call to revive primordial Russian speech was as absurd as the attempts to bring back old-fashioned homespun coats and caftans.

Shishkov need not have feared the demise of Russian uniqueness. While the Russian dandy externally resembled his European brothers, he nevertheless displayed distinctions that highlighted his national difference.

The Distinctions of Russian Dandies

First, Russian dandies trying to prove their affluence through their dress often misused expensive accessories: 'Certain Croesuses contrived to display their wealth by setting large diamonds in the center of each silk button.'[27] English dandies invariably condemned such examples of 'conspicuous consumption'; not for nothing George Brummell, at the very outset of his career, instructed the Prince of Wales to avoid what he considered to be the vulgar passion for diamonds. Russian dandies did not share Brummell's scorn, and they favoured expensive pins to fasten crimped cambric shirt frills, rings, and not one, but a pair of watches, preferably by the French firm Breguet. This 'pairing' was a distinctive departure from European fashion; Russian dandies always sought to wear two timepieces while Europeans were normally satisfied with just one. Watches were carried in special pockets inside one's waistcoat. The heavy gold watch chain was extracted for display, and loaded with pendants decorated with precious stones, or carved with the family emblem.

Secondly, Russian fashionable men (and women) were criticized for trying too hard, and their efforts were obvious to all. Since they viewed their clothing, in fact their entire outfit, as enormously important, they desperately saw to every detail, especially colours, and what was worse, having acquired the proper outfit, they frequently felt fettered by it, fearing that the tiniest unnecessary movement might spoil their toilet. In their desire to 'out-French' the French, they drew attention to their desperation to 'catch up'. The trend-setting dandies of Western Europe permitted themselves, as a rule, departures from the strict requirements of fashion in favour of personal taste or comfort. They affected tranquillity and relaxation, free poses, and gestures.

The third difference in the style of Russian dandies was linked with the necessities occasioned by wintry weather. Whatever the desire to imitate the French, they had to factor in the specifics of Russia's cold climate. For winter wear frock coats were made from heavy wool fabric, and over these were worn full, sleeveless cloaks or fur coats. Indeed, the general penchant for furs in winter always caught the notice of travellers and became an 'exotic' national feature. The fur for winter wear was called 'Russian fur' in France. Théophile Gautier, visiting Russia in 1858–1859, described street types very precisely:

> The young people who are neither military nor civil-service personnel are dressed in fur coats, the cost of which would surprise a foreigner, and our fashionable types would refuse to pay such prices. Not only are they made from fine cloth and marten or nutria furs, but they sew beaver collars on them that cost between 200 and 300 rubles, depending on how coarse or soft the fur is, how dark its color, and the number of white bristles still protruding from it. A coat with a price of a thousand is not regarded as exceptional, and many coats cost much more. This is a Russian luxury unknown to us. In St Petersburg you could say, 'Tell me what kind of fur you're wearing, and I'll tell you what you cost.' Fur coats mark one's status.[28]

The deliberate conspicuous consumption that made an impression on Gautier was connected to the demands of a harsh climate; no fabric then available could keep one as warm as fur (Figure 22).

Théophile Gautier on Russian Dandies

An experienced dandy,[29] Gautier understood the importance of an entire outfit and made note of the variations in combinations of headgear and fur coats.

> If, having renounced the useless elegance of a hat, you wear a cap of quilted cotton or mink, then you will not be bothered by a high fur-lined collar [pushing up against the hat brim]. Mature dandies, strict adherents to London or Paris fashion, cannot tolerate quilted, peaked caps and have made for themselves caps without flaps at the back but just a simple peak at the front. But do not even think of opening your collar then; the wind will blow on your bare neck and you will suffer an icy blade as perishing as the touch of steel to the neck of a condemned man.[30]

Figure 22 Paul Gavarni. Russian fur coat. 1830.

Forced to avoid the wide-brimmed hats that prevented them from raising their collars, Russian dandies refused to wear ugly cotton caps. This was their form of aesthetic compromise. Théophile Gautier himself, it should be noted, bought a beaver hat while in Russia!

The techniques of wearing fur coats even stimulated Gautier to write on Russian gestures. Gautier was fascinated by the way in which Russian dandies donned their coats while maintaining their poise.

> They throw on a fur coat, putting an arm in a sleeve and wrapping it deeply inside, placing a hand in a little pocket on the front. To know how to wear a fur coat is an art in itself, not learned overnight. With unnoticeable movement the coat slips across the back, a hand goes into a sleeve, the coat wraps itself around the body, like swaddling for a baby.[31]

As a perceptive observer, Gautier not only comments on external appearance but also probes the social distinctions manifesting themselves through dress. In the beginning of his passage on fur coats, he notes that these were worn by young men who were not military or civil servants. Army men and officials, of course, could not wear fur coats. Thus, in the same street,

> one instantly noticed the guards officers in their grey coats with epaulettes denoting their rank. Their chests almost always covered with medals, on their heads they wore helmets or peaked caps. Then came the civil servants in long riding coats with folds on the back, pushed together by their tightly fastened belts.[32]

The Debates between Slavophiles and Westernizers on Fashion

The ideological debates between Slavophiles and Westernizers left a special mark on Russian men's fashion in the nineteenth century. They continued in a new historical framework the dispute over old and new language and masculine national dress. For a time, one's choice of costume depended on one's position in this old quarrel. European style was favoured by liberal westernizers, and there were a number of devotees of dandyism among them.

The renowned liberal Petr Chaadaev was known for the 'unusual refinement' of his garments, according to Mikhail Zhikharev, his nephew.

> One may categorically say that he dressed like no one else. His outfits were not lavish, and he never wore accessories, or any trinkets known as 'bijoux'. Many people have I seen, who dress much more extravagantly. Yet never, before or since, have I encountered anyone dressed better, who could bring off their outfit perfectly thanks to the grace and noble attitude of their person. He had undoubted 'je ne sais quoi', an indefinable, elusive quality. Everything he wore appeared flawlessly fashionable. Never was one put in mind of pictures from a magazine, on the contrary, such thoughts could not have been further from one's mind.[33]
>
> 'I do not know,' he continued, 'how Mr Brummell and his analogues dressed, and so will refrain from any comparison with these world leaders of dandyism, but I conclude that Chaadaev raised the art of costume almost to historical significance.'[34]

In a similar vein, Yuri Lotman noted, commenting on Chaadaev's style, that

> Petr Chaadaev can be an example of exquisite fashion. His dandyism did not consist in the desire to follow fashion, but in the deep conviction that he set it. The area of extravagance in his dress was precisely its daring lack of extravagance.[35]

Chaadaev's coldness towards women evoked a great deal of curiosity from his contemporaries. Some critics, like Konstantin Rotikov, not troubling to seek specific evidence, consider that Chaadaev was gay,[36] but it is noteworthy that this coldness, in combination with an aesthetic minimalism in dress, was typical of English dandies of the first generation. The clearest example was George Brummell, who never took a female lover and who promoted a strict masculinity. In his case purism reigned both in clothing and erotic preference: economy and asceticism on all levels became a fundamental principle of his aesthetic system.

European dandyism, which contemporaries sensed in Chaadaev (revered, among others, by Pushkin), contrasted starkly with the Slavophile attempts to return to a Russian national costume. Although there were fashion plates among the zealots of national tradition, their attempts at fashion à la russe looked too contrived and artificial, inevitably arousing the irony of observers. The leading Slavophile Konstantin Aksakov, as recalled by Ivan Panaev, 'made a great fuss in Moscow appearing in blacked boots, a red *rubakha*, and a *murmolka*'.[37] His propaganda had more of a comic effect.

> It is time to become closer to our people, and in order to do that we must first throw off these stupid, short German outfits that divide us from the people (meanwhile Aksakov bowed toward the ground, took off his frock coat and contemptuously threw it away). Peter the

Great, tearing us away from our nationhood, forced us to shave off our beards; we should return to our nation and grow them back.[38]

It is funny that while propounding the value of Russian costume Aksakov was normally wearing a frock coat. Of course, he did then make a spectacle of himself by taking it off.

A passionate agitator, Aksakov would attempt to persuade high society belles to exchange their outfits for traditional costume. 'Cast aside that German dress!' he would suggest to the ladies, much to their confusion. 'Why would you wish to wear it? You could set an example for our women by putting on a sarafan! It would so become your beautiful face!'[39] On one occasion, as Aksakov was delivering his sermon to a society belle, she was approached by the military governor of Moscow, Prince Shcherbatov. The woman remarked to the prince that Aksakov was trying to convince her to don a sarafan. The governor smiled. 'Are we to wear kaftans, in that case?' he enquired not without sarcasm, glancing at Aksakov. 'Yes!' Aksakov agreed emphatically, eyes sparkling, clenching his fist. 'Soon the time will come, when we will all wear kaftans!' Seeing Aksakov's enthusiasm, Prince Shcherbatov thought good to make his retreat. 'What passed between Shcherbatov and Aksakov?' someone asked Chaadaev, who had witnessed the incident. 'I really do not know,' Chaadaev responded with a slight smile.

> I think Konstantin Sergeich was trying to convince the military governor to wear a sarafan… or something of the kind.[40]

Bearing in mind Chaadaev's manner as a dandy, his sarcastic smile does not come as a surprise.

Aksakov's dislike of European dress stemmed from his ideological objection to the aristocracy as followers of Western fashion and ideas. His distaste for these was apparent even in his student years.

> When we entered the third year, a lot of the new students came from so-called aristocratic families. They brought with them all the vulgarity, the superficial decorum, the soulless propriety of their environment, all its malignant sociability. These petty noblemen had their dapper little coats made for them, and were most contented, while the other students tried to wear uniform as little as possible… If, until then, the only language spoken by the students had been Russian, one now began to hear French in the auditorium, also. Our animosity was well-justified: their vulgar formality and refined appearance took over the university, yielding their rotten fruit.[41]

This passage presents a clear divide, with Westerner students speaking French and sporting dapper university coats, while Aksakov and his friends wore ordinary civil clothes and spoke Russian. Slavophiles did not express their ideological enmity towards dandyism frivolously. They were offended not just by differing attitudes towards national traditions, but the underlying structural principle embodied in dandyism. They resisted the idea of genuine dandy as an adept of self-discipline, constantly self-regarding from a distance, checking the refinement of his bearing.

Gender Aspects

In spite of discussions and resistance European dandyism became a widespread fashion for young Russians during the 1820s. Most were affluent noble youth from very old families, and the aristocratic rank of the Russian dandy not only gave him a clear social character but suggested reasons for different speculations about dandyish masculinity.

> These suspicions usually took the form of oblique accusations of effeminacy. Again, as in the times of Krylov, descriptions of fashionable men's outfits suggested an effete, foppish image. Even in winter, the young followers of fashion wore white hats. With the palest rays of sunlight, they hurried to put up umbrellas. The gentlemen of those times wore tight trousers and hussars' boots with tassels, opulent jabots, cloche hats, and coats with bright gold buttons and tall collars. Their watch chains hung heavy with massive pendants. Some wore discrete earrings.[42]

Elegant beaux were constantly being rebuked for excessive effeminacy and accused of homosexual tendencies.

Leonid Grossman, the author of 'Pushkin and Dandyism', an article in the spirit of sociological critiques that were so popular in the 1920s in Soviet Russia, noted:

> The exhaustion of an ancient pedigree, the eclipse of a family crest is often expressed in a feminine fragility among its last members. The refinement of the physical organization, the aggravation of the nervous system, the intensification of sensitivity, these are the typical signs of the last bearers of an ancient lineage.[43]

Grossman was writing about the eponymous hero of Pushkin's poem Eugene Onegin, whom Pushkin characterized as 'an exemplary pupil of fashion', comparing him with 'Coquettish Venus'.

Reflecting on this theme, F. F. Vigel' observed in his 'Notes':

> The affectedness that one encountered then in literature was also found in the manners and attitudes of many young people. Effeminacy was not counted as a complete disgrace, and grimaces that would have been revolting to see in women were regarded as the refinements of a society education. Those who traded in such things displayed a kind of delicacy that is indecent in our sex, not concealing any fear, and hardly being amusing, which was even more surprising.[44]

In order to understand this observation, it should be remembered that Filipp Filippovich Vigel' was himself gay and as a result experienced many difficulties in his professional life.[45] He was of course unable to discuss a gay aesthetic openly in his text and as a result there are many passages filled with cautious phrases: 'a kind of delicacy', 'not counted as a complete disgrace', and 'hardly being amusing'. Sensing the contradictions, Vigel' added a supplementary conclusion to the end of this discussion:

> The present age, destroying these forms among our young people, forms so abusive especially for Russians, takes them to the other extreme, and their masculinity frequently inspires loutishness (muzhikovatost').[46]

Trying to arrive at a compromise, Vigel' hinted at his spectrum of 'masculinity', from 'effeminacy' to 'loutishness', the latter regarded in his discourse as highly negative.

Such assessments of the gender value of masculine costume are typical of the responses of many members of the nineteenth-century Russian elite. Dandyism was received as a stable virtue if it emphasized masculinity, but with suspicion, if not negativity, if it invoked any shade of effeminacy. In these circumstances practically the only way for the Russian dandy to promote himself without offending public opinion was, however paradoxically, to appear in full dress uniform.

Military Uniforms

Many young noblemen served in privileged military guards' units, such as the elite Semenov and Preobrazhenskii regiments. The military uniform had long been considered prestigious and fashionable, and there were not a few devotees of fashion in this milieu. 'Officers went about strapped into corsets; to look more imposing, staff officers fashioned artificial shoulder pads, with thick epaulets firmly bristling on them.'[47] Corsets stayed in fashion for military men even after they had disappeared from civilian men's wardrobes.

Of all the kinds of uniforms, the most dandyish was considered to be the full military dress uniform. As L. E. Shepelev wrote,

> The attitude towards full dress uniform in Russia has always been enthusiastic, even loving. Dress uniform served to conjure up memories of battle valor, honor and the exalted feeling of comradeship. The military uniform was thought to be the most elegant and attractive of masculine garments. All of this pertained especially to the ceremonial uniform, worn on grand occasions and intended particularly for them.[48]

Russian emperors always appeared in public in ceremonial dress uniform and personally regulated the changes to military dress. As elsewhere in Europe, there was in Russia a practice of using dress uniforms as rewards; government officials were made honorary commanders of military units or were given high military ranks in recognition of long service.

The elegant dress uniform worn only on special occasions was an object of pride and concern for the military dandy.

> In 1886 Adjutant General Count A. P. Shuvalov, former head of the Third Section and leader of the corps of gendarmes, later ambassador to England, was awarded a dandyish "white dress uniform" - the uniform of the Life Guards Regiment of the Cavalry - because that is where he began his service. In November of that year Shuvalov "in full ceremonial cavalry uniform" attended the dedication festivities of the Semenov Regiment.[49]

Among the upper military ranks it was typical to have several dress uniforms and to wear various ones to receptions at court or on holidays, a practice known as 'gracing society with uniforms' ('liubeznichat mundirami').

Retired military men had a special motive for 'gracing society'; the various uniforms they were entitled to wear displayed the achievements of their careers. The 1886 social calendar of Prince A. I. Bariatinsky, governor-general of the Caucasus from 1856 to 1862, is a case in point:

> He told funny stories, joked and graced society with his various dress uniforms. The other day he lunched with their Imperial Highnesses in the uniform of a cuirassier in honor of the Empress; yesterday he apparently lunched wearing a hussar's garments in honor of His Majesty; today he wears an adjutant-general's dress since it is the birthday of Grand Prince Aleksei Aleksandrovich; on the sixth of the month, he will wear the kabarda to mark the regimental holiday.[50]

There were critics of too much freedom and effeminacy even in military dress. Mikhail Pyliayev has written:

> The fashion for earrings flourished especially among military men in cavalry regiments, and though it is hard to believe, hussars of bygone days, 'wicked friends round a bottle', all followed this feminine fashion, and not only officers, but the men too wore earrings. The first to object to this fashion was General Kul'nev, the commander of the Pavlograd Hussar regiment; he published an order that all rings should be removed from soldiers' and officers' ears and turned in to him. They say that the famous saying, 'for a good friend, even the ring from my ear' was thought up by soldiers at that time. Fifty years ago, it was not thought strange to whiten and powder the face, and some dandies so adorned their faces with powder that it was shameful to look at them.[51]

For military dandies, wearing dress uniform sometimes demanded certain sacrifices, since the outfits often

> hampered movement; it was hard or even impossible to sit down, for they were easily soiled. Trousers proved particularly inconvenient. In cavalry regiments, for example, white riding breeches made of elk skin had to be put on while damp, so that ideally, they would cling to the figure. Nicholas I, who took a dandy's interest in his dress, was forced to spend many days not appearing in public as a result of soreness produced by his military uniforms.[52]

Corsets caused similar suffering.

The dandy's enjoyment of the military uniform was a typical Russian phenomenon. For European dandies, on the other hand, wearing a uniform more often signified the suppression of their individuality in dress. George Brummell sought in vain to resign his commission in the Tenth Dragoons when his regiment was forced to transfer to Manchester, because he wanted to continue his high society life in London. The French writer and dandy Barbey d'Aurevilly in his penetrating fashion noted:

> It has been said, somewhat scornfully, that military uniforms must have carried an irresistible fascination for George Brummell, but that is to explain a Dandy in terms

of the instincts of a second lieutenant. A Dandy, who places his personal stamp on everything and who cannot exist without a 'certain exquisite originality' (lord Byron), must necessarily despise uniforms.[53]

The Guards officer Konstantin Aleksandrovich Bulgakov (1812–1865) was a famous dandy among military men at the beginning of the 1840s. He expressed his attitude towards the dress uniform in comic public performances. Avdotya Panaeva recalled:

> Once in March Bulgakov appeared on Nevsky Prospekt [a main street in St Petersburg] without an overcoat and caught the attention of passersby with his bright green, very long frock coat. The reason was that an order had been issued to change the black cloth in military coats to a greenish one and to lengthen the coats somewhat. Bulgakov was the first to have a new uniform made, but he deliberately overdid it.[54]

Bulgakov made his ironic protest in a purely dandyish way, using the language of clothing, applying hyperbole to the new outfit he disliked.

Opportunities for Dandy's Self-expression

In the terminology of modern art, Bulgakov's behaviour can be called a street performance, and it would not be an exaggeration to say that at this time the theatricalization of everyday life was a frequent occurrence. Yuri Lotman has emphasized the great significance of the code of behavioural theatricality that prevailed in the culture of the early nineteenth century.[55]

It is possible to extend this idea to later decades. Mikhail Pyliayev wrote:

> At the end of the 1840s the model for dandified dress was thought to be the actor playing the part of young, first-time lover. I think that today hardly anyone would slavishly follow the fashions of the young lovers of the Aleksandrinsky Theater and curl their hair tightly into ringlets, but then middle-class dandies, having few good examples to follow, copied actors in everything. In this era young lovers wore olive-colored dolman capes with red scarves at the neck in public and to public entertainments. It was considered chic to change the scarf frequently, retaining the rest of the outfit. Young theater-goers, imitating actors, also appeared in the streets in this apparel.[56]

Everyday pursuits such as promenading also offered ample opportunities to show off effete behaviour. Flaunting their outfits, flâneurs observed each other's manners and dress. Flânerie as a special urban pastime had been practised by Russia's beaux since the early nineteenth century. As Pyliayev wrote,

> in St. Petersburg, there was a free society for lovers of promenading. Their leader, quite well-known at that time, was Doctor Ivan Yastrebtsev. The master of ceremonies was Count Sollogub, and chief advisor to the society, P. Bezobrazov. The council censor was Vasily Sots, the secretary, invariably Osipov. Members of this society received very beautiful

diplomas with allegorical depictions of the seasons in the corners, and a handsome blue frame. A lorgnette on a black ribbon served to distinguish these honorable walkers, enabling them to stand out from ordinary strollers or mere passers-by… The reasons for the appearance of this society were, perhaps, of a hygienic nature. It may also have been created to ridicule the existing rules concerning the obligatory use of carriages. At that time [the 1820s – O.V.], walking was seen as petty bourgeois. Anyone of any station was to travel in a carriage, with particular signs of distinction according to their rank, introduced by Catherine the Great.[57]

Despite the playful overtones, this set-up carefully preserved the rituals and attributes of dandy flâneuring, even including the obligatory lorgnette.

In Gogol's 'Nevsky Prospect', the narrator wonders at the spectacle on display.

O Creator! what strange characters one meets on Nevsky Prospect! There is a host of such people as, when they meet you, unfailingly look at your shoes, and, when you pass by, turn to look at your coattails. To this day I fail to understand why this happens. At first I thought they were shoemakers, but no, that is not the case: for the most part they serve in various departments, many are perfectly well able to write an official letter from one institution to another; or else they are people occupied with strolling, reading newspapers in pastry shops—in short, they are nearly all decent people. At this blessed time, from two to three in the afternoon, when Nevsky Prospect may be called a capital in motion, there takes place a major exhibition of the best products of humanity. One displays a foppish frock coat with the best of beavers, another a wonderful Greek nose, the third is the bearer of superb side-whiskers, the fourth of a pair of pretty eyes and an astonishing little hat, the fifth of a signet ring with a talisman on his smart pinkie, the sixth of a little foot in a charming bootie, the seventh of an astonishment-arousing necktie, the eighth of an amazement-inspiring mustache.[58]

Here, typically of Gogol's grotesque poetics, the ironic list of pompous metonymies serves to liken humans to inanimate objects. Noting one main detail in each outfit, the flâneur's eye turns the wearer into a commodity, a product laid out for show. This view serves to distance the reader from the scene. The discerning gaze of the flâneur is trained in metonymy. Simultaneously focused and removed, it makes out key details which, more often than not, are situated in the marginal field, near the boundary of the main picture. This could be a ring on a person's finger, a shoe, a necktie, or sideburns.

The expression 'capital in motion' *(dvizhushchayasya stolitsa)* is also a fascinating choice of chronotope: the chronotope of the flâneur, the time when Nevsky truly represents the capital, as the beaux take their daily stroll. This key role was retained by Nevsky Prospect in later years, also. In the magazine Biblioteka Dlya Chteniya (The Reader's Library), its flâneurs were described thus:

Gentlemen, lions and dandies one encountered with every step. Just like ordinary mortals, they strode by with such confidence and ease, as if doing the rounds of their own estate. Calm and carefree, their countenances shone with the certainty that this was the very best time and place for a promenade.[59]

This confidence is the mark of beaux who stride through life along a well-established fixed route. They appear in all the right places, are seen with all the right people, wear the right dress and generally do all the things seen as prestigious by the circles in which they move. Such was the carefully constructed image, the ideal strategic performance of dandyism.

Overall, the opportunities for self-expression through masculine dress were rather limited, principally because the sphere of regulation of clothing in Russia was much wider than in European countries. Military personnel, civil servants, and nobility were not permitted to appear in public as they wished but were obliged to dress in accordance with the Table of Ranks introduced by Peter I in 1722.

The main social strata, titles, ranks, and corresponding uniforms were determined by the Table of Ranks. Its general regulations were followed by more specific instructions. In 1782, for instance, uniforms were introduced in the gubernii (governorates), with each administrative unit allocated its own colour. The main reason given was the desire to 'avoid ruinous luxury' and 'preserve prosperity'. The measure, in other words, was the Russian equivalent of ancient and medieval 'laws against luxury'. In 1794, an album of sketches representing the new uniforms was published.

By the nineteenth-century, a complex hierarchy had formed, including fourteen classes each of court and civil ranks, as well as military and court suite titles and, of course, the military itself. A man's coat could tell much of his tale: 'one's coat showed the wearer's type of work, department (or branch of the military), and the class of his rank (in military service).'[60]

At the court and in the gubernii, uniform dresses were introduced for women. All uniforms had to be made at the wearer's expense, which, for the poorer officials, constituted a heavy burden (recall the overcoat of Akaky Akakievich!) The lower ranks and non-commissioned officers struggled for years to repay the cost, which was kept back from their wages.[61]

If a man entered the civil service or acquired noble rank, dressing as he wished was no longer possible. Any innovations evoked suspicion and suggested disloyalty. When he was presented at court, Pushkin, regardless of his dandyism, had to wear the uniform of a gentleman of the bedchamber with lace trimmings, which he openly despised and criticized in his letters.

Ivan Panaev, another fashion plate, also fell into an ambiguous position because of his dislike of his Treasury Department uniform.

> Once I came to the department in dress uniform with colorful plaid trousers, which had only just appeared in St Petersburg at that time. I was one of the first to wear them and wanted to show them off at the office. The effect created by my trousers exceeded my expectations. When I passed a row of offices in my department, the clerks, both permanent and temporary, threw their work aside, smiled and nudged each other, pointing at me. That was the least of it. Many head clerks and even heads of departments came to my section to look at me; some of them approached me and said, 'May I ask what kind of trousers you are wearing?' and then they touched them. One of the head clerks, a humorist, observed, 'Yes, it seems that they are made of the same material that cooks have their aprons sewn from.' My trousers caused such a noise and stir in the department that V. M. Kniazhevich turned to my desk, looked at me askance, and then, passing in front of me, advised me that I was dressed indecently.[62]

The word 'indecently' in this context did not mean 'obscenely', but rather 'inappropriately for the workplace'. The dandy Panaev caused a sensation because instead of ordinary uniform trousers he wore pants made of Scottish plaid; that was not acceptable in the department. The tartan cloth, a novelty in Russia in the 1830s–1850s, became popular because of the influence of Sir Walter Scott's historical novels. Panaev's vestimentary experiments were not merely a youthful fling, but the mark of a serious passion. Later he began to run the fashion section of the journal 'Nash Sovremennik' and wrote a series of fashion articles with his wife Avdotya Panaeva.

The interest in and passion for fashion may well have been intensified by the government's regimentation of masculine dress. Prohibition spurs ingenuousness, and a number of cunning channels were set up to circumvent the regulations. For instance, in 1832, provincial uniform was replaced with one worn by all nobility, which lasted until the revolution. But on his own estate, a landowner could dress as he wished, yet in order to attend a meeting of the nobility, or any business in town, he had to wear uniform.

Perhaps as a consequence, menswear expressed a semiotic code of intensely rich meanings throughout the nineteenth century. It was not coincidental that practically all Russian authors devoted much attention to the costumes of their characters. How a man dressed not only suggested his financial position, but indicated what social type he was.

Ivan Goncharov's 'Letters of a Friend from the Capital to a Provincial Bridegroom'

The well-known writer I. A. Goncharov, in a series of sketches entitled 'Letters of a Friend from the Capital to a Provincial Bridegroom' (1840), laid out an interesting classification of fashionable types in Russian high society. Goncharov himself had a reputation as a dandy: he wore a morning coat, grey trousers striped on the outer seams, plum-coloured boots with patent-leather spats, and a short watch chain decked with intricate fobs. He addressed his letters to his older brother, whom Goncharov sought to teach 'savoir-vivre', or how to live. 'Savoir-vivre' for the author was a subtle science, comprehending the arts of personal appearance, of social interaction, and of a certain moral tone. He created his own classification of fashionable types according to these criteria.

The first fashionable type in his system was the *Fop* (frant), who only acquired the very simplest aspect of 'savoir-vivre', the art of dressing impeccably.

> In order to afford to wear trousers sewn only the day before yesterday, of the right color with side-stripes, or to exchange one watch chain for another, he agrees to eat meagerly for two months. He is prepared to stand on his feet for an entire evening rather than crease his white waistcoat by sitting down; to turn his head neither to left nor right so that he does not spoil his cravat.[63]

For the fop a good outfit was an absolute value, the basic technique of his self-identification, for which he was prepared to sacrifice all comforts and bodily needs. The straitened circumstances of the fop are visible in this neglect of his own body.

The Lion, in contrast to the Fop, distinguished his savoir-vivre with a different set of externals. His outfit was not the most significant aspect:

> He never looks over his clothing, does not adorn it, never adjusts his tie or hair; an impeccable toilet is not a quality, not a virtue in him, it is a necessary condition. He is brimming with confidence that he is dressed perfectly, consistent not just with current but with the very latest fashion.[64]

The lion paid similar attention to all aspects of fashion in his life. He ate well, smoked the best cigars, and had the most fashionable furniture in his home. He was a leader of fashion and was constantly imitated, because he had a feel for what was coming next. It was the lion in Goncharov's classification that most closely resembled the contemporary western dandy embodied by Brummell and Count d'Orsay.

> Lions are constantly in the public eye. Everyone notices which lady they favour, and she begins to receive universal attention. Everyone asks which of the new French novels he prefers, and begins to read that book. Even his domestic arrangements come under scrutiny, his furniture, his bronzes, his carpets, his trinkets – all are closely studied, his habits are copied by everyone, and even his bêtises come to be imitated.[65]

The true Lion's habits are always unique, and he remains impossible to emulate. With his degree of personal freedom, he trusts his own instincts. It is important for him to be the centre of attention: 'his massive, brilliant pretensions are to constantly remain in the public eye. He must never leave the pedestal, upon which he has been placed by his elegant taste.'[66] Under this definition by Goncharov, George Brummell is undoubtedly a lion. Like a talented newsmaker, the Beau was marvellously adept at maintaining public interest in his own person.

Describing the lion, Goncharov chooses the same word, 'chameleon-like', that Plutarch used with regard to Alcibiades. A lion's tastes change rapidly: able to adapt to new circumstances, he displays chameleonism, typical for many dandies. According to Goncharov, this feature also lends 'femininity' to his nature. Even while shaping social opinion, he is also swayed by, and dependent upon it.

The next character type in Goncharov's system is far more concerned with his own personal needs. *The man of bon ton*, he has good taste, and appreciates elegant things, yet his aim is not to produce an effect, but always to ensure his own comfort. He acts just as he pleases, showing that a person of bon ton does not need to follow fashion religiously.

> At times, he might allow his manservant or tailor to decide on the details of his toilet. He might remain ignorant of a new trend, and continue smoking the old cigars to which he is accustomed, taking his meals and choosing clothes in the places he prefers, guided by his own personal tastes.[67]

The main feature of a *man of bon ton*, however, is natural tact. Such men have an easy, appealing manner. As Goncharov explains, they have 'learned the art of living' not merely in its external aspects, but in their own internal space. Bon ton implies the ability 'to hold oneself *properly and appropriately* in the company of others' (author's italics – O.V.).[68]

> *A man of bon ton* will never have a sudden awkward outburst. He will never be rude or brazen, or look at anyone with excessive sentiment. On no account will he behave strangely or brutally towards anyone. When meeting a person for the first time, he will never, all of a sudden, turn cold or scornful, neither will he be unctuous. He will not seek to borrow money, nor, naturally, will he lend his own.[69]

It might be possible to catch the Lion unawares in circumstances in which he would throw off the mask of politeness, but the man of bon ton would always know how to divest himself of unpleasant persons in a light and deft manner, outwardly observing the rules of propriety.

The characteristics of a man of bon ton in Goncharov's sketch coincide with the general European ethos of the dandy in one significant aspect of behaviour – the imperative of reserve, the prohibition against the display of the individual's emotions. Thus, the complaint that such men were heartless was frequently heard, 'You will say that this is just a doll, an automaton, who has discarded from his straitened soul all sensation, all passion.'[70]

But Goncharov defended this hero:

> No, he has not discarded these; he merely does not make spectacles of them, so as to keep from disturbing others, to keep from embarrassing and worrying others with endless, constant demands. He expects and desires that kind of behaviour in himself and others.[71]

Here the stoic coldness of the dandy is transformed, in Goncharov's interpretation, into the cardinal virtue of intelligent behavior.

These rules of bon ton, and, to some extent, the imperative of masculine reserve, were the behavioural code of the westernizing Russian nobility during the entire nineteenth century. Consider the words of O. S. Murav'eva:

> The ability to conceal from others 'petty disappointments and resentments' was considered an indispensable trait of the educated person. K. Golovin, recalling Prince Ivan Mikhailovich Golitsyn, whom he considered 'one of the finest adornments of Petersburg salons', wrote, 'His indefatigable courtesy never became banal and never gave way to irritation.' And this despite the fact that everyone knew that the prince had plenty to be irritated about, his life being far from smooth and carefree.[72]

It was precisely on this point that the Russian nobility followed literally the commandments of bon ton developed by European etiquette. They were all avid readers of Lord Chesterfield's 'Letters' to his son, a widely published collection of advice on manners, on which we have already relied discussing the concept of vulgarity. Chesterfield stressed the importance of emotional control in gentlemanly behaviour.

> This knowledge of the world teaches us more particularly two things, both of which are of infinite consequence, and to neither of which nature inclines us; I mean, the command of our temper, and of our countenance. A man who has no *du monde* is inflamed with anger, or annihilated with shame, at every disagreeable incident; the one makes him act and talk like a madman, the other makes him look like a fool. But a man who has *du monde*, seems not to understand what he cannot or ought not to resent.[73]

Yet despite the European gloss, Goncharov's man of bon ton was not impeccable in a moral sense. He was 'a hero of respectability', but not 'a hero of the moral rules' and could, while calmly observing the external forms, enter into a deception, refuse to pay a debt, or dupe someone in a card game, violating the very same code of gentlemanly honour.

As foil to the man of bon ton, Goncharov set up the next type in his classification – *the honest man* (poriadochnyi chelovek). He possessed in full measure 'a close, harmonious combination of external and internal moral savoir-vivre',[74] in which the latter dominated. Like the *man of bon ton* he never violated external decencies, but his refined manners flowed from a genuine spiritual delicacy and an inborn sense of justice. He would not take up deception or otherwise violate the principles of a moral way of life. (Let us here recall Pyliayev's defence of Prince Kurakin, who, he stressed, never offended anyone in his life. In the nineteenth century, this criterion doubtless remained just as crucial.)

Goncharov admitted that the *honest man* was practically an ideal type, he was nevertheless convinced that to live among civilized people it was necessary to be an honest man:

> ...because select, refined society is the same everywhere in the world, whether in Vienna, Paris, London or Madrid. Like the Jesuit Order it is eternal, inextinguishable, indestructible, whatever the storms and shocks; just like that Order it has its doctrine, its own rules not accessible to everyone, and it possesses the same spirit, despite tiny differences in form, with one object always and everywhere: to spread across the face of the earth the great science of savoir-vivre.[75]

This utopian picture ceaselessly repeats itself in Russian culture as the idea of the spiritual brotherhood of noble people. During Goncharov's day this ideology was based on estate and was linked to aristocratic origin, but in a later era with the strengthening of a middle class in Russia, it became the property not only of a cultured nobility, but of all educated people.

After the revolution, aristocratic ideology of course was barely mentionable. Adopting decency, good manners and what Goncharov termed the 'moral ability to live' as its creed, the intelligentsia handed these principles down from generation to generation. Following them, steadfastly helped people to survive and retain their human dignity, even in times of extreme challenges. Even after the harrowing experiences to which many of its finest were subjected, the members of Russia's intelligentsia retained their dignified and respectful manners, their mental acuity, and their ability to rejoice at life. In the memoirs of those who went through Stalin's camps, one immediately senses this resilience.[76]

In Goncharov's system, there is an ascending hierarchy of types. To the untutored eye, it is obvious that he respected the *'honest man'* the most and the fop the least. Yet, there is another curious gradation present, in the authenticity of character and the degree of savoir-vivre. The *Fop* constantly seemed to pretend, he imitated the *Lion*, but did not really become one. The *Lion*, in his turn, possessed more savoir-vivre, but even he could be caught unawares in dismaying moments while trying to imitate the behaviour of the *man of bon ton*. The latter aspired to become like the *'honest man'*, who was the sole type to achieve both external and internal savoir-vivre and who was distinguished by the genuinely ethical basis of his character.

Goncharov also highlights attitudes towards money and material goods.

> The *fop* and the *lion* struggle without money. Without it, they are nothing. Deprived of the means of being a fop and a lion, they return to their natural, primordial state. Disappearing from high society, they lose all their importance.[77]

The *man of bon ton* and the *honest man*, however, are not dependent on money in order to remain true to themselves. Even in poverty and isolation, they retain their refined, pleasant manners, and the honest man always preserves his moral principles. 'Like precious diamonds, they can become lost in the dust, without ever losing their value.'[78]

Goncharov's essays can be seen as classical treatises on fashion. In Europe, this genre was represented by writers such as Balzac, Barbey d'Aurevilly, Baudelaire, and Théophile Gautier. The closest in spirit to Goncharov was perhaps Balzac, with his 'Treatise on Elegant Living' (1830); Goncharov, indeed, may have been familiar with this work. The key ideas of both texts are similar: recall, for instance, Balzac's definitions of elegance as 'grace in everything in and around us', and as the 'art of spending money wisely', or one of his favourite notions, that 'the elegant man is always able to receive guests… no visitor can catch him unawares'.[79]

Goncharov and Balzac appear to exhibit similar ways of thinking. Both writers were fond of establishing their own systems of classification, and based their reflections on these groups and types.

The Silver Age Masters of Elegance

European Influences

Looking at dandyism in Russia, we have always been aware of two clashing tendencies, the Westerners and the Slavophiles. The European trends tended to dominate, and not only in dress, as Russia's beaux followed the social habits of their western role models. Describing the fops, Goncharov notes, for instance, their love of flânerie: as he explains, they strove always to 'walk down the whole of Nevsky, never slowing their usual pace, without once taking their hand from their back coat pocket, or letting fall from their eye the adeptly inserted lorgnette'.[80]

Besides flânerie, Russia's beaux also took on English dandy habits such as practical jokes and bets. The well-known socialite and man of fashion Konstantin Bulgakov, whom we have already discussed, was a famous lover of bold escapades.

Bulgakov was quite the rake. On one occasion, in Pavlovsk, at a recital, he bet a friend of mine that he would walk past her arm-in-arm with the Grand Prince.[81] Our circle was convinced that he would lose, of course, yet he won. We watched as he approached the Grand Prince and said something to him, whereupon the Grand Prince allowed Bulgakov to take his arm. Bulgakov admitted to the Grand Prince that he was madly in love with a woman, and that if the Grand Prince would do him the favour of walking past her with him, he would make him the happiest man alive.[82]

Such tricks and manipulation of high-ranking personages cannot but put one in mind of Beau Brummell's insolent games with English aristocrats.

In the nineteenth-century Russian culture, two clear peaks of European influence can be seen. The first, in Pushkin's time, witnessed the heyday of Romanticism, and the second, at the end of the century and in the early 1900s, was the time of European decadence. In both periods, interest in dandyism rose.

At the end of the nineteenth and the beginning of the twentieth century, the culture of dandyism spread further and as a result became differentiated into mass and elite types. Specialized fashion periodicals enabled a mass character to emerge; one such journal was Dendi ('The Dandy'), published from 1910 in Moscow under the editorship of R. N. Brenner. Dendi appeared twice a month and bore the subtitle 'The Journal of Art and Fashion'. Dendi carried all the advertisements characteristic of the era – for eau-de-Cologne, for miraculous 'pneumatic trusses', for hypnosis, for the latest medical corsets, and so on. Nevertheless, the journal did justify its title; in articles on men's fashion an observer under the English pseudonym 'Jim' told men, in a dandyish spirit, how to dress.

Some of Jim's essays were illustrated with drawings by the artist Bernard Boutet de Monvel. In his series 'On Men's Fashion: What a Man Should Wear, and Where, and How, He Should Wear It', Jim offers both general thoughts on dress theory, and specific recommendations. His first essay, for instance, looks at contemporary men's clothing. It opens with an anecdote which clearly demonstrates the trend of simplification in male dress in the bourgeois period.

> Do you know why Parisians were obliged to abandon the stirrups which had ensured that the trousers of 1830 were such a perfect fit? Merely because the stockbrokers could not run up the steps of the temple of Gold with stirrups restraining their feet.[83]

According to Jim, the innovations of the busy stockbrokers were geared to the fast-paced life of the businessman. In the nineteenth century, old-fashioned aristocratic outfits, which required time to put together, became less elaborate, and more convenient. The stirrups introduced by Brummell in order to avoid the creasing of breeches no longer suited the needs of the fast-moving new times.

The author deliberately focuses on a single item of men's clothing, the tie. This, in Jim's opinion, is the sole keeper of past traditions.

> Having sacrificed all their former finery for new, cleaner lines, men retained a single detail with which they could not part: the tie. The modern tie, and in particular, its lonely, proud pearl, appeared, like some heady extract, to contain all the juices of ancient glory.[84]

Figure 23 Illustration from Russian magazine "The Dandy". 1910.

Contemporary men's fashion, indeed, had long ceased to be concerned with colour, having firmly opted for black. The focus, now, was on cut and silhouette (Figure 23). In this regard, Jim even quotes the Larousse dictionary.

> Referring to the tie, even the serious and virtuous Larousse dictionary observes that 'the art of dressing is now entirely concentrated in the art of wearing one's tie'.[85]

The tie is seen as imbued with special symbolism. 'Like a microscopic ruby set in a black pearl, the tie breathes life into a man's costume, lighting up the stern beauty of his face.'[86] With its Baroque detail and attention to precious stones, this description is typical of fin-de-siècle Aestheticism. The tie provides the final touch, the key detail through which an experienced man of fashion can express something of his own personality. In this way, he can proudly assume the title of 'modern dandy'. To this character, Jim addresses his final advice.

> The modern dandy should turn all his attention to the lines of his costume, since it is primarily in this area that he has the freedom to show his own taste, and only line can lend an outfit elegance and beauty.[87]

Yet the fullest expression of the dandy's ideology was not to be found in Jim's articles on menswear, but in a translation of the program manifesto of European dandyism of the 1840s. Beginning with its first edition, the journal serialized a Russian translation of Barbey d'Aurevilly's 'On Dandyism and George Brummell', the foundation text of European dandyism. Two years later Barbey's essay, translated by M. Petrovsky with minor amendments, was published as a separate book by Al'tsiona publishers.[88]

The author of the brief foreword to the treatise in the Dandy journal publication defined dandyism as 'aesthetic mysticism', a 'religion for "geniuses without briefcases" seeking any source to satisfy their immense thirst for power'.[89] Since Dandy journal was seen as a school of popular dandyism, the translation from Barbey d'Aurevilly was a perfect fit. There was serious and more than intermittent interest during the Russian Silver Age in Barbey's D'Aurevilly's work. Much quoted, the French author was highly popular in Russian intellectual circles. For many Russian writers, his dandy characters served as sources of inspiration and self-fashioning models. Maximilian Voloshin devoted three articles to Barbey D'Aurevilly, which is highly indicative. Voloshin saw in him an 'underground classic' of French literature: 'Of all the solitary minds he remained, perhaps, the most undervalued.'[90]

The start of the new century saw a similar rise in demand for books by Oscar Wilde and Charles Baudelaire. The new decadent culture in Russian was constructing its literary canon.

> There was unprecedented interest in Oscar Wilde. 'De Profundis', 'The Ballad of Reading Gaol', 'The Picture of Dorian Gray', and 'Salome' – all books disappeared immediately, the last two very expensive and magnificent Grif editions. The market literally clamoured for a new edition of 'Les Fleurs du Mal', along with every single line ever written by Baudelaire.[91]

Editions such as these were drawn up with the help of well-known Russian writers and philologists.[92]

The writer Mikhail Kuzmin, famous for his gay preferences, was asked to contribute a foreword to Barbey's book for the separate edition. He agreed to write about Barbey and Brummell because he was personally involved in the theme of dandyism. As memoirists have testified, Kuzmin loved to experiment with his appearance and outfits. After a period in 1906 when he dressed in a special Russian costume – a cherry-coloured poddevka (a man's light, tight-fitting coat) and a gold brocade rubakha (a traditional Russian shirt) – Kuzmin changed his style and from 1907 was hailed in St. Petersburg as a European dandy, admired for his brightly coloured waistcoats and even earning the nickname 'the Russian Oscar Wilde'.

In his correspondence with the student Ruslov, he takes pains to recreate the image of a dandy-aesthete. 'We see before us the Kuzmin who changes ties every day, and for whom the colour of a tie, or, more precisely, a cravat, means more than all the pearls of wisdom so valued by Vyacheslav Ivanov.'[93] Ivanov himself, of course, offered a flattering portrait of Kuzmin in his poem 'Anachronism', calling him a 'singer and peer of Antinous'.[94]

Kuzmin was frequently compared to Brummell in stories that circulated widely.

> Kuzmin is the king of the aesthetes, the lawgiver of fashions and tone. He is the Russian Brummell. He owns 365 waistcoats. In the morning at his place, lycee students, law students, and young guardsmen gather to greet him at his *petit lever*,

wrote the poet Irina Odoyevtseva.⁹⁵ When she actually met him, she found that the real Kuzmin fell far short of the reports about him.

> Under the striped trousers are bright green socks and worn-out patent slippers.... It is he, Kuzmin, prince of aesthetes and lawgiver of fashions. The Russian Brummell. In a rumpled, stained morning coat, in some kind of velvet Gogolesque waistcoat. Undoubtedly the other 364 vests were pretty much the same.⁹⁶

Irina Odoyevtseva's disappointment was understandable; the myth of Kuzmin-as-dandy was very popular at the time, so the memoirist repeated, with obvious irony, her previous characterization: such a Kuzmin clearly did not bear comparison with Brummell. But we must bear in mind that the second description refers to 1920, when the civil war had impoverished everyone in Petrograd, including the perpetual spendthrift Kuzmin.

The Dandies of the World of Art

The dandy's style was particularly valued by the famous circle of avant-garde artists called 'Mir iskusstva' (World of Art). Theirs was, of course, not the military style of dandyism of the mid-nineteenth century, but one rather more in the aesthetic, decadent vein. Stylistically derivative, it was oriented towards the nineteenth-century western literature of Charles Baudelaire, Joris Karl Huysmans and Oscar Wilde. The fundamental originality here was not to be found in everyday clothing or the behaviour of the 'miriskusniki' (members of the World of Art), but in their artistic innovations in painting and later in the design of scenery and costumes for the Ballets Russes, which had a real influence on European culture.⁹⁷ Nevertheless, it is worth examining the fashions of the World of Art.

The musicologist Alfred Nurok (1860–1919) had reputation as notorious dandy in the circle. Nurok was a big fan of Aubrey Beardsley and was the first to popularize the works of Beardsley in the World of Art circle. He was never seen without a book of Baudelaire in his pocket and liked to quote from Marquis de Sade, hence his nickname Silenus. His witty articles made him famous as a critical reviewer in the World of Art journal. He was always elegant and sardonic – this combination of qualities is seen in his portrait by Valentin Serov.

The publisher of the journal and famous ballet impresario Sergey Diaghilev was also a dandy (Figure 24), as recalled Sergey Makovsky:

> His top hat, his impeccable morning coat and jacket were noted by Petersburgers not without mocking envy. He carried himself with foppish looseness, he loved to flaunt his dandyism, he carried in his sleeve a scented silk handkerchief that he would remove coquettishly to place against his trimmed moustache. He could he deliberately impertinent, like Oscar Wilde, refusing to take account of the "prejudices" of good behavior and not hiding his unusual tastes in order to spite virtuous hypocrites'.⁹⁸

Figure 24 Lev Bakst. Portrait of Diaghilev. 1906. Wikimedia Commons.

These were clearly the games of European dandyism, by now an established technique of self-presentation. The same can be said of painter and scenery designer Lev Bakst, who also attracted attention with his dandyism. According to Igor Grabar',

> he was a dandy, spic-and-span in patent leather shoes, a marvelous necktie and a bright lilac hanky stuffed coquettishly in his shirtsleeve. He was a flirt (on byl koket): his movements were soft, his gestures elegant, his speech calm; everything in his manner was an imitation of society dandies with their lack of constraint and their artificially "English" dissipation.[99]

Even among the fashion plates of the World of Art, Valter Fedorovich Nuvel' (nicknamed 'Corsair' and 'Petronius') stood out with his elegance. He was one of the founders of the group and brought Diagilev, Konstantin Somov, and Alexander Benois into its ranks. His character recalled that of Brummell, sarcastic but without Brummell's coldness.

> Valechka Nuvel' was judged a 'magister elegantiarum'. But he would sooner have been regarded a 'shaker of foundations' since he had a poisonous and shattering skepticism. Yet it was all expressed in such amusing and brilliant, and sometimes merry and cynical, ways, and was so subtle and witty, that it was disarming and had something attractive in it.[100]

Benois' description of the exuberant Nuvel' puts one in mind of Barbey's depiction of Brummell, who was always guaranteed to provide entertainment for his noble English friends.

> Valichka! Oh my, he is the spice, without which all our luncheons would be mere rubbish. But not just the spice… he is like those little burners one places under a dish, although what burns in him is spirit, not tar, but still, he burns with his own flame, and a flame, be it in a night lamp, or the sun itself, is always a flame, it brings life, light and heat. A match can set ablaze an entire city, endless expanses of forest and steppe. I bow down before the match, the burning match…[101]

This lightning sequence of metaphors is built on images of fire and light, typical for descriptions of charisma. Similar things were said about Count D'Orsay.

Other Russian beaux, on the contrary, were known for their icy dandy sophistication.

> Sergey Sudeikin liked to shine in salons, where he was known as a society man, albeit, an immoral one. His manner was somewhat insolent: the actor Mgebrov recalls that Sudeikin, who always dressed like a dandy, could be contemptuous and disdainful, proclaiming his superficial nothings with great condescension. With his charisma and talent, however, he was nonetheless able to occupy a high position in society.[102]

The Dandies of the Middle Class

The brilliance of the personal style of the World of Art members is undeniable, yet it seems that the fundamental result of Russian dandyism is not to be found in these examples of elite fashionable style, but rather in the far more widespread phenomenon of the dandy of the middle class. These dandies, like the one in the photo, were typical in Russian society of the first decades of the twentieth century (Figure 25).

This snapshot from my family archive is of my paternal grandfather, Konstantin Borisovich Vainshtein. He had this picture taken in 1916 in a photography studio against a decorated background and for the occasion he wore a handsome Prince of Wales check three-piece suit and a walking stick, not forgetting his watch chain and his signet ring. He casually holds a cigar in the tips of his fingers, there is a carefully folded handkerchief in his pocket, and his shoes are polished until they shine. And while the suit does not quite hang perfectly on his frame, his whole appearance and the easy pose testify to his serious dandyish determination. It is clear that for Konstantin Vainshtein the dandy's style was a sign of self-confidence and self-control, a deliberate program of self-fashioning, designed to create the image of a man with taste and well-honed masculine manners, a lady killer.

In his efforts to create an image my grandfather was not alone. Thousands of middle-class young people in pre-revolutionary Russia used the code of the culture of the dandy when they wanted to create the best impression. For them, this code was already a convenient, well-polished stereotype of masculine elegance. In this popularized version of the dandy's code the 'dangerous' decadent connotations – of vanity, frivolousness,

Figure 25 Konstantin Vainshtein. 1916. © Olga Vainshtein, family archive.

and femininity – had been muffled; instead, the semantics of bourgeois masculinity – elegance, propriety, responsibility, reliability, and respectability – were accented.

Russian Dandyism: Constructing the Cultural Canon

The specific features of Russian dandyism, if one tries to define them in broad terms, are not so visible, because the formation of cultural canon was not completed and fully developed. Russian dandyism was not discursively constituted on a metanarrative level: the urbane folklore around the dandies hardly existed at all – almost no legends about the famous dandies, no stories about witty remarks (like 'Do you call this thing a coat?') or the secret recipes of good taste in clothes. Obviously, the art to produce narration, to fictionalize the trivialities of everyday life demanded the emergence of a more intensive cultural field.

One could find, of course, separate representations of dandies in literature, yet the philosophical essays on dandyism, like those by Barbey D'Aurevilly or Baudelaire in France, are significantly absent. 'Letters by the friend from the capital to the provincial bridegroom' (1848) by Ivan Goncharov remains one of the few theoretical essays on male fashion and society types in Russian nineteenth-century culture.

Dandyism in Russia was realized more as the practice of personal self-fashioning rather than general intellectual strategy, a set of cultural norms, like the European imperative 'Nil admirari' or the principle of conspicuous inconspicuousness in costume. This is one of the reasons why the description of individual cases presents the most articulate material: they abound in expressive details, like someone's passion for hygiene or collection of snuffboxes. But do such separate cases form a cultural tradition? As I see it, they rather reflect the process of its construction.

Dandyism after the Revolution (Pre-war Years)

After the Revolution, predictably, the concept of 'dandyism' in all its rich nuances lost any currency. The arduous material circumstances of everyday life made the dandy's life impossible for those fashionable men who stayed in Russia. The word itself remained in the lexicon of the intelligentsia, although now with a predominantly ironic shade. The new, fashionable Soviet man sought other means and other labels to construct his identity.

Known as a dandy before the revolution, the imaginist Anatoly Mariengof[103] contrived to retain his reputation among friends, even in Soviet times. In his memoirs, Mariengof recollects that Meyerhold once presented him with his photos,

> with the inscription 'to the only dandy in the Republic'. The 'dandy' owned but four handkerchiefs, and two shirts, yet both were French silk.[104]

In this context, the word 'dandy', indeed, begs to be used in inverted commas. How long Mariengof's silk shirts lasted, we do not know, yet towards the end of his memoirs, the author recalls asking Vasily Kachalov to show him his monocle. The famed actor had just returned to Soviet Russia from his tour of Europe and America.

> Do you still have your monocle in your waistcoat pocket, Vasya?' I asked. 'Of course, I do!' 'Would you put it in, please? I want to learn. I hate the idea of putting old man's spectacles on my nose, but I have to do something...' 'What a poor dandy you are!' and, deftly extracting his monocle from his waistcoat pocket with two fingers, he tossed it nonchalantly up, and caught it with his eye. 'Marvellous!'[105]

Small trifles such as monocles could still be found in the wardrobes of intellectuals ruined by the revolution, modest reminders of more opulent days.

> Annenkov is the only man in St. Petersburg who still wears a monocle. He never parts with it. Blushing and lowering her gaze, a young, pretty ballerina... assured me that he even sleeps with it in.[106]

Annenkov's overall appearance, Irina Odoyevtseva notes in her memoirs, was really quite eccentric. 'As always, he wore valenki [thick felt boots], his blue sheepskin jacket, and his monocle.'[107]

Amid the destitution of the early 1920s, even the most experienced beaux struggled to maintain an elegant appearance. In bohemian circles, fashion took a direct hit. As Odoyevtseva stated,

> An unexpected 'victory of the revolution': in the St. Petersburg arts world, as in the world of animals and birds, the males are now more glamorous and imposing than the females. Not everyone, naturally. Blok, Lozinsky, Georgy Ivanov, Adamovich, Dobuzhinsky, Lourié, Kozlinsky and the others are still doing their best to maintain their toned Petersburg aesthetic

looks. A lot of the students and actors and artists though are shamelessly donning the most extraordinary sheepskins, green hunting jackets, red velvet coats made from curtains, and quite remarkable breeches, to say nothing of the motley puttees and impossibly tall, shaggy hats. Where do they find these singular masquerade items?[108]

Frequently, the outlandish outfits were the result of simple lack of means. 'Do not worry, Kharms is wearing an extraordinary waistcoat at present (the waistcoat was red), as he does not have the means to buy an ordinary one.'[109] Should we see the red waistcoat of Kharms as a reference to Théophile Gautier's notorious pink doublet? If so, it is a reference made through historical irony – an unwitting, bitter pun.

In the same way, in his youth Vladimir Mayakovsky liked to use dress as a means to shock. His famed yellow Futurist jacket, for instance, appears in the poem 'The Fop's Blouse' (1914):

> I will make myself some black pants
> From the velvet of my voice.
> A yellow blouse from three arshins of sunset.
> Along the Nevsky of the world, with its glossy strips,
> I will stroll with the step of a Don Juan fop…[110]

The provenance of Mayakovsky's blouse was not so poetic, however. In his autobiography 'I, Myself', the poet recalls:

> I never owned suits. I had two blouses, both appalling. The tried and tested solution was to use a tie. I had no money. I got some yellow ribbon from my sister, and wound it around. It caused a furore. So, the tie is what's most noticed and most beautiful. Therefore, the bigger the tie, the bigger the furore. But the size of one's tie is limited, so I was cunning. I made a tie-shirt, a shirt-tie. I was irresistible.[111]

After the revolution, when Mayakovsky found favour with the new authorities, his dandy looks caused him to stand out from the impoverished intelligentsia. Mikhail Bakhtin, who saw him in 1920 or 1921, recalled:

> Then a tall man appeared. I realised at once that this was Mayakovsky. I had seen portraits of him, and had, perhaps, seen him in person, also. He was dressed extremely fashionably at a time when people were, on the whole, very poorly dressed. He had a flared coat, which was much in vogue. Everything he was wearing was so very fashionable, so very new, and one could tell that he was constantly aware of this, aware that he was dressed like a dandy! Like a dandy! Yet the true dandy, of course, is not constantly aware of his outfit. The very first rule of dandyism, indeed, is to wear your clothes in such a way as to show that you just don't care. He, however, was evidently very preoccupied with his flared coat, with the fact that he was so fashionably dressed, and that he cut such a figure. I didn't like it at all.[112]

This incisive description by Bakhtin not only helps us to picture Mayakovsky's personal style but it also serves to show the ineffectiveness of 'Soviet' dandyism. It is not by chance that in this conversation the words 'like a dandy' are repeated twice, followed by the comment 'he laughs': the critical irony of Bakhtin is more than obvious. In the beginning of 1920s, even for those who had the means and the flare to dress up, the dandyism as consistent cultural practice was simply no longer possible: the historical context was radically different. As a coherent strategy of self-fashioning, dandyism belonged in the past.

This inevitable conclusion is also evident in Alexander Blok's well-known essay 'Russian Dandies', penned on 2 May 1918. Its main hero is Valentin Stenich (that was his penname) or, to give him his real name, Valentin Smetanich (1897–1938), one of the few members of the intelligentsia who contrived to retain their 'toned aesthetic looks' in the challenging years following the revolution.[113] In his essay, Blok describes Stenich as an ostentatiously decadent homme de lettres. His generation, Stenich claims, is not interested in anything but poetry, and is 'empty, completely empty'.

Later, Stenich claimed that his exchange with Blok was merely a successful hoax. '"I pulled the wool over his eyes!" he crowed, gleefully.'[114] The young man had, it seems, hoped to impress Blok with his verse, and, when this failed to happen, had opted instead to make his mark as a striking 'bourgeois' aesthete.

> We are all drug addicts, opium-eaters, and our women are nymphomaniacs. We are a minority, yet amongst the youth, we hold sway. We laugh at those who are interested in socialism, work, revolution. We live only for poetry.[115]

At that time, Blok had just completed 'The Twelve', and was in the painful process of attempting to accept socialist ideology. Seeing his meeting with Stenich as a provocation, three months after the event, Blok wrote 'Russian Dandies'. His conversation with the twenty-year-old 'Neurastenich', as Mayakovsky nicknamed him, had been brief, yet it evidently made a lasting impression. Blok describes the dialogue in detail. Stenich's exaggerated decadence likely reminded the poet of his own youthful attitudes, yet its absurd excess caused him to recoil.

Stenich's stance, Blok claims, was that of a dandy. This was not Symbolism, or Aestheticism, or even decadence. 'I was afraid I would see too far into this narrow and terrible well... of dandyism', he writes.[116] Holding dear the literary tradition of the Silver Age, Blok himself, of course, was no stranger to dandyism. In the 1910s, many of his friends had adopted the dandy code of conduct. Of Stenich, he writes: 'Behind his words there was an indubitable truth, they possessed a value of their own.'[117] By then however, Blok's inner connection with decadent Symbolist attitudes had ended, and he desired nothing but to separate himself from its alien manners and gestures.

Within this context dandyism, for Blok, was fast turning into the epitome of all that was hostile and undesirable.

> So, there it is – Russian dandyism of the twentieth century! Its devouring flame was lit by a spark from a small part of the Byronic soul; throughout the whole troubled last century it smouldered in various Brummells, suddenly flaring up and scorching the wings of the winged: Edgar Poe, Baudelaire, Wilde; in it there was great seduction – the seduction of 'anti-philistinism'; yes, it alighted something on the waste-ground of 'philanthropy', 'progressiveness', 'humanitarianism' and 'utility', yet, having burnt there, it spread to

forbidden territory. From the 'Muscovite in Childe Harold's cloak', it raged on, drying out roots and turning the century-old maples and oaks of noble parks into the soft, rotten pulp of bureaucracy. A gust of wind – and the bureaucracy crumbles, leaving nothing but wood chips, dust, and deadwood. Yet the flames do not abate. As the blaze advances, it dries out the roots of our young people. Among the workers and the peasants, one already sees young dandies. This cannot but cause alarm. It is, after all, a kind of retribution.[118]

The metaphors used by Blok in this passage are somewhat unusual, with dandyism likened to a flame. In 1918, of course, Blok penned 'The Twelve', throughout which images of the fire of world revolution persist.

And, to spite the bourgeois,
We will fan a fire worldwide,
Worldwide fire steeped in blood,
May the good Lord bless us all!

In this fire engulfing the world, Blok's family estate Shakhmatovo was not spared. The poet's library, quite literally, burned down. For Blok, accepting the revolution required a tremendous effort of will. After torturous internal struggle, he finally made his choice: that same year, 1918, he published the article 'The Intelligentsia and the Revolution'. Yet even in 'Russian Dandies', notes of dramatic tension can be heard. The roots of ancient maples and oaks in the parks of the nobility, which flames are said to be drying out, are clearly described in affectionate, nostalgic language. Such sentiment is evidently at odds with the spirit of revolution: the unpleasant association, although muted, is nonetheless apparent.

As an overall metonymy, dandyism, for Blok, was used to represent too many negative phenomena. Starting out as a mere aesthetic opponent, Stenich rapidly evolves into an ideological and social enemy. The forced nature of this intellectual chain is also evident in the shifts in tone. If, at the outset, the mood is elevated and romantic (recall the 'spark from the Byronic soul', the 'wings of the winged'), towards the end, it becomes more critical, almost propagandist, reminiscent of post-war Soviet magazines' invectives of 'bourgeois' men of fashion and, later, of the Stilyagi.

On one point, however, Blok's intuition was completely correct. Stenich was of course a dandy. In his memoirs, Nikolai Chukovsky wrote of him thus:

He had every right to describe himself in Mayakovsky's words: 'And besides a freshly washed shirt, in all honesty, I need nothing'. His shirts, indeed, were always freshly cleaned. Like no one else, he was able to choose a perfect tie. On him, any jacket looked as if it had been specially made to order by the very best tailor. Without investing much effort or money, he was one of the most elegant men of his time.[119]

A master of irony, Stenich liked to do romantic melancholy, the dandy way. 'I would kill myself,' he would say, 'but I have just taken my white trousers to the cleaners, and they will not be ready until Friday'.[120] In his exchange with Blok, Stenich used the tried and tested dandy trick of absurd exaggeration, essentially playing a practical joke. He was famous for his 'sharp tongue'[121] and his cutting comments frequently resembled Brummell's.

A member of the Writers' Union once talked, in his hearing, about 'our brothers, the writers'. Turning to him immediately, Stenich exclaimed, 'Oh? You have a brother who is a writer?' On another occasion, in the Literaturny Sovremennik magazine headquarters, Stenich noticed a poet, busy working at a desk. Peeking over her shoulder, he saw she was correcting the proofs of her latest poem. 'What! They even publish *your* work here!' he exclaimed loudly, as if in complete horror.[122]

Implying a distancing from the 'object',[123] such jokes invariably stressed the speaker's superior position. In Soviet times, when dandies were rare, irony, which Schlegel described as 'the freest of all freedoms', remained one of the few accessible forms of inner independence.

Orange Jackets and Pea Green Pants: The Fashion of Stilyagi in the Soviet Post-war Culture

The phenomenon of 'Stilyaga'[124] belonged to alternative fashion movement that was part of unofficial cultural sphere existing in all periods of Soviet history. During the Second World War, it received a strong injection of Western influence through such wartime experience as the American lend-lease and the personal impressions of Europe of millions of Soviet soldiers. In the post-war years, Soviet society for a time maintained a degree of openness to the West. Most films shown in Soviet cinemas in the first years after the war were Hollywood and German trophy films. 'Sun valley serenade' was a hit, as well as 'One hundred men and a girl'. Fashion plates often modelled their images on those of film stars. As the well-known Leningrad fop Valentin Tikhonenko recalled:

> After the war there was a trophy film about the American spy who was sent to infiltrate the Gestapo. Naturally, he was fantastically captivating, and so my photograph (in the hat) – that's his style. I copied it from him just like that.[125]

In the post-war years, the clubs and houses of culture organized regular dancing to Western music, the orchestras played American jazz, Duke Ellington's 'Caravan' became a popular tune. Young people were in love with jazz, which was later labeled by official propaganda as 'music for fat' (meaning 'for capitalists'). Homemade music records satisfied the growing demand for jazz: they were known as 'music on the ribs',[126] as they were recorded on x-ray photos with the help of special machines made from old phonographs.

In this cultural context, a new type of young cool dressers appeared in big cities. They were the first advocates of an alternative style, the first devotees of foreign music, who became known as stilyagi (from Russian 'stil' – style) – a name designed by a soviet newspaper to sound derisive. The young fans of new fashion originally used the expression 'to dance in style' – meaning contemporary style of movement.[127] The preferred dances were foxtrot, boogie-woogie, later – twist and shake. Dances and clothes were the focal points of a new youth subculture, forming in big Soviet cities.

Stilyagi used a special jargon allowing them to distinguish themselves from others. For instance, 'bakhili' meant shoes, 'khata' – flat, 'laba' – music, 'nadibat' – to get, and 'kanat' – to go away. The knowledge of jargon also served as a means to recognize people belonging to stilyagi circles. The stylish young men called each other 'chuvak', while the term 'stilyaga' was used more by the journalists writing about them.

By the end of 1940s, stilyagi first made their public appearance. The official soviet press sensed the danger immediately: in 1949, the satirical magazine Krokodil published the article against stilyagi by Beliaev. It had the subtitle 'Social Types from the past'. Symptomatically, in the same issue appeared the first article against 'cosmopolitans without kin'. This was a start of political campaign against western influences, and the image of stilyaga figured as often, as an image of fat and wicked capitalist in a series of caricatures in the next decade. Nevertheless, in an ironical historical twist, stilyaga turned out to be a type with a rich cultural potential. The *stilyagi* were not the ones to recede into the past, but rather persisted into the future, continuing throughout the 1950s and lasting into the 1960s, although later they changed from calling themselves *stilyagi* to *shtatniki* ('Yanks' or 'Americans'). Just like Westward-looking Russian dandies in the nineteenth century (albeit without speaking to each other in French), they followed foreign fashions and looked to modern Western culture for guidance in all things.

The portrait of the earliest *stilyaga* from the late 1940s comes to us in part from satirical essayists and from Soviet literature. One of the first descriptions of stilyaga can be found in the above-mentioned article by Dmitry Beliaev:

> A young man appeared in the doorway. He had the most absurd appearance: the back of his coat was bright orange, while the sleeves and tails were green. I have never seen such broad, canary yellow and pea green pants, not even during the reign of the famous flared trousers. His boots were a cunning combination of black patent leather and red suede. The young man leaned against the door frame and, in an extraordinarily cheeky gesture, threw his right leg over his left, revealing his socks, whose brightness was blinding...[128]

This description is interesting not only for the fashion, but also for the young man's body language: his 'extraordinarily cheeky gestures' were carefully considered and far from accidental. Such stilyagi shaped their entire bodies into something highly refined and deliberately affected. Their new ways of moving – the head flung back, a haughty look from above down at those around them, and a special 'lurching' gait – marked them as bohemians. The stilyaga says: 'We are the first to discover that the main thing in dancing is not only the movement of legs but also face expression.'[129] So, the effects of face expression and specially trained gaze were part of alternative style.

The dandies of the nineteenth century used similar techniques, intentionally drawing out the pronunciation of words and cultivating a sluggish walk. Such movements were to some extent necessitated by the clothing. As Raisa Kirsanova notes, 'the unusual clothing forced one to move differently, and dance differently. The music, the new rhythms, were very likely behind this need to dress differently, to mark oneself'.[130]

Later in fiction stilyagi were depicted by Vasiliy Aksyonov in his novel 'Ticket to the Stars', published in 1961. The heroes of the novel got their ideas of western culture due to the World's festival of youth and students held in Moscow in 1957. Andrey Bitov also described stilyagi in a chapter of his novel 'Pushkin House' (1964–1971). Later, stilyagi became the main characters in the play by Slavkin 'Grown-up daughter of a young man', that was staged in 1972 and enjoyed tremendous success.

The stilyaga was living proof of just how significant fashion statements were for the west-oriented segment of Russian young men. He wore his hair short but made a special cock in front with the help of hair wax. Thin elegant moustache was called 'merzavchiki' – 'small scoundrels'. The stilyaga outfits changed with time – later stilyaga favoured narrow, straight legs pants (briuki-dudochki), which became fashionable after the wide trousers, long-checkered double-breasted jackets, oversized pointed shoes, a Hawaian shirt, sunglasses, and a bandana or wide tie of bright colours around his neck.

Many of these things were homemade – it was called 'samostrok' ('self-sewing') by analogy with 'samizdat' (self-publishing). White rubber shoe platforms – they were called 'semolina' because of the colour – were made by special order in small shoe repair shops, the jeans were sewn and stitched with yellow threads at home. According to Aleksey Kozlov, there were hair salons specializing in stilyaga's favourite hair styles with cocks and, special tailors sewing narrow pants and long jackets.[131] The ties with dragons came from China.

Stilyaga as Flaneur

The stilyagi normally gathered in the main street of the city – in Moscow it was the right side of Gorky Street from hotel Moskva to Pushkin square. It was called 'Brod', short form of 'Broadway' in New York. But for Russian ear the name also sounded as Russian word 'brod', meaning 'ford', thus creating a pun, a word play: walking along 'Broadway' in Moscow was as dangerous as finding a reliable ford in a river. 'It was fashionable to appear on Broadway in the evening, as dusk set in, and do what was called a *khil*, i.e. a stroll.'[132] In Leningrad 'Broadway' meant Nevsky Prospekt, and in Baku it was Torgovaya Street. A typical stilyaga would walk up and down the Broadway several times during an evening, stopping to talk to friends and glancing at the passers-by. The important part in this ritual flanerie was looking at other stililiaga's clothes, reading appearances and dresses, and recognizing the brand names. There were special techniques for showing off one's clothing in a supposedly accidental way. For example, one might put a hand in a jacket pocket to reveal the lining of a raincoat (as a name-brand raincoat was often recognized by the lining). Recognizing a brand while on the move was considered a first-class feat. Such brief sign of silent approval – exchange of glances with short nod – was called 'greeting the raincoat' (привет плащу). This was typical of *stilyaga* optics, inviting visual examination, be it fleeting or thorough.

Behaving as classical flaneur stilyaga also distinguished himself by a deliberate manner of walking. According to a former stilyaga, they walked

> With the head thrown back, held high and bouncing around as if we were constantly on the look out. And there was a reason for the stuck-up nose and the arrogant gaze; we considered ourselves much better informed than everyone else.[133]

The height of success was to become indistinguishable from foreigners, and to achieve this a *stilyaga* would even develop a special 'distracted' facial expression.

Among the general public, the image of the stilyaga was crystallized in an exaggerated form, and as such it was immortalized in Bitov's classic novel "Pushkin House":

> He was that same famous hepcat [*stilyaga*] of the early fifties. The very same trousers, that same green jacket drooping from shoulder to knee, apparently the same shoe soles glued on by an enterprising craftsman, the same necktie tied in a microscopic knot, the same ring, the same pomp hair, the same walk—straight caricature, even for that time, straight out of *Krokodil*...[134]

The social background of stilyaga could vary. There were kids from rich families, who had access to the western clothes and expensive things due to their parents. At the famous drawing by Boris Prorokov a young man is depicted standing in front of his father's prestigious car – 'Pobeda' (Victory), two bottles rolling out of the car.[135]

However, the group of stilyaga also included no small number of children from working-class families as well. The famous Valentin Tikhonenko, one of the first Leningrad stilyagi, was the son of a worker who had been a political prisoner. As an adolescent during the war, he had his arm blown off by a mine, but this did not keep him afterwards from racing motorcycles and dressing in the latest fashions. This was initially facilitated by items from the lend-lease program: 'From the things sent by Americans, I wore some very chic pants, for example, with hazy silvery white stripes. Those were interesting pants.'[136]

In post-war period, goods from abroad could be purchased from foreigners. Visitors from Finland often came to Leningrad, and could sell whole suitcases full of inexpensive clothing right from their tour bus or in their hotel. But the basic resource was buying from illegal traders or 'fartzovshik', who used to sell things either brought from the voyages abroad or bought from foreign tourists in the hotels. The subculture of 'fartzovshik' was secret and even now remains almost unexplored. In Moscow, there were 'fartzovshik' at every major hotel. This was referred to as 'ironing' (*utiuzhit*) foreigners. Some stilyagi did the 'ironing' themselves, while others merely bought things from 'fartzovshik' and black market 'whisperers'.

While buying clothes connoisseurs could identify brand-name items immediately: for instance, 'the genuine article was considered to be the square-toed American military boots that people wore when walking on Gorky Street'.[137] The trained eye could quickly discern the distinguishing features of a brand: 'the definitive little button in the back, the loop for hanging up a shirt'.[138]

Creating the expressive outfits, certain stilyagi with exquisite taste displayed not only awareness of trends but also a penchant for innovation:

> I was the number one fashion plate. Once I bought a Swiss overcoat, which I needed to advertise myself... It really was a fabulous Swiss coat... I went around in an American Stetson hat, all color coordinated, and a light blue overcoat down to my knees.[139]

The combination of a Swiss overcoat and a Stetson hat was no small matter. Western devotees of protest clothing also frequently selected ensembles in a similar avant-garde style. The stilyagi often experimented bravely in 'mix and match' manner, thus being the forerunners of contemporary street-style fashion. Mikhail German describes some of these experiments:

> The fops were no longer enamored of the capacious gabardine or covert cloth summer coats ('*mantels*'), either worn or thrown over the arm, which had previously been considered just as chic. Instead they paraded around in Czech knee-length raincoats, tied their neckties with microscopic knots, and even dared to sew tight trousers, which seemed slightly amusing but also excruciatingly marvelous. And there were already flickers of blue pants 'with seams on the outside,' as the irate old ladies said – the first blue jeans. The naïve poluboks[140] remained the mainstay of the conservatives: young men preferred to have their hair cut in 'polish' or 'canadian' style and it was considered very modern to carry a zippered folder (a 'bootlicker' - 'podkhalimka') instead of a bag, and a plaid cowboy shirt of a special new cut.[141]

Were There Women Stilyagi?

From the start the movement of stilyaga was mainly in men's fashion. Women-stilyagi were less visible, but they certainly existed. It was more difficult for them to find the sartorial key of innovative fashion. Fortunately, for ladies in the 1950s, mass fashion for women began to change: it became more democratic, fashion shows were organized in the House of Fashion in Moscow. Even the fashion collections of Christian Dior were shown in Moscow in 1959.[142] There was a revival of textile industry, new fashion magazines started to be published, new synthetic materials were all the rage.[143] According to Mikhail German,

> At that time the visage of our compatriots began very gradually to change. The ridiculous Soviet '*meningitka*,' (a round hat worn on the top of the head), just as enormous berets made of hard felt, billowing high over the forehead, known on the street as "I'm a fool," now accompanied cute shoulder-less dresses and wide skirts. A somber, practical staple still reigned, and the shaggy *torchon* and *éponge*,[144] along with the immortal crepe-back satin, matte on one side and shiny on the other, were still considered eccentric refinement but there was already the glimmer of a rare and unprecedented dream of the fashion places in the brocaded shine of taffeta! ... It was no longer a rarity to see foreign pointed-toe shoes, which were incredibly difficult and expensive to obtain, requiring torturous queuing or highly placed connections. Multicolored capron gloves were worn with great enthusiasm.[145]

New Look has influenced the fashion for women-stilyaga. But the modest attempts to introduce the elements of New Look could be done only with the help of home dressmakers. Urban women were very creative in their vestimentary efforts, and often had nice outfits sewn by dressmakers. Some dressmakers and tailors used to sew things for men too. The prices for this work were quite democratic and enthusiasts of fashion with modest income could afford having the beautiful outfits sewn by individual measures.[146]

The female version of the stilyaga was 'klievaya chuvikha'. In the satirical essay by Beliaev, we find her portrait in the character of Mumochka, the female friend of stilyaga, who dances with him the dance they invented themselves.

Later in the 1960s there appeared the new fashion type – 'ingenu', characterized by a childlike short hairstyle, a round turndown collar, a slight décolleté, a naïve gaze, achieved by outlining the eyes to make them round and wide, light pastel hues in make-up, a miniskirt, clothes that outlined the figure, and the mannerisms of a capricious child. In many respects this image corresponded to the tendencies dominating Western fashions of the time and exemplified by the British model Twiggy. In the 1970s, the sweet 'ingenu' was transformed into the more aggressive type of 'otviaznaya devitsa', who sported extra-wide trousers, gamine caps, and shoes with platforms – the new variant of old good white 'semolina' rubber shoes. As one might guess, this look was ideal target for bitter reproaches in masculinity, being 'not feminine enough'. The case with stilyaga's gender-bending got the symmetrical development on the women's side.

A special aspect of women's self-fashioning was hair style. The distinctive women's hairdos attracted public attention:

> The permanent wave was disappearing, hair was frizzing out naturally, women were wearing their hair in a circle with curls - ('corolla of the world') hairdo. Or else the hair was romantically unfurled in the 'Sorceress' style that was the height of fashion at the time, named after Marina Vlady, who starred in the film sensation of that name (made in 1956 by André Michel, based on Kuprin's *Olesya*). Intrepid young ladies insisted on indiscriminately churned up locks.[147]

Yet young women stilyagi did not develop their own recognizable separate style, as men did, but were instead content with a few original accents added to their clothing. They copied models from fashion magazines of socialist and Baltic countries, wearing skirts with slits, pants, silk blouses with flower prints, and pointed-toe shoes. In essence, any Western import in a woman's appearance automatically transformed her into a 'stilyaga'. Even attempts to diet for the sake of an attractive figure, or the extensive use of makeup, were seen as something suspect, a violation of the socialist standards of 'modesty', 'simplicity', and a 'sense of proportion'.[148] The slightest effort to look 'unlike everyone else' provoked a harsh ideological response from the official defenders of 'good taste':

> Fashionably emaciated, pale, her black eyes sunken into a thick black shadow on her exhausted face. Her rich hair was combed high above her head. Her dress with its dull black splotches also seemed as if it were drawn in china ink… As if straight from a picture in a Western magazine, this woman exuded the stench of that decaying world, where people know nothing of how to respect one another. No, this repellent way of painting one's face does not fit with our joyful, open-hearted, honest, good women![149]

But there were also times when the repression let up. The festival of young people and students in 1957 represented a brief triumph of the stilyagi. This event included a performance by the music group 'Deviatka TsDRI' (the Nine from the Central House for Art Workers), which had the famous jazz musicians Georgy Garanian, Konstantin Bakholdin, and Boris Rychkov. This group was the sensation of the festival and afterwards gained unprecedented popularity. This time period also saw the first jam sessions with foreign musicians. Ernest Hemingway was the cult writer, the first exhibition of Pablo Picasso in Moscow in 1956 was a huge success. This exhibition launched the public discussion about the figurative and abstract art, which continued through the decades, finishing with the famous speech of Khrushchev against abstractionism in 1962.

The New Generation: Shtatniki of the 1960s

The 1960s were one of the liveliest and more dynamic periods in the history of Soviet fashion: owing to Khrushchev's Thaw, with its comparative receptivity to the west, this decade witnessed the further flourishment of stilyagi fashion.

The so called 'shestidesyatniki' – generations of the 1960s, fighters for the liberal values, are the grown-up stilyagi, cool dressers who are already trying to look around, understand, and undertake social action. For a short time, the Westernizing trends of the stilyagi fitted into the mainstream. Since traveling to the west was impossible to the majority of citizens, most cultural information came by way of short wave broadcasts, and through soviet sailors returning from abroad on commercial ships, or from foreign tourists and diplomats. The next generation of stilyagi were in love with the Beatles and preferred what they called 'shtatnik look' – (from Shtati – the United States). This time the source was the film 'The Man in the Gray Flannel Suit' (1956) with Gregory Peck, shown in Soviet Union with typical delay. Shtatniki were dressing very differently from the modes of the 1950s. They tried to create the condensed image of 'American style' – wearing gray suits, wide gray jackets, black loafers, and smoking cigars.

As described by Bems, a renowned stilyaga who was the model for the protagonist in Slavkin's play 'The Adult Daughter of a Young Man':

> That's what we called ourselves – *shtatniki*, because we dressed in American fashions: wide gray jackets, these solid shoes, like unsinkable ships, raincoats with a button at the top… There were a lot of features we used to identify one another. Small things, like how a button was sewn on, how a seam was done, what kind of buckle you had…[150]

International Parallels and Influences

As we see, the dress of Soviet stilyagi changed markedly over time. In addition, there were also a number of local variations.[151] For example, the capital of Soviet Azerbaijan Baku had its own flourishing style. From the time of the Nobel Brothers and their oil extraction business, this port city had earned a reputation for cosmopolitanism. True connoisseurs looked down on the products of the local clothing factories. During strolls along Torgovaya Street, the fashion conscious displayed their regalia, purchased directly from Western tourists, and certainly not at the state-run retail outlet 'Beryozka'.

Baku's marginal position, far from the watchful eye of the Moscow censors, made it possible to hold festivals there on an unprecedented scale, including the 'Golden Autumn' event, which attracted talented musicians from all over the country. The city had a great many vocal and musical groups (Figure 26). In the 1960s and 1970s, the young people of Baku enjoyed listening to The Beatles and were well-versed in Jimi Hendrix. Led Zeppelin, Pink Floyd, and Deep Purple became popular in later years.

Figure 26 Stilyagi from Baku. Jazz-rock band of the faculty of physics of Baku University. From the left: Emil Gasanov, Hikmet Haji-zada, Vagif Aliev. 1976. © Bahar Haji-zada.

While the music tastes were dictated by English and American performers, fashion in clothes was more influenced by Italian style. The models of masculine elegance and unusual combinations of bright colours in outfits were partly borrowed from Italian fashion.

Although the clothing ensembles of the Soviet stilyagi were known for their unique eclecticism (which is understandable given the unfavorable conditions), there are also grounds for comparison with other types of alternative fashion that were popular in the West at the same time. One obvious parallel is the clothing of the English 'Teddy boys' of the early 1950s, who sported long jackets with velvet cuffs, tight pants and heavy-soled suede shoes, or brothel creepers.[152] Their hair were coiffed into a cock over their foreheads and their faces were flanked by impressive sideburns. The original idol of the Teds was King Edward VII, who was known as an inveterate dandy. The name 'Teddy boy' in fact came from the nickname for Edward. With a somewhat exaggerated version of the elegant neo-Edwardian style, these young men from the urban outskirts played at being gentlemen, diluting their parodically lofty dress with American borrowings (the 1953 film 'The Wild One' with Marlon Brando was popular at the time). The bow tie, for example, was quickly replaced by the bolo tie in imitation of American cowboys, and the tight pants were replaced with blue jeans. This outfit later became popular among fans of rock and roll.[153]

The public reaction to Teddy boys was very similar to the case of stilyagi. As Ted Polhemus notes,

> Needless to say, the powers that be were not pleased. At first the media treated these "New Edwardians" or "Teddy boys" as a joke, but the strategy soon switched to that of

questioning their masculinity… The Teds fought words with images. They might preen and strut like like peacocks but their macho demeanour left no one in doubt that these were 100 per cent male peacocks.[154]

This sort of concern regarding gender ambivalence resembled precisely the soviet criticism of 'stilyaga's woman's look' – the authorities sensed the implicit danger of subverting gender stereotypes.

The Teddies were also known for their exemplary behaviour. They might stop a train by pushing the emergency button to call the engineer, and they were known to pick fights. They were tried for disturbances of public order, and during one of these trials the judge attempted to teach them a lesson:

> You tried to get hold of money to pay for ridiculous things like Edwardian suits. They are ridiculous in the eyes of ordinary people. They are flashy, cheap and nasty, and stamp the wearer as a particularly undesirable type.[155]

As one might see, in their own time the English bourgeois public was not enamoured of the Teddies and their behaviour, but later their style became known as an urban fashion classic and was resurrected a number of times in later decades.[156]

Similar youth movements developed in the 1950s around the world: in Australia the Bodgies, forerunners of today's bikers were the leaders of alternative fashion. They wore pipe stem trousers and black leather jackets, while their girlfriends the Widgies bleached their beehive hair and showed off in skin-tight skirts.

Japan also had its fashion-forward youth, the Taiyozoku. Just as stilyagi, they preferred to wear pipe stem trousers, Hawaiian shirts, and black glasses. Extolling the 'cult of the sun', the Taiyozoku expressed a deliberate idleness in their dress, a relaxed resort feel, aimed at the day-to-day mundanity of the adult world. It seems likely that the colourful flippancy of Hawaiian shirts and neckties with monkeys was designed to have a similar provocative effect in the Soviet context.

An earlier predecessor of Soviet stilyaga fashion was the American 'zoot suit', comprised of baggy trousers and a long coat with extremely wide lapels. This caricature of a dress outfit with a dinner jacket was clearly meant as a shot at the American mainstream of the 1940s. The 'zoot suit' was a particular favourite among fashionable young black and Mexican men, who saw it as a convenient means of symbolic protest against the white establishment.[157] It was not uncommon to hear of fights in which the proponents of zoot suits were stripped to their underwear. The 'zoot suit riots' that occurred in 1943, when American military personnel and police attacked the wearers of these outfits, went down in history as a milestone in the minority rights movement. The grotesquely exaggerated style of the zoot suit, with its huge pants tapered at the bottom and a coat to the knees, in combination with a sombrero and long chains dangling and clinking, looked even more extravagant thanks to its bright theatrical coloration. This combative attempt to assimilate the proper dress jacket and distort it in a parodic form was a success, and thus was a wholly avant-garde movement inscribed into the conservative history of men's clothing.

The common factor that unites these various national manifestations of alternative youth fashion is the principle of 'mix and match': the combination of high and low style with distinctive irony: a dinner coat, but pink and with a sombrero; a Swiss overcoat, but sky blue and with a Stetson hat; an Edwardian jacket, but with a bolo tie. These were tests of a playful style in various combinations, a joyful nonconformity and war against accustomed patterns.

Thus the look of soviet stilyaga was a pastiche of several styles: besides the Teddy boys fashion, stilyagi sported Hawaian shirts, which were made popular by American tourists returning from Hawaii in the 1950s. The obvious link with exotic southern style was the socialist Cuba: flamboyance in colour, supported associations with jazz flash styles. Printed shirts and huge ties with tropical palms or monkeys carried the message of carefree, hedonistic lifestyle, proclaiming the easy, relaxed attitudes of 'golden youth'. And, finally, the habit of dressing up, typical of the next generation of stilyaga – who used to wear bow-ties and smoke cigars, was read as a summary image of 'bourgeois' style but sometimes could create the appearance of provincial theatricality.

Off course, when the soviet young men picked up on these styles they evolved them in a distinctive way – but in detailing. The extra upper button at the collar of a raincoat was considered chic, and the art of reading such details was part of stilyaga's sophisticated conspiracy. But gaining friend's respect was one thing, and the bold proclamation of an alternative style on the street was a completely different matter.

Public Reaction

Being fashionable under the soviet regime could be quite a risky adventure, and yet many young people managed to preserve individual style and resist the ideological control of their looks. Publicly violating the Soviet fashion etiquette, prescribing the principles of Modesty, Simplicity, and 'Sense of measure',[158] they invented the new dress codes.

This was a kind of conspiracy against state's surveillance. They developed their own modes of cultural production, openly opposing the official dress code.

The bright, bold, and casual style of stilyaga naturally attracted attention and many cool dressers were stopped in the streets by militia or indignant passers-by. The official authorities took measures against stilyagi – the students-stilyagi were turned out of institutes, some komsomol activists tried to catch stilyagi and cut off their hairs, or at least cut their narrow trousers at the bottom. So, the stakes in this game were high and many stilyagi paid the high price for their fashionable habits. Yet the game on the Broadway continued every evening.

Female *stilyagi* were subjected to the same persecution as the men, including being forced to cut their hair. As Aleksandr Shlepyanov, the London businessman and former Leningrad *stilyaga*, recalled:

> Once my wife Nina and I were walking on Nevsky Prospekt, and she looked different from all the other pedestrians because she had a skirt with slits made by her mother as instructed in the magazine Poland (Pol'sha), and she had her hair in a bouffant, as was fashionable

at the time. And I had on some sort of checked coat from Czechoslovakia, which I had bought at a consignment store for something like 8 rubles. This was enough to make the public order squad grab us and try to cut her hair, but fortunately for us the poet Yuri Golubensky was in this squad and he was 'one of us,' so he stepped in and got us off the hook somehow.[159]

The disapproving responses in the countries in question naturally varied in their degree of repressiveness, but a general irritation was evident in all cases.[160] In this context, one could conclude that the attacks on Soviet stilyagi were not a unique phenomenon: young people with alternative preferences were victimized in all countries, but with the key difference, of course, that in the Soviet Union a stilyaga could have his or her life drastically altered, being expelled from college and blacklisted, or arrested for unlawful currency transactions.

In Leningrad, there were serious administrative persecutions of the stilyagi. Fashionable youth were not only seized on the streets, but even kicked out of their schools. It is telling that those who came to the defence of these unfortunate students were the professors who had held not entirely orthodox Soviet positions, for example, 'the formalists'. Dissident scholars in the humanities and dissidents in fashion had little trouble recognizing one another.

> At university the only person who stood up against these crackdowns was Boris Mikhailovich Eikhenbaum, the famous literature scholar, who said that cropping the hair of girls because they adhered to a somewhat different fashion than that followed by our respected lawmakers was positively medieval, and our university should not do that... And at this professors Plotkin, Meilakh, and Makagonenko started screaming that he was going against the party line, and everything else that one was expected to scream in those days. Only one person, old professor Propp, the folklorist, supported Eikhenbaum.[161]

The reaction to the stilyagi in each particular instance was to some extent a litmus test, demonstrating the measure of conformity or dissidence.

To what extent was the vestimentary protest of the stilyagi a conscious resistance? As we saw, the cool dressers used all possible cultural resources for their potentially subversive self-fashioning practices: dress, body language, music, dance, and walking in the streets. The stilyagi themselves admitted that one of the motives was a clear desire to declare themselves different from others. As described by Igor Berukshtis, once a Moscow stilyaga: 'One needed to get some distance, some freedom from the usual people, or, to put it more pointedly, from the vulgar crowd.'[162] This romantic manifesto confirms, that the Soviet *stilyagi*, those hepcats, flaneurs, and Westernizers, managed to maintain the alternative fashion in the most adverse conditions.

In the contemporary culture, the phenomenon of Stilyaga continues to attract attention. In 2008, a musical film 'Stilyagi' was released (shot by a famous director Valery Todorovsky). The costumes for the movie were made by Aleksander Osipov. The movie was very successful, having grossed over 490 million of roubles in Russia. From that time starts the popularity of costume parties with 'stilyaga' dress code.

Thus, we see that the movement of Stilyagi is not only a chapter in the history of fashion but also continues to inspire the contemporary fops, fashionistas and fans of street style.

Notes

1. The author thanks Raisa Kirsanova for valuable suggestions made during the preparation of this chapter.
2. Mikhail Pyliayev, *Zamechatelnie chudaki i originali* [Memorable people and eccentrics] (Moscow: Interbuk, 1990), 90–91.
3. John Harvey, *Men in Black* (Chicago: University of Chicago Press, 1996).
4. Pyliayev, *Zamechatel'nye chudaki*, 91.
5. James Laver, *Costume and Fashion* (London: Thames & Hudson, 1986), 103–27.
6. Tamara Korshunova, *Kostium v Rossii XVIII - nachala XX veka: iz sobraniia gosudarstvennogo Ermitazha* [Russian Costume of XVIII-beginning of XIX centuries] (Leningrad: Khudozhnik RSFSR, 1970), 7–9.
7. Antioch Kantemir, *Sobranie Stikhotvoreniy* [Collected poems] (Leningrad: Sovetskiy Pisatel, 1956), 72.
8. On masculinity in the eighteenth and nineteenth century, see Vern L. Bullough and Bonnie Bullough, *Cross-Dressing, Sex and Gender* (Philadelphia: University of Pensylvania Press, 1993), 113–174. On the gender aspects of the dandy, see Jessica R. Feldman, *Gender on the Divide* (Ithaca and London: Cornell University Press,1993); Peter McNeil, 'Macaroni Masculinities', *Fashion Theory* 4, no. 4 (2000): 375–405.
9. Ivan Krylov, Mysli filosofa po mode [Thoughts of philosopher on fashion], in *Russkaia proza XVIII veka* [Russian Prose of XVIII Century] (Moscow-Leningrad: Khudozhestvennaya literatura, 1950), 2: 757.
10. Ibid., 754. Compare suspicious and disapproving attitudes towards English macaronies, discussed in Peter McNeil, 'That Doubtful Gender: Macaroni Dress and Male Sexualities', *Fashion Theory* 3, no. 4 (1999): 411–447.
11. Krylov, Mysli filosofa po mode, 753.
12. Filipp Vigel', *Zapiski* [Notes] (Moscow: Zakharov, 2000), 51.
13. See Laver, *Costume and Fashion*, 149–152.
14. Vigel', *Zapiski*, 78–79.
15. Pyliayev, *Zamechatel'nye chudaki*, 163.
16. For more detailed analysis, see Raisa Kirsanova, *Kostium v russkoi khudozhestvennoi culture* [Dress in Russian Arts and Culture] (Moscow: Rossiyskaya entsyklopedia, 1995), 131–132.
17. Pyliayev, Zamechatel'nye chudaki, 53.
18. Yuri Arnol'd, *Vospominaniya* [Memories] (Moscow: 1892), vol. 1, 9.
19. See Anne Hollander, *Sex and Suits* (New York: A. A. Knopf, 1995), 63–116.
20. Aleksander Pushkin, *Sochineniya* [Works] (Moscow: Khudozhestvennaya literatura, 1949), 312.
21. On Pushkin's dandyism, see Sam N. Driver, *Pushkin: Literature and Social Ideas* (New York: Columbia University Press, 1989); Monika Greenleaf, *Pushkin and Romantic Fashion: Fragment, Elegy, Orient, Irony* (Stanford: Stanford University Press, 1994); Leonid Grossman, Pushkin i dendizm [Pushkin and dandyism], in *Sobranie sochineniy* [Collected Works] (Moscow: Sovremennie problemi, 1928), 1: 14–45.
22. Yuri Lotman, Russkiy dendizm [Russian dandyism], in *Besedy o russkoi kul'ture* [Talks on Russian Culture] (St. Petersburg: Iskusstvo-Peterburg, 1994), 123–135.
23. Vigel', *Zapiski*, 78–79.
24. Pushkin, *Sochineniya*, 315.
25. Oleg Proskurin, *Poeziia Pushkina ili podvizhnyi palimpsest* [Pushkin's poetry or Mobile Palimpsest] (Moscow: NLO, 1999), 328–347.
26. Quoted from Raisa Kirsanova, *Kostium v russkoi khudozhestvennoi culture* [Dress in Russian Arts and Culture] (Moscow: Rossiyskaya entsyklopedia, 1995), 287.
27. Arnol'd, *Vospominaniya*, 10.
28. Théophile Gautier, *Puteshestvie v Rossiu* [Travel in Russia] (Moscow: Misl', 1990), 43–44.

29 Gautier was no casual observer of such trivial details. Famous for having worn a red (or in some sources, pink) waistcoat to the premiere of the Hugo's play 'Hernani', he was a dandy all his life and followed fashion strictly. In his novels he described his characters' costumes with detail and feeling. In his article 'On Fashion' (1858) he wrote intriguingly about the relationship between clothing and the body. Thus, Russian fur coats would have excited his imagination and he would have sympathised with the problems of winter outfitting encountered by Russian dandies.
30 Ibid., 68.
31 Ibid.
32 Ibid., 43.
33 Mikhail Zhikharev, *Dokladnaya zapiska potomstvu o Petre Yakovleviche Chaadaeve* [Note to offspring on Petr Yakovlevich Chaadaev], in *Russkoye obshchestvo 30-kh godov XIX veka. Liudi i idei. Memuary sovremennikov* [Russian Society of the 1830s. People and Ideas, Memoirs of Contemporaries] (Moscow: Izdatelstvo MGU, 1989), 56–57.
34 Ibid., 57.
35 Yuri Lotman, *Kultura i vzryv* [Culture and Explosion] (Moscow: Gnosis, 1992), 127.
36 Konstantin Rotikov, *Drugoi Peterburg* [Another Peterburg] (St. Petersburg: Liga plus, 2000), 252–259.
37 Ivan Panaev, *Literatnye vospominaniya* [Literary memories] (Moscow: Pravda, 1988), 197. A murnolka is a hat with a high crown narrowing upwards. A rubakha is a traditional, long shirt worn outside the pants and belted at the waist.
38 Panaev, 196–197.
39 Ibid.
40 Ibid.
41 Konstantin Aksakov, Vospominaniya studentstva 1832–1835 [Memories of studenthood, 1832–1835], in *Russkoye obshchestvo 30-kh godov XIX veka. Liudi i idei. Memuary sovremennikov* [Russian Society of the 1830s. People and Ideas, Memoirs of Contemporaries] (Moscow: Izdatelstvo MGU, 1989), 333.
42 Pyliayev, 163–164.
43 Grossman, *Sobranie sochineniy*, 1, 29–30.
44 Vigel', 66. On various forms of the 'feminine' in fashion, see also Marjorie Garber, *Vested Interests* (New York and London: Routledge, 1993).
45 Solomon Shtraikh, Istoriko-literaturnyi ocherk o Vigele [Historical-literary Essay on Vigel'], in Vigel', *Zapiski*, 554–580.
46 Vigel', 66.
47 Pyliayev, 163–164.
48 Leonid Shepelev, *Tituly, mundiry, ordena* [Titles, Uniforms, Orders] (Leningrad: Nauka, 1991), 93.
49 Ibid, 94.
50 Ibid., 94–95.
51 Pyliayev, 163–164.
52 Shepelev, 95.
53 Jules Barbey d'Aurevilly, *On Dandyism and George Brummell*. Trans. George Walden (London: Gibson Square book, 2002), 105.
54 Avdotya Panaeva, *Vospominaniya* [Memories] (Moscow: Pravda, 1988), 197.
55 Yuri Lotman, Teatr i teatral'nosl' v stroe kul'tury nachala XIX veka [Theatre and Theatricality in XIX century culture], in *Izbrannye stat'i v trekh tomakh* [Selected Articles in three volumes] (Tallinn: Aleksandra, 1992), 1: 269–287.
56 Pyliayev, 164.
57 Pyliayev, 204.
58 Nikolai Gogol, *The Collected Tales of Nikolai Gogol*. Translated and annotated by Richard Pevear and Larissa Volokhonsky (New York: Vintage Classics, 1999), 29.

59 Dmitry Grigorovich, Svistulkin. *Biblioteka dlya chteniya*, 129 (1855): 21–22. I am grateful to Professor Igor' Dobrodomov who brought this text to my attention.
60 Shepelev, 22.
61 See Alla Begunova, *Povsednevnaya zhizn' russkogo gusara v tsarstvovaniye Aleksandra I* [The Everyday Life of a Russian Hussar in the Reign of Alexander I] (Moscow: Molodaya Gvardiya, 2000).
62 Panaev, *Literaturnye vospominaniya*, 61.
63 Ivan Goncharov, Pis'ma stolichnogo druga k provintsialnomu zhenikhu [Letters by the friend from the capital to the provincial bridegroom], in *Felietony sorokovykh godov. Zhurnalnaya i gazetnaya proza I.A.Goncharova, F.M.Dostoevskogo, I.S.Turgeneva* [Feuilletons of the Forties. Magazine and Newspaper Articles by I.A.Goncharov, F.M.Dostoyevsky, I.S.Turgenev], eds. Yu. G. Oksman (Moscow-Leningrad: Academia, 1930), 41–42.
64 Ibid., 43.
65 Ibid., 43–44.
66 Ibid., 44.
67 Ibid., 45.
68 Ibid., 47.
69 Ibid., 47–48.
70 Ibid., 48.
71 Ibid.
72 Olga Murav'eva, *Kak vospityvali russkogo dvorianina* [The Upbringing of the Russian Nobleman] (St. Petersburg: Letniy Sad, 1998), 78–79.
73 Lord Chesterfield, *Letters to His Son and Others* (London: J. M. Dent, 1929), 258.
74 Goncharov, 51.
75 Ibid., 55.
76 See Eleazar Meletinsky, *Izbranniye statyi. Vospominaniya* [Selected Articles. Memoirs] (Moscow: RSUH, 1998).
77 Goncharov, 55.
78 Ibid., 56.
79 Honoré de Balzac, *Traité de la vie élégante*, ed. Marie-Christine Natta (Clermont-Ferrand: Presses Universitaire Blaise Pascal, 2000), 130.
80 Ivan Goncharov. Pisma stolichnogo druga k provintsialnomu zhenikhu [Letters by the friend from the capital to the provincial fiancé], in *Felietony sorokovykh godov. Zhurnalnaya i gazetnaya proza I.A.Goncharova, F.M.Dostoevskogo, I.S.Turgeneva* [Feuilletons of the Forties. Magazine and Newspaper Articles by I.A.Goncharov, F.M.Dostoyevsky, I.S.Turgenev], ed. Yu. G. Oksman (Moscow-Leningrad: Academia, 1930), 41–42.
81 The author is referring to Grand Prince Mikhail Pavlovich.
82 Avdotya Panaeva, *Vospominaniya* [Memories] (Moscow: Pravda, 1986), 95.
83 *Dendi* [Dandy], no. 1, (1910), 23.
84 Ibid., 23.
85 Ibid.
86 Ibid., 24.
87 Ibid.
88 Jules Barbey d'Aurevilly, *Dendizm i George Brummell* [On Dandyism and George Brummell]. Trans. Mikhail Petrovsky, Preface by Mikhail Kuzmin (Moscow: Al'tsiona, 1912).
89 M. L. *Predislovie* [Foreword to Barbey D'Aurevilly's Treatise "On Dandyism and George Brummell], *Dandy*, no. 1, (1910), 15.
90 Maximilian Voloshin, *Liki tvorchestva* [Faces of Creation] (Leningrad: Nauka, 1988), 41.
91 Nina Petrovskaya. Iz vospominaniy [Excerpts from Memoirs], in Valery Bryusov, *Literaturnoye Nasledstvo* [Literary Heritage] (Moscow: Nauka, 1976), 778.
92 In 1912, for instance, the four volumes of *Istoriya zapadnoi literatury 1800–1910* [History of Western literature 1800–1910] appeared, edited by Professor Fedor Batyushkov. Among the authors of this unique publication were Vyacheslav Ivanov, Sergey Soloviev, Vladimir

Nabokov, Ferdinand Georgievich de La Bart, Nestor Kotlyarevsky, Zinaida Vengerova, and Viktor Zhirmunsky.
93 Nikolay Bogomolov, *Mikhail Kuzmin* (Moscow: NLO, 1995), 190.
94 Viacheslav Ivanov, *Stikhotvoreniya i poemy* [Poems] (Leningrad: Sovetsky Pisatel, 1978), 179–180.
95 Irina Odoyevtseva, *Na beregakh Nevy* [On the banks of Neva] (Moscow: Khudozhestvennaya literatura, 1989), 96–97.
96 Odoyevtseva, 101.
97 Here I disagree with Julia Demidenko who considered the dandyism of the World of Art to be genuinely innovative; see Julia Demidenko, Russkie dendi [Russian Dandies], *Rodina* no. 8 (2000), 111–114.
98 Sergey Makovsky, Diaghilev, in *Sergei Diaghilev i russkoe iskusstvo* [Sergey Diaghilev and Russian Art, in two volumes] (Moscow: Izobrazitel'noe iskusstvo, 1982), 2: 309.
99 Igor Grabar', O Bakste [On Bakst], in *Sergei Diaghilev i russkoe iskusstvo* [Sergey Diaghilev and Russian Art, in two volumes] (Moscow: Izobrazitel'noe iskusstvo, 1982), 2: 290.
100 Mstislav Dobuzhinsky, *Vospominaniya* [Memories] (Moscow: Nauka, 1987), 203.
101 Quoted from Bogomolov, 217.
102 Éliane Moch-Bickert, *Kolombina desiatykh godov* [A 1910s Columbine] (Paris, St. Petersburg: Grzhebin Publishers, 1993), 39.
103 On Mariengof see Tomi Huttunen, *Imazhinist Mariengof: Dendi. Montazh. Tsiniki.* [Imazhinist Mariengof: Dandy. Montage. Cynics] (Moscow: Novoe Literaturnoe Obozrenie, 2007); Oleg Demidov, *Anatoly Mariengof: pervy dendi strani Sovetov* [Anatoly Mariengof: First Dandy of the Soviet Country] (Moscow: Redaktsia Eleni Shubinoy, 2019).
104 Anatoly Mariengof. Moy vek, moya molodost', moi druzya i podrugi [My times, my youth, my friends], in *Moy vek, moi druzya i podrugi. Vospominaniya Mariengofa, Shershenevicha, Gruzinova* (My Times, My Friends. The Memoirs of Mariengof, Shershenevich, and Gruzinov) (Moscow: Moskovsky Rabochy, 1990), 121.
105 Ibid., 290–291.
106 Odoyevtseva, *Na beregakh Nevy*, 240.
107 Ibid., 241.
108 Ibid., 241.
109 Lidiya Ginzburg is quoting Nikolai Oleynikov: Lidiya Ginzburg, *Zapisniye knizhki. Vospominaniya. Esse* [Notebooks. Memoirs. Essays] (St. Petersburg: Iskusstvo-SPB, 2002), 487.
110 Vladimir Mayakovsky, Kofta Fata (The Fop's Blouse), *Polnoye sobraniye sochineniy v 13 tomakh* [Collected Works in 13 vols] (Moscow: Gosudarstvennoye izdatelstvo khudozhestvennoi literatury, 1955), 1: 59 (translation of quotation by Sofia Horujaya-Cook).
111 Mayakovsky, Ya sam [I, Myself], *Polnoye sobraniye sochineniy v 13 tomakh*, 1: 21.
112 Viktor Duvakin, *Besedy V.V. Duvakina s M.M.Bakhtinym* [Conversations between V.Duvakin and M.Bakhtin] (Moscow: Progress, 1996), 128.
113 Valentin Smetanich was a poet and excellent translator of Dos Passos and Joyce. He was repressed and shot in prison in 1938. Nadezhda Mandelstam called Stenich 'a man with a great feeling for language and literature and an acute sense of the modern age' and wrote that 'he might have become a brilliant essayist or critic, but the times were not auspicious'. See Nadezhda Mandelstam, *Hope against Hope*. Trans. Max Hayward (New York: Atheneum, 1983), 314.
114 Nikolay Chukovsky, *Literaturniye vospominaniya* [Literary memoirs] (Moscow: Sovetsky Pisatel', 1989), 213.
115 Alexander Blok, *Sochineniya v odnom tome* [Works in one volume] (Moscow, Leningrad: OGIZ, Goslitizdat, 1946), 466.
116 Ibid.
117 Ibid.

118 Ibid. Translation taken in part from Polonsky R. *English Literature and the Russian Aesthetic Renaissance*. Cambridge University Press, 1998.
119 Chukovsky, *Literaturniye vospominaniya*, 224–225.
120 Ibid., 224.
121 Nadezhda Mandelstam, *Hope against Hope*, 314.
122 Chukovsky, *Literaturniye vospominaniya*, 224.
123 One might recall a similar comment from Captain Jesse. Noticing an acquaintance in an aristocratic salon, Jesse once exclaimed: 'Why, Mr. D--, are you here?' See William Jesse, *The Life of George Brummell, Esquire* (London: Saunders and Otley, 1844), 2: 52. The cutting nature of this comment, Jesse explains, was in fact ascribed to it by Brummell, who immediately saw Jesse as a kindred spirit, but nevertheless, a certain similarity would appear to suggest itself.
124 The word 'stilyaga' is derived from the word 'style' ('stil' in Russian). The plural form is 'Stilyagi'.
125 Olesya Guk, *Tarzan v svoem otechestve. Interv'iu s Valentinom Tikhonenko* [Tarzan in His Homeland. An Interview with Valentin Tikhonenko]. http://www.beliy.ru/work/stilyagifilm/-id%3D43.htm. Accessed 1.05.2022.
126 In 2017 the Moscow museum of contemporary culture Garage organised an exhibition '*Bone Music'* in Moscow presenting research by the X-Ray Audio project (London). The exhibition was about 'inventive Soviet music lovers who made illegal copies of banned music on used X-ray film from the late 1940s to the early 1960s'. According to Stephen Coates, curator of *Bone Music*, 'They are images of pain and damage inscribed with the sound of forbidden pleasure; fragile photographs of the interiors of Soviet citizens layered with the ghostly music they secretly loved'. The site of exhibition: https://garagemca.org/en/exhibition/bone-music. Accessed 1 May 2022.
127 Alexey Kozlov, Vospominaniya dzhazmena, perezhivshego vse stadii ottepeli [Memories of a jazzman, who survived through all stages of a Thaw], in *Ottepel'* [Thaw] (Moscow: Tretyakov gallery publishing, 2017), 303.
128 Dmitry Beliaev, 'Stilyaga', *Krokodil*, no. 7 (1949): 10. Quoted by Valery Slavkin, *Pamiatnik neizvestnomy stilyage* [*Monument to the Unknown Stilyaga*] (Moscow: ART Publishing House, 1996), 40–41.
129 Ibid., 41.
130 Raisa Kirsanova, 'Stilyagi', *Rodina*, no. 8 (1998): 72–75. For more on *stilyagi*, see Galina Orlova, Stilyagi. Biografiia veshshi [Stilyagi. Biography of a Thing], *in Ob"iat' obyknovennoe. Povsednevnost' kak tekst po-amerikanski i po-russki* (Moscow: MGU Publishing House, 2004), 205–218; Kristin Rot-Ai. 'Kto na p'edestale, a kto v tolpe? Stilyagi i ideia sovetskoi 'molodezhnoi kul'tury' v epokhu 'ottepeli' ['Who is on a pedestal and who is in the crowd? Stilyagi and the idea of Soviet "youth culture" in the thaw period'], *Neprikosnovennyi zapas*, no. 4 (2004): 36. https://magazines.gorky.media/nz/2004/4/kto-na-pedestale-a-kto-v-tolpe-stilyagi-i-ideya-sovetskoj-molodezhnoj-kultury-v-epohu-ottepeli.html. Accessed 1 May 2022.
131 Kozlov, 305.
132 Berukshtis, Igor'. 'Stilyagi'. Interview with Igor' Pomerantsev, *Ural*, no. 11, (1999): 124.
133 Quoted in Mark Allen Svede, Twiggy and Trotsky, in *Dandies. Fashion and Finesse in Art and Culture*, ed. Susan Fillin-Yeh (New York: New York University Press, 2001), 251.
134 Andrei Bitov, *Pushkin House* (Normal, IL: Dalkey Archive Press, 1987), 20.
135 The ironical sketch aims at the young stilyaga, using his father's expensive car: 'Pobeda' was a luxurious brand of Soviet cars.
136 Guk, ibid.
137 Vadim Makarevich, 'S dzhazom po zhizni. Interv'iu s Borisom Alekseevym' ['Through Life with Jazz. An Interview with Boris Alekseev'], *Nezavisimaia gazeta*, 20 June (2003): 13.
138 Makarevich, 13.
139 Guk, ibid.

140 Haircut with short back and sides cut with clippers.
141 Mikhail German, *Slozhnoe proshedshee* [Past Perfect] (Moscow: Pechatny dvor, 2000), 266.
142 *Ogonek*, 26, 21 June (1959).
143 Natalia Lebina, Konets epokhi bolshogo stilya: antistalinskie tendentsii v mode 1960 godov [End of Grand Style period: antistalinist tendencies in Soviet Fashion of 1960s], in *Ottepel'* [Thaw] (Moscow: Tretyakov gallery publishing, 2017), 177–191.
144 *Torchon* and *éponge* were the names of terrycloth-type dress fabrics popular in the Soviet Union.
145 German, 265–266.
146 See Olga Vainshtein, Fashioning woman: dressmaker as cultural producer, in *Para-sites. A Casebook against Cynical Reason*, ed. George Marcus (Chicago: The University of Chicago Press, 2000), 195–225.
147 German, 266.
148 For more on the cultural norms regarding women's fashions in the USSR, see Olga Vainshtein, Female fashion, Soviet style: Bodies of ideology, in *Russia – Women – Culture*, eds. H. Goscilo and B. Holmgren (Bloomington: Indiana University Press, 1996), 64–94.
149 Olga Rusanova, *Razdum'ia o krasote i vkuse* [Thoughts on Beauty and Taste, in Russian] (Moscow: Znanie, 1962), 133.
150 Valery Slavkin, *Pamiatnik neizvestnomy stilyage* (Moscow: ART Publishing House, 1996), 75.
151 For more on Latvian *stilyagi*, see Mark Allen Svede, 'Twiggy and Trotsky', in *Dandies. Fashion and Finesse in Art and Culture*, ed. Susan Fillin-Yeh (New York: New York University Press, 2001), 243–270. On East-European parallels see Djurdja Bartlett, Socialist Dandies International: East Europe, 1946-1959, *Fashion Theory* 17, no. 3 (2013): 249–299.
152 By the 1960s and 1970s when Teddy boy look became part of the more widespread as part of the rock-n-roll music scene, it had added frilly nylon shirts in a variety of colours and whiskers.
153 For more details, see Ted Polhemus, *Street Style* (London: Thames and Hudson, 1997), 33–37.
154 Polhemus, 34.
155 See also Chris Steele-Perkins, Richard Smith. *The Teds* (London: Dewi Lewis Publishing, 2002).
156 'Jamesie was looking enchanting, wearing a sort of Teddy boy evening-dress composed of tight black trousers, dark blue corduroy coat, white silk shirt, and purple choker'. Iris Murdoch, *The Unicorn* (London: Triad Panther, 1977), 135.
157 For more about zoot suits, see: Holly Alford, 'The zoot suit: its history and influence', *Fashion Theory* 8, no. 2 (2004): 225–237.
158 Olga Vainshtein, 'The concept of modesty in socialist dress and grooming: snapshot', in *The Berg Encyclopedia of World Dress and Fashion*, ed. Joanne B. Eicher, vol. 9, East Europe, Russia, and the Caucasus (Oxford and New York: Berg Publishers, 2010), 364–365.
159 Aleksander Shlepyanov, "Stilyagi". Interview with Igor' Pomerantsev. *Ural*, no. 11, (1999): 126.
160 For more on youth culture in the 1950s, see Mark Abrams, *The Teenage Consumer* (London: London Press Exchange, 1959); Tosco R. Fyvel, *The Insecure Offenders: Rebellious Youth in the Welfare State* (London: Pelican, 1961).
161 Berukshtis, 124. The names of Vladimir Propp and Boris Eikhenbaum are renowned among humanities scholars, and their works continue to be regularly republished.
162 Berukshtis, 123.

Chapter Eight

DANDYISM REVISITED

Three Periods of Nineteenth-Century European Dandyism

In the development of European dandyism, three significant periods should be outlined. The **first**, in Britain, covered the opening decades of the nineteenth century. The central figure here, naturally, was Beau Brummell, who departed for France in 1816. Through Brummell, the dandy image found its complete expression in corporeality, dress, and behaviour, as a new, understated, and neoclassical aesthetic of male dress emerged. Due to his authority as arbiter of fashion, Brummell was able to instate the Great Masculine Renunciation, a minimalist trend which came to dominate the first third of the nineteenth century.

Equally significant was the particular dandy rhetoric of performative behaviour, developed by Brummell, whose actions and gestures were automatically woven into the fabric of culture. The aesthetics of late Romanticism had already prepared the ground for social acceptance of individual creative fancy. Brummell's witticisms and sudden stylistic 'coups' invariably became the stuff of anecdotes and legends, forming a new layer of urban folklore. His self-fashioning practice was subsequently taken up and imitated by his many followers and admirers. In the Regency years, the main 'rules' of dandy behaviour, and norms of hygiene and corporeality, came into being. Finding its expression primarily through social practice, British dandyism of the first period mainly consisted in showing off and perfecting one's dress, manners, general appearance, and, ultimately, one's entire way of life. The dandy code of behaviour was flexible, leaving ample room for play, and disruption of social convention through practical jokes, scandal, insolence, and cutting.

In the late 1820s, the literary canon of dandyism began to form with the fashionable novels published by Henry Colburn. The silver fork novels, in which the main heroes were often dandies, came to be seen as textbooks in good manners and social etiquette. Following the sensational success of the series, dandies became firmly established not only as a social group, but as literary characters, with their clubs, salons, balls, and opera coming to be seen as familiar settings. Fashionable novels offered much-desired opportunities for 'virtual' aristocratism, with all necessary information on aristocratic manners and high society living.

In the 1830s, however, the development of dandyism began to be impeded by conservative trends emanating from publications such as Fraser's Magazine. Satirised by Carlyle in 'Sartor Resartus' (1831), and condemned by Thackeray, dandyism was all but brought to a halt by Victorian purism until the 1880s, which opened a new era of decadence. During the drab decades of stagnation, the key figure remained the Count D'Orsay, representing the type of Butterfly dandy. A brilliantly charismatic dandy who had spent the first part of his life in France, his charm ensured he remained at the heart of 1830s and 1840s London high society.

In the 1830s, the centre of European dandyism shifted from Britain to France. During this **second** period, a new version of dandyism emerged, shaped by translations of fashionable novels, and French Anglomania. Distinctly intellectual in flavour, the new trend was closely linked with the development of modern European society. By now a philosophy of urban life, dandyism came to be associated with flâneurs, being always in the public eye, and producing a positive impression. If the British strategy had centred around exclusivism, the new dandies were endowed with a practical toolkit for elegance. The black coat of George Brummell, previously an exclusive element of his own unique style, was now part of everyday middle-class dress. The growing popularity of ready-to-wear clothes played a significant part in this process, also affecting mechanisms of visual perception: key details in one's dress could now be used as 'clues' to the wearer's social status.

During this period, dandyism also came to be associated with a new body of text, including key treatises on fashion such as Balzac's 'Treatise on Elegant Living' (1830), Jules Barbey D'Aurevilly's 'On Dandyism and George Brummell' (1845), Théophile Gautier's 'On Fashion' (1858), and Charles Baudelaire's 'The Painter of Modern Life' (1863). In these seminal texts, the dandy appears as a modern hero with his own modus operandi fusing literature and fashion. Trying out new means of self-expression in everyday urban reality, this character spends time in cafes and boulevards. Practising vestimentary and social metamorphoses, he explores the 'theory of walking' as a flâneur, analyses passers-by, describing ladies' crinolines and cosmetics with excitement. This is the dandy as bohemian artist: founded on the gentleman's code of conduct, with the free artistic spirit of bohemian Paris, the dandy model of performative behaviour becomes more democratic.

The third period in the evolution of European dandyism is closely linked to the decadent movement. In literature, this stage was represented by novels such as Joris-Karl Huysmans's 'Against the Grain' ('A Rebours') (1884), Oscar Wilde's 'The Picture of Dorian Gray' (1891), and Max Beerbohm's 'Zuleika Dobson' (1911). In these key texts, the dandy makes the transition from bohemian artist to refined Aesthete. Among their main themes are artifice, faces and masks, and the battle with vulgarity and bad taste. The Dandy-Aesthetes actively promoted their ideology (recall Oscar Wilde's educational lectures) and served as patrons of the arts (count Robert de Montesquiou, for instance, supported many artists, including René Lalique). Important features of the Aesthetes were heightened sensitivity and deliberate development of different types of sensual awareness. Hence, their love of the exotic, and obsession with scent: recall the olfactory experiments of the heroes of Wilde and Huysmans. Such refined tastes, naturally, required changes in dress. The plain black coat now appeared banal and bourgeois. As leaders in fashion, dandies took the next step, creating Aesthetic dress with a variety of hues – count Robert de Montesquiou, for example, favouring grey. Around that time, the most significant portraits of dandies were painted by artists such as Whistler, Boldini, and Sargent. At the same time, the modernist tendency initiated by Baudelaire to objectivise personality, continued. The dandy image of that period was akin to an ideal emblem of a human 'object': in this, it anticipated the Camp aesthetic of Oscar Wilde and Max Beerbohm.

During this period, the connections between art and everyday life became exceptionally transparent, functioning as a two-way process. After de Montesquiou inspired Huysmans to create Des Esseintes, 'Against the Grain' played a key part in the appearance of 'The Picture of Dorian Gray', which itself became a source of inspiration for countless followers. The image of the Aesthete came full circle from life to literature, and back.

At times, the self-fashioning experiments of the Aesthetes were dramatically shaped by real events. The trial of Oscar Wilde lent decadent dandyism an element of risk, the appeal of forbidden fruit. Reminding of the romantic escapades and demonic moods of Lord Byron, paradoxically, this served to revive dandyism's protest potential. Due to these neoromantic moods, in the twentieth century, dandies came to be seen as rebels (as with Camus' 'hommes revoltés'), men on the fringes of society, artists of bohemian ways.

The main features of the decadent period could be summed up thus: (1) Dandyism was fully integrated into the processes of European modernisation. Through the Camp aesthetic, it mastered 'aggressive self-defence' strategies. (2) Following the trial of Oscar Wilde, the gender aspect of dandyism came into general focus. Issues of queer identity in dandyism, until then largely unnoticed, began to require their own discourse, 'language' within culture. (3) In the dandy aesthetic, the principle of artifice became paramount, bringing conscious self-fashioning to the fore.

In the twentieth century, dandyism as a single cultural phenomenon bringing together fashion, literature, and a code of behaviour, was largely transformed. Disparate traces could, naturally, still be discerned in the vestimentary experiments of fashionable people or in the many versions of Camp, yet we should be very cautious while using the word 'Dandy' and the concept of dandyism in modern culture.

Modern Dandies and Two Trends in the History of Dandyism

'A Dandy has to be a man of his time', said the Savile Row tailor Julio Mompó, discussing his vision of modern dandyism.[1] Undoubtedly, each historical epoch has its own set of dandies. But what are the distinctive features to distinguish the contemporary heirs of Beau Brummell?

It is always a challenge to define a modern dandy. Many authors tried to suggest their answers.[2] A variety of criteria is amazing: leader of society; an English gentleman; a devotee of sartorial minimalism; an aesthete designer; a darling of high society who sometimes plays risky games; a flaneur; a cleanliness fanatic; a connoisseur of perfumes – each facet of the dandy has the allure of deceptive clarity.

In the first half of the twentieth century, it was still possible with little effort to identify people who continued the tradition of classical dandyism: the writers Marcel Proust, Ronald Firbank, and Vladimir Nabokov; Count Boni de Castellane, the Duke of Windsor. For a long time in England, Quentin Crisp (1908–1999) was considered the number one dandy.[3] Aesthete, writer, and journalist, he was incredibly popular, and there is a wax figure of him at Madame Tussaud's. Despite his varied interests, Quentin's principal creation was said to be his own lifestyle, which was entirely unique and consisted in an ironical dandyism with a good dose of camp. His witticisms were quoted everywhere, and the television program 'An Evening with Quentin Crisp' invariably topped the ratings.

In recent memory, Fred Astaire, Cary Grant, and Neil Munro 'Bunny' Roger are often mentioned as sources of inspiration for modern dandies. Other lists of the dandies would include people of such disparate styles as the photographer Cecil Beaton, the dramatist Noel Coward, the writer Tom Wolfe, the musician Eric Clapton, the singer David Bowie, the philosopher Jacques Derrida... the list goes on and on.

However, if we try to trace back the particular features of historical dandyism, we will see that it is hardly possible to reproduce them today as an integral cultural system. As it evolved in the nineteenth century, the dandy style initially embodied minimalist elegance. The dandy's code of behaviour was difficult but absolutely mandatory, prescribing cold politeness and outbursts of irony, imperturbability, the art of frustrating expectations and instantly creating an impression, measured épatage, slowness as a style of dressing and strolling. Also important is the corporal aspect of dandyism as manifested in impeccable hygiene and grooming, activeness in sports (effete aesthetes being the lone exception), habitual gracefulness at social events, the art of dancing and horseback riding.

Even a simple list of these basic features of dandyism suggests that the entire complex is impossible to be replicated today – the contemporary life has changed too much. The dandy as an integral cultural type belongs rather to the nineteenth and beginning of the twentieth century.[4] Nevertheless, in contemporary society one could identify and trace separate aspects of dandyism, such as the art of virtual self-presentation in modern media, dandyism as a stylish performance in public space, and, of course, the traditional self-fashioning through elegant clothes (Figure 27).

Figure 27 Georgy Dobrovolsky (1928–1971), Soviet cosmonaut, commander of Souyz 11 spacecraft. Dobrovolsky on board the cruise ship 'Russia', 1952. © Marina Dobrovolskaya.

We shall further try to outline the cultural territories where the tradition of dandyism, although modified and transformed, is still recognizable and answers to the contemporary challenges.

Modern dandyism, as I see it, develops bifurcating into two incarnations that were, to be sure, dormant in the concept of the dandy from the very first. One is refinement and elegance elevated to high pitch, the other is subtle flamboyance and ostentation. These two strands I see embodied (but not essentialized because dandyism is anathema to an essence) in the English-style gentleman on the one hand, and the African sapeur on the other. Not only do these examples typify the clear directions of the dandy, they vouch for the religion of style that is so important for him (or her), while at the same time showing how the dandy can be used as an identity cipher for self-expression and asserting difference.

Thus, my discussion of contemporary dandyism is constructed around two such distinctive cultural zones – Savile Row tailoring in London and La Sape in the Congo, which generate a profound sense of collective identity. The first case study is focused around the New Bespoke Movement, represented by the British designers Timothy Everest and Ozwald Boateng. The second case study examines the subculture of the Congolese sapeurs.

In late nineteenth- and early twentieth-century European dandyism, two distinct trends may be observed. Tracing back to Beau Brummell and the minimalist tradition of the Regency dandies, the first covered fashion, corporeality, and behavioural norms. Producing the classic principle of 'conspicuous inconspicuousness', this trend was based on aesthetic minimalism, sartorial understatement in dress, and discipline and restraint in self-expression. It was continued in the twentieth century by the celebrated British dandy Max Beerbohm (1872–1956) – a unique 'link' between the Edwardian era and the postwar years. 'The first aim of modern dandyism is the production of the supreme effect through means the least extravagant. [Brummell] was most economical and scrupulous of means,' stated Beerbohm in his famous treatise 'Dandies and Dandies'.[5] Always in classic good taste, Beerbohm's suits showed meticulous attention to detail. 'An evening suit impeccably tailored in black wool and a soft brown smoking jacket trimmed with chocolate braid suggest a life lived permanently according to the stylish rituals of the 1890s—in flight from vulgarity,' writes Christopher Breward of the suits of Max Beerbohm.[6]

Savile Row style implying a perfect cut, structured look, skillful layering, sartorial understatement, and careful luxury of finish, has been repeatedly described as one of the last incarnations of classical Brummellian dandyism.[7] It is not by chance that wearing a Savile Row suit is frequently pronounced a form of symbolic empowerment. Thanks to the tailors of Savile Row the minimalist style of dandified clothes was able to find expression in sartorial culture (Figure 28). The distinctive trademark of Savile Row was a conservative, understated elegance. According to Breward, 'A combination of factors, including a well-judged sharpness in the making-up of seams, creases and darts, high-quality textiles and a relaxed ease of wear, identified a Savile Row pedigree of suit.'[8] Supporting the dandy tradition of conspicuous inconspicuousness, companies such as Henry Poole, Huntsman, Gieves & Hawkes, Kilgour and French,

Figure 28 Julio Mompó, Savile Row tailor. © Lee Osborne @sartorialee. 2023.

and Hardy Amies caused the trend to flourish throughout the twentieth century and in the first two decades of the twenty-first.

The second tendency in twentieth-century dandyism had its roots in nineteenth-century French men's style: an outstanding example was Alfred Guillaume Gabriel, Count D'Orsay. A passionate lover of vivid colours, this remarkable man of fashion espoused the spicy 'butterfly dandy' style. Combining bold hues in striking ways, he loved to invent new looks. Amid the somber men's outfits of the 1830s and 1840s, his pale blue coats and primrose waistcoats were extraordinarily striking. He wore wide-brimmed hats, gold chains, diamonds, and heavy golden rings on perfumed white gloves. This gaudy style tended to reemerge later in the twentieth century, be it the flamboyant stage costumes of Jimi Hendrix or the colourful male fashion of 1970s. Unlike Beau Brummell, Alfred D'Orsay adored silk and velvet. Far from conspicuous inconspicuousness, this was, on the contrary, ostentation itself. Count Robert de Montesquiou, a man with a penchant for eye-catching flair, maintained a similar reputation later, in the time of European decadence, but his style was less decorative and more nuanced. Favouring classic suits in shades of grey, he sometimes liked to wear eccentric items and accessories: fencing gloves, for instance, or tartan breeches. He adored period costume, styles reminiscent of Louis XIV, or professional uniforms, sometimes appearing in drivers' leather jackets.

Yet even without these outstanding figures, at the opening of the twentieth century, everyday French fashion was changing, with daring colours, unorthodox combinations, and extravagant looks. The shift can be traced in art through works such as Bernard Boutet de Monvel's series of drawings 'Les Elegantes,' 'La Froleuse' from 'Les Femmes de ce Temps' by Guy Arnoux, or Georges Villa's watercolor, 'A Couple of Lovers'. In all these illustrations, one sees typical examples of early twentieth-century French men's fashion: such would have been the suits worn by Frenchmen arriving at that time in the Congo. Through them, the archetype of 'Parisian chic' emerged, which was then reproduced and adapted by Congo's 'contemporary dandies' – the sapeurs.

The New Bespoke Movement

The New Bespoke Movement in men's fashion was born in the late 1990s. The term 'New Bespoke Movement' was first coined by public relations professional Alison Hargreaves, who has labelled three tailors as a 'new generation,' modernizing the school of Savile Row tailoring. Having learned their skills in Savile Row, the movement's founders, tailors Timothy Everest, Ozwald Boateng, and Richard James, opted to leave behind the centuries-old traditions of bespoke tailoring, and to develop instead their own style, as well as new marketing techniques. Maintaining a thorough approach to all the details, the trio sought to create a more modern and individual take on the classical men's suit, bringing a fashion designer approach to Savile Row. Designers of the New Bespoke Movement were not afraid to use a far broader range of colours than the customary dark tones, or to embark on innovative experiments with tailoring and design details. Their suits tended to show off the contours of the male body legitimizing a new model of masculine corporeality.

Timothy Everest

Being one of the founders of the New Bespoke Movement, Timothy Everest began his career in 1982, under the famous tailor Tommy Nutter, whose clients included The Beatles and The Rolling Stones. The suits worn by the Fab Four on the cover of their album Abbey Road were indeed created by Nutter. Later, in 1989, Everest decided to strike out on his own, deciding to go against tradition by opening his atelier in East London's Spitalfields, rather than in Savile Row. Depending on the needs and financial situation of his clients, the designer offered a range of approaches corresponding to different traditionally established types of work at Savile Row.

In first place was the bespoke suit: the most expensive and thoroughly crafted offering. Sewn entirely by hand, this was a unique garment made to fit its wearer only. Requiring three to four fittings, which were held in Everest's Spitalfields atelier, the entire process usually took around two months. The work on a bespoke suit normally takes at least 150 hours. The next best option was made to measure. A less costly variant, this offered a simpler, less personal approach. A standard-sized base pattern was used, which was customized with several individual body measurements to create a suit tailored to each specific client.

Finally, the most basic and cheapest option was the ready-to-wear suit. For many years, Timothy Everest's ready-to-wear could be purchased in a number of stores, such as Marks & Spencer (as part of the Autograph collection) and the Japanese multi-brand Oki-ni. Specializing in luxury menswear, the shop has now moved online. With ready-to-wear suits, no fittings are held; they are sold off-the-peg as finished items in standardized sizes. Occasionally, the store where one purchases the suit may offer an alteration service. Timothy Everest also had collaborations with brands such as Rapha, La Martina, and Superdry.

What were the distinguishing features of the Timothy Everest style? His suits combined high-quality tailoring, with a hint of non-conformity. The bold touch could be a windowpane check or a broad stripe, an insert on a shirt, a brightly coloured lining. For young professionals, Everest created a fitted suit with a single-breasted, two-button jacket and uncuffed trousers. The suit's slim fit flatters the wearer's figure. A special feature of Timothy Everest's design is his attention to detail: his company also made silk handkerchiefs, ties, and cufflinks.

Besides the New Bespoke Movement, Timothy Everest also spearheaded other innovative approaches to bespoke tailoring.[9] One of these, the so-called Bespoke Casual Movement, involved offering customers bespoke casual wear, such as casual shirts, jeans, T-shirts, and smart-casual jackets. The initiative allowed clients to acquire individually made, stylish, and smart-casual clothing created to Savile Row standards. Particularly successful were his tailored denim suits made as part of a collaboration with Levi's in 2004. With Everest's bespoke casual wear, the client's comfort is crucial, yet all items had to be not only comfortable but also elegant. The customer's wish was Everest's command: his company could, for instance, re-create one's favourite old shirt once it became overly worn.

Timothy Everest's diverse and highly successful experiments with the bespoke suit clearly demonstrate the high potential for transformations of the traditional men's suit. This 'remarkable capacity for reinvention' is surely in some part connected with the ability to adapt within different national settings. Nicolas Cambridge has demonstrated, for instance, that the British suit has played a significant role in the sartorial culture of Japan[10]. At present, many clients of Timothy Everest's come from the United States and Japan.

Ozwald Boateng

The contemporary British menswear designer Ozwald Boateng also belongs to the New Bespoke Movement. His distinctive style is the daring use of bright colours and rare colour combinations for men's suits. He easily produces green or pink suits, or pairs orange with blue. Indeed, his use of vibrant, exuberant colours for suits and linings became his trademark feature. His passion for colours obviously goes back to the French tradition of dandyism described earlier in this chapter. According to Boateng,

I've always wanted to take men into a place where they felt maybe they weren't comfortable before but realized they could be in the use of color and how they could wear it; when you use deep rich colors, any man can wear those colors.[11]

The designer's love for bright colours is also part of his African heritage: although Boateng himself grew up in north London's Muswell Hill, his parents were Ghanaian. Boateng's unique feel for colour was precisely the feature highlighted by the organizers of his solo retrospective exhibition at the Victoria and Albert Museum in 2005. Suzanne Lussier, curator of his show said, 'He was chosen because he has revolutionized Savile Row, fusing traditional skills in tailoring and expert cutting with this very modern use of colors.'[12] Boateng himself defined his style as 'Structured Classics', appealing to the sartorial traditions of Savile Row. This tendency is directly opposite to the more relaxed loose fit of the Italians, which tended to dominate in the 1980s. His signature chisel collar shirts also form a very recognizable item, as well as tribal print ties. The distinctive feature of his silhouetted cut is the effect of slimming, achieved by a close-fitting jacket with streamlined lapels and narrow trousers.

In 1994, Boateng became the first of the British Savile Row tailors to take part in Paris Fashion Week. In 2002, he opened his own shop at 12A Savile Row. To celebrate the opening, the designer held an unprecedented street fashion show, stopping the traffic in Savile Row. The only other celebrities ever to close the famous street to traffic were the Beatles, back in the 1960s. At different times, among Boateng's clients were Mick Jagger, David Bowie, Samuel L. Jackson, Keanu Reeves, Jimmy Paige, Jude Law, Spike Lee, Will Smith, Jamie Foxx, Leonardo DiCaprio, Daniel Day-Lewis, Richard Branson, and Barack Obama. In 2003, the president of LVMH Bernard Arnault made Boateng Creative Director of Menswear at Givenchy. Presenting his first collection for the French Fashion house, the designer opened the show with his first animation, a manga-style film he made specially for the purpose. Boateng was with Givenchy until 2007. The designer has also created a new look for British Airways staff. In 2019, he launched his own line of womenswear in New York. Named AI, the collection was presented in Harlem's famous Apollo Theater. Many of his collections are inspired by African style. 'Africa is a great source of inspiration for me and many creatives and we should all do more to celebrate our beautiful continent,' said Boateng.[13]

In 2018, he launched the Africanism collection. Trying to create an African aesthetic but with a modern twist, he designed not only the suits but also the fabrics. Using Kente cloth, Boateng aimed to explore Ghanaian heritage. Nevertheless, the designer picked solid colours, rejecting the multi-coloured pattern typical of Kente. 'There was a real focus on fusing traditional English fabrics, such as tweed and flannel, with the Kente and tribal fabric that I designed,' he wrote in his Vogue essay. An interesting feature of this collection is that it is almost fully unisex. 'A lot of the pieces in the collection were genderless and looked great on both the women and the men,' commented Boateng.[14]

The Sapeurs

My second case study is focused around the Congolese subculture known as La Sape, which has continued to fascinate academics and photographers for many years.[15] The acronym stands for La Société des Ambianceurs et des Personnes Elégantes, which can be translated as the Society of Tastemakers and Elegant People. The name derives from the French verb se saper, to dress up with style. Members of La Sape refer to themselves as sapeurs. While the Sape can scarcely be seen as a fashion trend, it does nonetheless constitute a subculture with a certain ideology and a way of life. The subculture is centered on the cities of Brazzaville, capital of the Republic of Congo, and Kinshasa – the capital of the Democratic Republic of the Congo (DRC).[16]

In general terms, the style of the Sape can be traced to European, primarily French, tradition of dandified menswear. The sapeurs, however, took things quite a few steps further, adding to Parisian chic their own most distinctive touch. The visual strategy of the Sape could, indeed, be described using the term coined by Katelyn Knox, 'self-spectacularization'.[17] When venturing out, a sapeur turns everything he does into a performance, a deliberate spectacle: moving in an ostentatiously theatrical manner, he greets his audience and delights it with a few witty jokes. Humor, irony, and sarcastic jibes are typical of members of the Sape. This is clear from sapeurs' nicknames, also: one Yves Ngatsongo was known as Yves Saint Laurent.

With a clear penchant for bright colours and daring combinations, the African dandies developed a fondness for bold details and accessories (such as pocket squares, canes, and cigars) combined with traditional suits. But there is a difference between the style of sapeurs from Brazzaville and those from Kinshasa. While the Brazzaville sapeurs favour a more classical look, the Kinshasa beaus tend to be more extravagant and flamboyant in their outfits, creating unusual combinations of colours. Among the distinctive features of the Sape style was a love of luxury brands and accessories. To the sapeurs, designer clothes were not unlike a fetish, serving to transport them to a land of dreams, and to assert their importance both to others and to themselves. Stylish dress helped sapeurs to erase class difference, overcome the constraints imposed by poverty, and rise above the daily humiliation of their badly paid jobs. Sporting luxury brands, the sapeurs were trying 'to gain access to the benefits of modernity'.[18]

The list of favoured brands, however, was a very particular one. Among the accessories always in high regard were shoes by Capobianco, J. M. Weston, Lobb, Church, and Alden. Cartier watches, Vuarnet sunglasses, Morabito scent, Valentino belts, and Burlington socks were likewise firm favourites. For clothing, European brands, such as Christian Dior, Jean-Paul Gaultier, Tierry Mugler, Versace, Prada, and Yves Saint Laurent, were preferred, with Japanese designers Kenzo and Yohji Yamamoto also popular, whereas jeans had to be by Marithé + François Girbaux. A limited number of other brands were also held in high esteem. The attitude towards renowned fashion designers among sapeurs is very personal: they frequently refer to them by first names – Yohji, Coco, Vivienne – as though they were old friends. Suits from Ozwald Boateng are explicably popular with many sapeurs. 'I feel comfortable in my Ozwald Boateng suit, so I wear it', said the sapeur Aime Champagne.[19]

In selecting their luxury brands, the sapeurs utterly rejected French middle-class Sunday suits used mainly for going to church. The dark tones of these stern outfits did not suit the sapeurs in the slightest. Neither did they favour formal office suits from brands such as Chevignon, Celio, Benetton, and Daniel Hechter – nor, indeed, classic British Savile Row. In their rejection of the traditional Sunday suit, the sapeurs were not unlike the Teddy Boys, who had refused to wear traditional middle-class English 'Sunday Best', opting for Edwardian style.

The African dappers preferred instead much brighter, more festive colours, and by skillfully combining them, they contrived to create an impression of bold Parisian chic. Their aim was to attract attention, to stand out. Somber, understated British minimalism was not at all down their street. Furthermore, in dark suits, the sapeurs would risk going unnoticed and merely fading into the crowd, which is hardly what they were after. The rule they were following might be called 'conspicuous conspicuousness', quite contrary to the principles of British dandyism, proclaiming conspicuous inconspicuousness.

The Sape was known for a number of fixed rules of dress. One of these was the law of three colours: an outfit was not to contain more than three different colours. Besides apparel, the rules governed certain aspects of behaviour also. A sapeur was never to be the first to start a dance, had always to have a pristine white handkerchief, and had always to be seen in the best shoes.[20] In the streets the sapeurs are frequently accompanied by a crowd of fans, greeting them or trying to imitate their style of walking. The typical walk of a sapeur was recognizable and conspicuous. This is a very confident walk, similar to a catwalk model's walk, when the feet are placed in one line. Striding along with rapid, long steps, they were better able to preserve their expensive luxury shoes in the dirty uncobbled streets.

Luxury brands serve as proof that a successful sapeur had reached his destination. His journey to achieve his ideal status within his community was complete. In this way, the brands can be seen as mythological totems, talismans, or fetishes: in bringing their owners confidence, they offered them psychological safety and protection. A sapeur appearing in luxury branded clothing implied his successful initiation: he had clearly made a productive trip to Europe, secured employment in a European country, and used his salary to purchase some expensive items before returning home. His appearance in the 'right' clothes put out a nonverbal message about the young man's victory and status. It was an act of 'claiming membership in the community of moderns'.[21]

At the same time, stylish clothing also reflects dreams of a better future, attempts to construct a better life for oneself. For this reason, the sapeurs' dress should primarily be seen as an example of aspirational fashion. Without his luxury brands, a sapeur loses his identity. As one observer notes,

> Africans who live here in Europe are careful. If they don't have anything to wear, they prefer not to return home for vacation. There are people who haven't gone back for 15 years! In 1982 I had a friend who spent two months down there, he couldn't go out during the day because he only had imitation clothing and shoes, not griffes [designer labels].[22]

More recently, however, the sapeurs have contrived to find a way out of such unfortunate situations thanks to the fashion for retro-style clothing. Purchasing vintage designer clothes, they might alter the garments slightly, giving them a new lease on life, or come up with new combinations of old items. This way, they support sustainable fashion while at the same time avoiding unnecessary expenditure.[23] A good example of this kind of activity would be the Kenyan designer duo '2manysiblings'. Brother and sister Velma Rossa and Oliver Asike, known as Papa Petit, use items found at flea markets and in second-hand shops to create bright, colourfully joyful outfits. In 2015, they organized the first Thrift Social festival – an annual event bringing together young African designers and followers of fashion.

On the History of La Sape and Dandyism in Africa

The style of the sapeurs is deeply rooted in the history of dandyism in Africa. It could be said to have been born in the 1910s. During the colonial regime, young servants would frequently receive the worn old suits of their masters as a gift, which they would proceed to show off in public, thereby confirming their master's social status and reputation. Some servants would even get paid in expensive European suits, rather than cash. According to Vannocci Bonsi,

> The Belgians and the French, giving European clothes to the Africans, were attempting to colonize them, domesticate them and civilize them through fashion. But the Congolese, instead of passively accepting European fashion, answered to this sort of clothing domination actively, reinterpreting it and translating subjection into emancipation.[24]

Together with the new style of dress, the local dappers became accustomed to a number of habits. They would frequently wear their outfits in several layers, thus clearly demonstrating their financial status, and finish them off with a top hat. Given the hot climate, the vogue for top hats proved short-lived, however, giving way instead to a fashion for panamas.

Little by little, a new subculture came into being. By the 1920s, visitors to Brazzaville could see fashionable men in the streets sporting European suits and accessories such as canes, monocles, gloves, and pocket watches with chains. Meeting in special clubs, they would discuss the latest fashions, enjoy an aperitif, and have a dance to some Cuban or European music. In fact, sapeurs create 'an alternative system of visibility that establishes communities of taste, where a shared passion for beauty encourages forms of mentoring and mutual assistance'.[25]

An important figure in 1920s La Sape culture was André Matswa (Matsoua), a political activist who fought against the colonial regime in French Congo. During his time in Paris, his elegant suits set the tone for African lovers of European fashion. In 1926, Matswa organized a special society to promote education and fashion among the Africans – L'Amicale des Originaires de l'Afrique Équatoriale. Its final goal was to achieve independence for colonial countries, but Matswa meant to act only by peaceful methods. Upon his return to French Congo, Matswa was arrested and thrown in jail. When apprehended, eyewitnesses claimed, he was wearing white trousers and a three-button blazer. Matswa's sartorial preferences were to signal a turning point in the semantics of dandyism in Africa. Thanks to Matswa, the sharp European suit came to be seen not as imitation but as a symbol of self-respect, a political statement against colonialism, even as a vehicle for political change, a sign of social protest.

The 1930s witnessed the emergence of another key fashionable type: the popo. A sophisticated follower of fashion, not satisfied with merely wearing another man's old suits, the popo would spend his entire wages, gradually assembling flawlessly stylish outfits. After purchasing a trendy hat, he would then buy a smart shirt to go with it; then, the chic shoes, saving up his earnings to put together his wardrobe.

> Do you know that in Brazzaville and in Kinshasa, all the gentlemen or young people dressed in popo style; which is to say they have a helmet worth 150 franks and a silk shirt, a poplin suit or a suit made of another fabric, worth at least around 250 or 300 franks and pants that go all the way to the heels of their feet.[26]

Having assimilated the European style of dress, the African dandies came to be known as 'whites with black skin'. Many sapeurs, indeed, even used various methods to try to lighten their skin, resorting to a range of medical and homemade creams in order to achieve a lighter olive complexion. As Frantz Fanon argued in his seminal book of 1952, the Black identity is frequently constructed after white cultural models for psychological reasons.[27] The Black skin is identified with impurity in colonial mentality,[28] and when this attitude is interiorized, the practices of cosmetic whitening become self-gratifying and are regarded as a possible social lift.

In 1960, the Democratic Republic of the Congo, then known as the Republic of the Congo, achieved independence. Under President Mobutu the country became ruled by nationalists who promoted the return to traditional values, including the authentic African dress. Therefore, European clothing acquired a new meaning, entering the category of alternative fashion: wearing the style of the former colonial authorities came to be seen as a form of political protest against the new government.

But was this fashion statement not attempting to assert the local dandies' independence? Katelyn Knox has argued that sapeurs 'can only be either subversive agents or unintentional victims of neo-colonialism.'[29]

Sapeurs from the Lari group, however, explained their clothing choices differently:

> We all come from the South, and it may appear paradoxical today but we were 'proud' to have been colonized by the French, who, penetrating into the Congo from the South, brought us education and western clothing. We all admired our grandparents, war veterans, who returned home in frock coats, bowler hats and gloves. And we sought the same clothing! The people in the North were still naked and hunting with bows and arrows.[30]

This reflects a history of voluntary cultural appropriation with all its unexpected twists and turns.

More typical historically is the case when the colonized people reject the uniform of colonizers as a sign of protest. 'Mohandas Gandhi—wearer of well-tailored outfits during his time in London as a law student—reverted to native dress in order to lead Indian people towards self-determination.'[31] The situation of La Sape, however, clearly presents us with a paradox. In imitating French style in male dress, the Sape was surely reproducing the colonial mentality it should have been seeking to undermine. The dialectics of this seeming contradiction could be described, as I suggest, through the concept of colonial mimicry analyzed by Homi Bhabha:

> Colonial mimicry is the desire for a reformed, recognizable Other, as a subject of a difference that is almost the same, but not quite. Which is to say, that the discourse of mimicry is constructed around an ambivalence; in order to be effective, mimicry must continually produce its slippage, its excess, and its difference. The authority of that mode of colonial discourse that I have called mimicry is therefore stricken by an indeterminacy: mimicry emerges as the representation of a difference that is itself a process of disavowal. Mimicry is, thus, the sign of a double articulation; a complex strategy of reform, regulation, and discipline, which 'appropriates' the Other as it visualizes power.[32]

The sartorial codes of La Sape demonstrate indeed this algorithm of 'almost the same, but not quite' in relation to the European luxury menswear. In a number of cases, the difference is visible in the choice of colours, in the arrangement of details and accessories, in the cut, and, ultimately, in the fit of the suits.

Appropriating the style of former colonizers, the sapeurs created a new postcolonial identity, transforming the discourse of power. So, the sartorial code of European menswear served for sapeurs as an instrument of symbolic empowerment. 'Ecstatic celebration of equality through the symbolism of dress', wrote Christopher Breward about the culture of sapeurs.[33] In this respect, the style of sapeurs is not unique. Other African national sartorial codes are also constructed through a nuanced cultural appropriation. Accordingly, Sasha Newell in his detailed study of Ivory Coast, argued that 'Ivoirian national identity has (somewhat paradoxically) been formed in part through such a culture of appropriating otherness.'[34]

Among the vestimentary practices of the sapeurs were a series of almost ritual gestures, allowing the wearers to expose the designer labels on their clothes to general view by way of dance, posture, and spectacular body movements. During la 'dance des griffes' sapeurs demonstrate their outfits through ritualized gestures and controlled movements of the body. The following is a description of how the sapeur Charlie Schengen performs his dance:

> He alternates slow, long strides with rapid sequences of heel-toe steps, loudly knocking his J.M. Weston triple sole shoes on the salon floor. He concludes by standing in the middle of the room with his arms wide open, taking in the admiration of the audience while a younger sapeur turns the label of his jacket to reveal the original Dolce & Gabbana label.[35]

In this regard, the sapeurs were not unlike the Soviet 'Stilyagi' dandies, who also developed special techniques for 'casually' showing off designer labels. Putting their hands in their jacket pockets, for instance, the Stilyagi would thereby expose the lining of their coats.[36] The Congolese dandies would often use the fast movement of the Rumba to fling open their jackets or pull up their trouser legs, showing off their designer socks. Another common gesture of this kind was casually flipping over one's tie in order to reveal the label on the reverse.

The dance of brands was described in fiction. For instance, Fessologue, one of the characters in Alain Mabanckou's Black Bazar, demonstrates his fashionable brands in Paris when he notes he is looked at: 'I undid three of my jacket buttons, which is a special technique I have for showing off my expensive belt Christian Dior to its best advantage.' The passers-by, however, react with insults, taking him for a striking laborer.[37]

The typical space where the 'dances' of the designer labels were performed in the Congo, were ngandas, apartments containing a bar and serving as a meeting place for the Sape. Sometimes at such gatherings the sapeurs would organize an improvised fashion show. Getting together, the sapeurs would pore over and value items of dress and accessories, discuss their adventures in European towns, and listen to Congolese rumba, whose music would often prompt a dance of designer labels. Sometimes, the sapeurs would meet in cafes, where they would gather in a circle, and take turns doing their special dance in the center. The importance of music in their subculture is another feature uniting the sapeurs and the Soviet Stilyagi. If the Congolese dandies came together over rumba, however, in the case of the Stilyagi, the music informing the subculture was jazz.

Sapeurs in Contemporary Culture

The past fifty years have seen significant changes in the way Africa's dandies have interpreted French fashion. The colours have grown brighter, while the cut of the garments has become bolder, more extravagant. This is especially true of the Kinshasa dandies. Some of the more brazen sapeurs would deliberately go against the accepted European standards of dress, subverting such rules that a suit should fit. Several generations ago the old suits were handed down by the masters, and now the contemporary dappers play over this custom, making a fad of wearing badly fitting attire. More often than not, these suits would be too big for the wearer.

Of the modern sapeurs, perhaps the best known was Papa Wemba, nicknamed Le Pape de La Sape. A popular Congolese musician and singer, Papa Wemba promoted the ideology and style of the Sape through his work and through his personal image. He was a celebrity: in 1995, he released the album Emotions, which went on to sell over 100,000 copies. The style of his music is generally described as rumba rock. From the late 1970s onward, the musician supported young sapeurs, taking them with him on tour. When addressing young followers of fashion, Papa Wemba liked to stress the importance of good personal hygiene, corporeal practices, a good shave, and grooming. 'Dressing well is not just a matter of money, not just something for

Westerners, but that we Africans also have elegance', the singer claimed.[38] He used to choose 'parliamentarians' among the best dressed sapeurs in every country where Congolese live, for them to be ambassadors of La Sape chic. Papa Wemba died on stage during a performance in 2016, aged sixty-six.

The bold outfits of the sapeurs were much loved by photographers. In 2003, the Spanish photographer Hector Mediavilla made a series of pictures of sapeurs in Brazzaville and Paris. Behind each of his images there is a name and a character. Take, for example, Mediavilla's photo of a famous sapeur Ben Mukasha, shot in his Paris restaurant La Sapelogie. Discussing La Sape with a customer, Ben has placed a bottle of luxury beer in a champagne ice bucket as an extra touch of glamor.

The Milanese photographer Daniele Tamagni (d. 2017)[39] began to work with Congolese dandies in 2006. His book, Gentlemen of Bacongo[40] succeeded in capturing the dramatic poses often struck by sapeurs, as well as the sharp contrast between their elegant dress and dilapidated urban setting. Creating the outstanding shots, he did not try to treat the African dandies as exotic, but took the time to get to know each of his models, learning about their lives and stories (Figure 29). Daniele Tamagni, sadly, died from cancer in 2017, but his photos remain one of the most beautiful and touching human documents of sapeurs' movement. In 2009, the first

Figure 29 Daniele Tamagni. Three 'Grand sapeurs' of Brazzaville: Willy Covary, Severin Mayembo, Germain le Doyen. 2008. © Daniele Tamagni, Courtesy Daniele Tamagni Foundation.

edition of his photos appeared with a preface by Sir Paul Smith.[41] The British designer was so impressed with the book, that Tamagni's pictures had a direct influence on his work. His collection for women (Spring/Summer 2010) was created in the style of La Sape images by Tamagni. The first model in this show demonstrated the pink suit from the book cover. Tamagni also worked with the singer Solange Knowles on the video to her song 'Losing You' (2012). The younger sister of Beyoncé, Solange was inspired by Tamagni's work to include a group of sharply dressed sapeurs in the clip.

In recent years, the Sape has acquired more female members. Among the new sapeuses are housewives, mothers of large families, policewomen, tailors, office workers, and many others. Like their male counterparts, the sapeuses show a preference for designer suits, luxury footwear such as Weston shoes, and Cartier watches. Spending some three thousand dollars on a suit, they may live in poverty, lacking food and basic necessities. Other sapeuses, however, hold high posts. Fascinatingly, when dressing up, sapeuses tend to prefer men's dress, adapted for female wear. In contrast to pachucas, who used to wear feminine outfits during zoot suit riots in the 1940s, the sapeuses usually choose menswear or gender-neutral accessories, such as ties, canes, dark glasses, watches, and bowties. Many smoke a pipe.

So why, instead of opting for luxury womenswear, do sapeuses turn instead to male dress? Dandyism, it appears, possesses a powerful semiotic code as a male culture. Most other well-known twentieth-century women dandies, such as Marlene Dietrich or Vesta Tilley, indeed, likewise favoured men's suits. In the African context, however, the European men's suits possess double power due to gender and nationality. And they are also marked as counterculture: during the Mobutu regime Congolese women were obliged to wear a traditional dress, a pagne, so sporting a masculine European suit was a double challenge. Interestingly, the young girls who adopt the Sape style likewise opt for men's suits.

Looking at the way sapeurs and stilyagi were treated by society in their respective countries, one cannot but notice a striking contrast. Sapeurs tended to be well respected: those around them would see it as an honour to shake their hand. When a sapeur appears in town in his best suit, he will not be laughed at. This a vivid spectacle of empowerment. In video clips, one may often see them striding proudly down the street or through a market, greeted on all sides by admiring onlookers. Members of the Sape appear as heroes, triumphant victors accorded the most deliberate signs of admiration. If we compare it to the Soviet society's reaction to the stilyagi, on the other hand, we see a very different picture. Shocked, disapproving looks, insults, unkind caricatures in the papers, and trouble with the police: the only allies these Soviet dandies could ever count on were their fellow fashionistas themselves.

Like the Soviet dandies, through their dress and way of life, the sapeurs created a concentrated European image, or, more specifically, a French one. Yet, as Didier Gondola notes, they should not be seen purely as imitators: this phenomenon is more about 'illusion and incarnation'.[42] At the same time, Elizabeth Kutesco has rightly maintained that, though African sartorialism was influenced by European fashions, La Sape did not replace a traditional local African culture.[43]

For the dandies of the Congo, the Sape is a means of self-expression, a creative search for collective identity. The philosophy of the group is to be polite, to avoid racism, to respect the aged, to practice nonviolence. If the movement does possess an element of protest, this is purely peaceful: interethnic and political conflict has cost both the DRC and the Republic of Congo dearly, with tensions still ongoing. Their bold, elegant suits can be seen as an effective means of protest against poverty and the tensions in society. This strategy could be interpreted as 'joy as resistance,' an old tradition of protest carnival marches. The sapeurs' approach is not unlike that of the recently emerged new movement Wide Awakes, who, in this latest phase of their history, are seeking to safeguard joy in our challenging time. The tradition of dressing up and organizing performances is kept in the diasporic culture of Congolese people based in London. They gather regularly in selected venues to socialize and display their outfits.

Contemporary London sapeurs belong mainly to the elder generation: they are in their forties and sixties. Benedetta Morsiani has consistently shown that most of the younger representatives of Congolese diasporic London do not follow the sapeur style and do not identify themselves with La Sape. They think the sapeur looks are too eccentric and extravagant but recognize La Sape as part of their cultural heritage.[44] Recently, researchers from Congo studied the attitudes among local students towards the sapeurs.[45] These were found to be basically positive, yet many respondents stated that sapeurs should buy more products from local designers instead of spending too much money on foreign luxury brands. Sustainable and locally oriented fashion remains a future challenge for the Sape.

As we have seen, for sapeurs, the art of clothing serves as an instrument of symbolic empowerment, a means of self-expression and distinctiveness. According to Bill Ashcroft, 'Here we find a fundamental postcolonial principle: the appropriation of dominant tools and technologies for the purposes of self-representation.'[46]

Dressing up for sapeurs and sapeuses remains a positive identity marker, epitomizing the search for modernity and emancipation. It is important to highlight that the sapeurs developed a remarkable art of wearing clothes as live assertive performance, a production of presence.[47] The performative aspect of the Sape is indeed unique and central. Also, their style has definitely influenced the contemporary shift towards colourful menswear. The flamboyant suits of Oswald Boateng would hardly have been possible without the aesthetics of the Sape.

Has dandyism realized its end point? Whether or not the Sape should be termed the last development of European dandyism is perhaps an unresolved question. However, it is clear that in using exuberant colours, the affirmative performance of wearing clothes, and the 'joy as resistance' strategies, the sapeurs managed to transform the sartorial code of modern menswear and change the landscape of contemporary dandyism.

Notes

1 Julio Mompó, A vision of a modern dandy, interview with Olga Vainshtein, in *Fashionable Masculinities: Queers, Pimp Daddies, and Lumbersexuals*, eds. Vicki Karaminas, Adam Geczy, and Pamela Church Gibson (New Brunswick, New Jersey: Rutgers University Press, 2022), chapter 16.
2 See, for instance: George Walden, *Who is a Dandy?* (London: Gibson Square Books, 2002).
3 See Rhonda Garelick, Quentin crisp: The last dandy?, in *Dandies. Fashion and Finesse in Art and Culture*. ed. Susan Fillin-Yeh. (New York: New York U.P, 2001), 270–280.
4 Olga Vainshtein, 'Walking the Turtles: Minimalism in European Dandy Culture in the Nineteenth Century,' *Fashion, Style & Popular Culture* 4, no. 1 (2017): 81–104.
5 Max Beerbohm, *Selected Prose* (Boston: Little, Brown/Atlantic Monthly Press, 1970), 188.
6 Christopher Breward, The dandy laid Bare, in *Fashion Cultures: Theories, Explorations and Analysis*, eds. Stella Bruzzi and Pamela Church Gibson (New York: Routledge, 2000), 234.
7 James Sherwood, *Bespoke: The Men's Style of Savile Row* (New York: Random House, 2010).
8 Christopher Breward, *Fashioning London: Clothing and the Modern Metropolis* (New York: Berg, 2004), 134–140.
9 On the current business of Timothy Everest see https://www.mbe.studio/bespoke-made-to-measure. Accessed 4 May 2022.
10 Nicolas Cambridge, 'New whistle and flute: orchestrating sartorial performances of contemporary masculinities,' *Fashion Practice: The Journal of Design, Creative Process & the Fashion Industry* 9, no. 2 (2017): 188.
11 Ozwald Boateng, 'Ozwald Boateng on Africanism', *Vogue*, 31 May 2018, https://www.vogue.co.uk/gallery/ozwald-boateng-africanism. Accessed 4 May 2022.
12 FashionUnited, 'Ozwald Boateng Exhibition at the V&A', *FashionUnited*, 22 November 2005, https://fashionunited.uk/news/fashion/ozwald-boateng-exhibition-at-the-v-a/2005112235907. Accessed 4 May 2022.
13 Ibid.
14 Ibid.
15 See, for instance, Keith Alexander Bryant, *Performing Black Masculinity: Race, Culture, and Queer Identity* (Plymouth: AltaMira Press, 2006); Shantrelle P. Lewis, *Dandy Lion: The Black Dandy and Street Style* (New York: Aperture, 2017); Monica L. Miller, *Slaves to Fashion: Black Dandyism and the Styling of Black Diasporic Identity* (Durham, NC: Duke University Press, 2009); Carol Tulloch, *The Birth of Cool: Style Narratives of the African Diaspora* (New York: Bloomsbury Academic, 2016).
16 The DRC gained independence from Belgium in 1960. Between 1971 and 1997, it was known as Zaire. A former French colony, the Republic of Congo also became independent in 1960. At present, both countries continue to rank among some of the poorest in the world.
17 Katelyn Knox, *Race on Display in 20th- and 21st-Century France* (Liverpool: Liverpool University Press, 2016), 44–71.
18 Sasha Newell, *The Modernity Bluff: Crime, Consumption, and Citizenship in Côte d'Ivoire* (Chicago: The University of Chicago Press, 2012), 19.
19 Eugenio Giorgianni, 'A Night Out with London's Sapeurs', *Al Jazeera*, 1 June 2016, https://www.aljazeera.com/features/2016/6/1/a-night-out-with-londons-sapeurs. Accessed 4 May 2022.
20 Enrica Picarelli, 'Elegance and Retrospective Sartorialism among Young African Males', *Clothing Cultures* 2, no. 2 (2015): 214.
21 Newell, *The Modernity Bluff*, 19.
22 Didier Gondola, 'Dream and drama: the search for elegance among Congolese youth', *African Studies Review* 42, no. 1 (1999): 34.
23 Picarelli, *Elegance and Retrospective Sartorialism*, 216–217.

24 Orsola Bonsi Vannocci, *La Sape: Cultural Appropriation as Identitarian Emancipation* (Rotterdam, the Netherlands: Roots & Routes, 2019), 5.
25 Picarelli, *Elegance and Retrospective Sartorialism*, 212–213.
26 Diata, quoted in Gondola, 'Dream and Drama', *African Studies Review* 42, no. 1 (1999): 27.
27 Frantz Fanon, *Black Skin, White Masks*. Trans. Richard Philcox (New York: Grove Press, 2008).
28 Fanon, ibid., ix.
29 Knox, *Race on Display*, 82.
30 Julia Ficatier, 'Au Congo, pays de la Sape,' *La Croix*, 13 April 1989, quoted from Gondola, *Dream and Drama*, 37.
31 Cambridge, *New Whistle and Flute*, 186.
32 Homi Bhabha, 'Of Mimicry and Man: The Ambivalence of Colonial Discourse', *October*, 28 (Spring 1984): 126.
33 Christopher Breward, *The Suit: Form, Function and Style* (London: Reaktion Books, 2016), 110.
34 Sasha Newell, 'Le Goût des Autres: Ivoirian fashion and alterity', *Etnofoor* 24, no. 2 (2012): 42.
35 Giorgianni, ibid.
36 Olga Vainshtein, 'Orange jackets and pea green pants: the fashion of stilyagi in Soviet postwar culture', *Fashion Theory* 22, no. 2 (2018): 173.
37 Knox, *Race on Display*, 84.
38 BBC News, *'Papa Wemba: Stars Remember the 'Voice of Africa'*, BBC News, 25 April 2016, https://www.bbc.com/news/world-africa-36128441. Accessed 4 May 2022.
39 See https://www.danieletamagni.com/. Accessed 4 May 2022. I would like to thank Giordano Tamagni, father of late Daniele Tamagni for the copyright permissions.
40 Daniele Tamagni, *Gentlemen of Bacongo* (London: Trolley Books: 2009).
41 Tamagni, ibid.
42 Gondola, Dream and Drama, 32.
43 Elisabeth Kutesko, 'Problems and tensions in the representation of the sapeurs, as demonstrated in the work of two twenty-first century Italian photographers', *Immediations: The Courtauld Institute of Art Journal of Postgraduate Research* 3, no. 2 (2013): 60–76.
44 Benedetta Morsiani, *Performing Cultural Identities and Transnational 'Imaginaries': Fashion and Beauty Practices as Diasporic Spaces among Young London Congolese* (PhD thesis, electronic version, University of Westminster, 2019), 112.
45 Basile Mulwani Makelele, Patrick Litalema Libote, and Boniface Aspan A Kasas, 'A Study on the Perception of Congolese Students towards Sape', *Research in Psychology and Behavioral Sciences* 5, no. 1 (2017): 12.
46 Bill Ashcroft, 'Towards a postcolonial aesthetics', *Journal of Postcolonial Writing* 51, no. 4 (2015): 415.
47 Hans Ulrich Gumbrecht, *Production of Presence: What Meaning Cannot Convey* (Stanford: Stanford University Press, 2004).

CONCLUSION

'Entelechy' is a philosophical term meaning the realization of a thing, usually to the potential immanent to it. Could there be an entelechy to the dandy? The first objection to be raised to this question is in the famous warning made in the first treatise on the dandy by Jules Barbey d'Aurevilly, that the dandy is vexingly hard to define. True enough, the dandy is the definition of a sartorial class – and a mode of being – that resists archetypes and reducible elements. But has the dandy evolved, like some organism, to define itself more promptly and more acutely?

In the cultural frame of nineteenth-century dandyism certain strategies were developed which assured this entelechy – actualization of dandyism as form-giving cause, smooth functioning of the dandy style in the future. In order to comprehend the contemporary developments of dandyism we must briefly outline the following strategies:

(1) Dandyism arose as the wave of Modernity swept over society, when fixed professional and social roles had broken down and upward mobility and the ability to adapt and switch had become a condition for success. The strategy of effective self-presentation and the principle of chameleonism legitimized changes of social masks and helped ambitious young people move upward. The inner connection between dandyism and modernity is evident in the fact that today as well dandyism is inseparable from modern urban culture and all its institutions – cafes, flânerie, advertising, and shopping.

(2) Another strategy is the ability to keep a distance that emphasizes the restricted access to the circle of the selected affiliates. The dandy always skilfully underscores his membership in an elite minority, whether the closed circle of the aristocracy or Bohemia. This is the source of the cold politeness that can instantly change to irony. Inaccessibility, snobbery, and the strategies of refusal are the instruments for maintaining an estranging distance. The Guermantes did not immediately invite the young Marcel into their home, and Beau Brummell was a master at 'not noticing' unsuitable people.

Connected with this is the standard criticism of vulgarity as consisting first of all in easy accessibility and second, excessively crude and direct strategies to create an impression. A liking for proverbs and loud colours in one's dress (an attribute of vulgarity according to Lord Chesterfield) could be compared to head-on statements, whereas the dandies' indirect messages are far more effective. Failure to follow the principle of minimalism in dress, behaviour, or speech in the nineteenth century would have been seen as a sign of vulgarity: an unseemly excess, an unnecessary luxury, and a lack of reserve.

(3) Dandyism has mastered the strategy of self-presentation through objectifying personality and transforming individual style into marketable properties. This strategy is connected above all with a special model of visualization: the dandy knows how to

look at others and to stand up under their looks. He is even especially attuned to this objectifying look, creating 'to be looked at' situations when out for flânerie, at a ball, in the parlour, sitting by the window of a club. An unhurried gait and 'immobile' face are evidence of self-control and personal dignity.

(4) Dandyism could be described through special techniques of the body requiring a 'slow life' and fixed spectacular poses. The dandy's body is intended for 'penetrating glances' and is prepared to withstand them. Here is where hygiene and sports come in. Most important of all, however, is to demonstrate voluntary power over the body, the ability to control it as an accurate and refined instrument, including the art of wearing clothes. And it is not so much a matter of the clothes themselves as the ability to wear them with nonchalance. Oscar Wilde's dress was already halfway to the aesthetics of camp – it was a style deliberately provocative but created to be imitated.

(5) Last but not least – aesthetic minimalism. First uphold by George Brummell as the principle of 'conspicuous inconspicuousness' in dress, minimalism became a universal criterion of sartorial understatement and reserved expressiveness, in which the functional construction and geometry of the basic form stripped of superfluous embellishment come to the fore. It can initially be compared with the ascetic art of refusal and estranged distancing in high society transferred to the sphere of aesthetics.

The aesthetic minimalism is the most important in our list as it enables to reveal the structural correspondences underlying dandyism as cultural system.

Yuri Lotman's famous definition of structure runs thus:

> A structural description is composed by noting in the object described, those elements of system and connection which remain invariant regardless of any homomorphic transformations of the object. Where such a description is concerned, it is precisely this invariant structure that represents the sole reality.[1]

Careful examination shows that this type of structure will yield correlation between different aspects of dandyism from dress and canons of elegance, to code of conduct, speech patterns, and personal hygiene. We have attempted to trace and summarize some parallels between the dandy code of conduct, dress style, and body techniques in the frame of aesthetic minimalism.

Minimalism as structural principle of dandyism: economy of expressive means	
Costume	'Conspicuous inconspicuousness', unobtrusive elegance, streamlined neoclassical silhouette, the art of distinctive detail
Body	Economic movements, minimal gestures, slow walking, new standards of cleanliness
Face	Inscrutable face, penetrating gaze, the use of optical devices
Speech	Aphorisms, laconic jokes, expressive pauses, 'cutting' remarks
Emotions	'Nil admirari', economy of emotions, understatement, self-control, stoical self-possession
Presence	Economy of presence, 'stay as long as you need to make an impression'; opposition to excessive ostentation and vulgarity

In the above table, one can see that the minimalist discourse pervades all layers of dandy culture. As we argued earlier, the principle of minimalism in classical art dictates that sharp contour and clear construction dominate over decorative detail and excessive ornament: thus, the main impression is formed by the basic construction. The historical development of the minimalist aesthetic in male dress in the early nineteenth century was heavily influenced by contemporary neoclassical trends. Stemming from neoclassicism, the minimalist aesthetics can be seen as a basic principle of dandy culture that applied not only to behaviour but also to the art of dress and to speech. The analysis of the workings of this universal canon, and the uncovering of invariant connections through structural description, were one of the main objectives of this book.

The minimalist aesthetic was not certainly the only cultural principle of the time, yet it was this canon that determined the basic traits of the first dandies who appeared in England in the late-eighteenth – early nineteenth century. The ladies' vogue for white neoclassical dresses was similarly a minimalist tendency.

The principles of 'conspicuous inconspicuousness' and of the great male renunciation in early nineteenth-century fashion could be said to have been totally new. This aesthetic laid the foundations for the arrival, in the 1830s and 1840s, of the ready-to-wear era, when basic dress, until then manufactured to special order only, entered mass production.[2]

Where the principles of behaviour are concerned, we have seen that dandy behaviour is governed by a set of clear rules. These rules are also based on the idea of economy of means of expression, and on the principle of minimalism. Governing an entire set of structural correlations, this principle could be said to be the very cornerstone of dandyism. Take, for instance, the second law of the dandy code of conduct: 'Maintaining composure, shock with the unexpected'. A semantic parallel can be drawn between this rule and the poetics of dandy dress. Just as the stoically composed dandy is allowed sudden unexpected cutting, so the simplicity and minimalism of his dress may be lifted with a single eye-catching detail, a small 'je ne sais quoi'. A fleeting glance, a small gesture, an insignificant trifle, could convey a clear message for those in the know. In the same way, casual insouciance and nonchalant lightness balanced out the formality of dress, leaving an overall impression of freedom and simplicity.

The dandy's laconic roundedness of gesture and abhorrence of fuss and bustle recall the principle of economy of presence enshrined in the third rule: 'Remain in society long enough to make an impression; once you have made it – leave!' In the sphere of body politics, minimalism was declared through the imperative of slow gestures and the static facial expression, the inhibition that prevented running and fussing (what Honoré de Balzac called *virvoucher* in his treatise 'Theory of walking' of 1833). Furthermore, the principle of slowness, which we observe in the unhurried dandy's promenade with his turtle, is likewise reflected in dandy's countenance, with his immobile face. Facial expression and gestures are naturally connected with emotional discipline, with the taboo on expression of emotion, especially surprise, and with the dandy's general preference for reserve and impenetrability. Minimalism can be compared with the dandy's stoical rule of economy of emotions – 'nil admirari', not to be surprised at anything.

Turning to speech patterns, we discovered that the dandies' deliberately brief appearances at social events, understated dress style and measured expression of emotion were matched with an equally economical manner of speaking, with terse, laconic remarks and a penchant for aphorisms. The rhetorical equivalent of minimalism is the genre of the aphorism, essentially involving the poetics of silence. This lapidary style influenced the literary writing of later dandy theoreticians such as Barbey D'Aurevilly, Balzac, and Baudelaire. Within the visual strategies of dandyism, the economy of minimalism revealed itself by means of intended blindness and selective insight.

Thus, we may conclude that dandy aesthetics can be seen as a cultural text open to systemic interpretation and showing consistency at multiple levels. It is thanks to this structural completeness that the classical dandy can be considered a recognizable and comprehensive cultural personage of nineteenth century. The structural completeness is also historically motivated, being connected to the multiple developments of modernity in the urban society in the nineteenth century. This extremely modern principle of minimalism not only determined the entire development of male dress for the ensuing centuries, it also underpins a whole range of trends in modern art. Minimalism indeed triumphed in the culture of modernity: suffice it to recall black-and-white photography, cubism in painting, constructivism in architecture, and the classical men's suit.

Naturally, throughout the nineteenth century Europe also saw other types of dandyism emerge, besides classical minimalism. For instance, Count d'Orsay and the Butterfly dandies, or the bohemian aesthetes of the Decadence formed a separate line of refined ostentation. With less austere dress and more relaxed behavioural codes, these groups created their own distinctive style which tended to reemerge in different decades. In the twentieth century, the African sapeurs continued this tradition of flamboyant dandies, developing the new cultural space where the practice of decorative dandyism is still alive and visible.

The tradition of classical dandyism, established by the first generation of Regency England dandies, was further developed in the English gentleman style represented by the Savile Row bespoke tailoring. This highly traditional craft turned out to be the site of constructing the multiple identities of contemporary dandies. Bespoke tailors, trained in Savile Row, work now in different countries (Figure 30). Indeed, the dandy is a convenient touchstone for historical tastes and trends from the beginning of the nineteenth century to our day.

In the abundance of roles offered by contemporary culture the originally clear and cold contours of the dandy, alas, are doomed to dissipate. As aptly observed by Baudelaire: 'Dandyism is a setting sun; like the declining star, it is magnificent, without heat and full of melancholy.'[3] Genuine dandyism, after all, is an ephemeral phenomenon that is slipping out of the conceptual schemes and economic systems of our pragmatic age. But the game goes on, and the twenty-first century is seeking out new transformations. And that is why writing about dandyism always presents a challenge for researchers. It was not for nothing that Barbey d'Aurevilly once

Figure 30 Ayres Gonçalo, bespoke tailor. © Lee Osborne @sartorialee. 2018.

remarked that the theme of dandyism requires a difficult balance: 'Deep minds have lacked the subtlety to do it, and subtle ones have lacked the depth.'[4]

Notes

1. Yuri Lotman, Dinamicheskaya model' semioticheskoy sistemi [The Dynamic Model of a Semiotic System], in *Izbrannie statyi v trekh tomakh* [Selected Writings in three volumes] (Tallinn: Alexandra, 1992), 1: 91.
2. See Christopher Breward, *The Hidden Consumer. Masculinities, Fashion and City Life 1860–1914* (Manchester: Manchester University Press, 1999).
3. Charles Baudelaire, The Painter of Modern Life, in *Selected Writings on Art and Artists*. Trans. P. E. Charvet (Cambridge: Cambridge University Press, 1972), 420–421.
4. Jules Barbey d'Aurevilly, *On Dandyism and George Brummell*. Trans. George Walden. George Walden, *Who is a Dandy?* (London: Gibson Square book, 2002), 87.

BIBLIOGRAPHY

Abrams, Mark. *The Teenage Consumer*. London: London Press Exchange, 1959.
Adams, Nathaniel, Rose Callahan, and Glenn O'Brien. *I Am Dandy: The Return of the Elegant Gentleman*. Berlin: Die Gestalten Verlag, 2013.
Adams, Nathaniel. *We Are Dandy: The Elegant Gentleman Around the World*. Berlin: Die Gestalten Verlag, 2016.
Addison, Joseph. *Selections from Addison's Papers Contributed to the Spectator*. Edited with Introduction and Notes by Thomas Arnold. Oxford: Clarendon Press, 1886.
Agamben, Giorgio. *Stanzas: Word and Phantasm in Western Culture*. Translated by Ronald L. Martinez. Minneapolis: University of Minnesota Press, 1993.
Aksakov, Konstantin. "Vospominaniya studentstva 1832–1835" [Memories of studenthood, 1832–1835]. In *Russkoye obshchestvo 30-kh godov XIX veka. Liudi i idei. Memuari sovremennikov* [Russian Society of the 1830s. People and Ideas, Memoirs of Contemporaries]. Ed. I. A. Fedosov. Moscow: Izdatelstvo MGU, 1989: 312–335.
Alford, Holly. "The zoot suit: its history and influence." *Fashion Theory*, 8, Issue 2 (2004), 225–237.
Anon. *The Dandies' Ball, or High Life in the City*. London: John Marshall, 1819.
Anon. *The Book of Fashion; Being a Digest of the Axioms of the Celebrated Joseph Brummell*. London: W.Kidd, 1835.
Arnold, Yuri. *Vospominaniya* [Memoirs]. Moscow: Yu.Lissner and E.Roman, 1892.
Ashcroft, Bill. "Towards a postcolonial aesthetics." *Journal of Postcolonial Writing*, 51, Issue 4, (2015), 410–421.
Babichev, Nikolay and Yakov Borovsky. *Slovar latinskikh krylatikh slov* [Dictionary of Commonly Used Latin Expressions]. Moscow: Russky Yazyk, 1988: 497–498.
Baillie-Cochrane, Alexandre (Lord Lamington). *In the Days of the Dandies*. London, Edinburgh: William Blackwood and Sons, 1890.
Balzac, Honoré. *Théorie de la démarche* (1833), http://www.ebooksgratuits.com/ebookslib/balzac1318.pdf. Accessed 27 April 2021.
Balzac, Honoré. *The Girl with the Golden Eyes*. Translated by Ernest Dowson. London: Leonard Smithers, 1896.
Balzac, Honoré. *Lost Illusions*. Translated by Herbert J. Hunt. London: Penguin Classics, 1976.
Balzac, Honoré. *Traité de la vie élégante*. Edited by Marie-Christine Natta. Clermont-Ferrand: Presses Universitaire Blaise Pascal, 2000.
Balzac, Honoré. *The Girl with the Golden Eyes*. Translated by Ellen Marriage. Auckland: The Floating Press, 2011.
Balzac, Honoré. *Scenes from a Courtesan's Life*. Translated by James Waring. Project Gutenberg e-book 1660. https://www.gutenberg.org/ebooks/1660. Accessed 26 April 2022.
Barbey D'Aurevilly, Jules. *Dendizm i Georges Brummell*. Preface by Mikhail Kuzmin. Moscow: Al'ciona, 1912.
Barbey D'Aurevilly, Jules. *The Anatomy of Dandyism: With Some Observations on Beau Brummell*. Translated from the French by D. B. Wyndham Lewis. London: Peter Davies, 1928.
Barbey d'Aurevilly, Jules. *On Dandyism and George Brummell*. Translated by George Walden. George Walden. *Who is a Dandy?* London: Gibson Square book, 2002.
Barthes, Roland. *Mythologies*. Translated by R. Howard and A. Lavers. London: Jonathan Cape, Ltd., 1972.

Bartlett, Djurdja. "Socialist Dandies International: East Europe," 1946–1959. *Fashion Theory*, 17, Issue 3, (2013), 249–299.

Batyushkov, Fedor, ed. *Istoriya zapadnoi literatury 1800–1910 v chetirekh tomakh* [History of Western literature 1800–1910, in 4 volumes]. Moscow: Mir, 1912–1917.

Baudelaire, Charles. *Selected Writings on Art and Artists*. Translated by P. E. Charvet. Cambridge, London: Cambridge University Press, 1981.

Baudrillard, Jean. *The System of Objects*. Translated by James Benedict. London, New York: Verso, 1996.

Beerbohm, Max. *Selected Prose*. Boston: Little, Brown/Atlantic Monthly Press, 1970.

Beerbohm, Max. *The Works of Max Beerbohm*. London: Charles Scribner's Sons, 1896.

Beerbohm, Max. *Dandies and Dandies*. https://standardebooks.org/ebooks/max-beerbohm/the-works-of-max-beerbohm/text/dandies-and-dandies. Accessed 20 March 2022.

Begunova, Alla. *Povsednevnaya zhizn' russkogo gusara v tsarstvovaniye Aleksandra I* [The Everyday Life of a Russian Hussar in the Reign of Alexander I]. Moscow: Molodaya Gvardiya, 2000.

Beliaev, Dmitry. "Stilyaga." *Krokodil*, 7, (1949), 10 March. P. 10.

Benjamin, Walter. *Selected Writings*. Vols. 1–4. Edited by Howard Eiland and Michael Jennings. Cambridge, MA: Belknap Press, 2002.

Berman, Elizaveta and Elena Kurbatova. *Russky Kostyum 1750–1917* ["Russian Dress 1750–1917"]. 5 Vols. Edited by Vadim Ryndin. Moscow: VTO, 1972.

Berne, Eric. *What Do You Say after You Say Hello? The Psychology of Human Destiny*. New York: Bantam Books, 1973. Open Library. https://archive.org/details/whatdoyousayafte00bern. Accessed 25 April 2022.

Berukshtis, Igor'. Stilyagi. Interview with Igor' Pomerantsev. *Ural*, 11, (1999), 123–124.

Bhabha, Homi. "Of mimicry and man: the ambivalence of colonial discourse." *October*, 28, Spring, (1984), 125–133.

Bitov, Andrey. *Pushkin House*. Normal, IL: Dalkey Archive Press, 1987.

Blanchot, Maurice. *Faux Pas*. Translated by Charlotte Mandell. Stanford: Stanford University Press, 2001.

Blessington, Marguerite. *The Idler in France: A Sequel to the Idler in Italy*. London: H. Colburn, 1842.

Blok, Aleksander. *Sochineniya v odnom tome* [Works in One Volume]. Moscow, Leningrad: OGIZ, Goslitizdat, 1946.

Boateng, Ozwald. "Ozwald Boateng on Africanism," *Vogue*, 31 May 2018. https://www.vogue.co.uk/gallery/ozwald-boateng-africanism. Accessed 4 May 2022; https://www.vogue.co.uk/gallery/ozwald-boateng-africanism?image=5d54bb3d506c0d0008cc3c60. Accessed 11 October 2020.

Boateng, Ozwald. https://ozwaldboateng.co.uk. Accessed 11 October 2020.

Bogomolov, Nikolay. *Mikhail Kuzmin*. Moscow: NLO, 1995.

de Bolla, Peter. "The visibility of visuality." In *Vision in Context*. Edited by Teresa Brennan and Martin Jay. New York: Routledge, 1996: 63–82.

Bonsi Vannocci, Orsola. *La Sape: Cultural Appropriation as Identitarian Emancipation*. Roots & Routes, 2019. https://www.roots-routes.org/la-sape-cultural-appropriation-as-identitarian-emancipation-orsola-vannocci-bonsi/. Accessed 4 November 2020.

Breward, Christopher. *The Hidden Consumer. Masculinities, Fashion and City Life 1860–1914*. Manchester: Manchester University Press, 1999.

Breward, Christopher. "The Dandy laid bare." In *Fashion Cultures: Theories, Explorations and Analysis*. Edited by Bruzzi, Stella and Pamela Church Gibson. London & New York: Routledge, 2000: 221–238.

Breward, Christopher. *Fashioning London: Clothing and the Modern Metropolis*. Oxford, New York: Berg, 2004.

Breward, Christopher. *The Suit: Form, Function and Style*. London: Reaktion Books, 2016.

Brewer, Jenny. *Alice Mann photographs African Men from London's La Sape*. https://www.itsnicethat.com/articles/alice-mann-la-sape-photography-120717. Accessed 12 July 2017.

Bryant, Keith Alexander. *Performing Black Masculinity: Race, Culture, and Queer Identity*. Plymouth: AltaMira Press, 2006.
Bullough, Vern L. and Bonnie Bullough. *Cross-Dressing, Sex and Gender*. Philadelphia: University of Pennsylvania Press, 1993.
Bulwer-Lytton, Edward. *Pelham; Or, the Adventures of a Gentleman*. Leipzig: Bernhard Tauchnitz, 1842.
Bulwer-Lytton, Edward. *Pelham*. Boston: Estes and Lauriat, 1891.
Bulwer-Lytton, Edward. *Pelham; Or, the Adventures of a Gentleman*. London: Henry Colburn, 1828.
Bulwer-Lytton, Edward. *Pelham; Or, the Adventures of a Gentleman*. London: Chapman and Hall, 1849.
Bulwer-Lytton, Edward. *Godolphin*. London: George Routledge and Sons, 1877.
Bury, Charlotte Campbell. *The Exclusives*. London: Henry Colburn and Richard Bentley, 1830.
Byron, George Gordon. *Letters and Journals of Lord Byron: With Notices of His Life*. Vol. 1. New York: J. & J. Harper, 1830.
Cambridge, Nicolas. "New whistle and flute: Orchestrating sartorial performances of contemporary masculinities." *Fashion Practice: The Journal of Design, Creative Process & the Fashion Industry*, 9, Issue 2, (2017), 183–199.
Campbell, Kathleen. *Beau Brummell: A Biographical Study*. London: Hammond, Hammond & Co, 1948.
Camus, Albert. *The Rebel*. Translated by Anthony Bower. New York: First Vintage International, 1991.
Carlyle, Jane Welsh. "Count d'Orsay Calls on Mrs. Carlyle," Letter, 7 April 1830. In *The Portable Victorian Reader*. Ed. Gordon S. Haight. London: Penguin, 1977: 20–22.
Chesterfield, Philip Dormer Stanhope. *Advice to His Son, on Men and Manners: Or, A New System of Education*. London, Philadelphia: T. Bradford and P. Hall, 1781; Ann Arbor: Text Creation Partnership, 2011, http://name.umdl.umich.edu/N13748.0001.001. Accessed 17 April 2022.
Chukovsky, Nikolay. *Literaturniye vospominaniya* [Literary memoirs]. Moscow: Sovetsky Pisatel, 1989.
Cole, Hubert. *Beau Brummell*. London: Granada Publishing, 1977.
Cole, Shaun and Miles Lambert, eds. *Dandy Style: 250 Years of British Men's Fashion*. New Haven, CT: Yale University Press, 2021.
Coleridge, Samuel Taylor. *The Portable Coleridge*. Edited by I. A. Richards. New York: Viking, 1950.
Collins, Wilkie. *Basil*. Oxford: Oxford University Press, 2008.
Conan Doyle, Arthur. *Rodney Stone*. London: Eveleigh Nash & Grayson, 1921.
Corbin, Alain. *The Foul and the Fragrant: Odor and the French Social Imagination*. Translated by M. Kochan, R. Porter, and C. Prendergast. Cambridge, Massachusetts: Harvard University Press, 1986.
Crary, Jonathan. *Techniques of the Observer: On Vision and Modernity in the Nineteenth Century*. Cambridge, London: MIT Press, 1996.
Dendi [*Dandy*], no.1 Moscow: R.N.Brenner, 1910.
Deleuze, Gilles. *The Fold: Leibniz and the Baroque*. London: The Athlone Press, 1993.
Demidenko, Julia. "Russkie Dendi" ["Russian Dandies"]. *Rodina*, 8, (2000), 111–114.
Demidov, Oleg. *Anatoly Mariengof: pervy dendi strani Sovetov* [Anatoly Mariengof: First Dandy of the Soviet Country]. Moscow: Redaktsia Eleni Shubinoy, 2019.
Deriège, Félix. *Physiologie du Lion*. Paris: Delahaye, 1841.
Disraeli, Benjamin. *Vivian Grey*. London: Longman's, Green and Co. 1892.
Disraeli, Benjamin. *Henrietta Temple. A Love Story*. New York: P. F. Collier, 1900 n.d.
Dobuzhinsky, Mstislav. *Vospominaniya* [Memories]. Moscow: Nauka, 1987: 203.
Donald, Diana, ed. *Followers of Fashion. Graphic Satires from the Georgian Period*. Prints from the British Museum. Newcastle: Hayward Gallery, 2002.
Driver, Sam N. *Pushkin: Literature and Social Ideas*. New York: Columbia University Press, 1989.
Dufourmantelle, Anne. *Of Hospitality. Anne Dufourmantelle Invites Jacques Derrida to Respond*. Bloomington: Stanford University Press, 2000.

Duvakin, Viktor. *Besedy V.V. Duvakina s M.M.Bakhtinym* [Conversations between V. Duvakin and M. Bakhtin]. Moscow: Progress, 1996.

Edgeworth, Maria. *Belinda*. Oxford: Oxford University Press, 1994.

Egan, Pierce. *Life in London, or Days and Nights of Jerry Hawthorne and His Elegant Friend Corinthian Tom, Accompanied by Bob Logic, the Oxonian, in Their Rambles and Sprees through the Metropolis*. London: Sherwood, Neeley and Jones, 1821.

Egan, Pierce. *Boxiana; Or, Sketches of Ancient and Modern Pugilism, From the Days of the Renowned Broughton and Slack, To the Championship of Cribb*. Vols. 1–3. London: Sherwood, Jones and Co, 1811–1830.

Elias, Norbert. *The Civilizing Process: The History of Manners*. New York: Pantheon, 1982.

Ellmann, Richard. *Oscar Wilde*. New York: Vintage, 1988.

Everest, Timothy. https://www.mbe.studio/bespoke-made-to-measure. Accessed 4 May 2022.

Fanon, Frantz. *Black Skin, White Masks*. Translated by Richard Philcox. New York: Grove Press, 2008.

FashionUnited. "Ozwald Boateng Exhibition at the V&A." *FashionUnited, 22 November 2005*. https://fashionunited.uk/news/fashion/ozwald-boateng-exhibition-at-the-v-a/2005112235907. Accessed 4 May 2022.

Favardin, Patrick and Laurent Bouëxière. *Le Dandysme*. Lyon: La Manufacture, 1988.

Feldman, Jessica R. *Gender on the Divide*. Ithaca and London: Cornell University Press, 1993.

Ficatier, Julia. "Au Congo, pays de la Sape." *La Croix*, 13, (1989), avril.

Fillin-Yeh, Susan, ed., *Dandies. Fashion and Finesse in Art and Culture*. New York: New York University Press, 2001.

Firbank, Ronald. *The Artificial Princess*. London: Duckworth, 1934.

Flügel, John Carl. *Psychology of Clothes*. London: Hogarth Press, 1930.

Fortassier, Rose. *Les Écrivains Français et la Mode*. Paris: PUF, 1978.

Forty, Adrian. *Objects of Desire. Design and Society Since 1750*. London: Thames and Hudson, Cameron Books, 1992.

Foucault, Michel. *Madness and Civilization: A History of Insanity in the Age of Reason*. London: Routledge, 2006.

Foulkes, Nick. *Last of the Dandies: The Scandalous Life and Escapades of Count d'Orsay*. London: Little Brown, 2003.

Freud, Sigmund. *The Standard Edition of the Complete Psychological Works of Sigmund Freud*. London: Hogarth Press, 1959.

Fyvel, Tosko R. *The Insecure Offenders: Rebellious Youth in the Welfare State*. London: Chatto and Windus, 1961.

Gagnier, Regenia. *Idylls of the Marketplace: Oscar Wilde and the Victorian Public*. Stanford: Stanford University Press, 1986.

Gamer, Michael. "A matter of turf: romanticism, hippodrama, and legitimate satire." *Nineteenth-Century Contexts*, 28, Issue 4, (2006): 305–334.

Garber, Marjorie. *Vested Interests*. New York and London: Routledge, 1993.

Garelick, Rhonda. *Rising Star: Dandyism, Gender and Performance in the fin de siècle*. Princeton, N.J.; Chichester: Princeton University Press, 1998.

Gaskell, Elizabeth. *Wives and Daughters*. London: Harper and Brothers, 1864.

Gautier, Théophile. *Mademoiselle de Maupin, A Romance of Love and Passion*. London: Gibbings & Co, 1899.

Gautier, Théophile. *Puteshestvie v Rossiu* [Travel in Russia]. Moscow: Misl', 1990.

Gebhardt, Lourens Loux. https://www.instagram.com/louxthevintageguru/?hl=en. Accessed 09 October 2020; https://louxthevintageguru.com/. Accessed 09 October 2020.

Ginzburg, Carlo. "Morelli, Freud, and Sherlock Holmes: clues and scientific method." In *The Sign of Three: Dupin, Holmes, Peirce*. Edited by Umberto Eco and Thomas A. Sebeok. Bloomington: Indiana University Press, 1984: 81–118.

Ginzburg, Lidiya. *Zapisniye knizhki. Vospominaniya. Esse* [Notebooks. Memoirs. Essays] St. Petersburg: Iskusstvo-SPB, 2002.

Giorgianni, Eugenio. *"A night out with London's Sapeurs,"Al Jazeera*, 01 January 2016. https://www.aljazeera.com/indepth/features/2016/05/nightlondon-sapeurs-drc-papa-wemba-160531084454216.html. Accessed 27 October 2020.

Goede, Christian. *The Stranger in England*. London: Mathews and Leigh, 1807.

Gogol, Nikolai. *The Collected Tales of Nikolai Gogol*. Translated and annotated by Richard Pevear and Larissa Volokhonsky. New York: Vintage Classics, 1999.

Goncharov, Ivan. "Pis'ma stolichnogo druga k provintsialnomu zhenikhu" [Letters by the friend from the capital to the provincial bridegroom]. In *Felietony sorokovykh godov. Zhurnalnaya i gazetnaya proza I.A.Goncharova, F.M.Dostoevskogo, I.S.Turgeneva* [Feuilletons of the Forties. Magazine and Newspaper Articles by I.A.Goncharov, F.M.Dostoyevsky, I.S.Turgenev]. Moscow-Leningrad: Academia, 1930. http://az.lib.ru/g/goncharow_i_a/text_0037.shtml.

Gondola, Didier. "Dream and drama: The search for elegance among Congolese youth." *African Studies Review*, 42, Issue 1, (1999), 23–48.

Grech, Nikolay. *Puteviye pisma iz Anglii, Germanii i Frantsii* [Travel Letters from England, Germany and France]. St. Petersburg: Tipografia N. Grecha, 1839.

Greenblatt, Stephen. *Renaissance Self-Fashioning: From More to Shakespeare*. Chicago: University of Chicago Press, 1980.

Greenleaf, Monika. *Pushkin and Romantic Fashion: Fragment, Elegy, Orient, Irony*. Stanford, Stanford University Press, 1994.

Grigorovich, Dmitry. "Svistulkin." *Biblioteka Dlya Chteniya* [Library for Reading], 129, 1855, 21–22.

Grossman, Leonid. *Sobranie sochineniy, tom 1–5* [Collected works in 5 volumes]. Moscow: Sovremennie problemi, 1928.

Guk, Olesya. "Tarzan v svoem otechestve. Interv'iu s Valentinom Tikhonenko" ["Tarzan in His Homeland. An Interview with Valentin Tikhonenko"]. 1997. https://www.beliy.ru/work/stilyagifilm/-id%3D43.htm. Accessed 27 July 2022.

Gumbrecht, Hans Ulrich. *Production of Presence: What Meaning Cannot Convey*. Stanford, CA: Stanford University Press, 2004.

Gurevich, Aron. "Dialektika sud'by u germantsev i drevnikh skandinavov" [The Dialectics of Fate among Germans and Ancient Scandinavians]. In *Poniatiye sudby v kontekste raznykh kultur* [*The Concept of Fate in the Context of Different Cultures*]. Ed. N. D. Arutyunova, Moscow: Nauka, 1994.

Gutkin, Len. *Dandyism: Forming Fiction from Modernism to the Present*. Charlottesville: University of Virginia Press, 2020.

Haedrich, Marcel. *Coco Chanel; Her Life, Her Secrets*. Translated by Charles Lam Markmann. Boston: Little Brown, 1972.

Harvey, John. *Men in Black*. Chicago: University of Chicago Press, 1996.

Hazlitt, William. *Essays*. Selected and edited by Frank Carr. London: Walter Scott, 1889.

Hazlitt, William. *Table-Talk*. London, Toronto: W. Dent, 1908.

Hazlitt, William. *The Complete Works in 22 Volumes*. Edited by P. Howe. London: J. M. Dent, 1934.

Hazlitt, William. *Brummelliana*. http://www.dandyism.net/hazlitts-brummelliana/. Accessed 10 April 2022.

Hogarth, William. *The Analysis of Beauty: Written with a View of Fixing the Fluctuating Ideas of Taste*. London: J. Reeves, 1753. http://name.umdl.umich.edu/004798055.0001.000. Accessed 23 April 2022.

Hollander, Anne. *Seeing Through Clothes*. Berkeley: University of California press, 1993.

Hollander, Anne. *Sex and Suits*. New York: A. Knopf, 1995.

Horace (Quintus Horatius Flaccus), *The Works of Horace: Consisting of His Odes, Satires, Epistles, and Art of Poetry*, Translated by P. Francis and P. Griffin. London: Doig and Sterling, 1815.

Huttunen, Tomi. *Imazhinist Mariengof: Dendi. Montazh. Tsiniki* [Imazhinist Mariengof: Dandy. Montage. Cynics]. Moscow: Novoe Literaturnoe Obozrenie, 2007.

Huysmans, Joris Karl. *Against the Grain*. Translated by John Howard. New York: Lieber & Lewis, 1922.

Ivanov, Viacheslav. *Stikhotvoreniya i Poemy* [Poems]. Leningrad: Sovetsky Pisatel, 1978.

Janes, Dominic. *British Dandies: Engendering Scandal and Fashioning a Nation*. Oxford: Bodleian Library Publishing, 2022.

Jesse, William. *The Life of George Brummell, Esq.* In 2 volumes. London: Saunders and Otley, 1844.

Johnson, Paul. *The Birth of the Modern: World Society 1815–1830*. New York: Weidenfeld and Nicolson, 1992.

Kantemir, Antioch. *Sobranie Stikhotvoreniy* [Collected poems]. Leningrad: Sovetskiy Pisatel, 1956.

Karaminas, Vicki, Adam Geczy, and Pamela Church Gibson, eds. *Fashionable Masculinities: Queers, Pimp Daddies, and Lumbersexuals*. New Brunswick: Rutgers University Press, 2022.

Kelly, Ian. *Beau Brummell: The Ultimate Man of Style*. New York: Free Press, 2006.

Kirsanova, Raisa. *Kostium v russkoy khudozhestvennoi kulture* [Dress in Russian Artistic Culture]. Moscow: Rossiyskaya Entzyklopedia, 1995.

Kirsanova, Raisa. "Stilyagi." *Rodina*, 8, (1998), 72–75.

Kirsanova, Raisa. "Chelovek v Zerkale Mira" [Man in the Mirror of the World, in Russian]. *Russkaya Galereya*, 49, Issue 2, (1998), 44–49.

Knox, Katelyn. *Race on Display in 20th- and 21st-Century France*. Liverpool: Liverpool University Press, 2016.

Korshunova, Tamara. *Kostium v Rossii XVIII – nachala XX veka: iz sobraniia gosudarstvennogo Ermitazha* [Russian Costume of XVIII-beginning of XIX centuries]. Leningrad: Khudozhnik RSFSR, 1970.

Kozlov, Alexey. "Vospominania dzhazmena, perezhivshego vse stadii ottepeli" [Memories of a jazzman, who survived through all stages of a Thaw]. In *Ottepel'* [Thaw]. Ed. A. S. Kurlyandtseva, Yu. V. Vorotintseva. Moscow: Gosudarstvennaya Tretyakovskaya Galereya, 2017: 301–316.

Krylov, Ivan. "Mysli filosofa po mode." In *Russkaia proza XVIII veka*, tom 1–2 [Russian Prose of XVIII Century, in 2 volumes]. Ed. A. V. Zapadov, G. P. Makagonenko. Moscow-Leningrad: Khudozhestvennaya literatura, 1950: 752–761.

Kutesko, Elisabeth. "Problems and Tensions in the Representation of the Sapeurs, as demonstrated in the work of two twenty-first century Italian photographers." *Immediations: The Courtauld Institute of Art Journal of Postgraduate Research*, 3, Issue 2, (2013), 60–76.

Larousse, Pierre. Grand Dictionnaire universel du XIX siècle, 6: 63. https://www.larousse.fr/dictionnaires/francais/dandy/21602. Accessed 22 May 2022.

Laver, James. *Costume and Fashion*. London: Thames & Hudson, 1986.

Lebina, Natalya. "Konets epokhi bolshogo stilya: antistalinskie tendentsii v mode 1960 godov" [End of Grand Style period: antistalinist tendencies in Soviet Fashion of 1960-s]. In *Ottepel'* [Thaw]. Ed. A. S. Kurlyandtseva, Yu. V. Vorotintseva. Moscow: Gosudarstvennaya Tretyakovskaya Galereya, 2017: 177–191.

Lecercle, Jean-Pierre. *Mallarmé et la Mode*. Paris: Librarie Seguire, 1989.

Lehmann, Ulrich. *Tigersprung: Fashion in Modernity*. Cambridge, MA: MIT Press, 2000.

Lestringuez, Pierre. *Le chevalier d'Orsay*. Montrouge: Draeger, 1944.

Lewis, Shantrelle P. *Dandy Lion: The Black Dandy and Street Style*. New York: Aperture, 2017.

Lotman, Yuri. "Dekabrist v Povsednevnoi Zhizni" [The Decembrist in Everyday Life]. In *Literaturnoe Nasledie Dekabristov*. Ed. V. G. Bazanov, V. E. Vatsuro. Leningrad: Nauka, 1975: 25–74.

Lotman, Yuri. *Izbrannye stat'i v trekh tomakh* [Selected Articles in three volumes]. Tallinn: Aleksandra, 1992.

Lotman, Yuri. *Kultura i vzryv* [Culture and Explosion]. Moscow: Gnosis, 1992.

Lotman, Yuri. *Besedi o russkoy culture* [Talks on Russian Culture]. Sankt-Peterburg: Iskusstvo, 1994.

M.L. *Predislovie* [Foreword to Barbey D'Aurevilly's Treatise "On Dandyism and George Brummell]. *Dandy*, no. 1, Moscow: R.N.Brenner, 1910.

Mabanckou, Alain. *Black Bazar*. Paris: Éditions du Seuil, 2009.

Makarevich, Vadim. "S dzhazom po zhizni. Interv'iu s Borisom Alekseevym" ["Through Life with Jazz. An Interview with Boris Alekseev"]. *Nezavisimaia gazeta*, 20 June, (2003), 13. http://www.ng.ru/saturday/2003-06-20/13_alekseev.html. Accessed 27.07.2022.

Makelele, Basile Mulwani, Patrick Litalema Libote, and Boniface Aspan A Kasas. "A Study on the Perception of Congolese Students towards Sape." *Research in Psychology and Behavioral Sciences*, 5, Issue 1, (2017), 6–12.

Mamardashvili, Merab. *Lektsii o Pruste* [Lectures on Proust]. Moscow: Ad Marginem, 1995.

Mandelstam, Nadezhda. *Hope against Hope*. Translated by Max Hayward. New York: Atheneum, 1983.

Mann, Phillip. *The Dandy at Dusk: Taste and Melancholy in the Twentieth Century*. London: Head of Zeus, 2018.

Mariengof, Anatoly. "Moy vek, moya molodost', moi druzya i podrugi" [My times, my youth, my friends]. In *Moy vek, moi druzya i podrugi. Vospominaniya Mariengofa, Shershenevicha, Gruzinova* [My Times, My Friends. The memoirs of Mariengof, Shershenevich, and Gruzinov]. Ed. S. Shumikhina, K. Yurieva. Moscow: Moskovsky Rabochy, 1990.

Martin-Fugier, Anne. *La Vie élégante, ou La Formation du Tout-Paris 1815–1848*. Paris: Perrin, 1990.

Mayakovsky, Vladimir. *Polnoye sobraniye sochineniy v 13 tomakh* [Collected Works in 13 vols]. Moscow: Gosudarstvennoye izdatelstvo khudozhestvennoi literatury, 1955.

McDowell, Colin. *The Man of Fashion*. London: Thames and Hudson, 1997.

McNeil, Peter. "'That doubtful gender': macaroni dress and male sexualities." *Fashion Theory*, 3, Issue 4, (1999), 411–449.

McNeil, Peter. "Macaroni Masculinities." In *The Men's Fashion Reader*. Edited by Peter McNeil and Vicki Karaminas. Oxford, New York: Berg, 2009: 54–71.

Mediavilla, Hector. http://www.hectormediavilla.com/sapeur.

Meletinsky, Eleazar. *Izbranniye statyi. Vospominaniya* [Selected Articles. Memoirs]. Moscow: izdatelstvo RGGU, 1998.

Melville, Lewis. *The Beaux of the Regency*, in 2 volumes. London: Hutchinson & Co, 1908.

Melville, Lewis. *Beau Brummell: His Life and Letters*. New York: G. H. Doran Co., 1925.

Mercier, Louis-Sebastien. *New Picture of Paris*. Dublin: Gale Ecco, 2018.

Merleau-Ponty, Maurice. *Basic Writings*. Edited by Thomas Baldwin. London: Routledge, 2004: 252.

Mertsalova, Maria. *Kostium raznykh vremen i narodov* [The Costume of Different Times and Peoples]. Vol. 1–4. Moscow: Akademiya Mody, 1996.

Miller, Monica L. *Slaves to Fashion: Black Dandyism and the Styling of Black Diasporic Identity*. Durham, NC: Duke University Press, 2009.

Mills, Jonn. *D'Horsay; or, the Follies of the Day*. London: William Strange, 1844.

Moch-Bickert, Éliane. *Kolombina desiatykh godov* [A Columbine of the 1910s]. Paris-St. Petersburg: Grzhebin Publishers, 1993.

Moers, Ellen. *The Dandy: Brummell to Beerbohm*. New York: The Viking Press, 1960.

Mompó, Julio. "A Vision of a Modern Dandy. Interview with Olga Vainshtein." In *Fashionable Masculinities: Queers, Pimp Daddies, and Lumbersexuals*. Edited by Vicki Karaminas, Adam Geczy, and Pamela Church Gibson. New Brunswick: Rutgers University Press, 2022: 223–226.

Montandon, Alain. Préface. In *Mythes et représentations de l'hospitalité*. Edited by Alain Montandon. Clermont Ferrand: Université Blaise Pascal, 1999.

Montandon, Alain. *Sociopoétique de la promenade*. Clermont-Ferrand: Presses Universitaires Blaise Pascal, 2000.

Monypenny, William Flavell and George Earle Buckle. *Life of Benjamin Disraeli, Earl Beakonsfield*, in 6 volumes. New York: Macmillan, 1910–1920.

Morgan, Sydney (Lady Morgan). *France in 1829–1830*. London: Saunders & Otley, 1831.

Morsiani, Benedetta. *Performing cultural identities and transnational 'imaginaries': fashion and beauty practices as diasporic spaces among young London Congolese*. Electronic version of a PhD thesis awarded by the University of Westminster. 2019. https://westminsterresearch.westminster.ac.uk/item/qxwyv/performing-cultural-identities-and-transnational-imaginaries-fashion-and-beauty-practices-as-diasporic-spaces-among-young-london-congolese. Accessed 27 July 2022.

Moscovici, Serge. *Mashina, tvoriashaya bogov* [The Machine that Makes Gods]. Moscow: Tsentr psykhologii i psikhoterapii, 1998.

Murav'eva, Olga. *Kak vospityvali russkogo dvorianina* [The Upbringing of the Russian Nobleman]. St. Petersburg: Letniy sad, 1998.
Murdoch, Iris. *The Unicorn*. London: Triad Panther books, 1977.
Neckclothitania; or Tietania: Being an Essay on Starchers. By One of the Cloth. London: Stockdale, 1818.
Nelson Evening Mail, XIII, Issue 58, 8 March (1878).
Newell, Sasha. *The Modernity Bluff: Crime, Consumption, and Citizenship in Côte d'Ivoire*. Chicago: The University of Chicago Press, 2012.
Newell, Sasha. "Le Goût des Autres. Ivoirian Fashion and Alterity." *Etnofoor*, 24, Issue 2, (2012), 41–56.
Newman, John Henry. "The definition of a gentleman." In *The Portable Victorian Reader*. Edited by Gordon S. Haight. London: Penguin, 1977: 464–468.
Odoyevtseva, Irina. *Na beregakh Nevy* [On the banks of Neva]. Moscow: Khudozhestvennaya literatura, 1989.
Onions, Charles Talbut. *A Shakespeare Glossary*. Enlarged by R. D. Eagleson. Oxford: Clarendon Press, 1986.
Orlova, Galina. "Stilyagi. Biografiia Veshi" ["Stilyagi. Biography of a Thing"]. In *Ob"iat' obyknovennoe. Povsednevnost' kak tekst po-amerikanski i po-russki* [Facing the Ordinary]. Ed. Tatiana Venediktova. Moscow: MGU Publishing House, 2004: 205–218.
Ortega y Gasset, José. *Toward a Philosophy of History*. Urbana: University of Illinois Press, 2002.
Panaev, Ivan. *Literatnye vospominaniya* [Literary Memories]. Moscow: Pravda, 1988.
Panaeva, Avdotya. *Vospominaniya* [Memories]. Moscow: Pravda, 1988.
Papa Wemba: *Stars remember the 'voice of Africa'*. 25 April 2016. https://www.bbc.com/news/world-africa-36128441. Accessed 27 July 2022.
Perrot, Philippe. *Les dessus et les dessous de la bourgeoisie*. Paris: Librairie Artheme Fayard, 1981.
Petrovskaya, Nina. "Iz vospominaniy" [Excerpts from memoirs]. In *Bryusov, Valery. Literaturnoye Nasledstvo* [Literary Heritage]. Ed. A. N. Dubovikov, N. A. Trifonov. Moscow: Nauka, 1976: 773–798.
Picarelli, Enrica. "Elegance and retrospective sartorialism among young African males." *Clothing Cultures*, 2, Issue 2, (2015), 209–223.
Plutarch. *Plutarch's Lives*. Translated by Bernadotte Perrin. Cambridge, MA: Harvard University Press; London: William Heinemann Ltd., 1916.
Pointon, Marcia. "The case of the dirty beau: symmetry, disorder and the politics of masculinity." In *The Body Imaged*. Edited by K. Adler and M. Pointon. Cambridge: Cambridge University Press, 1993: 175–189.
Polhemus, Ted. *Street Style*. London: Thames and Hudson, 1997.
Polonsky, Rachel. *English Literature and the Russian Aesthetic Renaissance*. Cambridge: Cambridge University Press, 1998.
Pool, Daniel. *What Jane Austen Ate and Charles Dickens Knew*. New York: Touchstone, 1994.
Proskurin, Oleg. *Poeziia Pushkina ili podvizhnyi palimpsest* [Pushkin's poetry or Mobile Palimpsest]. Moscow: NLO, 1999.
Proust, Marcel. *The Guermantes Way*. Translated by C. K. Scott Moncrieff. Edited and annotated by William C. Carter. New Haven and London: Yale University Press, 2018: 456.
Proust, Marcel. *The Guermantes Way*. Germany: Books on Demand, 2019. The Guermantes Way - Marcel Proust - Google Books, Accessed 17 April 2022.
Pushkin, Aleksander. *Sochineniya* [Works]. Moscow: Khudozhestvennaya literatura, 1949.
Pushkin, Aleksander. *Evgeniy Onegin*. Translated from Russian by Henry Spalding. London: Macmillan and Co, 1881. Project Gutenberg eBook 23997: https://www.gutenberg.org/files/23997/23997-h/23997-h.htm. Accessed 10 April 2022.
Pushkin, Aleksander. *Eugene Onegin*. Translated by A. S. Kline, 2009, chapter 6, https://www.poetryintranslation.com/PITBR/Russian/Onegin8.php#highlightonegin. Accessed 17 April 2022.
Pyliayev, Mikhail. *Zamechatelniye Chudaki i Originaly* [Memorable eccentrics and originals]. Moscow: Interbuk, 1990.
Raisson, Horace. *Code de la Toilette. Manuel Complet d'Elégance et d'Hygiène*. Paris: J.-P. Roret, 1829.

Richter, Jean Paul. *Horn of Oberon: Jean Paul Richter's School of Aesthetics*. Introduction and Translation by Margaret R. Hale. Detroit: Wayne State University Press, 1973.

Roget, Peter Mark. *The New Roget's Thesaurus in Dictionary Form*. Revised and edited by Norman Lewis. New York: Putnam, 1978.

Rot-Ai, Kristin. "Kto na p'edestale, a kto v tolpe? Stilyagi i ideia sovetskoi 'molodezhnoi kul'tury' v epokhu 'ottepeli'" ["Who is on a pedestal and who is in the crowd? Stilyagi and the idea of Soviet 'youth culture' in the thaw period"]. *Neprikosnovennyi zapas*, 4, Issue 36, (2004), 2–33.

Rothstein, Natalie, ed. *A Lady of Fashion: Barbara Johnson's Album of Styles and Fabrics*. New York: Thames and Hudson, 1987.

Rotikov, Konstantin. *Drugoi Peterburg* [Another Peterburg]. St Petersburg: Liga plus, 2000.

Rusanova, Olga. Razdum'ia o krasote i vkuse ["Thoughts on Beauty and Taste"]. Moscow: *Znanie*, 1962.

Ruskin, John. *Sesame and Lilies*. London: Smith, Elder & Co, 1865.

Russell, Bertrand. *Autobiography*. London and New York: Routledge, 1998.

Sadleir, Michael. *Blessington-d'Orsay. A Masquerade*. London: Constable & Co, 1933.

Sadoff, Diane. "The silver fork novel." In *The Oxford History of the Novel in English*. Edited by John Kucich and Jenny Bourne Taylor. Vol. 3. Oxford: Oxford University Press, 2012: 106–121.

Saint-Simon, Louis de Rouvroy. *The Memoirs of Louis XIV, His Court and of the Regency*. Project Gutenberg e-book 3875, 2004. https://www.gutenberg.org/ebooks/3875. Accessed 21 April 2022.

Sandberg, Mark. *Living Pictures, Missing Persons: Mannequins, Museums and Modernity*. Princeton: Princeton University Press, 2003.

Schlegel, Friedrich. *Werke in zwei Bänden*. Berlin und Weimar: Aufbau-Verlag, 1980.

Sennett, Richard. *The Fall of Public Man*. Cambridge: Cambridge University Press, 1977.

Shakespeare, William. *The Complete Works of William Shakespeare*. London: Odhams Press, 1932.

Shannon, Brent. *The Cut of His Coat: Men, Dress, and Consumer Culture in Britain, 1860–1914*. Athens: Ohio University Press: 2006.

Shepelev, Leonid. *Tituly, mundiry, ordena* [Titles, Uniforms, Orders]. Leningrad: Nauka, 1991.

Sherwood, James. *Bespoke: The Men's style of Savile Row*. New York: Random House Incorporated, 2010.

Shlepyanov, Aleksander. "'Stilyagi'. Interview with Igor' Pomerantsev." *Ural*, Issue 11, (1999), 125–126.

Shore, William Teignmouth. *D'Orsay or The Complete Dandy*. London: John Long, Limited, 1912.

Shtraikh, Solomon. Istoriko-literaturnyi ocherk o Vigele [Historical-literary essay on Vigel']. In *Vigel', Zapiski, Notes*. Ed. I. Zakharov. Moscow: Zakharov, 2000: 554–580.

Slavkin, Victor. *Pamiatnik neizvestnomy stilyage* [*Monument to the Unknown Stilyaga*]. Moscow: Artist. Rezhisser. Teatr, 1996.

Sontag, Susan. *Against Interpretation and Other Essays*. New York: Noonday, 1966.

The Spectator, no. 631, 10 December (1714). https://gutenberg.org/ebooks/12030. Accessed 20 March 2022.

Svede, Mark Allen. "Twiggy and Trotsky." In *Dandies. Fashion and finesse in Art and Culture*. Edited by Susan Fillin-Yeh. New York: New York University Press, 2001: 243–270.

Stafford, Barbara. *Artful Science*. Cambridge, MA: MIT Press, 1994.

Stanton, Domna. *The Aristocrat as Art*. New York: Columbia University Press, 1980.

Steele-Perkins, Chris and Richard Smith. *The Teds*. Manchester: Dewi Lewis Publishing, 2003.

Svelte, Dita. "'Do you call this thing a coat?': wit, the epigram and the detail in the figure of the ultimate dandy, Beau Brummell." *Fashion Theory*, 22, Issue 3, (2018), 255–282, DOI: 10.1080/1362704X.2017.1354436

Sue, Eugène. *The Mysteries of Paris*. Project Gutenberg e-book 33801, 2010, vol. 2:18. https://www.gutenberg.org/ebooks/33801. Accessed 21 April 2022.

Sue, Eugène. *The Mysteries of Paris*. Translated by Charles H. Town. New York: Harper and Brothers, 1843.

Tamagni, Daniele. *Gentlemen of Bacongo*. London: Trolley Books: 2009.

Tamagni, Daniele. https://www.danieletamagni.com/. Accessed 4 May 2022.
Tester, Keith, ed. *The Flaneur*. London, New York: Routledge, 1994.
Tietenberg, Anne Kristin. *Der Dandy als Grenzgänger der Moderne:Selbststilisierungen in Literatur und Popkultur*. Berlin: Lit, 2013.
Timbs, John. *Club Life in London with Anecdotes of the Clubs, Coffee-houses and Taverns of the Metropolis*, in 2 volumes. London: Richard Bentley, 1866.
Toll, Felix. *Nastolniy slovar' dlia spravok po vsem otrasliam znania*. [Table Dictionary for all Fields of Knowledge] Sankt Peterburg: Izdanie F.Tollya, 1864.
Tomes, Nancy. *The Gospel of Germs: Men, Women and the Microbe in American Life*. Cambridge, MA: Harvard University Press, 1998.
Tulloch, Carol. *The Birth of Cool: Style Narratives of the African Diaspora*. London, New York: Bloomsbury Academic, 2016.
Turchin, Valery. *Aleksandr I i stil neoklasssitsizma v Rossii* [Alexander I and Neoclassical Style in Russia]. Moscow: Zhiraf, 2001.
Uspensky, Boris. *Izbrannie trydi*. Tom 1-2. [Selected Works in Two Volumes]. Moscow: Gnozis, 1994.
Vainshtein, Olga. *Dendi: moda, literatura, stil' zhizni* [Dandy: Fashion, Literature, Lifestyle]. Moscow: New Literary Review, 2021.
Vainshtein, Olga. "Female fashion, Soviet style: bodies of ideology." In *Russia – Women – Culture*. Edited by H. Goscilo and B. Holmgren. Bloomington: Indiana University Press, 1996: 64–94.
Vainshtein, Olga. "Zhiznetvorchestvo v culture evropeyskogo romantizma" [Self-Fashioning in European Romantic Culture]. *Vestnik RGGU*. Vol. 2. Ed. Sergey Nekliudov. Moscow: Russian State University for the Humanities Press, 1998: 161–187.
Vainshtein, Olga. "Fashioning Woman: Dressmaker as Cultural Producer." In *Para-sites. A Casebook against Cynical Reason*. Edited by George Marcus. Chicago: The University of Chicago Press, 2000: 195–223.
Vainshtein, Olga. "The concept of modesty in socialist dress and grooming: snapshot." In *The Berg Encyclopedia of World Dress and Fashion*. Edited by Joanne B. Eicher. Vol. 9, East Europe, Russia, and the Caucasus. Oxford and New York: Berg Publishers, 2010: 364–365.
Vainshtein, Olga. "Dandy: a snapshot." In *Fashion History Reader. Global Perspectives*. Edited by Giorgio Riello and Peter McNeil. London, New York: Routledge, 2010: 329–332.
Vainshtein, Olga. "Walking the turtles: minimalism in European dandy culture in the nineteenth century." *Fashion, Style & Popular Culture*, 4, Issue 1, (2017), 81–104.
Vainshtein, Olga. "Orange Jackets and Pea Green Pants: The Fashion of Stilyagi in Soviet Postwar Culture." *Fashion Theory*, 22, Issue 2, (2018), 167–185.
Vainshtein, Olga. "The Latest Thing for Boys": Little Lord Fauntleroy and Children's Fashion. *Archivist Addendum*, 2021, 42–69.
de Viel-Castle, Horace. *Memoires de le regne de Napoleon III*. Vol. 2. Paris: Chez tous les libraires, 1883.
Vigarello, Georges. *Concepts of Cleanliness: Changing Attitudes in France Since the Middle Ages*. Translated by J. Birrell. Cambridge: Cambridge University Press, 1988.
Vigel', Filipp. *Zapiski* [Notes]. Moscow: Zakharov, 2000.
Visser, Jeroen. "Cultural dandyism." In *The New Man*. Edited by Jan Brand and José Teunissen. Arnhem: D'Jonge Hond, ArtEz Press, 2010: 79–90.
Vlasov, Viktor. *Stili v iskusstve* [Styles in Art]. St. Petersburg: Kolna, 1995.
Voloshin, Maximilian. *Liki tvorchestva* [Faces of Creation]. Leningrad: Nauka, 1988.
de Vugt, Geertjan. *Political Dandyism in Literature and Art: Genealogy of a Paradigm*. London, New York: Palgrave Macmillan, Springer International Publishing, 2018.
Walden, George. *Who is a Dandy?* London: Gibson Square Books, 2002.
White, Edmund. *The Flaneur: A Stroll through the Paradoxes of Paris*. London: Bloomsbury Publishing, 2001.
Wilde, Oscar. *The Complete Works of Oscar Wilde*. Edited by Russell Jackson and Ian Small. Oxford: Oxford University Press, 2000–2018.

Wilde, Oscar. *Phrases and Philosophies for the Use of the Young*. London: L. Smithers, 1903. https://www.sas.upenn.edu/~cavitch/pdf-library/Wilde_Phrases_and_Philosophies.pdf. Accessed 29 April 2022.
Wilde, Oscar. *The Complete Letters of Oscar Wilde*. Edited by Merlin Holland and Rupert Hart-Davis. New York: Henry Holt, 2000.
Wilde, Oscar. *The Collected Works of Oscar Wilde*. Herts: Wordsworth Editions Ltd., 2007.
Wilde, Oscar. *Interviews and Recollections*, Vols. 1–2. London: Macmillan, 1979.
Wilde, Oscar. *Selected Letters of Oscar Wilde*. Edited by Rupert Hart-Davis. Oxford: Oxford University Press, 1979.
Wilde, Oscar. *Essays and Lectures*. London: Methuen and Co, 1913.
Winckelmann, Johann Joachim. *On Art, Architecture, and Archaeology*. Translated by David Carter. Rochester: Camden house, 2013.
Wodehouse, Pelham Grenville. *Very Good, Jeeves*. London: Random House-Penguin, 2005.
Wölfflin, Heinrich. *Principles of Art History: The Problem of the Development of Style in Later Art*. Translated by M. D. Hottinger. NewYork: Dover Publications, 2012.
Woolf, Virginia. *Common Reader*, Second series. London: Hogarth Press, 1935.
Wordsworth, William. *The Prelude*. Edited by Ernest de Sélincourt and Helen Darbishire. Oxford: Oxford University Press, 1959.
Wyatt, James. *The Taylor's Friendly Instructor being an easy guide for finding the principal and leading points essential to the art of fitting the human shape, forming a complete system delineating the different parts according to the proportions of the human figures, illustrated with twenty four engraved models of different garments, designed on the principles of practical geometry, displaying in the most familiar manner the variety of forms produced by the variation of fashion; with notes containing the reason of every rule; also remarks on numerous systems in practice by different authors*. London: J. Harris, 1822.
Zaidi, Tariq. *Sapeurs: Ladies & Gentlemen of the Congo*. Heidelberg: Kehrer Verlag, 2020.
Zamyatin, Evgeny. *Mi* [We]. Huxley, Aldous. *Prekrasniy Novyi Mir* [The Brave new World]. Moscow: Khudozhestvennaya Literatura, 1989.
Zhikharev, Mikhail. "Dokladnaya zapiska potomstvu o Petre Yakovleviche Chaadaeve" [Note to offspring on Petr Yakovlevich Chaadaev]. In *Russkoye obshchestvo 30-kh godov XIX veka. Liudi i idei. Memuary sovremennikov* [Russian Society of the 1830s. People and ideas. Memoirs of Contemporaries]. Ed. I. A. Fedosov. Moscow: Izdatelstvo MGU, 1989: 48–120.
Zilbershtein, Ilya and Vladimir Samkov, eds. *Sergei Diaghilev i russkoe iskusstvo, v 2 tomakh*. [Sergey Diaghilev and Russian Art, in two volumes]. Moscow: Izobrazitel'noe iskusstvo, 1982.
Zola, Émile. *Nana*. Translated by Burton Rascoe. New York: Dover Publications Inc, 2007.

SUBJECT INDEX

A

albums 2, 4, 20, 159
aphorism 43, 44, 47, 145, 146, 234, 236
art of pleasing by displeasing 96

B

bucks 118, 119, 123

C

cane 16, 71, 82, 116, 123, 149, 154, 222, 224, 229
chameleonism 47–49, 181, 233
charisma 1, 49, 51, 52, 55, 57–62, 63n8, 190, 213
conspicuous inconspicuousness 13, 16, 39, 77, 81, 84, 116, 124, 191, 217, 218, 223, 234, 235
cravat 2, 16–20, 24n38, 39, 49, 78, 151, 180, 187
cutting 90, 91, 97, 99, 213, 234–235

D

dance 88, 115–116, 138, 196, 197, 200, 206, 223, 224, 226–227
dandy
    costume 1, 3, 7, 11–14, 16, 33, 42–43, 60, 69, 70, 75, 78, 79, 91, 114, 147–151, 156, 163–165, 167, 168, 172–173, 180, 186–188, 191, 206, 218
    definition of 1, 181, 233
    gaze 16, 51, 60, 70, 74, 178, 197
    gender 42, 48, 59, 67, 73, 136–137, 158, 165, 174, 175, 201, 204, 215, 229
    gestures 1, 32, 43, 67, 68, 76, 84, 85, 90, 114, 123–124, 137, 170–171, 189, 197, 213, 226, 234, 235
    rules 28, 39–40, 43, 65, 67–68, 85, 87–88, 91, 103, 105–107, 118, 120–122, 178, 182–183, 193, 213, 223, 225, 227, 235

F

fashionable novel 34–38, 40–41, 43, 145, 152, 213
flaneur 137, 198, 206, 215
frock coat 78, 164, 170, 172, 177, 178, 225

G

gloves 16, 28, 29, 49–50, 58, 149, 200, 218, 224, 225
great male renunciation 8, 213, 235

H

honest man 183–184
humour 28, 29, 45, 52, 54–55, 61, 83–84, 97, 99–101, 106, 145
hygiene 1, 29, 127–128, 130, 132–137, 143n78, 191, 213, 216, 227, 234

I

inscrutability 66, 67, 125–127
insolence 36, 89, 90, 92–98, 149, 213
interior 20–21, 136, 150, 157
irony 47, 155, 156, 160, 172, 193, 194

J

je ne sais quoi 20, 172, 235
justacorps 8–9

L

lion 75, 123, 178, 181–182, 184
lorgnette 70–71, 75, 126, 178, 184

M

macaroni 3, 7, 14, 70, 73, 160
man of bon ton 181–184
minimalism 43, 60, 67, 69, 77, 124, 168, 172, 215, 217, 223, 231n4, 233–235
monocle 37, 70–71, 76, 123, 126, 192, 224

N

neoclassicism 18, 23n7, 235
new bespoke movement 217, 220
nil admirari 65–66, 69, 126, 191, 234, 235

O

optical duels 73, 126

P

politeness 88, 92–96, 98, 182, 216, 233
practical jokes 99, 101–103, 105–107

R

races 34, 52, 120–123, 141n24, 215
romanticism 32, 185, 213
rudeness 90, 92–95

S

sapeurs 1, 217, 219, 222–230, 236
scandal 1, 30, 87, 89, 90, 92, 101, 106, 147, 213
secrets 16, 29–31, 34, 44, 51, 104
shirt 8, 12, 13, 17, 19, 41, 58, 124, 128, 148, 149, 151, 164, 166–167, 192, 193, 195, 198–200, 204–205, 220–221, 225
silver fork novel 34–35, 40–41, 213
slowness 1, 77, 88, 137–140, 216, 234, 235
sports 34, 117–118, 120–123, 131, 147, 216, 234
sprezzatura 93
stilyaga, stilyagi 28, 195–198, 200
stockings 8, 13–15, 42, 104, 117, 149–151, 168

T

trousers 8, 11–15, 18, 30, 36, 148, 159, 160, 167, 169, 174, 176, 179, 180, 185, 188, 195, 197–201, 204, 220–221

V

vest 8, 22, 23n1, 164, 169, 188
vulgarity 1, 81–86, 91, 145–146, 155, 157, 173, 214, 217, 233, 234

W

waistcoat 12–15, 28, 36, 40–42, 49, 58, 117, 119, 124, 148–151, 166–167, 170, 180, 187, 192–193, 218

NAME INDEX

A

Abercrombie, Patrick 76
Addison, Joseph 38
Against Nature (À Rebours) (Huysmans) 3, 42, 152
Albert Edward, Prince of Wales 146. *See also* Edward VII
Alcibiades 49, 97–99, 181
Aliabieva, Liudmila xi, 112
Almack's 3, 34, 37, 122
Apollinaire, Guillaume 41
Apollo 7, 10, 11, 13, 17, 33, 51
Apollo Theatre 221
Arden, William 33
Arkhipov, Dmitry xi
Arliss, George 76
Armine, Ferdinand 55
Arnold, Yuri 19, 168
Athenaeum Fragment 108 (Schlegel) 48
Austen, Ben 35
Austen, Jane 34
Austen, Sara 35–36

B

Babichev, Nikolay 65
Bakhtin, Mikhail 3, 193–194
Balzac, Honore 3, 18, 20, 27, 32, 41, 43, 51, 83, 116, 127, 129, 133–134, 138, 184, 214, 235
Barbey d'Aurevilly, Jules 3, 16, 23, 27–28, 32, 41, 43, 66, 78, 87, 98, 176, 184, 186–187, 190, 191, 214, 233, 236
Barrymore, John 28
Basil (Collins) 66
Bate, Henry 73
Baudelaire, Charles 3, 27, 32, 43–44, 47, 65–67, 81, 126, 137, 153, 158, 184, 187, 188, 191, 194, 214, 236
Baudrillard, Jean 21
Beau Brummell (Beaumont film) 28
Beau Brummell (Bernhardt film) 28
Beau Brummell (Woolf) 28

Beau Brummell: This Charming Man (Kelly television drama) 28
Beaumont, Harry 28
Bedford, 77, 131
Beerbohm, Max 14, 28, 32, 47, 113, 126, 146, 158–159, 214, 217
Belham, Patricia (Lady Patricia) 28
Belinda (Maria Edgeworth) 12
Berlioz, Hector 54
Bernhardt, Curtis 28
Bernhardt, Sarah 41
Bernini, Gian Lorenzo 17
Bertillon, Alphonse 78
Blanc, H 18
Blessington, Harriet 53
Blessington, Marguerite 20–21, 37, 53–59, 61
Book of Fashion; Being a Digest of the Axioms of the Celebrated Joseph Brummell, The 29
Book of Snobs (Thackeray) 35
Borges, Jorge Luis 53
Brooks, Romaine 76
Brummell, George Bryan 1, 3, 11, 13–20, 27–32, 35, 39, 41, 43–45, 49, 55, 60–61, 66–70, 73–74, 77, 79, 87–91, 97–99, 101, 116, 118, 121, 123–125, 128–132, 139–140, 145–146, 154, 158–160, 169, 172, 176, 181, 185–190, 194, 195, 213–215, 217–218, 233–234
Bulwer, Henry 36
Bulwer-Lytton, Edward 3, 32–34, 36–41, 51, 54, 56, 58, 60, 66, 74, 84, 126, 129
Byron, George Gordon 3, 11, 18, 19, 32–34, 43, 51, 53–54, 87, 98, 117–118, 128, 177, 194–195, 215

C

Carlyle, Jane 49, 56
Carlyle, Thomas 32, 38, 56, 213
Catherine II of Russia (Catherine the Great) 2, 164, 167, 178
Cavendish, Georgiana 51

Cecil, Or, The Adventures of a Coxcomb (Gore) 74
Chamberlain, Austen 76
Chardon, Lucien 20
Charlus, Baron Palamede 21
Chateaubriand, François-René 34
Chesterfield, George Stanhope 50
Chesterfield, Philip Dormer Stanhope 82–84, 86, 182, 233
Chevalier, Louis Vincent 75
Childe Harold (character) 33, 195
Childe Harold's Pilgrimage (Byron) 32
Cocteau, Jean 53
Colburn, Henry 34–37, 152, 213
Coleridge, Samuel Taylor 69, 79
Coleridge's Dream (Borges) 53
Collins, Wilkie 66
Conan Doyle, Arthur 78, 118, 120
Corelli, Marie 41
Crary, Jonathan 79
Cruikshank, George 4, 71, 85

D
Dandies and Dandies (Beerbohm) 28
David, Jacques-Louis 10, 122
Debrett's Peerage and Baronetage 35
Deffand, Marie Anne de Vichy-Chamrond 21
Deleuze, Gilles 17
Democritus 65
Deriège, Félix 76
Des Esseintes 22–23, 86, 160, 215
Detached Thoughts (Byron) 33
D'Horsay; or, the Follies of the Day (Mills) 60
Dickens, Charles 32, 54, 56
Disraeli, Benjamin 32, 36–37, 41, 50–52, 54–55, 74, 102
Dix, Otto 76
Doré, Gustave 54
Duke of Windsor 1, 215. *See also* Edward VIII
Dzhebrailov, Aydin xii

E
Eckermann, Johann Peter 27
Edgeworth, Maria 12
Edict of Nantes, The 21
Edward VII 203. *See also* Albert Edward, Prince of Wales
Edward VIII 1, 215. *See also* Duke of Windsor.
Elgin, Thomas Bruce 10

Elisabeth of Wied of Romania 41
Epicurus 65
Etiquette; Or, a Guide to the Usages of Society, With a Glance at Bad Habits (D'Orsay) 54
Euphorion, 34

F
Faust (Goethe) 34
Fitz-Gerall, George Robert 73
Flowers of Evil, The (Les Fleurs du Mal) (Baudelaire) 62, 187
Flugel, John Carl 8
Freud, Sigmund 78

G
Galton, Francis 78
Gautier, Théophile 42–43, 47, 126, 146, 152, 170–171, 184, 193, 214
Gavarni, Paul 54, 157
Geczy, Adam xi
George IV 28. *See also* George, Prince of Wales
George, Prince of Wales 28, 30. *See also* George IV
Gertrude (character) 36
Ginzburg, Carlo 78
Gippius, Zinaida 76
Girl with the Golden Eyes (La Fille aux yeux d'or) (Balzac) 51, 116
Glanville, Ellen 73
Glanville, Reginald 38, 73
Glenmorris, Lord (character) 70
Godolphin (Bulwer-Lytton) 51, 58
Goethe, Johann Wolfgang 27, 34
Goncharov, Ivan 11, 180–184, 191
Gore, Catherine Grace 74
Gramont, Antoine-Louis-Marie 53
Granby: A Novel (Lister) 33, 41, 74
Granger, Stewart 28
Grant, Bruce xi
Grech, Nikolay 12
Gronow, Rees Howell 32
Guiche, Antoine-Geneviève Héraclius de Gramont 53
Gusset, Miss (character) 36

H
Hamlet (Shakespeare) 81
Harden, Sylvie 76
Harlow, George Henry 33
Hartley, Elizabeth 73

Hazlitt, William 34, 45, 74, 77, 84, 85, 113, 125
Heath, William 79
Henrietta Temple (Disraeli) 51, 54
History of My Tea Gown, The (Bernhardt) 41
Hoffmann, Ernst Theodor 79–80
Holland, Elizabeth Vassall Fox 53
Hollander, Anne 23, 46, 79, 109, 207, 243
Holmes, Sherlock 78
Hook, Theodore 41, 101–103
Horace (poet) 65
Horujaya-Cook, Sofia xi
Huysmans, Joris Karl 3, 22, 32, 38, 42, 86, 146, 153, 188, 214

J
Jerome of Stridon (St. Jerome) 81
Jesse, William 13, 16, 27, 30–32, 41, 74, 128
Jim (columnist) 10, 185–186
Johnson, Barbara 2

K
Karaminas, Vicki xi
Keats, John 48
Kelly, Ian 28
Kirsanova, Raisa xi, 116, 197
Kurakin, Alexander 2, 163, 183

L
Laertes 81
Lamartine, Alphonse 54
Lamington, Alexander Baillie-Cochrane 51, 58, 59
Lanclos, Ninon 21
Landor, Walter Savage 54
Larina, Tatyana 33
Lawrence, Thomas 53
Ledoux, Claude-Nicolas 10
Lehmann, Ulrich 70
Leopardi, Giacomo 33
Lermontov, Mikhail 3
Lestringuez, Pierre 55
Letters, Sentences and Maxims (Chesterfield) 82
Lewis, Matthew Gregory 33
Lismore, Daniel 48
Lister, Thomas Henry 33, 40, 74
Liszt, Franz 54
Lost Illusions (Illusions perdues) (Balzac) 20
Loti, Pierre 32
Louis of Bavaria 47
Louis XIV of France 20, 47, 127, 164, 218
Louis XV of France 20

Louis-Napoleon 54, 58. *See also* Napoleon III
Loyola, Ignatius 67

M
Mackenzie, Henry 35
Maclise, Daniel 37
Macready, William 52, 60
Mademoiselle de Maupin (Gautier) 42
Maginn, William 56
Maintenon, Francoise d'Aubigne 21
Male and Female Costume (Brummell) 33
Mallarmé, Stéphane 41. *See also* Ponti, Marguerite (pseudonym)
Marie Antoinette 21, 47
Marsay, Henri 51, 116, 129
McNeil, Peter 3, 70
Men and Coats (Thackeray) 38
Merleau-Ponty, Maurice 70
Mildmay, Henry 33
Millington, Henry 40
Mills, John 60
Mirabel, Alcibiades (character) 51, 55
Moers, Ellen 77, 146
Montesquiou, Robert (Count Robert de Montesquiou) 1, 4, 21–22, 47, 158, 214–215, 218
Morgan, Sydney (Lady Morgan) 76
Moscovici, Serge 59
Mysteries of Paris, The (Les Mystères de Paris) (Sue) 83

N
Napoleon I 15, 18, 20, 49
Napoleon III 49. *See also* Louis-Napoleon
Neckclothitania; or Tietania: Being an Essay on Starchers. By One of the Cloth 18
Nekliudov, Sergei xi
New Literary Observer 4
Newman, John Henry 83, 86
Nike of Samothrace 12
Nurok, Ariadna xi

O
On Fashion (Gautier) 43, 214
Onegin, Eugene (character) 33
Onions, Charles Talbut 81
Orsay, Alfred Guillaume (Count d'Orsay) 1, 20–21, 28, 37, 49–62, 116, 123, 154, 158, 181, 218, 236
Orsay, Ida 53
Ouida 41

P

Painter of Modern Life, The (Le Peintre de la Vie Moderne) (Baudelaire) 27, 43–44, 214
Paulding, Miss (character) 68
Pelham (character) 37, 40, 66, 68, 126, 129, 139
Pelham, Lady (character) 84
Pelham, Or, The Adventures of a Gentleman (Bulwer-Lytton) 33, 34, 37–38, 40–41, 66–68, 74, 84, 126, 129, 139
Percival, Henry 12
Physiology of the Lion (Deriège) 75
Picture of Dorian Gray, The (Wilde) 3, 42, 62, 146, 152–153, 155, 157, 187, 214–215
Pierrepoint, Henry 33
Plato 47
Polonius 81
Ponti, Marguerite (pseudonym) 41.
    See also Mallarmé, Stéphane
Proust, Marcel 3, 21, 32, 85, 114–115, 158, 215
Pushkin, Alexander 3, 33, 85, 138, 168–169, 172, 174, 179, 185
Pythagoras 65

R

Raisson, Horace 13
Ramé, Maria Louise. *See* Ouida
Remembrance of Things Past (A la recherche du temps perdu) (Proust) 21
Richelieu, Or, The Conspiracy (Bulwer-Lytton) 60
Robert, Etienne-Gaspard (Robertson) 79
Rosalind (character) 42
Russelton, John 33, 41

S

Sartor Resartus (Carlyle) 38, 213
Schlegel, Friedrich 47–48, 196
Schopenhauer, Arthur 33
Sennett, Richard 78
Sévigné, Marie de Rabutin-Chantal 21
Shakespeare, William xii, 42, 70, 81–82
Simpson, Wallace 76
Southey, Robert 35
Staël, Germaine (Madame de Staël) 33, 34
Stendhal, 3, 32
Sue, Eugène 54
Symons, Arthur 41, 154

T

Talma, François-Joseph 10
Tankerville, Corisande Armandine 37
Taylor, Elizabeth 28
Thackeray, William Makepeace 35, 38, 52, 54–56, 102, 213
Tietania. See Neckclothitania; or Tietania: Being an Essay on Starchers. By One of the Cloth
Titus 12
Tiufiakina, Aleksandra 12
Toll, Felix 1
Treatise on Elegant Living (Traite de la vie elegante) (Balzac) 27, 41, 43, 184, 214
Trebeck (character) 33
Trelawny, Edward 54
Tremaine, Charles (character) 35
Tremaine, Or the Man of Refinement (Ward) 35–36, 41, 74
Trowbridge, Una 76
Twiss, Horace 33

U

Ustinov, Peter 28

V

Vainshtein, Boris v, 4, 115
Vainshtein, Konstantin x, 190
Velasquez, Diego 30
Vernon, John 58
Victoria (Queen) 41, 49
Victoria and Albert Museum 2, 221
Vigny, Alfred 54
Vivian Grey (character) 36–37, 66
Vivian Grey (Disraeli) 36, 74, 102
Voltaire 12

W

Ward, Robert Plumer 35–36, 41, 74
Watier's (club) 33, 44, 118, 130
Weber, Max 52, 59
Wellington, Arthur Wellesley 54
White's (club) 31, 35, 44, 69, 123
Whole Art of Dress or, the Road to Elegance and Fashion, The (A Cavalry Officer) 2–3
Wilde, Oscar 3, 32, 38, 41–43, 47, 62, 73, 86, 145–158, 160, 187–188, 194, 214–215, 234
William IV 49

Willis, Nathaniel Parker 57
Wilson, Harriette 32
Winckelmann, Johann Joachim 10–12, 18
Wölfflin, Heinrich 10
Woolf, Virginia 28, 32
Wordsworth, William 80

Y

Yellowplush Papers (Thackeray) 35
Yes and No: A Tale of the Day (Phipps) 41

Z

Zeno of Citium 65
Zurbaran, Francisco 17

Milton Keynes UK
Ingram Content Group UK Ltd.
UKHW041817130823
426812UK00001B/2